Bra

DREAM TRIP

ALEX & GARDÊNIA ROBINSON

CONTENTS

THIS IS
BRAZIL

Like many travellers to South America I left Brazil until last. And I've spent the last decade wondering why. While the Andes are well tramped and well used to tourists, Brazil remains Latin America beyond the brochures, and beyond the crowds. It's a country big enough to swallow Australia, France and the UK. A country to lose yourself in. To explore. In Brazil you can have miles of palm-shaded, reef-fringed beaches all to yourselves. You can be lost on a river so large that water stretches to every horizon and flows round islands as big as Switzerland. Or you can paddle on tiny streams through dense forest cut by Coca-Cola-coloured rivers and studded with dome-shaped boulder-mountains. Outside Africa, there is nowhere better to see wildlife than Brazil's vast Pantanal wetlands. No country has waterfalls more magnificent than Iguaçu, or a city with a more unforgettable setting than Rio.

And this is to say nothing of Brazil's greatest asset. It's people. Take even half a step off the beaten track and you will find that Brazilians are warm and welcoming without technical courtesy or vested interest. They are a people who brush 'then' and 'when' aside to live life now, seizing the moment. And they are a people more ethnically and culturally diverse than the rest of Latin America combined. Brazil is a fevered mingling of the world cooked up and rendered utterly its own, united by the lilting music of the Portuguese language, the rhythms of Africa and the spontaneity of a country bathed in perennial sunlight. Bierfests, sushi bars, Bauhaus architecture, cowboys and *capoeira* are as Brazilian as the girl from Ipanema and World Cup football. Portugal, France, Holland and Britain all laid claims here and left their cultures to mingle with the indigenous nations and the greatest numbers of Africans in the Americas. The south was haven for US confederates, the Amazon a colony for the Irish, and São Paulo still retains the largest populations of ethnic Japanese outside Japan.

Yet while the world comes together in Brazil, it fades into a distant memory, existing only somewhere out there in what Brazilians call 'the exterior'. Brazilians are not a people in search of an identity. They know who they are and they love to share the beat and the beauty of their diverse and divergent culture with those who finally make it here. And even if they've left Brazil until last, a visit is almost invariably only the first of many.

Alex Robinson

FIRST STEPS
PUTTING IT ALL TOGETHER

You could spend a year in Brazil without exhausting the sights.

Brazil is huge, with space inside its borders for Australia, France and the UK combined, and it has a continent's worth of things to see and do. It's important to be realistic about travel plans – you could spend a year in Brazil without exhausting the sights. These suggested itineraries cover large swathes of the country – but they leave whole regions to explore. None are set in stone so feel free to be creative both with the routes and attractions, and if you have enough time try and link a few together. Getting around Brazil is straightforward. There is an extensive domestic flight network, and while you may have to change planes in São Paulo, Rio, Brasília or Salvador, it's usually easy to find a good-value flight which will take you close to wherever you want to go. In addition, Brazil has a number of international gateway cities, including Rio, São Paulo, Belo Horizonte, Salvador, Natal, Manaus and Fortaleza, all of which feature in our itineraries.

These include Rio de Janeiro, a city many first-time visitors to Brazil are eager to get to know. An itinerary which starts and finishes here will take in much of the country's beautiful southeast – including Rio itself, the gorgeous beaches and forest-swathed islands of the Costa Verde and the pretty World Heritage-protected Portuguese colonial cities of Minas Gerais state. Brasília, the country's modernist capital can be easily visited on a side trip from this route.

With the louche delights of Brazil's biggest carnival, the lush and languid loveliness of the coconut-shaded coast and the luxe baroque beauty of Salvador, Bahia state merits an itinerary all of its own. There is a wealth of things to do here – from trekking in

→ DOING IT ALL

Rio de Janeiro → Ilha Grande → Paraty → Parque Nacional Itatiaia → São João del Rei → Tiradentes → Cogonhas do Campo → Ouro Preto → Mariana → Belo Horizonte → Diamantina → Brasília → Iguaçu → São Paulo → Campo Grande for Southern Pantanal → Cuiabá for Northern Pantanal → Cristalino Rainforest Reserve → Manaus → Belém → São Luís → Parque Nacional Lençóis Maranhenses → Jericoacoara → Fortaleza → Natal → Recife → Olinda → Fernando de Noronha → Salvador → Parque Nacional Chapada Diamantina → Porto Seguro → Parque Nacional Marinho dos Abrolhos → Rio de Janeiro

1 Rio de Janeiro 2 Scarlet macaw, Amazon

Recife and its enchanting pastel-paint and cobbled twin town of Olinda lie at the heart of one of Brazil's most exciting and culturally vibrant states, Pernambuco.

the Diamond hills of the Chapada Diamantina, to watching calving humpback whales off Caravelas or diving and snorkelling over pristine reef in the Abrolhos islands.

A short plane hop north from Salvador will bring you to Recife, the gateway city for our northeastern itinerary. Recife and its enchanting pastel-paint and cobbled twin town of Olinda lie at the heart of one of Brazil's most exciting and culturally vibrant states, Pernambuco. Come here for carnival and an unforgettable caper and then head north into Rio Grande do Norte, Ceará and Maranhão to relax on South America's most spectacular coast – where coconut-palm coves are interspersed with vast dune-scapes as dramatic and wild as those of Namibia across the water.

Wilder still is the itinerary beginning in São Paulo, which passes from that city's concrete jungle to Manaus and Belém, in the far lusher Amazon, via the spectacular Iguaçu Falls and the Pantanal wetlands. The latter is the best location in the Americas for spotting wildlife.

3 Praia do Forte, Salvador **4** Sagrado Coração de Jesus, São Paulo

DREAM TRIP 1
RIO → OURO PRETO → RIO

Best time to visit
The climate in Brazil's southeast is tropical, with temperatures in the high 20s and low 30s all year round. However, it is influenced by cold weather fronts sweeping up from the Southern Ocean. When there's a cold front it can rain at any time. The wettest months are December to March and the driest June to November. Things can get pretty busy over peak holiday time in Brazil – running from mid-December to early January and the 10 days on and around Carnival (the weekend before Shrove Tuesday) and in July. Prices can more than double in Rio over New Year and Carnival.

A TRIP OF ONE TO TWO WEEKS is enough to see a little of Rio, visit a destination on the Costa Verde and one of the colonial cities of Minas Gerais. Allow at least two days for Rio (page 35), taking a full day to visit the Christ Corcovado mountain and the Sugar Loaf. Be sure to enjoy an ice cold coconut on the beach in the early morning, take a stroll through the Botanical Gardens (nestled under Corcovado) and dance a few hours away in a Lapa samba club.

Save some valuable time by booking a direct transfer to one of the sights on the Costa Verde (page 78). If you have just a week, make it Paraty and stay for two days. With two weeks you can visit Ilha Grande too for two or three days, to walk in the rainforest and while away the hours on a beautiful tropical beach.

You'll need to double back to Rio and, if you only have one week, you could skip the road trip to Minas Gerais and fly straight to Belo Horizonte (page 105). You should then take a bus the same day to Ouro Preto (page 97), which you can see comfortably in two days. With two weeks you could also take side trips from Ouro Preto to Congonhas (page 94) and Mariana (page 102), and visit Pampulha (page 109) in Belo Horizonte, which is crammed with Oscar Niemeyer's modernist buildings.

1 Church of São Francisco de Assis, Pampulha, Belo Horizonte **2** Paraty **3** Copacabana beach

Allow at least two days for Rio, taking a full day to visit the Christ Corcovado mountain and the Sugar Loaf.

4 Sugar Loaf and Botafogo Bay from the Dona Marta viewpoint **5** Cristo Redentor, Corcovado

Consider taking an excursion to the mock-Mediterranean beaches in Búzios, discovered by Brigitte Bardot and her Brazilian boyfriend in the 1960s.

A THREE- TO FOUR-WEEK TRIP will allow enough time to explore the route in more depth. You can take four days to see more of Rio (page 35) – including the Tijuca forest, the Dona Marta favela and perhaps the wonderful sunset views of the city from Niterói across the bay. You might even think about joining the cheering crowds in the Maracanã stadium for a football game. Consider taking an excursion to the mock-Mediterranean beaches in Búzios, discovered by Brigitte Bardot and her Brazilian boyfriend in the 1960s. You'll need a week to explore the Costa Verde (page 78) at a relaxed place, to hike on Ilha Grande, take boat trips around Paraty and look for wildlife in Itatiaia National Park (page 84), whose thick rainforests are cut with trails leading to plunging waterfalls and high alpine grasslands and peaks. You can then double back to Rio for the road trip to São João del Rei (page 89) and its twin town of Tiradentes. Allow two days for the towns and be sure to take the miniature Maria Fumaça steam train which runs between them. Then head north to Ouro Preto, the jewel in colonial Brazil's crown and the best base for visiting the baroque towns and villages of central Minas Gerais state. Allow three days to see Ouro Preto (page 97), Mariana (page 102) and Congonhas (page 94). You might also think about a side trip to Diamantina (page 108) in the north of Minas Gerais which, like Ouro Preto, is World Heritage-listed but which sees almost no visitors, thus retaining a sleepy village feel.

There's no need to base yourself in Belo Horizonte. You can see Oscar Niemeyer's suburb of Pampulha (page 109) in a half day, then, perhaps, fly on to see its bigger brother Brasília (page 109) for a couple of nights. Or you can take a bus to Parque Nacional Caparaó (page 110), where you should allow two days to see the rainforests before heading back to Rio for the flight home.

1 Steam train between São João del Rei and Tiradentes 2 Tijuca forest, Rio de Janeiro 3 Black-pencilled marmoset, Ilha Grande
4 Lapa, Rio de Janeiro 5 Ouro Preto 6 Rio de Janeiro

→ GOING FURTHER

Explore the pristine rainforest of Parque Nacional de Itatiaia and, from Belo Horizonte, head north to the pretty colonial town of Diamantina or to Brazil's space-age capital, Brasília. → p84, p108, p109

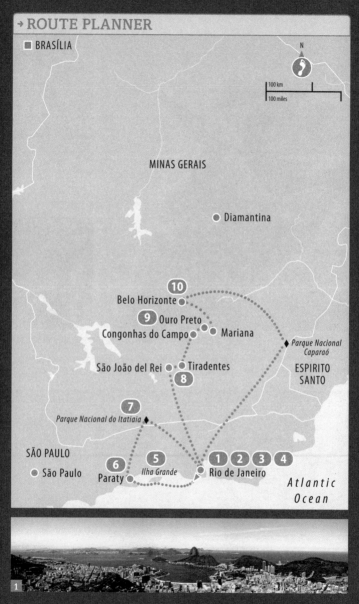

☐ BRASÍLIA

N

100 km
100 miles

MINAS GERAIS

● Diamantina

⑩

Belo Horizonte ●

⑨ Ouro Preto ●

Congonhas do Campo ● ● Mariana

◆ *Parque Nacional Caparaó*

ESPIRITO SANTO

São João del Rei ● ● Tiradentes

⑧

⑦

Parque Nacional do Itatiaia ◆

SÃO PAULO

⑥ ⑤ ① ② ③ ④

São Paulo ● Paraty *Ilha Grande* Rio de Janeiro

Atlantic Ocean

1

1 Rio de Janeiro panorama **2** Ipanema, Rio de Janeiro

→ WISH LIST

1 Take the Trem do Corcovado funicular railway from Cosme Velho through the rainforest to Corcovado and spend a few hours admiring the superb views over Rio's myriad beaches, bays and islands. 2 Dance the night away in one of the many samba clubs in Rio's bustling and bohemian Lapa neighbourhood. 3 Book an early-morning helicopter flight over Rio to see the mesmerizing cityscape from the air and hover over Ipanema, the Sugar Loaf and Christ on Corcovado in the soft morning light. 4 Take a walking tour through Santa Marta favela, having lunch with the locals and enjoying some of the best views of the Christ and Sugar Loaf mountain in the city. 5 Hike from the tiny village of Abraão on the emerald island of Ilha Grande through the tropical forest to a string of gorgeous beaches. 6 Take a boat trip from the pretty Portuguese colonial port town of Paraty to snorkel, sunbathe and eat sumptuous seafood on the islands and beaches of the southern Costa Verde. 7 Bring your binoculars and a zoom lens to spot brilliantly coloured hummingbirds, tiny marmoset monkeys and, if you're lucky, an ocelot or jaguar in the thick rainforests of Itatiaia National Park. 8 Take the toy-sized Maria Fumaça steam train between the twin colonial towns of São João del Rei and Tiradentes in the state of Minas Gerais. 9 Stroll through the cobbled streets of colonial Ouro Preto to see some of the finest Portuguese buildings, baroque art and decorative sculpture in the Americas. 10 Visit Oscar Niemeyer's architectural complex in Pampulha – his prototype for a new capital, and then take a side trip to Brasília to marvel at monumental buildings – a 1960s vision of the space age in concrete and clay.

DREAM TRIP 2
SALVADOR → CHAPADA DIAMANTINA → ABROLHOS ISLANDS

WITH ONE TO TWO WEEKS you will be able to take a whistle-stop tour of Salvador, the Chapada Diamantina and one of the northern Bahian beaches, such as Morro de São Paulo. Take a full day to explore Salvador's (page 115) historical centre, and if you have more than a week spend a day or two learning capoeira, sampling the city's nightlife and taking a day trip to the Recôncavo (page 133) region to the west, where much of modern Afro-Brazilian culture was born. Then fly or take a bus to the Chapada Diamantina (page 139) and spend two to three days exploring the park's waterfalls, cerrado forests, caves and table-top mountains. If you have time take a day or even a multi-day trek to get out into the park's wilds and absorb the magnificent scenery.

You will then have to return to Salvador to visit the Bahian coast. Fast catamarans leave from the city docks for the idyllic island of Tinharé (page 145) where you can relax in the sun for a few days. Morro de São Paulo, the island's main village, sits on a small cape next to a series of magnificent beaches and has a lively nightlife and a broad choice of restaurants and places to stay. Life is so tranquil in Tinharé's other main village that even climbing out of a hammock seems strenuous.

1 Morro de São Paulo **2** Whale watching, Ilhas Abrolhos **3** Salvador

With two weeks you can extend your trip to the little beach town of Itacaré (page 147), where locals take time out from surfing to sell hippy-chic handicrafts on the town's single main street, and myriad coconut-lined sandy bays seclude some of the most luxurious beach hotels in Brazil. From here it's straightforward to organize a side trip to the lonely beaches and bays of the Peninsula de Maraú, just to the north.

Extend your trip to the little beach town of Itacaré, where locals take time out from surfing to sell hippy-chic handicrafts.

4 Chapada Diamantina

Learn some capoeira in Arraial or watch the daily afternoon football match on the Quadrado village green in Trancoso.

1 Carnival decorations, Salvador **2** Bay of Itacaré **3** Monastery of São Francisco, Salvador **4** Barra fort, Salvador da Bahia
5 Chapada Diamantina National Park

→ GOING FURTHER

Head north from Bahia through the charming states of Sergipe and Alagoas to connect this itinerary with the Recife to São Luís route. → **p153**

A THREE- TO FOUR-WEEK trip will allow enough time to visit southern Bahia, where Brazil began in 1500 when a ship full of Portuguese explorers were blown off course to a sugary beach backed by rainforest and came across Brazil's indigenous people.

Many of southern Bahia's beaches still feel as unspoilt and unknown to Westerners as they must have felt in 1500. Using the beach towns of Arraial d'Ajuda (page 150) (which is a suburb of Porto Seguro) or Trancoso (page 151) as a base, take a day to explore these beaches by bus or hire car – driving south on the dirt road to tiny Caraíva. Learn some capoeira in Arraial or watch the daily afternoon football match on the Quadrado village green in Trancoso. Browse that town's fashionable little boutiques and restaurants or sample Arraial or Porto Seguro's energetic beach-based nightlife. And spend a morning wandering around the old colonial centre of Porto Seguro (page 150), and an afternoon visiting the indigenous Pataxó community at Jaqueira, just to the north of that port. After a few days of activity interspersed with doing not very much at all, take two more days to drive south. Spend one day driving through forests and along lonely stretches of coast to Caravelas (page 153), where you can overnight. The following day take a trip to the rocky, reef-ringed Abrolhos islands (page 154), perhaps seeing humpback whales along the way.

Porto Seguro is well connected to Salvador, as well as to Rio, São Paulo and Belo Horizonte from where you can connect to other itineraries in this book or to a flight home.

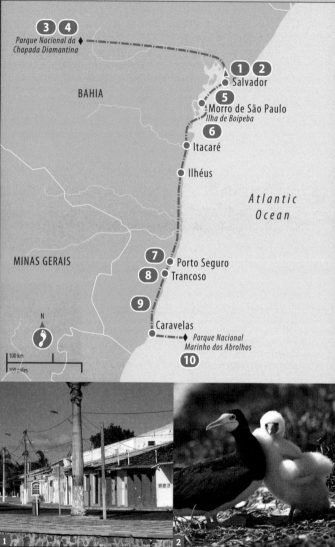

3 **4** ♦
Parque Nacional da
Chapada Diamantina

BAHIA

1 **2**
△ Salvador

5
Morro de São Paulo
Ilha de Boipeba

6
● Itacaré

● Ilhéus

Atlantic Ocean

MINAS GERAIS

7 ● Porto Seguro
8 ● Trancoso

9

● Caravelas
10 ♦ *Parque Nacional Marinho dos Abrolhos*

N

100 km
100 miles

1 Porto Seguro **2** Parque Nacional Marinho dos Abrolhos **3** Morro de São Paulo

→ WISH LIST

1 Spend a morning wandering the cobbled streets of Salvador's old colonial centre, the Pelourinho. Lunch on moqueca de camarão, the quintessential Bahian dish, in the Axego restaurant and then visit the magnificent World Heritage-listed baroque monastery of São Francisco. 2 Take a capoeira lesson and learn the swinging ginga – the first step towards mastering those mesmerizing acrobatic movements. 3 Climb to the top of the Morro do Pai Inácio in the late afternoon for sweeping views over the Chapada Diamantina national park warmed by golden light. 4 Book a day trip in the Chapada – visiting spectacular caves, plunging waterfalls hundreds of metres high and the cerrado woodlands. 5 Relax on an idyllic beach in Morro de São Paulo or Ilha de Boipeba. 6 Learn to surf the waves in Itacaré and take a side trip to the lonely beaches north of town along the Peninsula de Maraú. 7 Discover where Brazil was born with a wander around the old colonial centre of Porto Seguro. 8 Spend a day relaxing on the beach in Trancoso, followed by a candlelit dinner in Capim Santo or Cacau, two of the best restaurants in Bahia. 9 Visit the Jaqueira indigenous community near Porto Seguro and learn about the traditional way of life of the Pataxó people, who have lived in the Atlantic Coastal rainforest for millennia. 10 Take a boat trip to the Abrolhos islands to swim over pristine coral reefs, see vast colonies of nesting birds and, in the Brazilian spring, watch calving humpback whales.

3

DREAM TRIP 3
RECIFE → NATAL → FORTALEZA → SÃO LUÍS

Best time to visit
Brazil's northeast has a climate similar to Bahia's with warm temperatures all year round. Rain is heaviest between January and April and north of Fortaleza there are strong perennial prevailing winds, creating dunes and perfect conditions for kite and wind-surfing (especially between July and December). The dune lakes of the Lençóis Maranhenses national park are only full between May and September, making this the best time to enjoy this route.

WITH ONE TO TWO WEEKS you'll have to cherry pick locations from the itinerary and fly between locations. Allow at least a day to see the colonial buildings and sample the music and nightlife at a bar in Olinda (page 166) or Old Recife (page 159). Two days will allow you to visit the Instituto Brennand to see Francisco Brennand's bizarre sculptures. Fly from here to Fortaleza (page 181) for a connection to Jericoacoara (page 186). Spend at least two days here, visiting the many lakes and dunes, relaxing on the beach and trying your hand at kitesurfing. If you can spare the time, spend two days travelling the coastal route to the Lençóis Maranhenses (page 192), then a day visiting the dunes from the little town of Barreirinhas. From here it's an easy transfer to São Luís (page 193). Leave in the early morning then spend an afternoon exploring the old colonial centre before flying back to Fortaleza or Recife for the flight home.

A THREE- TO FOUR-WEEK TRIP will give you plenty of time to explore the region in more depth. Take a week to see Recife (page 159) and Olinda (page 166) and around, going on two side trips – one to the arts and crafts town of Caruaru (page 169) and another to spend a few days on Fernando de Noronha (page 171) island, which has some of the best beaches and diving in South America.

Leave Recife for Natal – a morning's journey – and from there take a short trip south to Praia da Pipa (page 175) where you can relax on the beach, visit the Atlantic coastal forest and sea-kayak with dolphins. Continue north to southern Ceará state where you can

Allow at least a day to see the colonial buildings and sample the music and nightlife at a bar in Olinda or Old Recife.

1 Praia das Minas near Praia da Pipa 2 Recife and Olinda 3 São Luís

stay in an indigenous or fishing community for a few days, learn how to sail a *jangada* boat and sand-surf on the dunes. After a day in Fortaleza (page 181) move on to Jericoacoara (page 186) for three to four days' kitesurfing.

Take the overland jeep route to the Lençóis Maranhenses, stopping off along the way to explore the labyrinthine waterways of the Delta do Parnaíba (page 191). Look out for green iguana and howler monkeys in the trees, and four-eyed fish, with their eyes half in, half out of the water, in the shallow streams and brooks. Allow three days to see the Lençóis Maranhenses (page 192), visiting the dunes from Barreirinhas and the fishing communities of Caburé and Atins, both set on a wild and windswept coast with a remote, end-of-the-world feel.

Take a morning bus to São Luís (page 193), then spend two or three days there, admiring the crumbling azulejo-fronted buildings of the old colonial centre, the sweltering sugar boom town of Alcântara (page 198) and the city's long, white-sand beaches.

São Luís has regular flights to Fortaleza and Recife (on this route) as well as to Belém, Manaus, Rio and São Paulo.

1 Recife Carnival **2** Sunset on Fernando de Noronha **3** Barreirinhas **4** Fortaleza dos Reis Magos, Natal

Look out for green iguana and howler monkeys in the trees, and four-eyed fish, with their eyes half in, half out of the water, in the shallow streams and brooks.

5 Lençóis Maranhenses

→ ROUTE PLANNER

1 Bumba-Meu-Boi celebration, São Luís do Maranhão   2 Baia de São Marcos

1 Spend a morning or an afternoon ambling through the streets of Portuguese Olinda, visiting the gilt- and azulejo-covered baroque churches and stopping on the cathedral hill to take a photograph of terracotta-tiled roofs and coconut coast set against the skyscrapers of Recife. **2** Spend a Friday or Saturday night in Old Recife sampling the music and nightlife or, better still, come to the city during the Mardi Gras carnival, which is free, frenetic and tremendous fun. **3** Hire a surf board and plunge into the glassy clear waves on Cacimba do Padre beach on Fernando de Noronha island, one of the most beautiful stretches of sand in Latin America. **4** Relax in Pipa, just south of Natal, a little resort with a string of idyllic beaches, two lovely boutiquey beach hotels and a handful of decent restaurants. **5** Stay with a traditional jangada fishing community or with indigenous people in a beachside village in southern Ceará. Book through Rede Tucum. **6** Spend a few days kitesurfing in Jericoacoara, making an afternoon pilgrimage to watch the sunset from the towering dune just outside town and enjoying a caipirinha-fuelled night out at one of the town's two samba and forró clubs. **7** Travel from Jericoacoara to the Lençóis Maranhenses along the spectacular coast, passing miles of deserted, dune-backed beaches and taking ferries big enough for a single car across lakes and rivers. **8** Spend a day crossing the Delta do Parnaíba – a watery wilderness of mangrove-fringed islands, deserted beaches and tiny fishing villages. **9** Marvel at the sweeping brilliant-white sand dunes, dotted with aquamarine and emerald lakes in the Lençóis Maranhenses National Park. **10** Join in the Afro-Brazilian Bumba-Meu-Boi celebrations in the old colonial city of São Luís, which reach their peak in June.

2

DREAM TRIP 4
SÃO PAULO ➜ IGUAÇU ➜ PANTANAL ➜ AMAZON ➜ FORTALEZA

Best time to visit
This long route cuts through the heart of Brazil. The best time to visit is when the Pantanal is in its dry season, which runs from April to November. The Amazon can be visited at any time of year – both when it floods (March to August) and when it recedes (September to February), exposing river beaches. The climate is warm and humid all year round. Rain can come at any time and wildlife is always tough to spot. São Paulo is wet and windy between December and March and dry for much of the rest of the year. The best time to visit Iguaçu is May or September, when the water flow is fairly strong and the crowds are thinner.

WITH ONE TO TWO WEEKS you'll have to sample highlights from this long itinerary. Allow a day for São Paulo (page 203) and be sure to see the city lights from the top of the Edifício Italia. Then fly to Foz do Iguaçu (page 225) for a whistle-stop day trip of both the Brazilian and Argentinean side of the waterfalls. Fly from Foz de Iguaçu to Cuiabá and spend a few days in a fazenda in the northern Pantanal (page 241) – one of the best places in the Americas for wildlife spotting. If you have more than a week then take the short flight north to Alta Floresta and spend two to three days at Cristalino Jungle Lodge (page 247), one of the best places to see Amazon wildlife in South America. Then return from Cuiabá to São Paulo for the flight home.

A THREE- TO FOUR-WEEK trip will allow you to enjoy the route at leisure. Spend a couple of days in São Paulo (page 203) to see the museums and sights, shop in the best fashion boutiques in South America, and enjoy a gourmet meal in a São Paulo restaurant.

A full day is enough to see the Iguaçu Falls (page 225) themselves. Two days will allow you to see the bird park as well, and to take a helicopter flight over both the falls and the rainforest. It's a long bus ride (or a flight via São Paulo) from Foz do Iguaçu to Campo Grande – the access point for the southern Pantanal (page 236). Allow three days for a Pantanal safari or a stay in a traditional Pantaneiro fazenda ranch house, or take a boat safari. You'll need two days to see the crystal-clear streams, caverns and bird-filled forests around Bonito (page 238), one of the best family-friendly wildlife destinations in Brazil.

Take a quick flight or a long bus ride north to Cuiabá (page 242) for a three-day jaguar safari in Porto Jofre, the best location to see the cats in South America. Consider taking a side trip to the table-top mountains of the Chapada dos Guimarães (page 245)

1

1 São Paulo city from the Banespa building 2 Foz do Iguaçu 3 Red-billed toucan 4 Black spider monkey

1 Jaguar, northern Pantanal 2 Blue-crowned motmot, Amazon 3 Guamá river, Belém

whose vertiginous cliffs drip with beautiful waterfalls. Or visit the clear-water rivers in Nobres (page 246) which are filled with brightly coloured freshwater stingrays.

Another flight from Cuiabá will bring you to Manaus (page 253) in the heart of the Brazilian Amazon. Allow a day to see the city. Wander the city centre which is crowned with the imposing and opulent Teatro Amazonas opera house and take a boat trip to the Museu Seringal, a reconstruction of an old rubber baron mansion set on a creek just north of the city. Spend a few days at a jungle lodge, on a river cruise, or in a homestay with *caboclo* people. If you have enough time and money journey up the jet-black Rio Negro (page 260) to swim with bubble-gum pink Amazon river dolphins.

Allow four days for Belém (page 262) and its environs. Take a day for the city sights – which include another opulent opera house and the Ver-o-Peso market which overflows with Amazon produce, from energy berries to bizarre fish and medicinal herbs. And allow three days for the Ilha de Marajó (page 265) – a vast sand island in the mouth of the Amazon River with extensive tracts of rainforest and broad, white-sand beaches.

Belém is well connected to cities on other Dream Trip itineraries, with at least daily flights to Manaus, São Luís, Fortaleza, Recife, São Paulo and Rio, and it is connected by road to São Luís.

Spend a few days at a jungle lodge, on a river cruise, or in a homestay with caboclo people.

4 Amazonas Theatre, Manaus **5** Bonito waterfall **6** Howler monkey, Pantanal

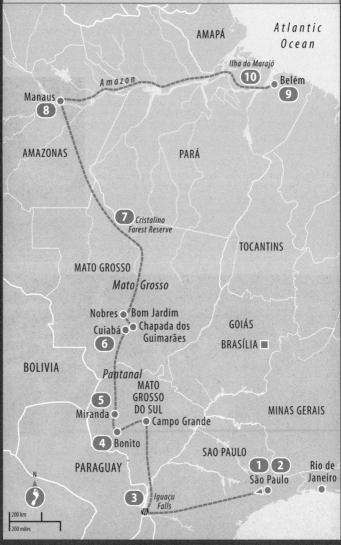

AMAPÁ

Atlantic Ocean

Amazon

Ilha do Marajó
⑩

Belém
⑨

Manaus
⑧

AMAZONAS

PARÁ

⑦ Cristalino Forest Reserve

TOCANTINS

MATO GROSSO

Mato Grosso

Nobres • Bom Jardim
Cuiabá • Chapada dos Guimarães
⑥

GOIÁS

BRASÍLIA ■

BOLIVIA

Pantanal

MATO GROSSO DO SUL

⑤
Miranda

Campo Grande

MINAS GERAIS

④ Bonito

SAO PAULO

① ②
São Paulo

Rio de Janeiro

PARAGUAY

③ Iguaçu Falls

N

200 km
200 miles

1 Rio Negro meets the Amazon
2 Museu Nacional Honestino Guimarães (foreground) and the cathedral (background), Brasilia

→ WISH LIST

1 Get a bird's-eye view of São Paulo's seemingly endless stretches of skyscrapers, flashing neon signs, whirring helicopters and rushing cars from the top of the Edifício Italia or Banespa building. 2 Spend a day visiting São Paulo's art galleries and sights. Begin with the Pinacoteca and Sacred Art museum in Luz to see Brazilian art ancient and modern. Move on to browse the most illustrious collection of European paintings in the southern hemisphere. Wind-up with a romantic gourmet meal in Alex Attala's D.O.M restaurant, voted the fourth best in the world in 2012 by Restaurant Magazine. 3 Be overwhelmed by the thundering Iguaçu Falls, making sure you visit both the Brazilian and Argentinean sides. 4 Snorkel the family-friendly, fish-filled clear-water streams in Bonito which are safe enough for small children. 5 Stay in a fazenda farmhouse in the heart of the southern Pantanal, spotting wildlife, learning how to lasso a steer and enjoying a barbecue grill under a canopy of stars. 6 Search for jaguars, giant anteaters and caiman in the rivers around Porto Jofre, the best place in the world to see South America's most elusive big cat. 7 Enjoy Brazil's best rainforest safaris at Cristalino Jungle Lodge, set in pristine Amazonian wilderness in northern Mato Grosso state. 8 Spend a few days with a caboclo river community in the Amazon near Manaus – either on a homestay and jungle lodge programme or on a river cruise. 9 Eat well and party hard in Belém, which boasts some of the finest food and one of the liveliest music scenes in Brazil. 10 Harness a buffalo on the Ilha de Marajó island and explore the beaches, mangrove forests and ranch houses around Soure, keeping your eyes peeled for rare birds and mammals.

1

DREAM TRIP 1:
Rio de Janeiro→Ouro Preto→Rio de Janeiro 21 days

Rio de Janeiro 3 nights, page 35

Ilha Grande 3 nights, page 78
Bus/shuttle from Rio to Angra dos Reis
(2-3 hrs), then boat (2 hrs)

Paraty 3 nights, page 79
Bus from Rio (3-4 hrs) or Angra dos Reis
(1 hr)

Parque Nacional de Itatiaia 2 nights,
page 84
Bus from Paraty (2 hrs) or bus from Rio
or Paraty via Angra dos Reis and Resende
(3½-4 hrs)

São João del Rei 1 night, page 89
Bus from Rio (8 hrs)

Tiradentes 2 nights, page 91
Bus from São João del Rei (30 mins),
steam train (30 mins)

Cogonhas do Campo Day trip, page 94
Bus from São João del Rei (2 hrs) and
walk (25 mins) or taxi

Ouro Preto 3 nights, page 97
Bus from Cogonhas do Campo (2 hrs)

Mariana 1 night, page 102
Bus from Ouro Preto (30 mins)

Belo Horizonte 1 night, page 105
Bus from Ouro Preto (1½ hrs) or Mariana
(1½ hrs)

Parque Nacional Caparaó 2 nights,
page 110
Bus from Belo Horizonte to Manhuaçu
(6 hrs), bus to Caparaó (40 mins)

Rio de Janeiro 1 night, page 35
Bus from Manhuaçu (11 hrs) or flight
from Belo Horizonte

GOING FURTHER

Diamantina page 108
Bus/flight from Belo Horizonte
(5 hrs/45 mins)

Brasília page 109
Bus/flight from Belo Horizonte
(12 hrs/1 hr)

DREAM TRIP 1
Rio de Janeiro→Ouro Preto→Rio de Janeiro

From the swoon-inducing views from the Christ on Corcovado mountain, through the sugary white-sand beaches and lush rainforests of the Costa Verde to colonial towns rich with gold leaf and bountiful baroque buildings, this route takes in a large chunk of Brazil's magnificent southeast. It begins and ends in Rio de Janeiro, South America's most spectacular city, whose natural beauty is complimented by exhilarating nightlife and vibrant culture. It then continues along the Costa Verde, or 'green coast', which stretches, beach after beach – from palm-fringed coves to long swathes of talcum-fine sand – for some 150 tortuous kilometres. The sea is dotted with forest-covered islands, including mountainous, emerald-green Ilha Grande, cut by numerous forest trails which run to long sandy beaches. The cobbled streets of Paraty at the western end of the Costa Verde are lined with Portuguese whitewash and terracotta houses, hiding chic *pousadas* and gourmet restaurants.

The route then cuts inland from here through Brazil's oldest national park Itatiaia where jaguars and pumas still prowl through the rainforests, before cutting into Brazil's colonial heartland, Minas Gerais. This inland state is home to a string of UNESCO-protected Portuguese colonial mining towns, studded with stunning baroque buildings and decorated with some of the finest baroque art in the Americas. They include Ouro Preto and Congonhas do Campo, which showcase sculptures and paintings by celebrated early Brazilian artists, such as Aleijadinho and Mestre Athayde. The route returns to Rio through the beautiful Caparaó National Park, whose forests protect scores of endemic tropical mammal and bird species.

It is also possible to visit the delightful and UNESCO World Heritage-listed colonial town of Diamantina and Brazil's 1960s space-age capital, Brasília, as extensions to this itinerary.

RIO DE JANEIRO

According to Cariocas – the people of Rio de Janeiro – God made the world in six days and then spent the seventh lying on the beach in Ipanema. For in a city as beautiful as this, they say, only the philistine or the ungrateful would do anything else. Indeed, photographs cannot prepare you for Rio. There is far more to the city than Corcovado capped with Christ or the Sugar Loaf; these are overtures to the grand symphony of the scene. Rainforest-covered boulder mountains as high as Snowdon rise sheer from the sea around the vast Guanabara Bay and stretch to the horizon. Their curves and jags are broken by long sweeping beaches of powder-fine sand pounded by the dazzling green ocean, or by perfect half-moon coves lapped by the gentle waters of the bay. The city clusters around them, climbing over hills and crowding behind beaches and lakes. Its neighbourhoods are connected by tunnels bored through the ancient rock or across winding double-decker highways that cling vertiginously to the cliffs above the fierce Atlantic Ocean.

Against this magical backdrop, the famous Carioca day leisurely unwinds. When the sun is up the middle classes head for the beach, wearing nothing but tiny speedos or bikinis. Here they surf, play beach volleyball or football, or soak up the rays between occasional dips into the waves, with the working day just a brief interruption. When the sun is down, still wearing almost nothing, they head for the botecos (street bars) for an ice-cold draught beer or chope. Then they go home, finally put some clothes on and prepare to go out until the early hours of the morning.

From high on the hills, the other Rio watches over the middle classes. Here lie the favelas – slum cities where the poor and predominantly black communities live. These are Rio's engine of blue-collar work, but also its cultural heart; carnival, samba and Brazilian football were born here. Favelas are at the core of the country's cinema resurgence and the soul of the music of Seu Jorge and Afro-reggae. Brazil's joyful spirit can be felt most strongly in the favelas, alongside its greatest misery and its most shocking violence.

→ARRIVING IN RIO DE JANEIRO

GETTING THERE

Air Rio is served by two airports. **Aeroporto Internacional Tom Jobim** ① *Ilha do Governador, 15 km north of the city centre* (formerly known as Galeão and often still called by this name), receives international and domestic flights. There are *câmbios* in the departure hall and on the first floor of international arrivals. The **Banco do Brasil** on the third floor (open 24 hours) has better rates of exchange. There are also ATMs for major Brazilian banks, several of which accept Visa and MasterCard. Duty-free shops are well stocked and open to arrivals as well as departures. There are **Riotur** information booths in the domestic arrivals hall of Terminal 1 (T021-3398 4077, daily 0600-2300), and in the international arrivals hall in Terminal 2 (T021-3398 2245, daily 0600-2400), which provide maps and can book accommodation. **Santos Dumont Airport** ① *in the city centre on Guanabara Bay*, is used for Rio–São Paulo shuttle flights, a handful of other domestic routes, private planes or air taxis. For more information visit www.infraero.gov.br and click on 'aeroportos'.

Taxis can be booked from within the airports or picked up at the stands outside the terminals. Fixed-rate taxis charge around US$30 from Jobim to Copacabana and Ipanema and US$25 to the city centre and Santa Teresa (about half as much from Santos Dumont); buy a ticket at the counter. Metered taxis cost around US$25 from Jobim to Copacabana, but beware of pirate taxis, which are unlicensed. Fixed-price taxis leave from the first floor of both terminals and have clearly marked booths selling tickets.

There are frequent buses between the two airports, the *rodoviária* (interstate bus station) and the city; the best are the air-conditioned **Real Auto**, T0800-240850, www.realautoonibus.com.br, which leave from outside arrivals on the first floor of terminals 1 and 2 at Tom Jobim (aka Galeão) and run 0500-2400, US$3. There are two routes: *Linha 2018 via Orla da Zona Sul*, runs every 30 minutes, to the Terminal Alvorada bus station in Barra da Tijuca and back again, stopping at the *rodoviária*, Avenida Rio Branco in the centre, Santos Dumont airport, Flamengo, Copacabana, Ipanema, São Conrado and Barra's Avenida das Americas. (This should not be confused with the *Linha 2018 via Linha Vermelha*, which runs a sporadic circular route via Barra and nowhere else of any use to foreign tourists.) *Linha 2145* runs every 25 minutes to Santos Dumont airport and back again, calling at Avenida Rio Branco along the way. Buses can be flagged down anywhere along their route and passengers can request to jump off at any time. There is also a standard Rio bus running along the 2018 line with similar frequency, US$2. Ordinary city buses also run from the airport to various locations in Rio – from the first floor of both terminals. These are far less secure and are not recommended.

Bus International and interstate buses arrive at the **Rodoviária Novo Rio** ① *Av Francisco Bicalho 01 at Rodrigues Alves, Santo Cristo, T021-3213 1800, www.novorio.com.br*. There is a **Riotur information centre** ① *T021-2263 4857, daily 0700-1900*, which can help with orientation and accommodation. Left luggage costs US$5. There are *câmbios* (cash only) and ATMs. From the *rodoviária* it is best to take a taxi to your hotel or to the nearest metrô station (Metrô Estácio); taxis can be booked at the booth on the ground floor. The metrô runs south as far as Copacabana (Metrô Cantagalo); for Ipanema and Leblon head to Metrô Siqueira Campos and take a taxi from there, or take a bus marked 'Metrô-Gávea'.

The **local bus terminal** is just outside the *rodoviária*: turn right as you leave and run the gauntlet of taxi drivers. The bus station attracts thieves, so exercise caution. The air-conditioned **Real bus** (opposite the exit) goes along the beach to São Conrado and will secure luggage. If you need a taxi collect a ticket from the office inside the entrance as this protects against over-charging; a taxi to Flamengo costs approximately US$12.

MOVING ON
Whether you are heading to **Ilha Grande** or **Paraty** on the Costa Verde (see pages 78 and 79) or **São João del Rei** and the colonial cities of Minas Gerais (see page 89), your bus will leave from the Rodoviária Novo Rio (see above). To get to the **Parque Nacional de Itatiaia** you will need to take a bus from Rodoviária Novo Rio to the town of Resende, from where there are connections (see page 84). You can also reach Resende from Angra dos Reis or from Paraty (with a change of bus in Cunha).

GETTING AROUND
The city is made up of separate districts connected by urban highways and tunnels heavy with traffic, so it's best to use public transport or taxis to get around. An underground railway, the **Metrô** ① *T0800-2595 1111, www.metrorio.com.br, Mon-Sat 0500-2400, Sun and holidays 0700-2300 and 24 hrs during Carnaval, tickets US$1.60 for a 1-way journey, US$2 for metro and connecting Gávea/Barra bus*, runs from the outer suburbs of the Zona

Norte (not of tourist interest), through the city centre (including the Sambódromo and the Maracanã stadium), Glória, Flamengo, Botafogo, Copacabana, the Lagoa to the Arpoador end of Ipanema. The Metrô–Barra buses connect at the penultimate station – General Osório (aka Tom Jobim or Ipanema) – for Leblon, Gávea and Barra. Metrô stations often have a number of different access points. **Buses** run to all parts, but should be treated with caution at night, when taxis are a better bet. Buses are usually marked with the destination and any going south of the centre will call at Copacabana and generally Ipanema/Leblon. **Minivans** run from Avenida Rio Branco in the centre as far south as Barra da Tijuca and have the destination written on the window. **Taxis** should always be booked through a hostel or hotel, or caught from a designated taxi *posto*; the name of the *posto* should be written in navy blue on the side of the taxi. Avoid freelance taxis hailed in the street or those without a taxi rank inscription. Santa Teresa is reached by **tram**, which leaves from the Largo da Carioca, near the metrô station and the cathedral, passing over the Lapa viaduct and running along all the main streets in Santa Teresa and eventually reaching either Dois Irmãos or Paula Mattos at the far end of Santa Teresa (see page 55).

BEST TIME TO VISIT

Rio has one of the healthiest climates in the tropics, with trade winds keeping the air fresh. June, July and August are the coolest months, with temperatures ranging from 22°C (18°C in a cold spell) to 32°C on a sunny day at noon. December to March is hot and humid, with temperatures of 32-42°C. October to March is the rainy season; the annual rainfall is about 1120 mm. **Carnaval** is a movable feast, running for five riotous days from the Friday afternoon before Shrove Tuesday to the morning hangover of Ash Wednesday.

TOURIST INFORMATION

Riotur ⓘ *Praça Pio X, 119, 9th floor, Centro, T021-2271 7000, www.rioguiaoficial.com.br*, is the city's government tourist office. There are also booths or offices in **Copacabana** ⓘ *Centro de Atendimento ao Turista, Av Princesa Isabel 183, T021-2541 7522, Mon-Fri 0900-1800*, and **Copacabana Posto Seis** ⓘ *Av Rainha Elizabeth 36 at NS de Copacabana, T021-2513 0077, Mon-Fri 0900-1800*. The helpful staff speak English, French and German and can provide good city maps and a very useful free brochure. There are further information stands at **Corcovado** ⓘ *R Cosme Velho 513, T021-2258 1329 ext 4, on the upper and lower levels of the elevator*, and at the international airport and Novo Rio bus station. There is also a free telephone information service, *Alô Rio*, in Portuguese and English, T021-2542 8080 or T021-2542 8004.

The state tourism organization is **Turisrio** ⓘ *R da Ajuda 5, 6th floor, Centro, T021-2215 0011, www.turisrio.rj.gov.br, Mon-Fri 0900-1800*. The private sector **Rio Convention and Visitors Bureau** ⓘ *R Visconde de Pirajá 547, suite 610, Ipanema, T021-2259 6165, www.rio conventionbureau.com.br*, also offers information and assistance in English. **Embratur** ⓘ *R Uruguaiana 174, 8th floor, Centro, T021-2509 6017, www.braziltour.com*, provides information on the whole country.

Guidebooks *Trilhas do Rio*, by Pedro da Cunha e Menezes (Editora Salamandra, second edition), US$22.50, describes walking trips around Rio. For a light-hearted approach to living in Rio, see *How to be a Carioca*, by Priscilla Ann Goslin. Danusia Barbara's *Restaurantes do Rio* (Senac Rio) is a widely respected gastronomic guide. Casa da Palavra publishes a

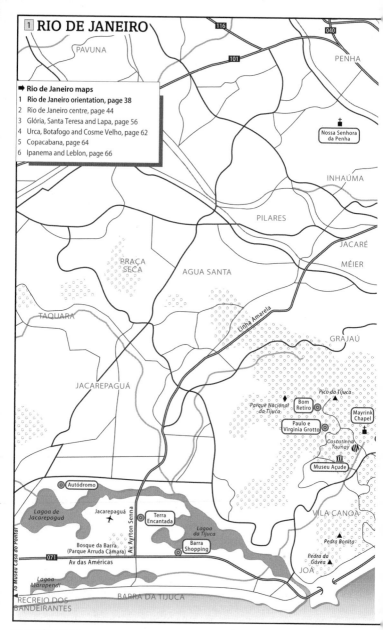

1 RIO DE JANEIRO

PAVUNA

PENHA

116

101

040

Nossa Senhora da Penha

INHAÚMA

PILARES

PRAÇA SECA

AGUA SANTA

JACARÉ

MÉIER

TAQUARA

Linha Amarela

GRAJAÚ

JACAREPAGUÁ

Parque Nacional da Tijuca

Pico da Tijuca

Bom Retiro

Paulo e Virginia Grotto

Mayrink Chapel

Cascatinha Taunay

Museu Açude

Autódromo

Lagoa de Jacarepaguá

Jacarepaguá

Av Ayrton Senna

Terra Encantada

Lagoa da Tijuca

VILA CANOA

Bosque da Barra (Parque Arruda Câmara)

Barra Shopping

Pedra Bonita

071

Av das Américas

Pedra da Gávea

Lagoa Marapendi

JOÁ

To Museu Casa do Pontal

RECREIO DOS BANDEIRANTES

BARRA DA TIJUCA

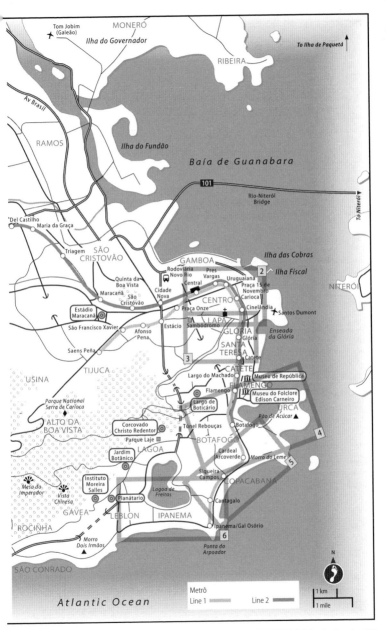

series of architectural guides to Rio, *Guia da Arquitetura*, in Portuguese and English. Many hotels provide guests with a useful free tourist booklet, *Guia do Rio*, which is published quarterly and has the most up-to-date listings.

Maps The *Guia Quatro Rodas – Rio* map book is the only completely comprehensive street map and is essential if you are driving. It can be bought at most newsstands.

Newspapers and magazines Advertisements in the classified sections of dailies *O Globo* and *Jornal do Brasil* proffer apartments for rent and other such services. Both have entertainments pages too; *O Globo* has a travel section on Thursday; the *Jornal do Brasil's Programa* on Friday is an essential 'what's-on' magazine. Even better is the Rio supplement to *Veja*, a weekly news magazine. *Caro Amigos*, http://carosamigos.terra.com.br, is Brazil's most influential centre-left magazine.

Websites www.brazilmax.com is by far the best site, with very useful and incisive cultural information, events listings and articles in English on the whole country; www.ipanema.com has practical information about Rio; www.samba-choro.com.br has information about Carioca music, venues and new releases; www.guiadasemana.com.br is an excellent entertainment site, with cinema, theatre and restaurant listings (in Portuguese). There are internet cafés throughout the city and 90% of hotels and hostels offer internet access.

→BACKGROUND

The coast of Rio de Janeiro was first settled about 5000 years ago. When the Europeans arrived, the indigenous inhabitants belonged to the Tupi or Tupi-Guarani, Botocudos, Puri and Maxacali linguistic groups. Tragically, no indigenous people in this region survived the European incursions.

The Portuguese navigator, Gonçalo Coelho, landed at what is now Rio de Janeiro on 1 January 1502. Mistaking the Baía de Guanabara (the name the local people used) to be the mouth of a great river, they called it the 'January River'. But the bay wasn't settled until 1555 when the French, under the Huguenot Admiral Nicholas Durand de Villegagnon, occupied Lage Island. They later transferred to Seregipe Island (now Villegagnon), where they built the fort of Coligny. The fort has been demolished to make way for the Escola Naval (naval college), and the island itself, since the narrow channel was filled up, has become a part of the mainland. Villegagnon set up a colony as the starting point for what he called Antarctic France.

In 1559-1560, Mem de Sá, the third governor of Brazil, mounted an expedition from Salvador to attack the French, who were supported by the indigenous Tamoio. The Portuguese succeeded in capturing the French fort and putting an end to Antarctic France, but did not colonize the area until 1567 when they transferred their settlement to the Morro de São Januário. This is generally considered the date of the founding of the city of São Sebastião do Rio de Janeiro, so called in honour of the Portuguese prince who would soon assume the throne.

Though constantly attacked by local indigenous groups, the new city grew rapidly and when King Sebastião divided Brazil into two provinces, Rio was chosen as capital of the southern captaincies. Salvador became sole capital again in 1576, but Rio again became the southern capital in 1608 and the seat of a bishopric. There was a further French incursion in 1710-1711 as a result of the tension between France and Portugal during the War of Spanish Succession, and because of the flow of gold out of Minas Gerais through Rio. Rio de Janeiro was by now becoming the leading city in Brazil. Not only was it the port out of which gold was shipped, but it was also the focus of the export/import trade of the surrounding agricultural lands. On 27 January 1763, it became the seat of the viceroy. After Independence, in 1834, it was declared capital of the empire and remained so for 125 years.

THE SHAPING OF A CITY

Rio went from a colonial capital to the capital of a large Empire when King João and the entire Portuguese court fled to Brazil in 1808 in fear of Napoleon, abandoning Portugal to a caretaker British Army General. The ideas they brought with them from Europe began to transform Rio. New formal gardens and stately *praças*, graced with faux-European fountains were built to accommodate the court's more refined tastes and lavish mansions and palaces were built to house the royals and their retinue. Despite his fear of Napoleon, King João invited an artistic mission from France to found academies of fine art and music in Rio in 1816. The architect Grandjean de Montigny, the painter Jean-Baptiste Debret and sculptor Nicolas Antoine Taunay began an artisitic relationship which continued into the 20th century through Le Corbusier and Levi-Strauss and which provided the template for modern Brazil's artistic and academic development. The city also expanded geographically, growing north into São Cristóvão and Tijuca and south through Glória, Catete, Flamengo and Botafogo. It also grew in prosperity, with wealthy coffee barons building *chacaras* – or country houses – in the hills around Tijuca and Santa Teresa, a trend which continued into Independence. By the time Brazil had become a republic in 1889, Rio was by far the most important city in the country politically, culturally and economically.

The new Republic was founded on French positivist principles, which were resolutely pragmatic and functionalist – as expressed by the new national motto 'Order and Progress'. The old past were discarded. Sadly it included much of colonial Rio whose beautiful terracotta tiled roofs, old alleys, churches and mansion houses were razed to the ground and replaced by poor versions of US office blocks, lining broad new avenues such as the 33-m-wide Avenida Central (later renamed Avenida Rio Branco). The disenfranchised poor Brazilian majority, many of whom were recently freed African Brazilian slaves, began to cluster on the hills in ungainly shanty towns, or favelas.

In 1960 Brazil entered an era of order and progress when new president Juscelino Kubitschek declared that his country would leap 50 years in just five – equivalent to his term of office. Kubitschek shifted the nation's capital several thousand kilometres inland to the new purpose-built Jetson age Brasília, sending the country into bankruptcy and Rio into decline. The commercial centre crumbled, the bright lights of Lapa and Cinelandia flickered and went dim and wealthy Cariocas left for the beaches around Ipanema and São Conrado. Resurrection began in the 1990s, when a new mayor, Luiz Paulo Conde, embarked on a massive programme of regeneration, remodelling the bayside suburbs and attracting residents, artistic endeavours and small businesses to neglected districts. Lapa emerged again as a nightlife centre and Rio began to find its cultural feet again. But years of neglect had left a toll. Contemporary Rio, with a population of eight million, has literally hundreds of favelas and is chronically divided between the haves, who live in the Cidade Maravilhosa, and the have-nots, who live in the Cidade de Deus or similar slum communities.

Hot and sweaty central Rio spreads back from Guanabara Bay in a jumbled grid of streets between Santos Dumont airport and the Jesuit Mosteiro São Bento. It dates from 1567, but much of its architectural heritage has been laid waste by successive waves of government intent on wiping out the past in favour of dubious and grandiose visions of Order and Progress. Nevertheless it remains the centre of Rio's history as well as the city, with some distinguished colonial buildings, Manueline follies and elaborate neoclassical façades huddled together under totalitarian blocks of flats and Le Corbusier-inspired concrete. All watch over a mass of cars and a bustle of people: business suits on lunch, beggars, skateboarders dressed in would-be New York oversized jeans and baseball caps, street performers and opportunists looking to snatch a purse. It can all feel a bit hectic and bewildering. But don't give up. There is plenty to explore here and a wealth of air-conditioned havens in which to escape for respite and a coffee.

The greatest concentration of historic buildings is in the south of the centre, near Santos Dumont airport and around **Praça 15 de Novembro**, from where Rio de Janeiro grew in its earliest days. Here you'll find most of the museums, some of the city's more beautiful little churches and colonial buildings such as the **Paço Imperial** and the **Palácio Tiradentes**. More colonial buildings lie at the centre's northern extremity around the Morro de São Bento. These include the finest baroque building in Rio, the **Mosteiro de São Bento**, and the city's most imposing church, **Nossa Senhora da Candelária**.

The city's main artery is the **Avenida Presidente Vargas**, 4.5 km long and more than 90 m wide, which divides these northern and southern sections. It begins at the waterfront, splits around the Candelária church, then crosses the Avenida Rio Branco in a magnificent straight stretch past the **Central do Brasil** railway station. Vargas is dissected by two important arterial streets. **Avenida Rio Branco**, nearest to the sea, was once lined with splendid ornate buildings, which were quite the equal of any in Buenos Aires. These have largely been razed to the ground but a few remain around **Cinelândia**. **Avenida 31 Março**, further to the west beyond the railway station, leads to the **Sambódromo** and the Carnaval district. Some of the better modern architecture is to be found along Avenida República do Chile, including the conical 1960s **Catedral Metropolitana de São Sebastião**.

ARRIVING IN CENTRAL RIO AND LAPA
For Praça 15 de Novembro, Largo do Carioca, Cinelândia and Lapa take the metrô to Carioca in Cinelândia. For Candelária and São Bento take the metrô to Uruguiana. For the Cidade Nova and Sambódromo take the metrô to Praça Onze. Opening times for churches, museums and public buildings change frequently. All museums close during Carnaval.

PRAÇA 15 DE NOVEMBRO AND THE IMPERIAL PALACES
Originally an open space at the foot of the Morro do Castelo – a hill which has now been flattened – the Praça 15 de Novembro (often called Praça Quinze) has always been one of the focal points in Rio de Janeiro. Today it has one of the greatest concentrations of historic buildings in the city. Having been through various phases of development, the area underwent major remodelling in the late 1990s. The last vestiges of the original harbour, at the seaward end of the *praça*, were restored. Avenida Alfredo Agache now goes through an underpass, creating an open space between the *praça* and the seafront and giving easy

access to the ferry dock for Niterói. The area is well illuminated and clean and the municipality has started to stage shows, music and dancing in the *praça*. At weekends an antiques, crafts, stamp and coin fair (Feirarte II) is held 0900-1900. The rather modest colonial former royal palace, **Paço Imperial** ① *on the southeast corner of Praça 15 de Novembro, T021-2533 4407, www.pacoimperial.com.br, Tue-Sun 1200-1800*, is one of the centre's landmarks. It was built in 1743 as the residence of the governor of the Capitania and was made into the royal palace when the Portuguese court moved to Brazil. After Independence it became the imperial palace. It fell into disuse in the mid-20th century to be resurrected as a temporary exhibition space and arts centre. There's often something interesting on display here, and two decent air-conditioned café-restaurants, the **Bistro** and **Atrium**, provide respite from the heat. Just north of the palace is the **Chafariz do Mestre Valentim**, or Chafariz do Pirâmide; a fountain designed by the famous sculptor.

Beside the Paço Imperial, across Rua da Assembléia, is the grand neoclassical **Palácio Tiradentes** ① *T021-2588 1411, Mon-Sat 1000-1700, Sun and holidays 1200-1700, guided visits by appointment only, T021-2588 1251*. It was named in honour of the former dentist (*tiradentes* means teeth-puller), Joaquim José da Silva Xavier, who is often seen as the symbolic father of Brazilian Independence, and who was held prisoner here and executed nearby. The building itself was constructed between 1922 and 1926 and is now the state legislative assembly. A **statue of Tiradentes** by Francisco de Andrade stands in front.

LARGO DA MISERICÓRDIA AND THE MUSEUMS

There is a cluster of interesting little museums south of Praça XV on the way to Santos Dumont airport that can be reached by the Largo da Misericórdia, which runs immediately south of the Palácio Tiradentes. At the end of the *largo* is the **Ladeira da Misericórdia**; the oldest street in Rio and now just a severed stump on the side of the grand Santa Casa da Misericórdia hospital. This hill was once crowned by a magnificent monastery and fort that watched out over the bay. Next door to the hospital, in a series of handsome buildings, is the **Museu Histórico Nacional** ① *Praça Marechal Âncora, T021-2550 9224, www.museuhitoriconacional.com.br, Tue-Fri 1000-1700, Sat and Sun 1400-1800, US$3, free on Sun*. This is one of the city's more distinguished museums, with a collection of magnificent carriages, historical treasures, colonial sculpture and furniture, maps, paintings, arms and armour, silver and porcelain. It also retains a rampart from that first fort that crowned the former Morro do Castelo hill from the 1603 until the 20th century. The building was once the war arsenal of the empire, and was partly constructed in 1762 (this part is called the 'Casa do Trem'). The **Museu da Imagem e do Som (MIS)** ① *at the moment split between 2 centres: R Visconde de Maranguape 15, Largo da Lapa, T021-2332 9508 and Praça Luiz Souza Dantas (aka Praça Rui Barbosa) 01, Praça XV, T021-2332 9068, Mon-Fri 1100-1700, www.mis.rj.gov.br, free, visits by appointment only*, is scheduled to move into a swanky, purpose-built new building in Copacabana in 2012. It currently houses a collection of cinema images, photos of Rio and of Carioca musicians, and recordings of popular music, including early *choro* by artists including Jacob do Bandolim. There are booths for listening to music and a small cinema for watching the 16 mm and 35 mm film archive.

TRAVESSA DO COMÉRCIO AND THE CARMELITE CHURCHES

North of Praça XV, the **Travessa do Comércio** and its continuation to the left, the **Rua do Ouvidor**, are reached via the **Arco do Teles** directly across from the palace. The arch is all

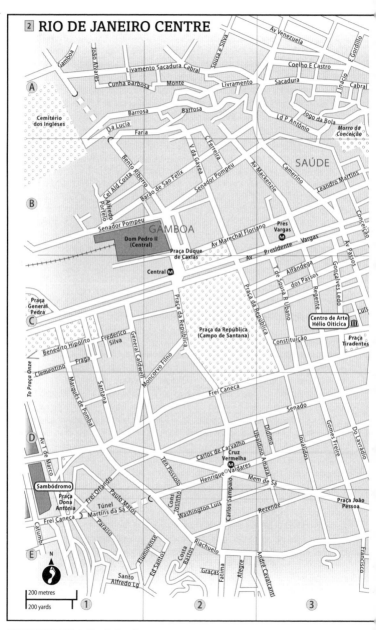

2 RIO DE JANEIRO CENTRE

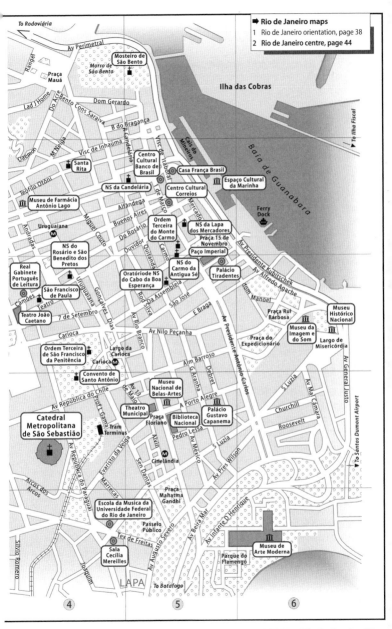

➡ Rio de Janeiro maps
1 Rio de Janeiro orientation, page 38
2 Rio de Janeiro centre, page 44

To Rodoviária

Av Perimetral

Rangel

Praça Mauá

Morro de São Bento

Mosteiro de São Bento

Lad J Home

Do Acre Cons Saraiva

Dom Gerardo

Ilha das Cobras

B do Bragança

Daemon   M Reiga

Visc de Inhaúma

Cais dos Mineiros

To Ilha Fiscal

Teófilo Otôni

Santa Rita

Centro Cultural Banco de Brasil

NS da Candelária

Casa França Brasil

Centro Cultural Correios

Espaço Cultural da Marinha

Baía de Guanabara

Museu de Farmácia Antônio Lago

Andradas

Uruguaiana Ⓜ

Alfândega

Buenos Aires

Do Rosário

Ordem Terceira do Monte do Carmo

NS da Lapa dos Mercadores

Ferry Dock

Maciel Couto

Ouvidor

Praça 15 de Novembro

Paço Imperial

Av Presidente Kubitschek

Real Gabinete Português de Leitura

NS do Rosário e São Benedito dos Pretos

Ouvidor

Ouvidor

Oratório de NS do Cabo da Boa Esperança

NS do Carmo da Antiga Sé

Palácio Tiradentes

Av Alfredo Agache

São Francisco de Paula

Uruguaiana

Gonçalves Dias

Rosa Da Assembléia

São José

Dom Manoel

Teatro João Caetano

Camões   Teatro

7 de Setembro

E Braga

Praça Rui Barbosa

Museu Histórico Nacional

Carioca

Av Nilo Peçanha

Av Presidente Antônio Carlos

Museu da Imagem e do Som

Largo da Carioca

Praça do Expedicionário

Largo de Misericórdia

Ordem Terceira de São Francisco da Penitência

Carioca Ⓜ

Av General Justo

Convento de Santo Antônio

Museu Nacional de Belas-Artes

Alm Barroso

G Aranha

Débret

S Luzia

Av Mal Câmara

IV 13 de Maio

A Porto Alegre

Palácio Gustavo Capanema

Churchill

Catedral Metropolitana de São Sebastião

Av República do Chile

Theatro Municipal

Praça Floriano

Biblioteca Nacional

Av México

S Luzia

Roosevelt

To Santos Dumont Airport

Tram Terminus

Pedro Lessa

Arcos dos Arcos

Av República do Paraguai

Evaristo da Veiga

Sen Dantas

Cinelândia Ⓜ

Av Pres Wilson

Silvio Romero

Praça Mahatma Gandhi

Escola da Música da Universidade Federal do Rio de Janeiro

Passeio Público

Av Infante D Henrique

Av Beira Mar

Museu de Arte Moderna

Tex de Freitas

Sala Cecília Meireles

Av Augusto Severo

Parque do Flamengo

Joaquim

LAPA

To Batafogo

4   5   6

that remains of an 18th-century construction, now incorporated into a modern building, and the two streets give an idea of how most of Rio must have looked in the 19th century. Little bars and restaurants line the streets and are very lively after 1800. These include the **Arco Imperial**, where Carmen Miranda lived between 1925 and 1930 (her mother kept a boarding house). There are also some interesting bookshops and one of Brazil's prettiest little baroque churches, **Nossa Senhora da Lapa dos Mercadores** ① *R do Ouvidor 35, T021-2509 2239, Mon-Fri 0800-1400*. This began life as a street oratory erected in a blind alley by market vendors who traditionally petitioned Our Lady of Lapa for help in hard times; it became a church in 1750, was remodelled in 1869-1872 and has now been fully restored.

The busy thoroughfare of Rua 1 de Março cuts across the top of Praça XV and Rua Ouvidor and is littered with Carmelite churches, all of them worth a quick look. The most famous is at the northwestern corner of the *praça*: **Nossa Senhora do Carmo da Antiga Sé** ① *R 1 de Março at R 7 de Setembro 14, T021-2509 2239, Tue-Thu 0900-1700, Sat 1100-1700*, has one of the finest baroque interiors in Rio and occupies the site of the original founding Carmelite chapel, which stood here between 1590 and 1754. The current church dates from 1761. After the arrival of the Portuguese court in 1808 it became the designated Royal Chapel and subsequently the city's first cathedral – between 1900 and 1976. The crypt allegedly holds the remains of Pedro Alvares Cabral, the European discoverer of Brazil, a claim disputed by the town of Santarém in Portugal. Just north of this church and right in front of the end of Rua Ouvidor is the **Igreja da Ordem Terceira do Monte do Carmo** ① *R 1 de Março s/n, Mon-Fri 0800-1400, Sat 0800-1200*. This was built in 1754, consecrated in 1770 and rebuilt in the 19th century. It has strikingly beautiful portals by Mestre Valentim, the son of a Portuguese nobleman and a slave girl. He also created the main altar of fine moulded silver, the throne and its chair and much else. At the rear of the old cathedral and the Igreja da Ordem Terceira do Monte do Carmo, on Rua do Carmo, is the **Oratório de Nossa Senhora do Cabo da Boa Esperança**; one of the few remaining public oratories from the colonial period in Rio.

CANDELÁRIA AND AROUND

Rio's most imposing church lies on an island in a sea of traffic some 500 m north of Praça XV. The mock-Italianate **Igreja de Nossa Senhora da Candelária** ① *Praça Pio X, T021-2233 2324, Mon-Fri 0800-1600, Sat 0800-1200, Sun 0900-1300*, has long been the church of 'society Rio'. Celebrities still gather here in the marble interior for the city's most prestigious weddings. The church is modelled on the Basílica da Estrela in Portugal. The tiles in the dome are from Lisbon, the marble inside is Veronan and the heavy bronze doors were commissioned from France. All were shipped across at vast expense in the late 18th century, during an era when even though such materials were readily available in Brazil at similar quality and far lower prices, snob value demanded that they be imported. The church was built on the site of a chapel founded in 1610 by the Spaniard Antônio Martins Palma who arrived in Rio after surviving a terrible storm at sea. He erected the chapel in homage to Nuestra Señora de Candelária, the patron saint of his home, La Palma island in the Canaries. There are a number of cultural centres near the church. The **Centro Cultural Correios** ① *R Visconde de Itaboraí 20, T021-2253 1580, www.correios.com.br, Tue-Sun 1200-1900, free*, in a smart early 20th-century building with a little private park, is a good stop for an air-conditioned juice or coffee. It has a theatre, a 1000-sq-m concert hall and spaces for temporary exhibitions and cultural events, and a postage stamp fair on Saturdays. Just opposite, with entrances on

Avenida Presidente Vargas and Rua 1 de Março 66, is the **Centro Cultural Banco do Brasil** (**CCBB**) ① *R 1 de Março 66, T021-3808 2020, www.bb. com.br/cultura, Tue-Sun 1000-2100*, in a fine early 19th-century neoclassical building with a beautiful glass domed roof. The centre hosts many of the city's large and distinguished art shows, including some excellent photographic exhibitions. It also has an arts cinema, library, multimedia facilities and lunchtime concerts (around US$5). The restaurant is air-conditioned and the food respectable. At the corner of Rua Visconde de Itaboraí (No 253) and Avenida Presidente Vargas, just opposite Candelária, is the **Casa França-Brasil** ① *R Visconde de Itaboraí 78, T021-2253 5366, www.casafrancabrasil.com.br, Tue-Sun 1000-2000*, a Franco-Brazilian cultural centre designed by one of the key players in the 19th-century French cultural mission to Rio, Grandjean de Montigny. It holds temporary exhibitions exploring the long relationship between the two countries. The newest of the cultural centres near Candelária is the **Espaço Cultural da Marinha** ① *Av Alfredo Agache, on the waterfront, T021-2104 6025, www.sdm.mar.mil.br/espaco.htm, Tue-Sun 1200-1700, free*. This former naval establishment, built on a jetty over the bay, now contains museums of underwater archaeology and navigation. *Galeota*, the boat used by the Portuguese royal family for sailing around the Baía de Guanabara is kept here and a Second World War submarine and warship, the *Bauru* (not to be confused with the sandwich of the same name), is moored outside. The museum is very popular with Brazilian children and is crowded at weekends.

Just offshore, but connected to the mainland by a causeway to Ilha das Cobras, is the **Ilha Fiscal** ① *Av Alfredo Agache, T021-2233 9165, boats leave Thu-Sun at 1300, 1430 and 1600, closed 1 Jan, Carnaval, Holy Week and Christmas; when the sea is too rough transport is by van*. It was built as a customs house at the emperor's request, but he deemed it too beautiful, and said that it should be used only for official parties. Only one was ever held – a masked ball hosted by the viscount of Ouro Preto in honour of the crew of the Chilean warship, *The Admiral Cochrane*, five days before the republic began. It is now a museum, linked with the Espaço Cultural da Marinha. The island is passed by the ferry to Niterói.

MOSTEIRO DE SÃO BENTO

① *R Gerardo 68, T021-2516 2286, www.osb.org.br, daily 0700-1730, free, guided tours Mon-Sat 0900-1600; modest dress, no shorts; taxi from the city centre US$6.*

The **Praça Mauá**, which lies north of Avenida Presidente Vargas, marks the end of Centro and the beginning of the port zone. Many of the empty warehouses here are used as workshops by the samba schools for the construction of their beautiful carnival floats. The area would be unremarkable were it not for the Mosteiro de São Bento, whose sober Brazilian baroque façade sits on a promontory looking out over the bay. It is widely publicized as a World Heritage Site, which it is not. But of all the city's colonial buildings this is the most worth visiting, both for its magnificent interior and for its significance as the most important Benedictine monument outside Europe. The church began life in 1586 with a group of monks who arrived in Rio from Salvador and it grew to become the most powerful monastery in the city. It preserves a lavish gilt baroque interior but is very poorly lit (the church charges an absurd US$5 to put on all of the electric lights). However, in the gloom it is possible to make out that not an inch remains unadorned. The three doors sculpted by Father Domingos da Conceição, which give access to the nave, and the sculptures of St Benedict, St Escolastica and Our Lady of Monserrat are particularly remarkable. The last, which is also by Domingos de Conceição, has painted birds' eggs for eyes. The painting is as wonderful as the carving; particularly the panels in the Blessed Sacrament chapel by Inácio Ferreira Pinto and *O Salvador*, the masterpiece of Brazil's first painter, Frei Ricardo do Pilar, which hangs in the sacristy. The enormous candelabra are attributed to Mestre Valentim, Rio's most celebrated church artisan, and are made from solid silver especially imported from Peru and the mines of Potosí in Bolivia at a price higher than Brazil's own gold. The monastery's library (open to men only) preserves a number of priceless religious manuscripts alongside 200,000 other books.

São Bento can be reached either by a narrow road from Rua Dom Gerardo 68, or by a lift whose entrance is at Rua Dom Gerardo 40. Both routes lead to a *praça* with tall trees, but arriving in the lift is more magical as you are whisked from the heat and bustle of the dock area to an oasis of calm, which sets the mood beautifully for a wander around the monastery buildings. If you would rather walk, the monastery is a few minutes from Praça Mauá, turning left off Avenida Rio Branco; Rua Dom Gerardo 68 is behind the massive new RBI building. Every Sunday at 1000 there is a Latin Mass with plainsong. Arrive an hour early to get a seat. On other days, Mass is at 0715 and the monks often sing at vespers.

LARGO DA CARIOCA AND AROUND

This higgledy-piggledy street of colonial churches, modern buildings and street stalls sits between Rua da Carioca and the Carioca metrô station about 1 km south of Praça XV along Rua da Assembléia. There is a variety of interesting sights here within a very small area. The **Convento de Santo Antônio** ① *T021-2262 0129, Mon, Wed, Thu, Fri 0730-1900, Tue 0630-2000, Sat 0730-1100 and 1530-1700, Sun 0900-1100, free*, the second oldest in Rio, sits on a little hill off the Largo da Carioca. You will often see single women here gathered to pray: there are many more women than men in Brazil and St Anthony is traditionally a provider of husbands. The church interior is baroque around the chancel, main altars and two lateral altars, which are devoted to St Anthony, St Francis and the Immaculate Conception respectively. The beautiful sacristy is decorated with *azulejos* (tiles) and adorned with paintings depicting scenes from St Anthony's life. Many members of the Brazilian imperial family are buried in the mausoleum. Separated from this church only by a fence of iron railings is one of Rio's least-known baroque jewels: the little church of the **Ordem Terceira de São Francisco da Penitência** ① *T021-2262 0197, Mon-Fri 0900-1200 and 1300-1600, free*, which was built between 1622 and 1738. It has a splendid gilt interior by Francisco Xavier de Brito, who is largely credited with introducing baroque to Brazil and who was probably Aleijadinho's teacher in Ouro Preto. There's also a fine panel depicting the glorification of St Francis by Caetano da Costa Coelho Behind the church is a tranquil catacomb-filled garden.

A couple of streets north, at the end of Rua do Ouvidor and dominating the square that bears its name, is the twin-towered **Igreja de São Francisco de Paula** ① *Largo São Francisco de Paula, Mon-Fri 0900-1300, free*, with some fine examples of Carioca art including carvings by Mestre Valentim, paintings by Vítor Meireles and murals by Manuel da Cunha. Across the Largo de São Francisco and on the corner of Rua Uruguaiana 77 and Ouvidor is the **Igreja de Nossa Senhora do Rosário e São Benedito dos Pretos** ① *T021-2224 2900, Mon-Fri 0700-1700, Sat 0700-1300, free*. Since the 17th century this church has been at the centre of African Christian culture in Rio. During the 19th century it was the site of an elaborate festival that recreated scenes from the courtly life of the king of Congo. A king and queen were crowned and they danced through the nearby streets followed by long parades of courtiers in fancy dress; a precursor perhaps for Carnaval. It was here that the announcements for the final abolition of slavery were prepared. The church once had a fabulous gilt interior but this was sadly destroyed in a fire in 1967. Next to the church is a small museum devoted to slavery in Brazil, whose collection of instruments of subjugation speaks starkly of life for black people in the last Western country to abolish the slave trade.

The **Real Gabinete Português de Leitura** ① *R Luís Camões 30, T021-2221 3138, www.realgabinete.com.br, Mon-Fri 0900-1800, free*, sits just to the north of Largo São Francisco de Paula on Rua Luís de Camões. This is one of the city's hidden architectural treasures and one of the best pieces of mock-Manueline architecture in Brazil. Manueline architecture is usually described as Portuguese Gothic and takes its name from King Manuel I who ruled Portugal between 1495 and 1521. It is unlike any other European Gothic style, drawing strongly on Islamic and nautical themes – a lavish fusion of Islamic ornamentalism and sculpted seaweeds, anchors, ropes and corals, typified by the Cristo monastery in Tomar and the Mosteiro dos Jerônimos in Lisbon. The modest exterior of the Real Gabinete, which was designed by Portuguese architect Rafael da Silva e Castro in 1880, was inspired by the façade of Jerônimos. It is decorated with statues of Camões, Henry the Navigator, Vasco da Gama and Pedro Álvares Cabral, who claimed Brazil for Portugal. More interesting, however, is the magnificent reading hall built around the oldest central steel structure in Rio. Towering arches decorated with Islamic flourish ascend via coiled wooden ropes to an elaborate painted ceiling with skylights from which a massive iron chandelier is suspended. There are some 120,000 books in the library's collection, many of them very rare. The magnificent belle-époque coffee house, **Confeitaria Colombo**, is a short walk to the east, at Rua Gonçalves Dias 32.

PRAÇA TIRADENTES AND THE CATHEDRAL

One long block behind the Largo da Carioca and São Francisco de Paula is **Praça Tiradentes**, old and shady, with a **statue to Dom Pedro I** carved in 1862 by Luís Rochet. The emperor sits on horseback shouting his famous 1822 Declaration of Independence, the Grito de Ipiranga: 'Liberty or Death'. The **Teatro João Caetano** sits on the northeastern corner of the *praça* and is named after a famous 19th-century actor. Prince Dom Pedro first showed the green and yellow Brazilian flag in the original building, which was an important venue for meetings discussing Brazilian Independence. The current theatre was constructed in 1920 after the original had fallen into disrepair. Two canvases by one of the city's most celebrated artists, Emiliano Di Cavalcanti, hang on the second floor. Just north of the *praça*, in a handsome salmon pink colonial building, is the **Centro de Arte Hélio Oiticica** ① *R Luís de Camões 68, Mon-Fri 1000-1800*, named after another famous Carioca artist and now a smart contemporary art exhibition space with six galleries, a good art bookshop and an air-conditioned café. Important national and international artists exhibit here. Shops in nearby streets specialize in selling goods for *umbanda*, the Afro-Brazilian religion. The **Catedral Metropolitana de São Sebastião** ① *Av República do Chile, T021-2240 2669, www.catedral.com.br, daily 0700-1900, Mass Mon-Fri 1100, Sun 1000*, lies just south of the Praça Tiradentes and the Largo da Carioca; bordering Cinêlandia to the east and Lapa to the south. It is an oblate concrete cone fronted by a decorative ladder and replete with rich blue stained glass, which looks like a modernist Mayan temple. The design could be mistaken for a Niemeyer, but is in fact by another Brazilian Le Corbusier disciple, Edgar de Oliveira da Fonseca, with heavy modernist statues and panels by Humberto Cozzi. It's best to visit in the late afternoon when the sunlight streams through the immense monotone stained-glass windows. There is a small sacred art museum in the crypt, which has a handful of relics including Dom Pedro II's throne and the fonts used for the baptizing of imperial Brazilian babies. The *bonde* (tram) to Santa Teresa leaves from behind the cathedral, the entrance is on Rua Senador Dantas (see page 55). Soon after leaving the station the tram traverses the Arcos da Lapa offering wonderful views.

One of the city's quirkier museums lies only a short walk from the cathedral. The **Museu de Farmácia Antônio Lago** ① *R dos Andradas 96, 10th floor, T021-2263 0791, www.abf.org.br/museu.html, Mon-Fri 1430-1700 by appointment only via email abf@abf.org.br, US$2*, is a reproduction of a 17th-century Brazilian apothecary's shop, complete with Dr Jekyll cabinets and rows of dubious-looking herbal preparations in glass and porcelain vessels.

CINELÂNDIA AND AVENIDA RIO BRANCO

The area around Praça Floriano was the liveliest part of the city in the 1920s and 1930s when Hollywood hit Brazil. All of the best cinemas were situated here and their popularity became so great that the *praça* was named after them. Today **Cinelândia** remains lively, especially at the end of the week, owing to its proximity to the city's nightlife capital, Lapa. The 30-m-wide **Avenida Rio Branco**, which bisects Cinelândia, is the financial heart of the city. Lined by an untidy mishmash of modernist and art deco skyscrapers it was built at the turn of 20th century under the 'tear it down' regime of Mayor Pereira Passos. Rio once had long stately avenues that rivalled the best of Buenos Aires but only clusters have survived. Although it has seen better days, the **Theatro Municipal** ① *Praça Floriano, T021-23329191, www.theatromunicipal.rj.gov.br, Mon-Fri 1300-1700, bilingual guided tours by appointment T021-2299 1667*, remains a splendid piece of French-inspired, lavish neoclassical pomp. The tour is worth it to see front of house and backstage, the decorations and the machine rooms – a luxuriously ornate temple to an early 20th-century Carioca high society. On either side of the ostentatious colonnaded façade are rotundas, surmounted by cupolas. The muses of poetry and music watch over all, alongside an imperial eagle, wings outstretched and poised for flight. The interior is a mock-European fantasy of Carrara-marble columns, crystal chandeliers and gilt ceilings fronted by a vast, sweeping, *Gone With the Wind* staircase. The stage is one of the largest in the world. The theatre was designed by Francisco de Oliveira Passos, son of the contemporaneous city mayor, who won an ostensibly open architectural competition together with French architect Albert Guilbert.

Opposite, on the other side of Avenida Rio Branco, is the refurbished **Museu Nacional de Belas-Artes** ① *Av Rio Branco 199, T021-2219 8474, www.mnba.org.br, Tue-Fri 1000-1800, Sat and Sun 1200-1700, US$3, free on Sun*. Fine art in Rio and in Brazil was, as a whole, stimulated by the arrival in 1808 of the Portuguese royal family. In 1816 the Academia de Belas-Artes was founded by another Frenchman, Joaquim Lebreton. This building was constructed 1906-1908 to house the national gallery and contains the best collection of art in the country. This includes depictions of Brazil by European visitors such as Dutchman Frans Post and Frenchman Jean-Baptiste Debret, and the best of

20th-century Brazilian art by important names such as modernist and social realist Cândido Portinari, Emiliano Di Cavalcanti (famous for his iconographic images of black Cariocas at a time when racism was institutionalized in Rio), Tarsila do Amaral (founder of the first major school of Brazilian Art, *antropofagismo*, which strongly influenced *tropicália*) and the brutalist art deco sculptor Victor Brecheret. Another gallery contains further works by foreign artists and the temporary exhibition hall houses many of Rio de Janeiro's most important international exhibitions.

Another of Cinelândia's stately neoclassical buildings is the **Biblioteca Nacional** ① *Av Rio Branco 219/239, T021-3095 3879, www.bn.br, Mon-Fri 0900-2000, Sat 0900-1500, free*, an eclectic Carioca construction, this time with a touch of art nouveau. The library is fronted by a stately engaged portico supported by a Corinthian colonnade. Inside is a series of monumental staircases in Carrara marble. The stained glass in the windows is French. The first national library was brought to Brazil in 1808 by the Prince Regent, Dom João, from a collection in the Ajuda Palace in Lisbon. Today the library houses more than nine million items, including a first edition of the *Lusiad of Camões*, a 15th-century Moguncia Bible and Book of Hours, paintings donated by Pedro II, scores by Mozart and etchings by Dürer.

Nearby, in the former Ministry of Education and Health building, is the **Palácio Gustavo Capanema** ① *R da Imprensa 16, off the Esplanada do Castelo, at the junction of Av Graça Aranha and R Araújo Porto Alegre, just off Av Rio Branco, T021-2220 1490, by appointment only, Mon-Fri 0900-1800*. Dating back to 1937-1945, it was the first piece of modernist architecture in the Americas and was designed by an illustrious team of architects led by Lúcio Costa (under the guidance of Le Corbusier) and included a very young Oscar Niemeyer – working on his first project. Inside are impressive murals by Cândido Portinari, one of Brazil's most famous artists, as well as works by other well-known names. The gardens were laid out by Roberto Burle Marx who was responsible for many landscaping projects throughout Rio (including the Parque do Flamengo) and who worked with Costa and Niemeyer in Brasília.

LAPA

Only a decade ago Lapa, which lies just south of the cathedral on the edge of Cinelândia, was a no-go area; tawdry and terrifying, walked only by prostitutes, thugs and drug addicts chasing the dragon in the crumbling porticoes of the early 20th century and art nouveau buildings. The area can still feel a little edgy, especially on weekdays after dark. But it has undergone an unimagined renaissance. This was once the Montmartre of Rio; the painter Di Cavalcanti wrote poetically of wandering its streets at night on his way home to Flamengo, past the little cafés and ballrooms and the rows of handsome town houses. Now the cafés are alive once more, spilling out onto the streets, and the ballrooms and town houses throb with samba and electronica. Opera is once more performed in the concert halls of the Escola de Música, and the area's once notorious thoroughfare, Rua do Lavradio, is now lined with smart little restaurants and clubs, playing host to one of the city's most interesting bric-a-brac and antiques markets on Saturdays.

Although the area is best just for a cautious wander after 2000 at the end of the week, or for the Saturday market, there are a few interesting sights. The most photographed are the **Arcos da Lapa**, built in 1744 as an aqueduct to carry water from Santa Teresa to the Chafariz da Carioca, with its 16 drinking fountains, in the centre of the city. The aqueduct's use was changed at the end of the 19th century, with the introduction of electric trams in

Rio. Tracks were laid on top of the arches and the inaugural run was on 1 September 1896. The tram is still in use today and is one of the city's most delightful journeys; it leaves from behind the Catedral de São Sebastião and runs to Santa Teresa, see page 55.

Bars huddle under their southern extremity on **Avenida Mem de Sá**, one of Rio's most popular nightlife streets. Street performers (and vagrants) often gather in the cobbled square between the *arcos* and the cathedral. There are a number of moderately interesting buildings off this square. The eclectic baroque/neoclassical **Escola da Musica da Universidade Federal do Rio de Janeiro** ① *R do Passeio 98, open officially just for performances*, has one of the city's best concert halls. A stroll away is the bizarre baroque façade of another prestigious classical concert hall, the **Sala Cecília Mereilles** ① *Largo da Lapa 47*. More picturesque are the mosaic-tiled **Ladeira do Santa Teresa** stairs, which wind their way steeply from the square and from the back of Rua Teotônio to Santa Teresa. These are much beloved of music video directors and fashion photographers who use them as a backdrop to carefully produced gritty urban scenes. The steps are tiled in red, gold and green and bordered by little houses, many of which are dishevelled and disreputable but wonderfully picturesque. Be vigilant here.

North of Avenida Mem de Sá is **Rua do Lavradio**. This was one of urban Rio's first residential streets and is lined with handsome 18th- and early 20th-century town houses. These are now filled by samba clubs, cafés, bars and antiques shops. Any day is good for a browse and a wander, and on Saturdays at the end of the month there is a busy antiques market, live street tango, no cars and throngs of people from all sections of Carioca society. Some of the houses here were once grand. Number 84 once belonged to the marquis who gave the street its name. Further along is what was once Brazil's foremost Masonic lodge, the imposing **Palácio Maçônico Grande Oriente do Brasil**, which tellingly has had as its grand masters King Dom Pedro I and one of the country's most important Republican politicians, José Bonifácio Andrada e Silva.

CENTRAL DO BRASIL RAILWAY STATION

Central do Brasil or **Dom Pedro II** railway station, as it is also known, once served much of the country but now serves only Rio. This brutal 1930s art deco temple to progress was one of the city's first modernist buildings and was made famous by the Walter Salles film *Central do Brasil* (Central Station). The film's thronging crowd scenes were set here. For similar shots come with your camera in the morning or evening and watch hundreds of thousands of people bustle in and out of trains leaving for the northern and western parts of Rio.

GAMBOA, CIDADE NOVA AND THE SAMBÓDROMO

In the early 20th century, after the Paraguayan war and the abolition of slavery but before the warehouses were built in **Gamboa**, this northern dockland area was known as 'Little Africa' due to the high number of resident Bahian immigrants. With them, the African-Bahian rhythms of the *candomblé* religion were introduced into the Carioca community and the next generation spawned a host of famous local musicians that included Donga, Chico da Baiana and João de Baiana.

The streets and backyards of Gamboa became the birthplace of a new music: samba, born of Angolan *semba* rhythms fused with European singing styles and instruments. Donga and João da Baiana used to gather on the Pedra do Sal stairs close to the Praça

Mauá to play and hold impromptu music and samba dance parties. Later the dance was incorporated into an alternative Mardi Gras festival as a counterpart to the ballroom dances of the white elite. Street parade clubs were formed by another young Carioca, Hilário Jovino Ferreira. Their structure was copied later by the much larger samba schools that still produce the Carnaval parades today.

In 2008 the city government inaugurated the **Cidade do Samba (Samba City)** ⓘ *R Rivadávia Corréa 60, Gamboa, T021-2213 2503, http://cidadedosambarj.globo.com, Tue-Sat 1000-1900*, both to celebrate samba and to bring the administrative and production houses of the samba schools under one roof. The famous samba schools from the **Liga Independente das Escolas de Samba (LIESA)** now have a permanent carnival production centre of 14 workshops, each of them housed in a two-storey building. Visitors can watch floats and costumes being prepared or watch one of the year-round carnival-themed shows. A visit here is a wonderful experience and a real eye-opener, offering the chance to see how much painstaking work goes into create the floats, costumes and dances of schools such as the **Primeira Estação de Mangueira**, for one night's lavish display. Rio's carnival is nailed, glued, stitched and sewn over an entire year. Much of the work is undertaken by **AMEBRAS**, www.amebras.org.br, an association of serious, stern older women who enrol, train and employ dozens of would-be artisans and dressmakers from the favelas. Thus carnival is an industry that revitalizes poor Rio. In the words of Amebras president Célia Regina Domingues "there's no fooling about here – everything we do, from hat-making to foam-sculpting for the floats, is directed towards a profession, post-carnival. People leave our project with real skills." There is a gift shop at the Cidade do Samba where it is possible to buy carnaval costumes and souvenirs many by AMEBRAS, or you can request a visit through their website as part of a visit to the Cidade. The Cidade da Samba has weekly samba shows, tickets for which can be purchased at the booths near the main entrance.

Carnaval happens right next to Gamboa in the **Cidade Nova**. Oscar Niemeyer's 650-m stadium street, the **Sambódromo** ⓘ *R Marquês de Sapucaí s/n, metrô Central or metrô Praça Onze, Cidade Nova, T021-2502 6996, Mon-Fri 0900-1700*, was purpose-built for the annual parades and is well worth a visit at any time (see box, page 74).

Near the Sambodromo, in the Boca do Lixo, an area best reached only by booked taxi, is the **Crescer and Viver circus** ⓘ *R Boca do Lixo, every Thu-Sat from Aug to late Nov, tours are available, see www.crescereviver.org.br; Metrô Praça Onze, but do not walk in this neighbourhood – come by cab*, another of Rio's inspiring community projects. "If it weren't for our circus", says Vinícius Daumas of projeto Crescer and Viver, "I can honestly say that many of these teenagers would be dead. For sure some would be in a trafficking gang." Instead, some 2000 kids from the deprived communities of the Boca do Lixo neighbourhood have gone to circus school and learnt their three Rs whilst also mastering the trapeze and the flic-flac. The current company perform a spectacular show to music composed by Luíz Gonzaga's grandson, Daniel, in a tent in the Boca do Lixo.

Nearby, **Praça Onze** is today the terminus of the city's main thoroughfare, Avenida Presidente Vargas. But it was once a square and an established meeting place for *capoeristas* whose acrobatic martial art to the rhythm of the *berimbau* and hand clap inspired much Carnaval choreography. A replica of the head of a Nigerian prince from the British Museum, erected in honour of **Zumbi dos Palmares**, sits on Avenida Presidente Vargas itself. Zumbi was a Bantu prince who became the most successful black slave emancipator in the history of the Americas, founding a kingdom within Brazil in the 19th century. The **Centro de Memória do Carnaval** ① *Av Rio Branco 4, 2nd floor, T021-3213 5151, www.liesa.com.br, visits by appointment only*, is a research centre and preserves one of the largest repositories of international and Brazilian carnival images, documents and publications in the world.

→NORTHERN RIO

CEMITÉRIO DOS INGLESES

Over the Morro da Providência, between the Estação Dom Pedro II and the bay, is the **Cemitério dos Ingleses** ① *R da Gamboa 181*. The cemetery, the oldest in Rio, was granted to the British community by Dom João, Regent of Portugal, in 1810. Catholics who could afford a burial were laid to rest inside their churches (see the numbers on the church floors, marking the graves), but the British in Rio, being non-Catholic, were not allowed to be buried in the religious establishments. There are other interesting cemeteries in Rio, notably **O Cemitério São João Batista** ① *R Real Grandeza, Botafogo, T021-2539 7073*, where many of the city's most famous are buried, including Machado de Assis, Heitor Villa-Lobos, Carmen Miranda, Santos Dumont, Clara Nunes and Tom Jobim. The grand sculptures and mansion-sized mausoleums, many by Brazil's most celebrated sculptors, contrast with the concrete boxes and plastic flowers of the lower middle classes.

NOSSA SENHORA DA PENHA

① *Largo da Penha 19, T021-2290 0942, www.santuariodapenhario.com.br, Tue-Sun 1000-1600*. The church of Nossa Senhora da Penha is one of the most important pilgrimage centres in the whole country, especially for black Brazilians. It sits on an enormous rock, into whose side 365 steps have been carved. Pilgrims ascend these on their knees during the festival month of October. The church in its present form dates from the early 20th century, but it was modelled on an early 18th-century chapel and a religious building has been on this site since the original hermitage was built in 1632. There are great views from the summit.

To get there take the metrô to Del Castilho. Leave the station to the left, walk down the passageway and catch microbus (micro-ônibus) No 623 labelled 'Penha-Shopping Nova América 2' to the last stop. Get off at the shopping centre, in front of Rua dos Romeiros, and walk up that street to the Largo da Penha from where there are signposts to the church.

MARACANÃ STADIUM

① *Av Prof Eurico Rabelo, T021-2334 1705, www.suderj.rj.gov.br/visitacao_maracana.asp, daily 0900-1700; independent visit Gate 15, guided tour of the stadium from Gate 16 (in Portuguese or English, daily 0930-1700, US$11). Take the metrô to Maracanã station on Linha 2, one stop beyond São Cristóvão. Bus Nos 238 and 239 from the centre, 434 and 464 from Glória, Flamengo and Botafogo, 455 from Copacabana, and 433 and 464 from Ipanema and Leblon all go to the stadium. Trips to football matches can be organized through www.bealocal.com. It is not advisable to drive in this part of Rio. One wrong turn could take you into a dangerous favela.*

Whilst tour guides proclaim Maracanã the largest sports stadium in the world, in fact there are several larger stadiums, including Indianapolis in the USA and Strahov stadium in Prague, Czech Republic. But Maracanã was the largest when it was first built and remains impressive – not least because it is the hallowed temple to the most important religious practice in Brazil – the worship of football. This is where Pelé scored his 1000th goal in 1969. His feet, as well as those of Ronaldo and other Brazilian stars, are immortalized in concrete outside the stadium. The stadium hosted the largest crowd ever to see a football match in 1950 when Brazil lost to Uruguay in front of about 200,000 spectators – an event that shook the national psyche and which is known as the Maracanazo tragedy.

In 2007 the Maracanã was refurbished. The stands were replaced with seats resulting in the decrease of the total capacity to less than 90,000. A further refurbishment is scheduled for the 2014 World Cup, shrinking it even further to less than 80,000 seats. This will take place between September and November 2012, when Maracanã will be closed. The project is controversial, for whilst modest in its aims, it is expected to cost an astounding US$400 million and include the construction of 14,000 new parking spaces, 3000 of which are are going to be allocated inside Quinta da Boa Vista park.

Even if you're not a football fan, matches are worth going to for the spectators' samba bands and the adrenalin-charged atmosphere – especially a local or Rio-São Paulo derby, or an international game. There are four types of ticket: *Cadeira Especial* (special seats), the most expensive; *Arquibancada Branca* (white terraces), which give a good side view of the game; *Arquibancada Verde e Amarela* (green and yellow terraces), with a view from behind the goal; and *Cadeira Comum*. Prices vary according to the game, but it's more expensive to buy tickets from agencies than at the gate or via the internet; it is cheaper to buy tickets from club sites on the day before the match. Average prices are roughly US$46, US$23, US$17 and US$11 respectively. Popular games are more expensive.

Don't take valuables or wear a watch and take special care when entering and leaving the stadium. The rivalry between the local clubs Flamengo and Vasco da Gama is intense, often leading to violence, so it is advisable to avoid their encounters. If you buy a club shirt or favour, don't be tempted to wear it on match day: if you find yourself in the wrong place, you could be in trouble.

→SANTA TERESA

The journey to boho Santa Teresa on one of the pretty yellow trams has long been as captivating as the neighbourhood itself. For decades the trams clattered out of a station next to the cathedral, across the Arcos de Lapa viaduct and up the steep cobbled streets of Santa Teresa itself. But, following a serious accident in 2011, the service was suspended; it is due to re-commence in mid-2013. Even without the tram ride Santa Teresa is well worth visiting – for the attractive streets lined with pretty belle époque houses and lavish mansions, the great restaurants, arty ambience and the stunning views of Rio at every turn. The neighbourhood spreads around the **Largo dos Guimarães** and the **Largo das Neves**, little *praças* of shops and restaurants that feel as if they belong to a village green rather than a large city, where most of the restaurants and hotels are situated.

A sense of separation is reflected not only in the suburb's geography, but also its history. In 1624, Antônio Gomes do Desterro chose the area both for its proximity to Rio and its isolation, and erected a hermitage dedicated to Nossa Senhora do Desterro. The name was changed from Morro do Desterro to Santa Teresa after the construction in 1750 of a convent of that name dedicated to the patroness of the order. The convent exists to this day, but it can only be seen from the outside.

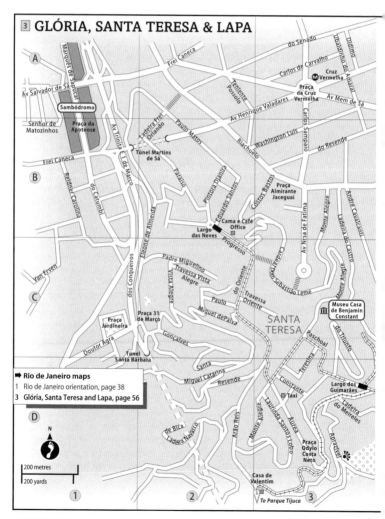

3 GLÓRIA, SANTA TERESA & LAPA

➡ **Rio de Janeiro maps**
1 Rio de Janeiro orientation, page 38
3 Glória, Santa Teresa and Lapa, page 56

200 metres
200 yards

ARRIVING IN SANTA TERESA

Getting there and around The traditional open-sided tram, the *bondinho* was not running as this book went to press, but is due to recommence in mid-2013. Trams run from the terminus next to the Catedral Metropolitana or from Cinelândia: take the metrô to Cinelândia station, go to Rua Senador Dantas then walk along to Rua Profesor Lélio Gama (look for **Banco do Brasil** on the corner); the station is up this street. Take the Paula Mattos line; the fare is around US$1 one way. Bus Nos 206 and 214 run between Avenida

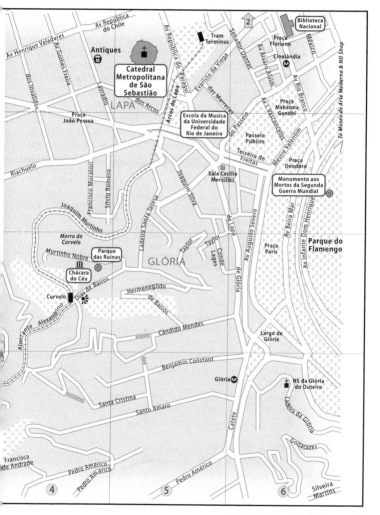

Rio Branco in the centre and Santa Teresa. At night, take a taxi (about US$15 to the centre or Ipanema). In recent years, Santa Teresa has had a reputation for crime; however, the area is much more heavily policed nowadays. Be vigilant with your camera and be particularly wary after dark. Steer clear of any steps that lead down the hill and on Rua Almirante Alexandrino or at the Tijuca end of Largo dos Guimarães.

PLACES IN SANTA TERESA

Santa Teresa is best explored on foot: wander the streets to admire the colonial buildings or stop for a beer in a little streetside café and marvel at the view. The better colonial houses, most of which are private residences, include the **Casa de Valentim** (a castle-like house in Vista Alegre), the tiled **Chácara dos Viegas** in Rua Monte Alegre and the **Chalé Murtinho**. This was the house in which Dona Laurinda Santos Lobo held her famous artistic, political and intellectual salons at the turn of the 20th century. The house was in ruins until it was partially restored and turned into a cultural centre called **Parque das Ruínas** ① *R Murtinho Nobre 41, daily 1000-1700*. It has superb views of the city, an exhibition space and an open-air stage (live music on Thursday). Next door is the **Chácara do Céu**, or **Museu Castro Maya** ① *R Murtinho Nobre 93, T021-3970 1126, www.museuscastromaya.com.br, Wed-Mon 1200-1700, US$1*, housed in the former home of the Carioca millionaire and art collector, Raymundo Ottoni de Castro Maya. It has a wide range of works by modern painters, including Modigliani and important Brazilian like Di Cavalacanti. There are wonderful views out over Guanabara Bay. To get to both the Chácara and the Parque das Ruínas take the Santa Teresa tram to Curvelo station, walk along Rua Dias de Barros, following the signposts to Parque das Ruínas. There are also superb views from the **Museu Casa de Benjamin Constant** ① *R Monte Alegre 225, T021-2509 1248, Wed-Sun 1300-1700*, the former home of the Carioca military engineer and positivist philosopher who helped to found the Republic.

→GLÓRIA, CATETE AND FLAMENGO

The city centre is separated from Copacabana and the other ocean beaches by a series of long white-sand coves that fringe Guanabara Bay and which are divided by towering rocks. The first of the coves is the **Enseada da Glória**, fronting the suburb of the same name and sitting next to the Santos Dumont airport. Avenida Infante Dom Henrique, a broad avenue lined with an eclectic mix of grand houses and squat office blocks, leads from here to what was once the city's finest beach, **Flamengo**, a long stretch of sand separated from the rest of southern Rio by the Morro da Viúva (widow's peak). The suburb of **Catete** lies just behind Flamengo. These three areas were once the heart of recreational Rio; the posing-spots of choice for the belle-époque middle and upper classes and perhaps the most coveted urban beaches in the world. These days the water is polluted and swimming ill-advised, but the suburbs are pleasant for a stroll.

ARRIVING IN GLÓRIA, CATETE AND FLAMENGO

Bus No 119 from the centre or No 571 from Copacabana serve the neighbourhoods, as does the metrô. The centrepiece of the three suburbs are the gardens of the Parque do Flamengo, on Avenida Infante Dom Henrique, reached from metrô Glória, Catete, Largo de Machado or Flamengo. Closed to traffic on Sunday. Be careful after dark.

PLACES IN GLÓRIA, CATETE AND FLAMENGO

Before the pollution became too much, Burle Marx, Brazil's 20th-century Capability Brown, designed the **Parque do Flamengo**, a handsome stretch of waterfront to separate Avenida Infante Dom Henrique from the city's most glorious beach, and gave it ample shade with a range of tropical trees and stands of stately royal palms. The gardens stretch from Glória through to the Morro da Viúva at the far end of Flamengo; they were built on reclaimed land and opened in 1965 to mark the 400th anniversary of the city's founding. The lawns and promenade are favourite spots for smooching lovers, especially at sundown. There are children's play areas too and a handful of monuments and museums. These include the impressive postmodern **Monumento aos Mortos da Segunda Guerra Mundial** ① *Av Infante Dom Henrique, Tue-Sun 1000-1700 for the crypt museum; beach clothes and flip flops not permitted*, the national war memorial to Brazil's dead in the Second World War. The gently curved slab is supported by two slender columns, representing two palms uplifted to heaven and guarded by soldiers from the adjacent barracks. In the crypt are the remains of the Brazilian soldiers killed in Italy in 1944-1945. At the far northern end of the Parque do Flamengo is the **Museu de Arte Moderna** ① *Av Infante Dom Henrique 85, T021-2240 4944, www.mamrio.com.br, Tue-Fri 1200-1800, last entry 1730, Sat-Sun 1200-1900, last entry 1830, US$4*, another striking modernist building with the best collection of modern art in Brazil outside São Paulo. Works by many well-known Europeans sit alongside collections of Brazilian modern and contemporary art including drawings by Cândido Portinari and etchings of everyday work scenes by Gregório Gruber.

The beautiful little church on the Glória hill, overlooking the Parque do Flamengo, is **Nossa Senhora da Glória do Outeiro** ① *T021-2225 2869, Tue-Fri 0900-1200 and 1300-1700, Sat and Sun 0900-1200, guided tours by appointment on the 1st Sun of each month*. Built 1735-1791, it was the favourite church of the imperial family and Dom Pedro II was baptized here. The building is polygonal, with a single tower. It contains some excellent examples of the best *azulejos* (tiles) in Rio and its main wooden altar was carved by Mestre Valentim. Next door is the small **Museum of Religious Art** ① *T021-2556 6434, same hours as church*.

Behind Glória and Flamengo is the rather down-at-heel suburb of Catete, which is dotted with museums. The best of these is the **Museu da República** ① *R do Catete 153, T021-3235 2650, www.museudarepublica.org.br, Tue-Fri 1000-1700, Sat-Sun and holidays 1400-1800, US$4, free Wed and Sun, free for children up to 10 years old and adults above 65, students with ID pay half*, the former palace of a coffee baron, the Barão de Nova Friburgo. The palace was built 1858-1866 and, in 1887, it was converted into the presidential seat, until the move to Brasília. The ground floor of this museum consists of the sumptuous rooms of the coffee baron's mansion. The first floor is devoted to the history of the Brazilian republic. You can also see the room where former president Getúlio Vargas shot himself. Behind the museum is the **Parque do Catete**, which contains many birds and monkeys and is a popular place for practising Tai Chi.

The **Museu do Folclore Edison Carneiro** ① *R do Catete 181, T021-2285 0441, Tue-Fri 1100-1800, Sat and Sun 1500-1800, free*, houses a collection of amusing but poorly labelled small ceramic figures representing everyday life in Brazil, some of which are animated by electric motors. Many artists are represented and displays show the way of life in different parts of the country. There are also fine *candomblé* and *umbanda* costumes, religious objects, displays about Brazil's festivals and a small but excellent library, with helpful staff who can help find books on Brazilian culture, history and anthropology. Flash photography is prohibited.

The **Museu Carmen Miranda** ① *Parque Brigadeiro Eduardo Gomes (Parque do Flamengo), Flamengo, T021-2334 4293, Tue-Fri 1100-1700, Sat and Sun 1300-1700, US$1,* has more than 3000 items related to the famous Portuguese singer forever associated with Rio, who emigrated to Brazil as a child and then moved to Hollywood. The collection includes some of her famous gowns, fruit-covered hats, jewellery and recordings. There are occasional showings of her films.

→BOTAFOGO, URCA AND PÃO DE AÇÚCAR (SUGAR LOAF)

Pão de Açúcar, or the Sugar Loaf, looms over the perfect wine-glass bay of Botafogo, the next of the Guanabara Bay coves after Flamengo. Huddled around the boulder's flanks is the suburb of Urca, home to a military barracks and the safest middle-class houses in Rio. Remnant forest, still home to marmosets and rare birds, shrouds the boulder's sides and a cable car straddles the distance between its summit, the Morro de Urca hill and the houses below, making one of the continent's most breathtaking views easily accessible. Urca and Botafogo have a few sights of interest and make convenient bases with decent accommodation and restaurant options, particularly in the lower price ranges.

ARRIVING IN BOTAFOGO, URCA AND PÃO DE AÇÚCAR (SUGAR LOAF)

Botafogo has a metrô station. Buses that run between Copacabana and the centre stop in Botafogo, so take any bus marked 'Centro' from Copacabana or 'Copacabana' from the centre. Bus No 107 (from the centre, Catete or Flamengo) and No 511 from Copacabana (No 512 to return) take you to Urca and the cable-car station for the Sugar Loaf. Alternatively, walk 10 minutes northeast from behind the Rio Sul shopping centre to the cable-car station, which lies on Praça General Tiburcio, next to the Rio de Janeiro federal university. The rides themselves go up in two stages, the first to the summit of Morro da Urca, the smaller rock that sits in front of the Sugar Loaf, and the second from there to the top of the Sugar Loaf itself. Allow at least two hours for your visit.

PÃO DE AÇÚCAR (SUGAR LOAF)

The western hemisphere's most famous monolith rises almost sheer from the dark sea to just under 400 m, towering over Botafogo beach and separating Guanabara Bay from the open Atlantic Ocean. The views from the top, out over Copacabana, Ipanema and the mountains and forests of Corcovado and Tijuca are as unforgettable as the view from New York's Empire State Building or Victoria Peak in Hong Kong. The **cable car** ① *Av Pasteur 520, Praia Vermelha, Urca, T021-2461 2700, www.bondinho. com.br, daily 0800-1950, US$25, free for children under 6, aged 6-12 half price, every 30 mins,* runs to the top where there are extensive paths, plentiful shade and snack bars. Come early for the clearest air, best views and smallest crowds.

Paths up and around the Sugar Loaf There is more to Sugar Loaf than the views from the top. The surrounding rocks hide secluded little beaches, remnant forest and small colonial suburbs well worth seeing. The best place to begin is at **Praia Vermelha**, the beach to the south of the rock where there is a simple restaurant, the Círculo Militar da Praia Vermelha (no sign) with wonderful views. The walking track, **Pista Cláudio Coutinho** ⓘ *daily 0700-1800*, runs from here along the waterfront around the foot of the rock. You'll see plenty of wildlife at dawn, especially marmosets and colourful tanagers, along with various intrepid climbers scaling the granite. About 350 m from the beginning of the Pista Coutinho is a turning to the left for a path that winds its way up through the forest to the top of **Morro de Urca**, from where the cable car can be taken for US$10. You can save even more money by climbing the **Caminho da Costa**, a path to the summit of the Pão de Açúcar. Only one stretch of 10 m requires climbing gear; wait at the bottom of the path for a group going up. You can then descend to Morro de Urca by cable car for free and walk the rest of the way down. There are 35 rock-climbing routes up the boulder. The best months for climbing are April to August.

BOTAFOGO

The Funai-run **Museu do Índio** ⓘ *R das Palmeiras 55, T021-3214 8702, www.museudo indio.org.br, Mon-Fri 0900-1730, Sat and Sun 1300-1700, US$2.50, free on Sun, 10-min walk from Botafogo metrô or bus No 571 from Catete*, preserves some 12,000 objects from more than 180 Brazilian indigenous groups, including basketry, ceramics, masks and weapons as well as 500,000 documents and 50,000 photographs. Very few are on display and the museum's few rooms are mostly devoted to information panels and short film shows. The garden includes a Guaraní *maloca* and there is a small, well-displayed handicraft shop and a library of ethnology.

The **Museu Villa-Lobos** ⓘ *R Sorocaba 200, T021-2266 3845, www.museuvillalobos. org.br, Mon-Fri 1000-1700, free, lunchtime concert US$6-17*, is a block east of the Museu do Índio. Such was the fame and respect afforded to Latin America's most celebrated composer that the museum was founded just one year after his death in 1960. Inside the fine 19th-century building is a collection of his personal objects including instruments, scores, books and recordings. The museum has occasional concerts and temporary shows and supports a number of classical music projects throughout Brazil.

The **Dona Marta viewpoint**, which sits in the forest immediately above Botafogo and is connected by road to Corcovado, offers the best views of the Sugar Loaf in the city. Do not visit after 1730 as robbers from the nearby favelas frequent the roads.

→CHRIST STATUE AT CORCOVADO AND COSME VELHO

Few famous sights in the world live up to the high expectations overexposure has placed on them. The view from **Corcovado mountain** is one of them. Come, if you can, for dusk. Almost 1 km above the city and at the apex of one of the highest pinnacles in Tijuca forest stands **O Redentor** – Christ the Redeemer – lit in brilliant xenon and with arms open to embrace the urban world's most breathtaking view. At his feet to the west are a panoply of bays, fringed with white and backed by twinkling skyscrapers and the neon of myriad street lights. To the east as far as the eye can see lie long stretches of sand washed by green and white surf. And in front and to the south, next to the vast ocean beaches, is the sparkle of Niterói watched over by low grey mountains and connected to Rio by a 10-km-long sinuous bridge that threads its way across the 10-km expanse of Guanabara Bay. As the light fades, the tropical forest at Christ's back comes to life in a chorus of cicadas and evening birdsong loud enough to drown even the chatter of 1000 tourists.

At the base of the mountain is the sleepy suburb of **Cosme Velho**, leafy and dotted with grand houses, museums and a little artist's corner called the Largo do Boticário. The two are linked by a 3.8-km railway, opened in 1884 by Emperor Dom Pedro II.

ARRIVING IN CHRIST STATUE AT CORCOVADO AND COSME VELHO

There are several ways to reach the top of Corcovado. A cog railway and a road connect the city to the mountain from the suburb of Cosme Velho. Both are on the northern side of the Rebouças tunnel, which runs to and from the Lagoa. From the upper terminus of the **cog railway** ① *R Cosme Velho 513, T021-2558 1329, www.corcovado.com.br, daily every 30 mins 0830-1830, 10 min-journey, US$8 one way, US$15 return*, there is a climb of 220 steps to the top or you can take the newly installed escalator, near which there is a café. Mass is held on Sunday in a small chapel in the statue pedestal. There is a museum at the station with panels showing the history of the statue and the railway.

To get to the cog railway station take a taxi or bus to Cosme Velho and get off at the station. **Buses** are as follows: from the centre or Glória/Flamengo bus No 180; from Copacabana bus Nos 583 or 584; from Botafogo or Ipanema/Leblon bus Nos 583 or 584; from Santa Teresa take the micro-ônibus. **Taxis**, which wait in front of the station, also offer tours of Corcovado and Mirante Dona Marta and cost around US$25.

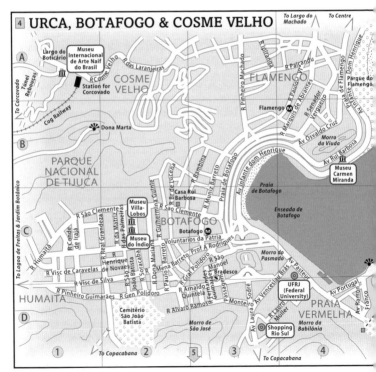

If going **on foot**, take bus No 206 from Praça Tiradentes (or No 407 from Largo do Machado) to Silvestre, where there is a station at which the train no longer stops. It is a steep 9-km walk from here to the top, along a shady road. Take the narrow street to the right of the station, go through the gate used by people who live beside the tracks and continue to the national park entrance. Walkers are charged entrance fees, even if you walk all the way you still have to pay for the van – it is an illegal charge, but in a country with as high a level of corruption as Brazil they can get a way with it. Allow a minimum of two hours (up to four hours depending on fitness).

By **car**, drive through Túnel Rebouças from the Lagoa and then look out for the Corcovado signs before the beginning of the second tunnel and off to your right. Ignore the clamour of the touts at the beginning of the Corcovado road. They will try to convince you that the road is closed in order to take you on an alternative route and charge a hefty fee. If going by car to Corcovado, avoid going on weekends and public holidays – the slow traffic and long queues are overwhelming. Cars cannot go all the way to the parking outside entrance, which is only for authorized cars and vans, instead you have to park halfway in a designated car park and then either walk or take a van, although you have to pay for the van anyway. Avoid returning after dark; it is not safe.

Almost all the hotels, even the hostels, offer organized **coach trips** to Corcovado, which usually take in Sugar Loaf and Maracanã as well. These offer a fairly brief stop on the mountain and times of day are not always the best for light. **Helicopter tours** are available though these leave from the Sugar Loaf or the Lagoa.

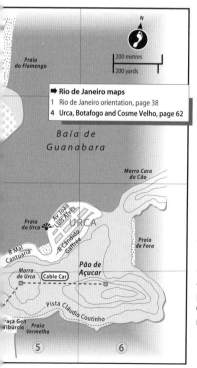

COSME VELHO

The **Museu Internacional de Arte Naif do Brasil (MIAN)** ① *R Cosme Velho 561, on the same street as the station for Corcovado, T021-2205 8612, www.museunaif.com.br, Tue-Fri 1200-1800, weekends 1200-1900, US$7.50,* is one of the most comprehensive museums of naïf and folk paintings in the world with a permanent collection of 8000 works by naïf artists from 130 countries. The museum also hosts several thematic and temporary exhibitions through the year. Parts of its collection are often on loan around the world. There is a coffee shop and a souvenir shop where you can buy paintings, books, postcards and T-shirts. Courses and workshops on painting and related subjects are also available.

➡ Rio de Janeiro maps
1 Rio de Janeiro orientation, page 38
4 Urca, Botafogo and Cosme Velho, page 62

The **Largo do Boticário** ⓘ *R Cosme Velho 822*, is a pretty, shady little square close to the terminus for the Corcovado cog railway and surrounded by 19th-century buildings. It offers a glimpse of what the city looked like before all the concrete and highways. That the square exists at all is thanks to concerned residents who not only sought to preserve it but were also instrumental in rebuilding and refurbishing many of the buildings, using rubble from colonial buildings demolished in the city centre. Many of the doors once belonged to churches. The four houses that front the square are painted different colours (white, pale blue, caramel and pink), each with features picked out in decorative tiles, woodwork and stone. Many artists live here and can often be seen painting in the courtyard.

→COPACABANA AND LEME

Copacabana, which is called Leme at its northern end, epitomizes Rio both for better and for worse. Like the city as a whole, it is breathtakingly beautiful from afar and a little ugly close to. At first sight it looks magnificent. The beach is a splendid broad sweeping crescent of fine sand stretching for almost 8 km, washed by a bottle-green Atlantic and watched over by the **Morro do Leme** – another of Rio's beautiful forest-covered hills. Behind it is a wide neon- and argon-lit avenue lined with high-rises, the odd grand hotel and various bars,

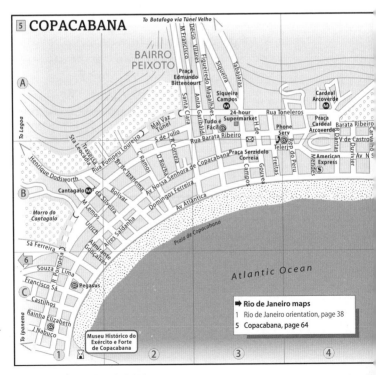

➡ **Rio de Janeiro maps**
1 Rio de Janeiro orientation, page 38
5 Copacabana, page 64

restaurants and clubs. The tanned and toned flock all around in little bikinis, *sungas* and colourful beach wraps, playing volleyball on the sand and jogging along the wavy black and white dragon's tooth pavements, while others busk, play capoeira and sell their wares. But, like much of Brazil, the devil is in the detail and up close Copacabana is a lot less appealing. The sand may be clean enough but those bottle-green waves are far from it. Many of the bars and hotels are tatty and tawdry, some frequented by a Pattaya-type crowd of young, thin Cariocas and fat older foreigners looking to buy more than a drink. And at night Copacabana can be dangerous. Soliciting is rife and muggings are not uncommon.

ARRIVING IN COPACABANA AND LEME
Buses are plentiful and cost US$1.35; Nos 119, 154, 413, 415, 455 and 474 run between the city centre and Avenida Nossa Senhora de Copacabana. If you are going to the centre from Copacabana, look for 'Castelo', 'Praça XV', 'E Ferro' or 'Praça Mauá' on the sign by the front door. 'Aterro' means the expressway between Botafogo and downtown Rio (not open on Sunday). From the centre to Copacabana is easier as all buses in that direction are clearly marked. The 'Aterro' bus takes 15 minutes. Numerous buses run between Copacabana and Ipanema; the two beaches are connected by Rua Francisco Otaviano or Rua Joaquim Nabuco, immediately west of the Forte de Copacabana. Copacabana has metrô stations a

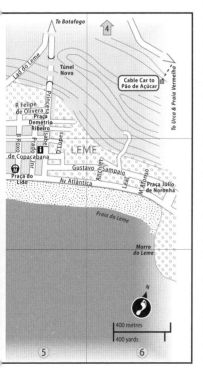

few blocks inland from the beach at Cardeal Arcoverde, Siqueira Campos and Cantagalo. Copacabana metro is linked to Lapa, Centre and Ipanema.

PLACES IN COPACABANA AND LEME
Copacabana has always been a beach and beyond it there are no sights of any note. The area exploded in population after the construction of the **Túnel Velho** (Old Tunnel) in 1891 and the **New Tunnel** in the early 20th century and has been growing, mostly upward, ever since. Streets are lined with high-rise flats that huddle together even on the seafront, crowding around the stately neoclassical façade of the **Copacabana Palace** hotel, which was the tallest building in the suburb until the 1940s.

Apart from New Year's Eve, when the whole suburb becomes a huge party venue and bands play along the entire length of the beach, Copacabana is a place for little more than landscape and people-watching. It's possible to swim in the sea when the current is heading out from the shore, but otherwise not advisable. The best way to enjoy the area is to wander along the promenade from *posto* (lifeguard post) to *posto*, perhaps stopping to enjoy a coconut at one of the numerous beachfront snack bars, and noting the different crowd at each one. Everyone looks at everyone in Rio so don't be afraid to subtly stare.

At the far end of the beach is the **Museu Histórico do Exército e Forte de Copacabana** ⓘ *Av Atlântica at Francisco Otaviano, Posto 6, T021-2521 1032, www.fortedecopacabana. com, Tue-Sun and bank holiday 1000-1800, US$2.30*, which charts the history of the army in Brazil through the colonial, imperial and republican periods, with cases of military artefacts and panels in Portuguese on campaigns such as the one fought at Canudos against Antônio Conselheiro. There are good views over the beaches from the fort and a small restaurant.

→IPANEMA AND LEBLON

Like Copacabana and Leme, Ipanema and Leblon are essentially one long curving beach enclosed by the monolithic Dois Irmãos rocks at the western end and the Arpoador rocks to the east. And, like Copacabana and Leme, they have few sights beyond the sand, the landscape and the beautiful people. Comparisons, however, end there. Ipanema and Leblon are as fashionable and cool as Copacabana is grungy and frenetic. If Copacabana is samba, then Ipanema is bossa nova: wealthy, sealed off from the realities of Rio in a neat little fairy-tale strip of streets and watched over by twinkling lights high up on the flanks

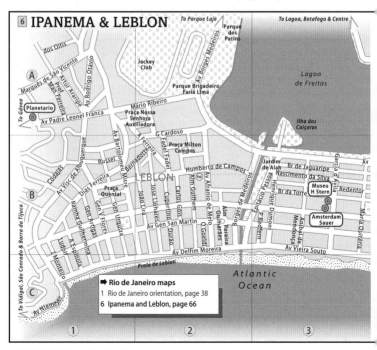

of the Morro Dois Irmãos. They look so romantic that it is easy to forget that they come from the world's largest favela.

Closeted and cosseted though it may be, these are the beach suburbs in which to base yourself whilst in Rio. Almost all of the city's best restaurants and bars are here (and in the suburbs of Gávea and Lagoa, which lie behind). The streets are fairly clean and usually walked by nothing more dangerous than a small white poodle; there is plenty of reasonable accommodation, which doesn't rent by the hour at the lower end of the market; and the sea is good for swimming.

ARRIVING IN IPANEMA AND LEBLON

There is a metro station in Ipanema, General Osório, and an overground metro that runs from Ipanema/General Osório to Gávea along Rua Visconde de Pirajá in Ipanema and Avenida Ataulfo de Paiva in Leblon. The destination for buses is clearly marked but, as a rule of thumb, any buses heading east along the seafront go to Copacabana or, if going west, to Barra da Tijuca; those going inland will pass by the Lagoa or Gávea.

PLACES IN IPANEMA AND LEBLON

Like Copacabana, Ipanema and Leblon are places for people-watching. A half-day wandering around Ipanema/Leblon followed by a half-day wandering Copacabana/Leme can be most interesting. The crowds are quite different. While Copacabana attracts

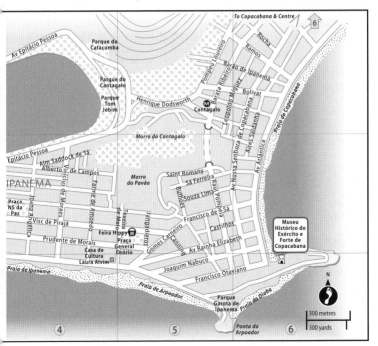

ON THE ROAD

Rio's sun worshippers

Ipanema and Copacabana are the most famous beaches in the world and there can surely be no people more devoted to lazing in the sun than Cariocas. But it wasn't always so. In the 19th century Brazilians would only go near sea water if they had been ordered to do so by a doctor. Even then it would only be for a quick dip at the beginning or the end of the day when the sun was weak. A tan was regarded as unhealthy and a sign of being lower class; to actually sit in the sun was a serious breach of social propriety.

All this began to change when the famous French actress Sarah Bernhardt came to Rio in 1886 to star in *Frou Frou* and *The Lady of the Camelias* at the São Pedro theatre. During her time off she caused a scandal, appalling the great and the good by travelling to then distant Copacabana, throwing on a swimsuit, sunbathing and even swimming in the sea. By the turn of the 20th century others had begun to follow suit, and by 1917 going to the beach had become sufficiently fashionable that the city established strict rules and regulations to govern sun worship. People were permitted to bathe only between 0500-0800 and 1700-1900, had to wear appropriate dress and be quiet and discreet; failure to do so resulted in five years in prison. Official attitudes only began to change in the 1920s with the building of the Copacabana Palace and the arrival of more foreigners who ignored Rio's prudishness and convinced Cariocas to begin to enjoy the beach.

a real cross-section of Rio society, Ipanema and Leblon are predominantly haunts of the fashionable peacocks, who strut along the beachfront promenade, especially around **Posto Nove**. Beyond the people and the breathtaking landscape, there is little to see here but plenty to do, especially for avid consumers. Shopping is best on and around Garcia D'Avila and at the **Feira Hippy**, where you will find everything from high-quality Brazilian designer swimwear to seed bracelets and Bob Marley T-shirts. Those seeking culture but unwilling to leave the beach should head for the **Casa de Cultura Laura Alvim** ① *Av Vieira Souto 176, T021-7104 3603, www.casadelaura.com.br*, comprising an arts cinema, galleries (temporary exhibitions), workshop spaces and a bookshop. If it's pouring with rain you could watch diamonds being cut and set at the **Museus H Stern** ① *R Garcia D'Avila 113, T021-2106 0000*, or **Amsterdam Sauer** ① *R Garcia D'Avila 105, T021-2512 1132*, or hang out at **Garota de Ipanema**, the bar where the *Girl from Ipanema* was written in the late 1950s.

→GÁVEA, LAGOA AND JARDIM BOTÂNICO

Just inland from Ipanema and Leblon, nestled under the forested slopes of Corcovado and the Tijuca National Park and spread around the picturesque saltwater lagoon of Lagoa Rodrigo de Freitas, are these three mainly residential suburbs. There are a few sights of interest and all have lively top-end nightlife. **Gávea** tends to attract the young and wealthy, while the 30-somethings dine in the restaurants in **Lagoa** overlooking the lagoon and go out to clubs in **Leblon** or to the exclusive **Jockey Club**.

ARRIVING GÁVEA, LAGOA AND JARDIM BOTÂNICO

Buses from the centre are marked 'Gávea', or for the Jardim Botânico, Leblon, Gávea or São Conrado 'via Jóquei'. Bus Nos 571 and 170 from the centre go to the Jardim Botânico or No 172 from Flamengo or Botafogo. Bus No 584 runs between Jardim Botânico and Copacabana. Bus Nos 176 and 178 run from the centre and Flamengo and bus Nos 591 and 592 from Copacabana go to the planetarium.

LAGOA DE FREITAS

The Lagoa is another of Rio de Janeiro's unfeasibly beautiful natural sights and has long been admired. Darwin and German naturalists Spix and Martius mention it in their accounts. It is best seen in the early evening when thick golden sunlight bathes the rainforest-clad slopes of the **Serra da Carioca**, which rise high above it to reach their spectacular pinnacle with the distant xenon-white statue of Christ.

Like Copacabana and Guanabara Bay, it could be even more beautiful if only it were looked after a little better. The canal that links the lake to the sea is far too narrow to allow for sufficient exchange of water; pollution makes it unsafe for swimming and occasional summer algal blooms have led to mass fish deaths.

The lake is surrounded by a series of parks. Immediately next to it is the **Parque Tom Jobim** and contiguous are **Brigadeiro Faria Lima**, **Parque do Cantagalo** and **Parque das Taboas**. All have extensive leisure areas popular with roller skaters and volleyball players. There are live shows and *forró* dancing in the **Parque dos Patins** and kiosks serve a variety of food. Nearby is the **Parque Carlos Lacerda** ① *Av Epitacio Pessoa, daily 0800-1900*, an open-air art gallery with sculptures by local artists in a landscaped park shaded by ornamental trees.

JARDIM BOTÂNICO (BOTANICAL GARDENS)

① *R Jardim Botânico 1008, T021-3874 1808, www.jbrj.gov.br, daily 0800-1700, US$3.*

These extensive 137-ha gardens protect 9000 rare vascular plants and are home to 140 species of birds, and butterflies including the brilliant blue morphos. There are stately stands of 40-m-high royal palms, large tropical ficus and ceiba trees and pau brasil, from which the country gets its name. Giant Amazonian victoria regia lilies cover many of the ponds and there are views up to Corcovado through the trees. The gardens were founded in 1808 by the king, Dom Joao VI, as a nursery for European plants and new specimens from throughout the world. When the electric tram line arrived in this part of the city, housing and industries soon followed, but the gardens, then as now, remained a haven of peace. There is a herbarium, an aquarium and a library as well as the **Museu Botânico**, housing exhibitions on the conservation of Brazilian flora, and the **Casa dos Pilões**, the first gun-powder factory in Brazil. A new pavilion contains sculptures by Mestre Valentim. Many improvements were carried out before the 1992 Earth Summit, including a new *orquidario*, an enlarged bookshop and a smart café. Birdwatchers can expect to see rarities including the social flycatcher, great and boat-billed kiskadees, cattle tyrants, sayaca, palm and seven-coloured (green-headed) tanagers, over 20 kinds of hummingbird, roadside hawks, laughing falcons and various toucans and parakeets. There are marmosets in the trees.

Less than 1 km from the gardens is the little-visited **Parque Laje** ① *R Jardim Botânico 414, daily 0900-1700, free*, which is more jungle-like than the Jardim Botânico and has a series of small grottoes, an old tower and lakes, as well as the **Escola de Artes Visuais** (visual arts school) housed in a large colonial house in the grounds.

FESTIVALS

20 January The festival of São Sebastião, patron saint of Rio, is celebrated by an evening procession, leaving Capuchinhos church in Tijuca and arriving at the cathedral of São Sebastião. On the same evening, an *umbanda* festival is celebrated at the *Caboclo* monument in Santa Teresa.

February Carnaval (see box, page 74).

June The Festas Juninas are celebrated throughout Brazil. In Rio they start with the **festival of Santo Antônio** on 13 Jun, when the main event is a Mass, followed by celebrations at the Convento do Santo Antônio and the Largo da Carioca. All over the state, the **festival of São João** is a major event, marked by huge bonfires on the night of 23-24 Jun. It is traditional to dance the *quadrilha* and drink *quentão*, *cachaça* and sugar, spiced with ginger and cinnamon, served hot. The Festas Juninas close with the **festival of São Pedro** on 29 Jun. Being the patron saint of fishermen, his feast is normally accompanied by processions of boats.

October This is the month of the feast of **Nossa Senhora da Penha** (see page 54).

30-31 December Less hectic than Carnaval, but very atmospheric, is the **festival of Yemanjá** when devotees of the *orixá* of the sea dress in white and gather at night on Copacabana, Ipanema and Leblon beaches, singing and dancing around open fires and making offerings. The elected Queen of the Sea is rowed along the seashore. At midnight small boats are launched as offerings to Yemanjá. The religious event is dwarfed, however, by a massive New Year's Eve party, called **Reveillon** at Copacabana. The beach is packed as thousands of revellers enjoy free outdoor concerts by big-name pop stars, topped with a lavish midnight firework display. It is most crowded in front of the Copacabana Palace Hotel. Another good place to see the fireworks is at the far end of the beach in front of R Princesa Isabel, famous for its fireworks waterfall at about 0010. Many followers of Yemanjá now make offerings on 29 or 30 Dec and at Barra da Tijuca or Recreio dos Bandeirantes to avoid the crowds and noise of Reveillon.

The **Planetario** ① *R Padre Leonel Franco 240, Gávea, www.rio.rj.gov.br/planetario, by appointment, free*, has a sculpture of the Earth and Moon by Mário Agostinelli. On Wednesday evenings at dusk, in clear weather, astronomers give guided observations of the stars. At weekends there are shows for children at 1630, 1800 and 1930. There are occasional *chorinho* concerts on Thursday or Friday.

The **Instituto Moreira Salles** ① *R Marquês de São Vicente 476, Gávea, T021-3284 7400, www.ims.com.br, Tue-Fri 1300-2000, Sat and Sun 1300-1800, free*, is a cultural centre in a modernist mansion with gardens landscaped by Burle Marx. There are exhibition halls for photographic shows and an auditorium for concerts and films.

Rough paths lead to the summit of the flat-topped **Pedra da Gávea** and to magnificent views. Hang-gliders fly to the beach at São Conrado from the **Pedra Bonita** behind the Pedra da Gávea.

This rapidly developing district, modelled on Miami, is one of the city's principal middle-class residential areas. It focuses on a 20-km sandy beach that is renowned for its surfing, especially at its far westernmost end: **Recreio dos Bandeirantes**. There are countless bars and restaurants, concentrated at both ends, as well as campsites, motels and hotels. Budget accommodation tends to be self-catering.

ARRIVING IN BARRA DA TIJUCA AND BEYOND

Buses from the city centre to Barra are Nos 175 and 176; from Botafogo, Glória or Flamengo take No 179; from Leme Nos 591 or 592; and from Copacabana via Leblon (45 minutes to one hour). A taxi from the centre costs US$25 (US$35 after 2400) or US$15 from Ipanema. A comfortable bus, **Pegasus**, goes along the coast from the Castelo bus terminal to Barra da Tijuca and continues to Campo Grande or Santa Cruz, or take the free 'Barra Shopping' bus. Bus No 700 from Praça São Conrado goes the length of the beach to Recreio dos Bandeirantes.

PLACES IN BARRA DA TIJUCA AND BEYOND

The **Bosque da Barra/Parque Arruda Câmara** ① *junction of Av das Américas and Av Ayrton Senna, daily 0700-1700*, preserves the vegetation of the sandbanks that existed on this part of the coast before the city took over. The **Autódromo** (motor-racing track) is behind Barra and the Lagoa de Jacarepaguá, in the district of the same name. The Brazilian Grand Prix was held here during the 1980s before returning to Interlagos, São Paulo.

Terra Encantada ① *Av Ayrton Senna 2800, T021-2430 9800, www.terra-encantada. com.br, Thu-Sun 1000-2300*, is a 300,000-sq-m theme park in Barra themed according to the different cultural heritages of Brazil: indigenous, African and European. Among the attractions are roller coasters, river rapids, a cinema and shows. Rides close at 2200 and on the main street restaurants, bars and nightspots open.

A bit further out is the **Museu Casa do Pontal** ① *Estrada do Pontal 3295, Recreio dos Bandeirantes, T021-2490 3278, www.museucasadopontal.com.br, Tue-Sun 0930-1700*. Located in a little wood near Recreio dos Bandeirantes beach, this is one of the finest collections of Brazilian folk art in the country. There are over 5000 works by more than 200 artists from 24 different Brazilian states, accumulated French designer Jacques van de Beuque over a 40-year period. Recommended.

① *Daily 0600-2100, see map, page 38.*
Corcovado is situated within Tijuca National Park; one of the largest areas of urban rainforest in the world. It is a haven for city-weary Cariocas, as well as for some 200 species of birds, numerous small mammals and primates and hundreds of species of endangered Atlantic coast rainforest plants. The forest has a number of natural springs, many of which have been diverted through bamboo channels to form natural showers – be sure to bring swimming gear. There is plenty of shade and the views from the various vantage points are almost as impressive as those from Corcovado.

GOING FURTHER

Búzios

Since it was visited by a young Brigitte Bardot and her Brazilian lover in the 1960s, Búzios has grown from tiny fishing village to mock-Mediterranean tourist resort and cruise ship port. At weekends and over holiday periods its single cobbled street, bustling bars, numerous condos and beaches buzz with people and buggies. There's little to do in Búzios but laze in the sun and take a bay cruise; the beaches are less spectacular than the rainforest-fringed coves of the Costa Verde, but they remain popular nonetheless and the town is a just a few hours' drive or bus ride from Rio.

There are 25 beaches in total. The most visited are **Geribá** (many bars and restaurants; popular with surfers), **Ferradura** (deep-blue sea and calm waters), **Ossos** (the most famous and close to the town centre), **Tartaruga** and **João Fernandes**. The better surf beaches, such as **Praia de Manguinhos** and **Praia de Tucuns**, are further from the town centre. To help you to decide which beach suits you best, you can join one of the local two- or three-hour schooner trips, which pass many of the beaches, or else hire a beach buggy (available from agencies on Rua das Pedras – the main street in tiny Búzios town – or through most hotels and hostels). These trips cost around US$20-25 and can be arranged through **Buziana Tour**, T022-2626 6760, www.buzianatour.com.br. There's plenty of accommodation in Búzios, details of which can be found at www.buziosonline.com.br.

The vegetation in the Parque Nacional da Tijuca is not primary; most is natural regrowth and planned reforestation. It is a testament to what humans can do to regenerate lost forest. The first Europeans to arrive in the area cut down trees for use in construction and as firewood. The lower areas were cleared to make way for sugar plantations. When coffee was introduced to Rio de Janeiro in 1760 further swathes were cut down for *fazendas*. But the deforestation destroyed Rio's watershed and in 1861, in one of the world's first conservation projects, the imperial government decided that Tijuca should become a rainforest preserve. The enormous task of reforesting the entire area was given to an army major, Manuel Gomes Archer, who took saplings from other areas of Atlantic forest and replanted Tijuca with native trees and a selection of exotics in fewer than 13 years. The names of the six slaves who did the actual manual work is not known. Reforestation was continued by Tomas de Gama. In 1961 Tijuca was joined to several other patches of remnant forest to form a national park of 3300 ha.

ARRIVING PARQUE NACIONAL DA TIJUCA
To get to the park entrance, take bus No 221 from Praça 15 de Novembro, No 233 ('Barra da Tijuca') or No 234 from the *rodoviária* or No 454 from Copacabana to Alto da Boa Vista. There is no public transport within the park and the best way to explore is by trail, tour, bicycle or car. If hiking in the park other than on the main paths, a guide may be useful if you do not want to get lost. Contact the **Sindicato de Guías**, T021-267 4582.

VISITING PARQUE NACIONAL DA TIJUCA
One of the best walks is to the **Pico da Tijuca** (1022 m). Views from the top are wonderful and the walk offers the chance to see plenty of animals. Allow two to three hours. To get to the trailhead enter the park at **Alto da Boa Vista** and follow the signposts (maps are displayed) to **Bom Retiro**, a good picnic place (1½ hours' walk). At Bom Retiro the road ends and there is another hour's walk up a fair footpath to the summit (take the path from the right of the Bom Retiro drinking fountain, not the more obvious steps from the left). The last part consists of steps carved out of the solid rock. There are several sheer drops at the summit which are masked by bushes – be wary. The route is shady for almost its entire length. The main path to Bom Retiro passes the **Cascatinha Taunay** (a 30-m waterfall) and the **Mayrink Chapel** (1860). Panels painted in the Chapel by **Cândido Portinari** have been replaced by copies and the originals will probably be installed in the Museu de Arte Moderna. Beyond the chapel is the wonderful little restaurant **Os Esquilos**, which dates from 1945. Allow at least five hours for the walk.

Other viewpoints include the **Paulo e Virginia Grotto**, the **Vista do Almirante**, the **Mesa do Imperador** and the **Vista Chinesa** (420 m), a Chinese-style pavilion with a view of the Lagoa Rodrigo de Freitas, I panema and Leblon. **Museu Açude** ① *Estrada do Açude 764, Alto da Boa Vista, T021-2492 2119, www.museuscastromaya.com.br, Thu-Sun 1100-1700, Sun brunch with live music 1230-1700*, is in the former home of tycoon Castro Maia with some impressive murals and *azulejos* (tiles).

ON THE ROAD

Carnaval

Rio's Carnaval focuses on a designated parade, taking place over a number of days and contained within the Sambódromo stadium. Alongside the showcase in the Sambódromo are a number of street carnival parades run by locally based troupes or *blocos* occurring throughout the city, *bailes* (parties) held within designated clubs and street shows like those held around Praça Onze. The main show in the Sambódromo features a competition between the famous Rio samba schools in Rio, which are divided into two leagues. The 14 schools of the premier group, the **Grupo Especial** parade on Sunday and Monday. These are the most spectacular and expensive shows – the ones featured on television. The less flamboyant **Grupos de Acesso A and B** parade on Saturday and Friday respectively. There is also a mirins parade (younger members of the established schools) on Tuesday. Judging takes place on Wednesday afternoon and the winners of the groups parade again on the following Saturday. Tickets to these winners' parades are always easy to get hold of even when all others are sold out.

Each Grupo Especial school comprises 2500-6000 participants divided into *alas* (wings), each with a different costume and parading on or around five to nine *carros alegóricos* (beautifully designed floats). Each school chooses an *enredo* (theme) and composes a samba that is a poetic, rhythmic and catchy expression of the theme. The *enredo* is further developed through the design of the floats and costumes. A *bateria* (percussion wing) maintains a reverberating beat that must keep the entire school, and the audience, dancing throughout the parade. Each procession follows a set order with the first to appear being the *comissão de frente* (a choreographed group that presents the school and the theme to the public). Next comes the *abre alas* (a magnificent float usually bearing the name or symbol of the school). The *alas* and other floats follow as well as *porta bandeiras* (flag bearers) and *mestre salas* (couples dressed in 18th-century costumes bearing the school's flag), and *passistas* (groups traditionally of mulata dancers). An *ala of baianas* (elderly women with circular skirts that swirl as they dance) is always included as is the *velha guarda* (distinguished members of the school) who close the parade. Schools are given between 65 and 80 minutes and lose points for failing to keep within this time. Judges award points to each school for components of their procession, such as costume, music and design, and make deductions for lack of energy, enthusiasm or discipline. The winners of the **Grupos de Acesso** are promoted to the next higher group while the losers, including those of the **Grupo Especial**, are relegated to the next lowest group. Competition is intense and the winners gain a monetary prize funded by the entrance fees.

The Carnaval parades are the culmination of months of intense activity by community groups, mostly in the city's poorest districts. Rio's *bailes* (fancy-dress balls) range from the sophisticated to the wild. The majority of clubs and hotels host at least one. The **Copacabana Palace**'s is elegant and expensive whilst the Scala club has licentious parties. It is not necessary to wear fancy dress; just join in, although you will feel more comfortable if you wear a minimum of clothing to the clubs, which are crowded, hot and rowdy. The most famous are the **Red and Black Ball** (Friday) and the **Gay Ball** (Tuesday), both of which are both televised. Venues for these vary.

Bandas and *blocos* can be found in all neighbourhoods and some of the most popular and entertaining are: **Cordão do Bola Preta** (meets at 0900 on Saturday, Rua 13 de Maio 13, Centro); **Simpatia é Quase Amor** (meets at 1600 on Sunday, Praça General Osório, Ipanema) and the transvestite **Banda da Ipanema** (meets at 1600 on Saturday and Tuesday, Praça General Osorio, Ipanema). It is necessary to join a *bloco* in advance to receive their distinctive T-shirts, but anyone can join in with the *bandas*. The expensive hotels offer special Carnaval breakfasts from 0530. **Caesar Park** is highly recommended for a wonderful meal and a top-floor view of the sunrise over the beach.

TICKETS AND RESERVATIONS

Sambódromo, R Marquês de Sapucaí s/n, Cidade Nova. http://carnaval.rioguiaoficial.com.br and www.rioguiaoficial.com.br. The nearest tube is Praça Onze.

The Sambódromo parades start at 1900 and last about 12 hrs. Gates open at 1800. There are *cadeiras* (seats) at ground level, *arquibancadas* (terraces) and *camarotes* (boxes). The best boxes are reserved for tourists and VIPs and are very expensive or by invitation only. Seats are closest to the parade, but you may have to fight your way to the front. Sectors 4, 7 and 11 are the best spots (they house the judging points); 6 and 13 are least favoured (being at the end when dancers might be tired) but have more space. The terraces, while uncomfortable, house the most fervent fans and are tightly packed; this is the best place to soak up the atmosphere but it's too crowded to take pictures. Tickets start at US$120 for *arquibancadas* and are sold at travel agencies as well as the Maracanã Stadium box office (see page 54). **Travel agency: Carnaval Turismo**, Av Nossa Senhora de Copacabana 583, T021-2548 4232, www.carnavalinrio.com.br. Tickets should be bought as far as possible in advance; they are usually sold out before Carnaval weekend but touts outside can often sell you tickets at inflated prices. Samba schools have an allocation of tickets which members sometimes sell, if you are offered one of these check the date. Tickets for the champions' parade on the Saturday following Carnaval are much cheaper. Many tour companies offer Rio trips including Carnaval, but tickets are at inflated prices.

Be sure to reserve accommodation well in advance. Virtually all hotels raise their prices during Carnaval, although it is usually possible to find a reasonably priced room.

TAKING PART

Most samba schools will accept a number of foreigners and you will be charged from US$200 up to US$450 for your costume depending on which school of samba you choose. This money helps to fund poorer members of the school. You should be in Rio for at least two weeks before Carnaval.

TRANSPORT

Taxis to the Sambódromo are negotiable and will find your gate; the nearest metrô is Praça Onze.

USEFUL INFORMATION

Guia do Rio, http://rioguiaoficial.com.br/rio-carnaval and www.rio-carnival.net, have more information on the events in any particular carnival year.

RIO DE JANEIRO LISTINGS

WHERE TO STAY

Rooms in Rio are not good value. If you want to stay near a beach that is clean enough to swim from, opt for Ipanema or Copacabana, both of which have rooms for all budgets. Other attractive areas include Botafogo (for backpackers) and *boho* Santa Teresa, which, while isolated from public transport, feels like a village within the city and affords stunning views. **Cama e Café** (www.camae cafe.com.br) offer accommodation with locals or in private flats in Santa Teresa and on the beaches. **Hidden Pousadas Brazil** (www.hiddenpousadasbrazil.com) have great options in carefully selected small mid- to upper-end hotels and homes throughout the city and beyond. **Hostel World** (www.hostel world.com) offers a broad and well-reviewed choice of budget accommodation.

Ipanema, Copacabana and around
$$$$ Fasano Rio, Av Vieira Souto 80, Ipanema, T021-3202 4000, www.fasano. com.br. A Philippe Starck-designed luxury boutique hotel has the plushest rooms with a view in Rio. If your budget will accommodate, opt for the ocean view deluxe. The best are on the upper floors on the building's corners. There's a spectacular rooftop terrace, pool, fitness centre, sauna and massage, a good bar with live music, limousine service for airport transfers, one of the city's best restaurants and exorbitant in-room Wi-Fi.
$$$$ La Maison, R Sergio Porto 58, Gávea, T021-3205 3585, www.lamaisonario.com. This fashionable, French-owned boutique hotel, sits in a period townhouse in an upmarket residential suburb 10 mins' cab ride from Ipanema. Modish, spacious rooms are decorated in bright primary colours and faux-baroque and there are wonderful views of Corcovado from the open-sided breakfast area and pool.

$$$ Copacabana Sol, R Santa Clara 141, T021-2549 4577, www.copacabanasolhotel. com.br. This newly refurbished tower hotel 5 mins' walk from the beach is well kept and well run, with tiled, a/c rooms all with cable TV, Wi-Fi, safes and en suite bathrooms with marble commodes and showers.
$$$ Santa Clara, R Décio Vilares 316, T021-2256 2650, www.hotelsantaclara.com.br. Bright, newly refurbished rooms a few blocks back from the beach. Spartan but friendly service. Well maintained, discreet and good value, at the lower end of this price range.
$$-$ Casa 6, R Barão da Torre 175, casa 6, Ipanema, T021-2247 1384, www.casa6 ipanema.com. This French-owned B&B in 2 townhouses sits on a street filled with hostels, 3 blocks from the beach. It offers attractive long-stay rates and the small, fan-cooled rooms with en suites are decorated in wood and tile.
$$-$ Stone of a Beach hostel, R Barata Ribeiro 111, Copacabana, T021-3209 0348, www.stoneofabeach.com.br. Very popular and well-run hostel with spacious, clean dorms and doubles, a lovely pool and bar on the terrace and one of the best ranges of tours in Rio, including surf classes.

Botafogo and the bay beaches
$$-$ Sun Rio Hostel, R Praia de Botafogo 462, casa 5, Botafogo, T021-2226 0461, www.sunriohostel.com.br. A/c dorms, doubles and en suites, all very well kept and clean. Shared kitchen, internet, bike rental and tours organized. Friendly owner Daniela is very welcoming. Several other similar hostels in this street if full.

Santa Teresa
$$$$-$$$ Quinta Azul and Quinta Rosa, R Almirante Alexandrino 256, T021-3253 1021,

www.quintazul.com, and R Santa Cristina 104, T021-2221 3221, www.quintarosa.com. 2 newly refurbished and revamped very attractive 19th-century townhouses with a range of simple, elegant rooms, pools, discreet, friendly service and plenty of lounging space. **Quinta Azul** has the best views and location – next to the fashionable Espírito Santa restaurant. Quinta Rosa is quieter, more private and more up-market. **$$-$ Casa Áurea**, R Áurea 80, T021-2242 5830, www.casaaurea.com.br. Tranquil, friendly, arty hostel and boutique hotel in a colonial house in a Santa Teresa backstreet.

RESTAURANTS

There's an eatery on every corner in Rio. Enjoy an energizing *açai* or tangy tropical juice at the numerous *casas de suco* near the beach, Brazilian tapas (*petiscos*) in a botequim bar, or a fresh coconut by the sea at one of the many booths on Ipanema or Copacabana. Per kilo resturants offer the best value.

$$$ Aprazível, R Aprazível 62, T021-2508 9174, www.aprazivel.com.br. Seafood, steaks and Brazilian staples may be pricier than their worth, but restaurant views don't get any better – Sugar Loaf, the bay and the lights of Rio twinkle at your feet. Book a chunky wood table in the tropical garden and come at sunset for pre-dinner *caipirinha* cocktails.

$$$ Carlota, R Dias Ferreira 64, Leblon, T021-2540 6821, www.carlota.com.br. The best of many on a street lined with restaurants and bars. Great unpretentious Mediterranean food in an elegant, casual all-white dining room.

$$$ Roberta Sudbrack, R Lineu de Paula Machado 916, Jardim Botânico, T021-3874 0139, www.robertasudbrack.com.br. If you love food and want to fine dine in Rio this is the best option. Roberta was the private chef for President Henrique Cardoso and cooked for all the visiting international dignitaries who dined with him during his term of office. Her tours-de-force are the degustations, showcasing Brazilian flavours and ingredients and utilizing molecular gastronomy.

$ Empório Saúde, R Visconde de Pirajá 414, Ipanema, T021-2247 6361, www.emporioesaude.com.br. Closed Sun and evenings. One of Rio's few veggie options, with a variety of meat-free comfort-cooking from quiches to stews in a wholefood shop inside a shopping gallery.

WHAT TO DO

André Albuquerque, T021-7811 2737/ 2427 3629, andrealbuquerque@yahoo.com.br. Private driver tours of Rio and beyond with an accredited English speaking guide. Friendly, reliable and helpful.

Be A Local, T021-9643 0366, www.bea local.com. Walking trips of Rocinha favela, trips to *baile* funk parties and football matches in Maracanã.

Helisight, R Visconde de Pirajá 580, loja 107, Térreo, Ipanema, T021-2511 2141, www.helisight.com.br. Helicopter sight-seeing tours. Well worth the high price.

Favela Santa Marta Tour, T021-9177 9459, favelasantamartatour.blogspot.co.uk. Visits with locals to a beautifully situated favela; fascinating insights into the community and stunning views of Corcovado and Sugar Loaf.

Rio Hiking, T021-2552 9204 and T021-9721 0594, www.riohiking.com.br. Walking and hiking tours around Rio city and state, including Tijuca and Itatiaia national parks.

COSTA VERDE

The Rio de Janeiro–Santos section of the BR-101 is one of the world's most beautiful highways, hugging the forested and hilly Costa Verde southwest of Rio. The Serra do Mar mountains plunge down to the sea in a series of spurs that disappear into the Atlantic to reappear as a cluster of islands offshore. The most beautiful of these is Ilha Grande: an 80,000-ha mountain ridge covered in rainforest and fringed with wonderful beaches. Beyond Ilha Grande, further down the coast towards São Paulo, is one of Brazil's prettiest colonial towns, Paraty, which sits surrounded by long white beaches in front of a glorious bay of islands. Seen from the harbour in the morning light, this is one of Brazil's most photographed sights.

TRAVELLING ALONG THE COSTA VERDE

The BR-101 is paved all the way to Santos, which has good links with São Paulo. Buses from Rio run to Angra dos Reis, the jumping-off point for Ilha Grande, Paraty, and further south. Some are direct, others take the *via litoral* and go through Copacabana, Ipanema and Barra (US$10, 2½ hours). Sit on the left for the best views. The route is busy at weekends. Hotels and *pousadas* have sprung up all along the road, as have expensive housing developments, though these have not spoiled the views. The drive from Rio to Paraty should take four hours, but it would be better to break the journey and enjoy some of the attractions. The coast road has lots of twists and turns so, if prone to motion sickness, get a seat at the front of the bus to make the most of the views.

→ILHA GRANDE

Ilha Grande is a mountain ridge covered in tropical forest protruding from the emerald sea and fringed by some of the world's most beautiful beaches. There are no cars and no roads, just trails through the forest, so the island is still relatively undeveloped. With luck it will remain so, as much of Ilha Grande forms part of a state park and biological reserve, and cannot be visited.

That the island has so much forest is largely a fluke of history. It was a notorious pirate lair in the 16th and 17th centuries and then a landing port for slaves. By the 20th century it was the site of an infamous prison for the country's most notorious criminals, including the writer Graciliano Ramos, whose *Memórias do Cárcere* relate his experiences. The prison closed in 1994 and is now overgrown. Since then Ilha Grande has been a well-kept Brazilian secret, but is gradually becoming part of the international backpacker circuit.

ARRIVING ON ILHA GRANDE

Getting there Fishing boats and ferries (**Barcas SA**, T021-2533 7524) leave from Angra dos Reis, Conceição de Jacareí and Mangaratiba, taking two hours or so to reach Vila do Abraão, the island's only real village. From Angra there are four daily yachts and catamarans and one ferry (at 1000) leaving between 0730 and 1600, and an extra ferry at 1330 on weekends and public holidays. From Conceição de Jacareí there are seven yacht sailings daily between 0900 and 1815, with an occasional late boat at 2100 on busy Fridays. From Mangaratiba there is a ferry at 0800 and a yacht at 1400. Schedules change frequently and it's well worth checking for the latest on www.ilhagrande.org, which details the names and phone numbers of all boats currently sailing. Ferries cost US$4 on weekdays and double that on weekends, yachts US$8 and catamarans US$30. All the towns are served by **Costa Verde** buses leaving from the *rodoviária* in Rio.

Easy Transfer, T021-7753 2190, offer a van and boat service from Rio to Ilha Grande; door to door from the city (US$40) and from the airport (price depends on flight times and numbers); and from Ilha Grande to Paraty (US$25). There are discounts on multi-trips (eg Rio–Ilha Grande–Paraty–Rio).

Moving on Buses and shuttles run along the BR-101 from Angra dos Reis to Paraty (see page 80).

Tourist information The weather is best from March to June and the island is overrun during the Christmas, New Year and Carnaval periods. There is a small tourist office on the jetty at Abraão. Further information and pictures can be found at www.ilhagrande.org. Be aware that undercover police may be searching for backpackers smoking cannabis on Ilha Grande's beaches.

BEACHES AND WALKS

The beach at **Abraão** may look beautiful to new arrivals but those further afield are far more spectacular. The two most famous are: **Lopes Mendes**, a long stretch of sand on the eastern (ocean side) backed by flatlands and patchy forest; and **Aventureiro**, fringed by coconut palms and tropical forest, its powder-fine sand pocked with boulders and washed by a transparent aquamarine sea. Lopes Mendes is two hours' walk from Abraão; Aventureiro is over six hours, but it can be reached by boat. A few fishermen's huts and *barracas* provide food and accommodation here but there is no camping. Good beaches closer to Abraão include the half-moon bay at **Abraãozinho** (15 minutes' walk) and **Grande das Palmas**, which has a delightful tiny whitewashed chapel (one hour 20 minutes' walk). Both lie east of the town past **Hotel Sagu**. There are boat trips to **Lagoa Azul**, with crystal-clear water and reasonable snorkelling, **Freguesia de Santana** and **Saco do Céu**.

There are a couple of good treks over the mountains to **Dois Rios**, where the old jail was situated. There is still a settlement of former prison guards here who have nowhere to go. The walk is about 13 km each way, takes about three hours and affords beautiful scenery and superb views. Another three-hour hike is to **Pico do Papagaio** (980 m) through forest; it's a steep climb for which a guide is essential, but the view from the top is breathtaking. **Pico da Pedra d'Água** (1031 m) can also be climbed.

→PARATY

With a population of 30,000, Paraty is one of Brazil's prettiest colonial towns and one of Rio de Janeiro state's most popular tourist destinations. It is at its most captivating at dawn, when all but the dogs and chickens are sleeping. As the sun peeps over the horizon the little rectilinear streets are infused with a rich golden light, which warms the whitewash and brilliant blue and yellow window frames of the colonial town houses and the façades of the Manueline churches. Brightly coloured fishing boats bob up and down in the water in the foreground and behind the town the deep green of the rainforest-covered mountains of the Serra da Bocaina sit shrouded in their self-generated wispy cloud. The town was founded in the 17th century as a gold port and most of its historic buildings date from this period.

At the weekend Paraty buzzes with tourists who browse in the little boutiques and art galleries or buy souvenirs from the indigenous Guarani who proffer their wares on the cobbles. At night they fill the numerous little bars and restaurants, many of which, like the *pousadas*, are owned by the bevy of expat Europeans who have found their haven in Paraty and who are determined to preserve its charm. During the week, especially off season, the town is quiet and intimate, its atmosphere as yet unspoilt by the increasing numbers of independent travellers.

The town's environs are as beautiful as Paraty itself. Just a few kilometres away lie the forests of the **Ponta do Juatinga Peninsula**, fringed by wonderful beaches, washed by little waterfalls and still home to communities of Caiçara fishermen who live much as they have done for centuries. Islands pepper the bay, some of them home to ultra-rare animals such as the tiny golden lion tamarin monkey, which is found nowhere else. The best way to visit these destinations is on a boat trip with one of the town's fishermen from the quay.

ARRIVING IN PARATY

Getting there and around There are direct bus connections with Rio (241 km, 3¾ hours, US$8.10) several times daily, and with a number of destinations along the coast, including Angra dos Reis (98 km, 1½ hours, US$4) if you are coming from Ilha Grande. On public holidays and in high season, the frequency of bus services usually increases. The *rodoviária* is at the corner of Rua Jango Padua and Rua da Floresta. Taxis charge a set rate of US$4 from the bus station to the historic centre, which is pedestrianized and easily negotiable on foot.

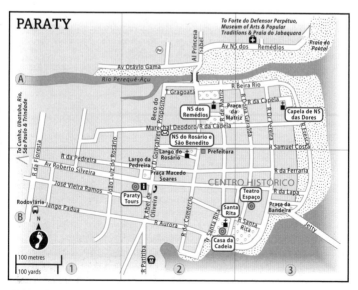

Easy Transfer, T021-7753 2190, offer a door-to-door van and boat service from Rio to Paraty; from the city (US$40) and from the airport (price depends on flight times and numbers); and from Ilha Grande to Paraty (US$25). There are discounts on multi-trips (eg Rio–Ilha Grande–Paraty–Rio).

Moving on From Paraty, you may want to make your way to the **Parque Nacional de Itatiaia** (see page 84). Alternatively, you can return to the *rodoviária* in Rio and head north on a bus to **São João del Rei** (see page 89) and the colonial cities of Minas Gerais.

Tourist information Staff at the Centro de Informações Turísticas ① *Av Roberto Silveira, near the entrance to the historic centre, T024-3371 1266,* are friendly and helpful and some speak English. There is a good town map in the *Welcome to Paraty* brochure, www.eco-paraty.com. More information is available at www.paraty.com.br. The wettest months are January, February, June and July. In spring, the streets in the colonial centre may flood, but the houses remain above the waterline.

PLACES IN PARATY

In keeping with all Brazilian colonial towns, Paraty's churches were built according to social status and race. There are four churches in the town, one for the 'freed coloured men', one for the blacks and two for the whites. **Santa Rita** (1722), built by the 'freed coloured men' in elegant Brazilian baroque, faces the bay and the port. It is probably the most famous picture postcard image of Paraty and houses a small **Museum of Sacred Art** ① *Wed-Sun 0900-1200, 1300-1800, US$1.* **Nossa Senhora do Rosário e São Benedito** ① *R do Comércio, Tue 0900-1200,* (1725, rebuilt 1757) built by black slaves, is small and simple; the slaves were unable to raise the funds to construct an elaborate building. **Nossa Senhora dos Remédios** ① *Mon, Wed, Fri, Sat 0900-1200, Sun 0900-1500,* is the town's parish church, the biggest in Paraty. It was started in 1787 but construction continued until 1873. The church was never completely finished as it was built on unstable ground; the architects decided not to add weight to the structure by putting up the towers. The façade is leaning to the left, which is clear from the three doors (only the one on the right has a step). Built with donations from the whites, it is rumoured that Dona Geralda Maria da Silva contributed gold from a pirate's hoard found buried on the

beach. **Capela de Nossa Senhora das Dores** ① *Thu 0900-1200* (1800), is a chapel facing the sea. It was used mainly by wealthy 19th-century whites.

There is a great deal of distinguished Portuguese colonial architecture in delightful settings. **Rua do Comércio** is the main street in the historic centre. It was here that the prominent traders lived, the two-storey houses having the commercial establishments on the ground floor and the residences above. Today the houses are occupied by restaurants, *pousadas* and tourist shops.

The **Casa da Cadeia**, close to Santa Rita Church, is the former jail, complete with iron grilles in the windows and doors. It is now a public library and art gallery.

On the northern headland is a small fort, **Forte do Defensor Perpétuo**, built in 1822, whose cannon and thick ruined walls can be seen. From the fort there are good views of the sea and the roofs of the town. It's about 15 minutes' walk from the centre. To get there, cross the Rio Perequê Açu by the bridge at the end of the Rua do Comércio; climb the small hill, which has some attractive *pousadas* and a cemetery, and follow the signs. Also here is the **Museum of Arts and Popular Traditions** ① *Wed-Sun*, in a colonial-style building. It contains carved wooden canoes, musical instruments, fishing gear and other items from local communities. On the headland is the gunpowder store and enormous hemispherical iron pans that were used for extracting whale oil, which was used for lamps and to mix with sand and cement for building.

BOAT TRIPS AND BEACHES

The most popular trip, and highly recommended, is a five-hour **schooner tour** around the bay for swimming (US$15, lunch is an optional extra). Smaller boats are available for US$10 an hour or US$20 for three hours. Many beautiful beaches are visited.

Praia do Pontal is the town beach, five minutes' walk from the historic centre: cross the bridge and turn right along the river. The water and sand are not very clean but the handful of *barracas* under the trees are a nice place to hang out. **Praia do Jabaquara** is about 20 minutes away on foot: cross the bridge and continue straight up the hill. There are a few *barracas* here and the sand is cleaner, but the water tends to be muddy.

There are other beaches further from town, many of which make worthwhile excursions. Scruffy **Boa Vista** is just south of town and beyond this (reachable only by boat) are, in order, the long, broad and clean stretches of **Praia da Conçeicao**, **Praia Vermelha** and **Praia da Lula**, all of which have simple restaurants and are backed by forest and washed by gentle waves. The **Saco da Velha**, further south still, is small and intimate, protected by an island and surrounded by rainforested slopes.

The small town of **Paraty Mirím**, is 17 km away and has a vast sweeping beach with a Manueline church built on the sand and some ruined colonial buildings. It is reached by boat or by four buses a day (three on Sunday) and has simple restaurants and places to camp. Fishing boats leave from here for other islands and beaches including the **Praia do Pouso da Cajaíba**, which has lodgings of the same name, and the spectacular sweep at **Martim do Sá**. The **Saco do Mamanguá** is a long sleeve of water that separates the Ponta da Juatinga and Paraty Mirím, which has good snorkelling.

GOING FURTHER
Parque Nacional de Itatiaia

Deep valleys shrouded in pristine rainforest hiding rocky clear-water rivers and icy waterfalls; winding trails through a swathe of different ecosystems, watched over by some of world's rarest birds and mammals; hotels and guesthouses to suit all budgets. And all within easy reach of Rio. Itatiaia is a must if you wish to see Brazilian forest and animals and have a restricted itinerary or limited time. This 30,000-ha mountainous park is Brazil's oldest. It was founded in 1937 to protect Atlantic coast rainforest in the Serra de Mantiqueira mountains, and important species still find a haven here, including jaguars and pumas, brown capuchin and black-faced titi monkeys. This is good hiking country with walks through subtropical and temperate forests, grasslands and *paramo* to a few peaks just under 3000 m. The best trails head for Pedra de Taruga, Pedra de Maçã and the Poranga and Véu de Noiva waterfalls. The Pico das Agulhas Negras and Serra das Prateleiras (up to 2540 m) offer good rock climbing.

ARRIVING IN PARQUE NACIONAL DE ITATIAIA

To drive to Itatiaia from Paraty (two to three hours) you will need to take the precarious Estrada Cunha dirt road which leaves Paraty to the north of town climbing inland through the Serra do Mar mountains. While spectacular, the road is steep and ridden with potholes and you'll need a car with plenty of clearance. There are no direct buses from Paraty to Itatiaia. There are two ways of getting there by bus. You can take one of two daily buses (morning and evening) from Paraty to Cunha (2½ hours). Then a handful of daily buses connect Cunha with Guaratinguetá (one hour), from where there are connections to Itatiaia (every hour, one hour). An easier option is to take a bus from Paraty to Angra (90 minutes) from where there are connections to Resende (90 minutes) for Itatiaia (buses every 15 minutes, 20 minutes). For the latest Paraty bus schedules, see www.paratytrindade.com.br.

Itatiaia is just off the main São Paulo–Rio highway, the Dutra. A bus marked '504 Circular' runs from Itatiaia town to the park four times a day, calling at the hotels in town. The bus can also be caught at Resende, at the crossroads before Itatiaia. Tickets are sold at a booth in the large bar in the middle of Itatiaia main street. There is another bus (used mostly by park employees) that goes to the park; it leaves at 0700 from the road that leads to the park gate and takes about 30 minutes (about R$3); stay on the bus until the last stop and check out the return time in advance. Guides provide their own transport. A local guide for this trek costs US$20 per person. The best way to see the park is to hire a car or to go with a tour operator. There is only one way into the park from Itatiaia town and one main road within it -- which forks off to the various hotels, all of which are signposted. **Ralph Salgueiro** ① *T024-3351 1823/024-9952 5962, www.ecoralph.com*, takes general tours (leaving from Itatiaia or Resende); **Edson Endrigo** ① *www.avesfoto.com.br*, one of Brazil's foremost birding guides, offers wildlife tours in Itatiaia and throughout Brazil. English is spoken by both.

Tourist information Entry per day is US$10 per car. Basic accommodation in cabins and dormitories is available in the village strung along the road leading to the park. There are some delightful options inside the park but they are more expensive. Avoid weekends and Brazilian holidays if wildlife watching is a priority. Information and maps can be obtained at the **Administração do Parque Nacional de Itatiaia (park office)** ① *Estrada Parque Km 8.5,* *www.ibama.gov.br/parna_itatiaia*, which operates a refuge in the park, which acts as a starting point for climbs and treks. Information can also be obtained from **Ibama** ① *T024-33521461 for the local HQ, or T021-3224 6463 for the Rio de Janeiro state depart- ment*. Information on trekking can be obtained from **Clube Excursionista Brasileiro** ① *Av Almirante* Barroso 2, 8th floor, Rio de *Janeiro, T021-2252 9844, www.ceb.org.br*.

FLORA AND FAUNA

The park has a list of more than 350 bird species, with scores of spectacular tanagers, hummingbirds (including the rare Brazilian ruby, with emerald wings and dazzling red chest), cotingas (including the black and gold cotinga, which as far as we are aware has never been photographed) and manakins. Guans squawk and flap alongside the park roads.

The vegetation is stratified by altitude so that the plateau at 800-1100 m is covered by forest, ferns and flowering plants (such as orchids, bromeliads, begonias), giving way on the higher escarpments to pines and bushes. Higher still, over 1900 m, the distinctive rocky landscape has low bushes and grasses, isolated trees and a great variety of lichens.

HIKING IN PARQUE NACIONAL DE ITATIAIA

The park also offers excellent trail walking. There are peaks with magnificent views out over the Atlantic coastal forest and the Rio de Janeiro coastline and a series of beautiful waterfalls, many of which are easily accessible from the park road. The trails, most of which begin just behind the **Hotel Simon** or around the visitor centre, cut through the forest, bushland and up into the alpine paramo. The views from here are breathtaking. Be sure to take plenty of water, repellent and a fleece for the higher areas; temperatures can get well below 0°C in the winter. The visitor centre has maps and gives directions to all the trail heads (though English is poor).

Maçico das Prateleiras peak, one of the highest in the park (2548 m) is a full day's walk for experienced hikers. When there is no mist the views are magnificent. To get there, take the trail from Abrigo Rebouças mountain lodge, reached from the BR354 road that heads north out of Engenheiro Passos – the next town beyond Itatiaia on BR116 (The Dutra). From here it is around 1½ hours. **Pico das Agulhas Negras** is the highest point in the park (2787 m) and is reached via the same route, but with a turn to the east at the Abrigo Rebouças (instead of west). The upper reaches are only accessible with a rope and moderate climbing experience. This is another full day's walk. **Tres Picos** is a six-hour walk, leaving from a trail signposted off to the right, about 3 km beyond the visitor centre. It is one of the best for a glimpse of the park's various habitats. The first half of the trail is fairly gentle, but after about an hour the path gets progressively steep. An hour or so beyond the steep trail is the **Rio Bonito** – a great place for a break, where there is a beautiful waterfall for swimming and refreshment. There are wonderful views from the top (45 minutes further on). The **Piscina do Maromba** is a natural pool formed by the Rio Campo Belo and situated at 1100 m. It's one of the most refreshing places to swim in the park. Trails leave from behind Hotel Simon.

There are a number of **waterfalls** in the park; most of which have pools where you can swim. The most accessible is **Cachoeira Poranga** – left off the park road about 3.5 km beyond the visitors' centre. **Itaporani** and **Véu da Noiva** are reached by a path just beyond the Poranga trail; which leaves from next to the road bridge and divides after about 1 km – left for Véu da Noiva, right for Itaporani.

CAMINHO DO OURO (GOLD TRAIL)

This partly cobbled trail through the mountains was built by slaves in the 18th century to bring gold down from Ouro Preto before transporting it to Portugal. Recently restored (www.caminhodoouro.com.br), it can be visited, along with the ruins of a toll house, on foot or horseback as a day trip. Tours leave at 1000 from the **Teatro Espaço** ① *R Dona Geralda 327, T024-3371 1575*.

There are several *cachoeiras* (waterfalls) in the area, such as the **Cachoeira da Penha**, near the church of the same name. It is 10 km from town on the road to Cunha; take a local bus from the *rodoviária*, US$1, there are good mountain views on the way. The tourist office and travel agencies have details on the waterfalls and hikes.

A recommended excursion is to **Fazenda Murycana** ① *T024-3371 3930 for tours and information*, an old sugar estate and 17th-century *cachaça* distillery with original house and waterwheel. You can taste and buy the different types of *cachaça*; some are aged in oak barrels for 12 years. Try the *cachaça com cravo e canela* (with clove and cinnamon). There is an excellent restaurant and horse riding is available but English is not spoken by the employees. Mosquitoes can be a problem at the *fazenda*, take repellent and don't wear shorts. To get there, take a 'Penha/Ponte Branca' bus from the *rodoviária*, four a day; alight where it crosses a small white bridge and then walk 10 minutes along a signed, unpaved road. There is a good chance of hitching a lift back to Paraty.

COSTA VERDE LISTINGS

WHERE TO STAY

Angatu, www.pontadocorumbe.com.br, offer charming accommodation around Paraty. **Hidden Pousadas Brazil**, www.hiddenpousadas brazil.com, have accommodation throughout the Costa Verde. **Hostel World**, www.hostel world.com, offer a broad and well-reviewed choice of budget accommodation.

Ilha Grande

$$$ Estrela da Ilha, Praia Pequena da Freguesia de Santana, www.estreladailha.com, (or with **Hidden Pousadas**). Magnificent ocean views from airy, rustic but romantic wood rooms, on-site yoga and healthy food and easy access to snorkelling sites and broad sandy beaches more than make up for this pretty *pousada*'s isolated location. Full board.
$$ Aritinga Inn, Vila do Abraão, www.aratinga ilhagrande.com.br (or with **Hidden Pousadas**). The simple furnishing in the rooms (little more than a bed and a table) are more than made up for by the location – in a lush tropical garden dotted with boulders right under the brow of Papagaio peak, and the excellent service which includes Anglo-Australian afternoon tea.

Paraty

$$$$ Pousada do Ouro, R Dr Pereira (or da Praia) 145, T024-3371 1311, www.pousada ouro.com.br. Near Paraty's eastern water-front and built as a private home with a fortune made on the gold route. Plain annexe rooms and suites in the main building. The tropical garden houses an open-air poolside pavilion. Pictures of previous guests, such as Mick Jagger and Tom Cruise, adorn the lobby.
$$$ Vivenda & Maris, R Beija Flor 9 and 11, Caboré, www.vivendaparaty.com and www.marisparaty.com.br. These identical *pousadas*, with lovely garden chalet rooms clustered around a jewel-like pool offer friendly, personal service and quiet, intimate accommodation 10 mins' walk from the centre.
$$ Pousada Arte Colonial, R da Matriz 292, T024-3371 7231, www.pousadaarte colonial.com.br. One of Paraty's best deals. An elegant colonial building in the centre decorated with style by its French owner, with artefacts and antiques from all over the world. Friendly, helpful and with breakfast.

Parque Nacional de Itatiaia

$$$ Hotel Donati, T024-3352 1110, www.hoteldonati.com.br. Mock-Swiss chalets set in tropical gardens visited by animals. A series of trails leads off from the grounds and the hotel can organize professional wildlife guides. Decent restaurant and 2 pools.

WHAT TO DO

Ilha Grande

Boat trips to the various sights and snorkelling spots leave from the quay in Vila do Abraão and can be organized directly there or through of the hotels and hostels.
Trekking The path from Abraão to Lopes Mendes is straightforward; allow 2 hrs. It's easy to get lost on other trails.
João Pontes, T(24) 8816-9212, is a reliable guide.

Paraty

Boat trips are easy to organize through fishermen on the quay (US$30-40 if the boat is full). The *Rei Cigano*, T024-9831 2098, is costlier but it's a beautiful 60-ft-long wooden schooner with cabins for overnight trips.
Hikes and excursions Paraty Tours, Av Roberto Silveira 11, T024-3371 1327, www.paratytours.com.br. From hikes on the gold trail to bike and jeep excursions, diving and boat trips. Can also arrange transfers.

COLONIAL CITIES OF MINAS GERAIS

Streets of whitewashed 18th-century houses with deep-blue or yellow window frames line steep and winding streets leading to lavishly decorated churches with Manueline façades and rich gilt interiors. Behind lies a backdrop of grey granite hills and green forests, still filled with tiny marmoset monkeys and flocks of canary-winged parakeets. The colonial gold-mining towns of southern Minas are the highlights of any visit to the state: islands of history and remnant forest in an otherwise dull agricultural landscape. They make a far more charming and restful base than Belo Horizonte and we recommend spending your time here, with just a quick stop in the state capital towards the end of your trip.

BACKGROUND

Like the Spanish, the Portuguese looked to their colonies for easy money. Outside the Jesuit reduction cities, there were never plans to invest in empire, only to exploit the land and the local people as ruthlessly as possible. At first it was wood that attracted the Portuguese, and then indigenous slaves for the cane plantations that stretched along the northern coast. But it was the ultimate in rich pickings that led to colonial Brazil becoming more than a coastline empire. In 1693, whilst out on a marauding expedition, a Paulista *bandeirante* found *ouro preto* – gold made black by a coat of iron oxide – in a stream south of modern Belo Horizonte. When news reached home, an influx of adventurers trekked their way from São Paulo through the forests to set up makeshift camps along the gold streams. These camps developed into wealthy towns such as Ouro Preto and Mariana. Later, with the discovery of diamonds and other gemstones, a captaincy was established and named, prosaically, 'General Mines'.

The wealth of Minas was reflected in its streets and in the baroque churches, whose interiors were covered in gold plate and decorated with sculptures by the best artisans in Brazil. And with the wealth came growing self-importance. The Inconfidência Mineira (see box, page 94), the most important rebellion in colonial Brazil, began in Ouro Preto in the late 18th century under a group of intellectuals educated in Portugal who were in contact with Thomas Jefferson and English industrialists. The Inconfidência never got beyond discussion but it was decided that the only non-aristocratic member of the group, José Joaquim da Silva, would be in charge of taking the governor's palace, occupied by the hated Visconde of Barbacena, who was responsible for levying the imperial taxes. Da Silva was derisively known as Tiradentes (tooth-puller) by his compatriots. Today he is the only Inconfidênte rebel that most Brazilians can name and he is celebrated as a folk hero – one of the common people who dared to challenge the powerful elite, and who was cruelly martyred as a result.

After Brazil changed from an empire into a republic, Minas Gerais vied for power with the coffee barons of São Paulo and, in the 20th century, produced two Brazilian presidents. Juscelino Kubitschek, an establishment figure chosen by the electorate as the best alternative to the military, opened up Brazil to foreign investment in the 1960s, and founded Brasília. Tancredo Neves also opposed the Brazilian military, was elected to power in 1985. A few days before his inauguration, he died in mysterious circumstances. His last words were reportedly "I did not deserve this". He was replaced by José Sarney, a leading figure in the Brazilian landowning oligarchy.

São João del Rei (population: 79,000) lies at the foot of the Serra do Lenheiro, astride what once must have been a winding little stream. This has now sadly been transformed into a concrete gutter with grass verges. Eighteenth-century bridges cross the stream leading to streets lined with colonial buildings and plazas with crumbling churches, the most interesting and best preserved of which is the church of **São Francisco**. The town feels far less of a tourist museum piece than nearby Tiradentes. There is a lively music scene, with two renowned orchestras and an annual arts festival in July, and the bars are filled with locals rather than tourists waiting for their coach. There is a good view of the town and surroundings from **Alto da Boa Vista**, where there is a **Senhor dos Montes** (Statue of Christ).

ARRIVING IN SÃO JOÃO DEL REI

Getting there and around To reach São João del Rei from Paraty or Itatiaia on public transport, you will need to return to Rio and catch a bus (Monday to Friday, three buses

daily, Saturday and Sunday two buses daily; see www.saojoaodelrei.mg.gov.br for the most up-to-date schedules). The *rodoviária*, 2 km west of the centre, has a telephone office, toilets, luggage store, *lanchonetes* and a tourist office.

Many streets seem to have more than one name, which can be a little confusing, but as the town centre is not large, it is hard to get lost. The **Secretaria de Turismo** ① *in the house of Bárbara Heliodora, T032-3372 7338, open 0900-1700*, provides a free map.

Moving on São João is a good base for visiting **Tiradentes** (see page 91), or vice versa; it's less than 30 minutes away by bus or at weekends via one of Brazil's most memorable steam train rides. You can get to **Congonhas do Campo** (see page 94) from São João. However, if you prefer, you can get a bus from São João to Ouro Preto (see page 97), and then visit Congonhas do Campo on an excursion from there.

PLACES IN SÃO JOÃO DEL REI

The Córrego do Lenheiro, a stream with steep grassy banks, runs through the centre of town. Across it are two fine, stone bridges, and on either side are colonial monuments, which are interspersed with modern buildings. On the north side are many streets with pleasant houses, but in various states of repair. **Rua Santo Antônio** has many single-storey eclectic houses from the imperial period, which have been restored and painted. **Rua Santo Elias** has several buildings all in the same style. Behind the church of Nossa Senhora do Pilar (see below), the **Largo da Câmara** leads up to **Mercês church**, which has quite a good view. Throughout the city you will see locked portals with colonial porticos. These are *passinhos*, shrines that are opened in Holy Week. They can be seen on **Largo da Cruz** and **Largo do Rosário**.

São Francisco de Assis ① *Praça Frei Orlando, Tue-Sun 0830-1700, US$1*, built in 1774, is one of the most beautiful churches in Brazil. Although often attributed to Aleijadinho, it was designed and decorated by two almost completely undocumented artists, Francisco de Lima Cerqueira and Aniceto de Souza Lopes (who also sculpted the Pelourinho in the Largo da Câmara). The magnificent but modest whitewash and stone façade sits between two cylindrical bell towers and is decorated with an ornately carved door frame and a superb medal of St Francis receiving illumination. The *praça* in front is shaped like a lyre and, in the late afternoon, the royal palms cast shadows that interconnect to form the lyre's strings. The six carved altars inside have been restored, revealing fine carving in sucupira wood. The overall shape of the nave is elliptical, the gold altar has spiralling columns and an adoring St Francis kneels atop.

The cathedral, **Basílica de Nossa Senhora do Pilar** ① *R Getúlio Vargas (formerly R Direita), daily 1000-1600*, was built in 1721, but has a 19th-century façade which replaced the 18th-century original. It has rich altars and a brightly painted ceiling (Madonna and Child in the middle, saints and bishops lining the sides). Note the androgynous gold heads and torsos within the eight columns set into the walls either side of the main altar. There is a profusion of cherubs and plants in the carving. This abundance and angelic innocence contrasts with the images of suffering of the Passion and the betrayal of the Last Supper before the altar.

The **Memorial Tancredo Neves** ① *R Padre José Maria Xavier 7, Wed-Fri 1300-1800, weekends and holidays 0900-1700, US$1*, is a homage to the man and his life. A short video on São João del Rei is shown. It also holds exhibitions and has a bookshop. Also worth exploring is the **Museu Ferroviário (Railway Museum)** ① *Av Hermílio Alves 366, T032-371 8004, US$0.50*, which traces the history of railways in general and in Brazil in brief. For the steam train to Tiradentes, see page 93.

→TIRADENTES

Aside from Ouro Preto, Tiradentes (population 6000) is the most visited of the Minas colonial towns. Its winding, hilly streets lined with carefully restored baroque Portuguese churches and neat whitewashed cottages huddle around the Santo Antônio river, beneath the rugged hills of the Serra de São José. Inside are art galleries, restaurants, souvenir shops and *pousadas*, all busy with tourists even during the week. Horse-drawn carriages clatter along the cobbles and at weekends a steam train towing Pullmans full of delighted children puffs its way slowly below the mountains to the pretty colonial town of São João del Rei.

ARRIVING IN TIRADENTES

Getting there Tiradentes and São João del Rei lie within less than 30 minutes of each other and buses leave every 30 to 40 minutes (US$3). Far more enchanting is the Maria Fumaça steam train, which takes 30 minutes (see page 93). Tiradentes is the more twee; São João is uglier but more of a real town. Tiradentes has a far greater choice of accommodation. The **tourist office** ① *R Resende Costa 71*, is in the *prefeitura*.

Moving on To get to Congonhas do Campo, you'll need to return to São João del Rei and catch a bus from there (see page 94). São João also has better bus connections with Rio, São Paulo, Belo Horizonte, Mariana and Ouro Preto.

PLACES IN TIRADENTES

A suggested walking tour is as follows. From the main *praça*, **Largo das Forras**, take Rua Resende Costa up to the Largo do Sol, a lovely open space where you'll find the simple church of **São João Evangelista** ① *Wed-Mon 0900-1700*. Built by the *Irmandade dos Homens Pardos* (mulattos), it has paintings of the four Evangelists and a cornice painted in an elaborate pattern in pink, blue and beige. Beside the church is the **Museu Padre Toledo**, the house of this leader of the Inconfidência Mineira, which is now a museum protecting some handsome colonial furniture and a painted roof depicting the Five Senses. The **Casa de Cultura** in the row of 18th-century houses on Rua Padre Toledo, which leads from Largo do Sol to the Igreja Matriz de Santo Antônio, is protected by the same organization.

The **Igreja Matriz de Santo Antônio** ① *daily 0900-1700, US$1, no photography*, first built in 1710 and enlarged in 1736, contains some of the finest gilded woodcarvings in the country. The main church is predominantly white and gold. Lamps hang from the beaks of golden eagles. The symbols on the panels painted on the ceiling of the nave are a mixture of Old Testament and medieval Christian symbolism (for instance the phoenix, and the pelican). A carved wooden balustrade separates the seating in the nave from richly carved side chapels and altars. The principal altar is also ornately decorated, as are the walls and ceiling around it. The church has a small but fine organ brought from Porto in the 1790s. The upper part of the reconstructed façade is said to follow a design by Aleijadinho. In front of the church, on the balustrade which overlooks the main street and the town, are also a cross and a sundial by him.

From Santo Antônio, it is well worth taking a detour up to the **Santuário da Santíssima Trindade**. The chapel itself is 18th century while the Room of Miracles associated with the annual Trinity Sunday pilgrimage is modern.

Heading back down past Santo Antônio along Rua da Câmara, you come to the **Casa da Câmara e Antigo Fórum**. Here the road divides, the left-hand street, Jogo de Bola, leads to the Largo do Ó (which rejoins the main street), while Rua da Câmara goes to the crossroads with Rua Direita. At this junction is the **Sobrado Ramalho**, said to be the oldest building in Tiradentes. It is believed to be where the gold was melted down, and contains many soapstone carvings. It has been beautifully restored as a cultural centre.

Before taking Rua Direita back to Largo das Forras, carry straight on towards the river and cross the bridge to the magnificent **Chafariz de São José** (public fountain), installed in 1749. The water is brought by a stone aqueduct from springs in the forest at the foot of Serra São José. It is still used for drinking, washing and watering animals.

Rua Direita has some interesting old buildings. The charming **Nossa Senhora do Rosário** ① *Praça Padre Lourival, Wed-Mon 1200-1600, US$0.50*, has fine statuary and ornate gilded altars. On its painted ceiling colonnades rise to heaven; two monks stand on a hill and the Virgin and Child are in the sky. Other ceiling panels depicting the life of Christ are in poor shape. The church contains statues of black saints, including São Benedito, patron saint of cooks; in one of the statues he is holding a squash. The church dates from 1727, but building by the 'Irmandade dos Pretos Cativos' (black slave brotherhood) began as early as 1708.

Opposite Praça Padre Lourival, is the **Antiga Cadeia** (18th-19th century) which now contains the **Museu de Arta Sacra**. Rua Direita meets the Largo das Forras at the

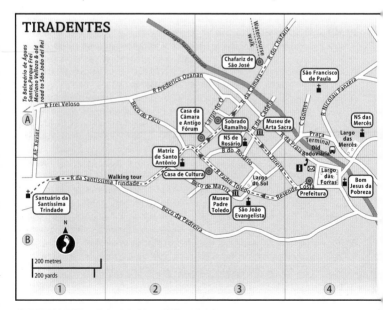

Prefeitura Municipal, a two-storey building with an extra room under the roof. It now houses the tourist, post and phone offices.

If you have any energy left, there are other churches and chapels in the town, including the **Igreja de Bom Jesus da Pobreza**, on the Largo das Forras. Across the river, the 18th-century **Nossa Senhora das Mercês** ① *Largo das Mercês, Sun 0900-1700*, has an interesting painted ceiling and a notable statue of the Virgin. On the grassy Morro de São Francisco is the small chapel of **São Francisco de Paula** (mid-18th century).

EXCURSIONS FROM TIRADENTES

The **Maria Fumaça steam trains** ① *Fri-Sun and holidays, 1000 and 1500 from São João del Rei, returning from Tiradentes at 1300 and 1700, US$16 one way, US$25 return, children 6-12 half price, under 6s go free*, which run on the 76-cm gauge track between São João del Rei and Tiradentes (13 km) have been in continuous operation since 1881 – a testament to the durability of the rolling stock and locomotives made by the Baldwin Company of Philadelphia. The maximum speed is 20 kph. To get to the railway station from the centre of the village you have to cross the river and head out of town on the Rua dos Inconfidêntes. Follow this road until it becomes the Rua Antônio Teixeira Carvalho, which carries on to the bridge over the Rio das Mortes.On the opposite bank is a small park and the station. There's a **railway museum** ① *Tue-Sun 0900-1100 and 1300-1700*, at the railway station in São João del Rei.

A recommended walk from Tiradentes is to the protected forest on the **Serra de São José**. The easiest access is from behind the *chafariz*, where a black door in the wall is opened at 0730 (Wednesday to Sunday). In just five minutes you are in the forest following the watercourse, where monkeys and birds can be seen. Alternatively, you can walk up into the **Serra** from behind the Mercês Church; ask for directions. It is recommended that you take a guide if you wish to walk along the top of the Serra.

There is a good one- or two-hour walk from Tiradentes to the **Balneário de Águas Santas**, which involves crossing the Serra. At the *balneário* is a swimming pool, a lake and a *churrascaria*, **Senzala**. A map can be obtained from the **Solar da Ponte**, or ask locally for directions (taxi US$15). On the way you pass **Parque Frei Mariano Vellozo**, which contains the Cachoeira do Mangue falls. It is busy at weekends and can be reached by car on the old road to São João.

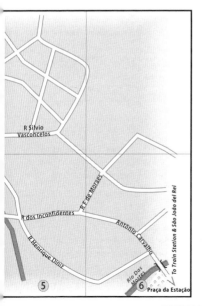

ON THE ROAD

Tiradentes and the Inconfidência Mineira

In the last quarter of the 18th century, Vila Rica de Nossa Senhora do Pilar do Ouro Preto was a dynamic place. Gold had brought great wealth to the city and this was translated into fine religious and secular buildings. Much of the artistry that went into these constructions and their decoration was home-grown, such as the genius of O Aleijadinho. In conjunction with this flowering of the arts an intellectual society developed. And yet all this went on under the heavy hand of the Portuguese crown, which demanded its fifth share (the *quinto*), imposed punitive taxes and forbade local industries to operate. While the artists and artisans could not travel and had to seek inspiration in what was around them, the intellectuals were often from families who sent their young to Europe to further their education. So, when the gold yields began to decline and the Portuguese demands became even more exorbitant, some members of society began to look to Europe and North America for ways to free Minas Gerais from the crown.

One side of the argument was the view of the governor, the Visconde de Barbacena, who refused to admit that the mines were exhausted and that poverty was beginning to affect the community. As far as he was concerned, there was no gold because it was being smuggled out of the captaincy and there was no economic problem, just a large unpaid debt to the Portuguese crown. On the other side was the idea, as expressed by the French poet Parny, that Brazil was a paradise on earth, with everything except liberty. The Jesuit Antônio Vieira, who lived in the previous century, put it thus: "the cloud swells in Brazil and it rains on Portugal; the water is not picked up from the sea, but from the tears of the unfortunate and the sweat of the poor, and I do not know how their faith and constancy has lasted so long."

In the late 1780s a group of people began to have secret discussions on how to resolve the intolerable situation. It included the poets Cláudio Manuel da Costa, Tomás Gonzaga and Ignacio de Alvarenga, the doctors Domingos Vidal Barbosa and José Alvares Maciel,

→CONGONHAS DO CAMPO

In the 18th century, Congonhas was a mining town. Today, it has a population of 42,000 and, in addition to the business brought by the tourists and pilgrims who come to the sanctuary, it is known for its handicrafts. There is little need to stay in Congonhas as the town's main sight, Aleijadinho's beautiful church and chapel-lined stairway, can be seen in a few hours between bus changes. Leave your bags at the information desk in the bus station.

ARRIVING IN CONGONHAS DO CAMPO

Getting there All public transport leaves from São João del Rei, a few kilometres from Tiradentes (see page 89). To reach Congonhas from São João del Rei, you will have to take the Belo Horizonte bus and asked to be dropped at the entrance to Congonhas village, where you can catch a taxi (US$15 round trip) or walk to the sanctuary (around 25 minutes). Buses are not scheduled to stop at Congonhas and if the driver is unwilling to drop you at Congonhas then get off at the town immediately before Congonhas – Conselheiro Lafaiette

Padres Toledo and Rolim and the military officers Domingos de Abreu Vieira, Francisco de Paula Freire de Andrade and José de Resende Costa. Into this group came Joaquim José da Silva Xavier, a junior officer, who was born at the Fazenda de Pombal near São João del Rei in about 1748. He was also a dentist and became known by the nickname Tiradentes – tooth-puller. Already dissatisfied with the way the army had treated him, by failing to promote him among other things, in 1788 he was suspended from active duty because of illness. The subsequent loss of pay roused him further. In trying to get reinstated he met Freire de Andrade and Alvares Maciel and later conversations prompted him to tell them of his idea of an uprising against the Portuguese. The Inconfidência grew out of these types of meeting, some planning action, others the future political and economic organization of a new, independent state.

The conspirators worked to gain support for their cause, but one soldier they approached, Coronel Joaquim Silverio dos Reis, used the information he had been given to betray the cause. The governor received reports from other sources and began to build up a picture of what was going on. Tiradentes was the first to be arrested, at the beginning of May 1789, in Rio de Janeiro. It seems that the plotters at this time still had no clear idea of what their ultimate aim was, nor of the importance of their attitudes. They never got the chance anyway because all were arrested soon after Tiradentes. They were imprisoned and kept incommunicado for two years while the case against them was prepared. Tiradentes was singled out as the most important member of the group and, under questioning, he did not disabuse his captors, taking full responsibility for everything. A defence for the Inconfidêntes was prepared, but it almost totally ignored Tiradentes, as if he were being made a scapegoat. It made no difference, though, because the defence lost; 11 Inconfidêntes were sentenced to death in November 1791. Soon afterwards the authorities in Brazil read out a surprising letter from the queen, Dona Maria I, commuting the death sentence for 10 of the conspirators to exile in Portugal or Africa. The 11th, Tiradentes, was not spared. On 21 April 1792 he was hanged and his body was quartered and his head cut off, the parts to be displayed as a warning against any similar attempts to undermine the crown.

– which is some 15 km from Congonhas. From here there are local buses and taxis (the latter charge around US$40 for a round trip). Alternatively, it is possible to visit Congonhas as an excursion from Ouro Preto (see page 97) either by bus or on an organized tour.

Moving on It's easy enough to catch a bus from Congonhas do Campo to Ouro Preto, the next place on the itinerary, unless of course you have decided to base yourselves in Ouro Preto and visit Congonhas as an excursion (see page 97) .

Getting around The *rodoviária* is 1.5 km outside town; a bus to the centre costs US$0.60. In town, the bus stops in Praça JK from where you can walk up Praça Dr Mário Rodrigues Pereira, cross the little bridge, then go up Rua Bom Jesus and Rua Aleijadinho to the Praça da Basílica. A bus marked 'Basílica' runs every 30 minutes from the *rodoviária* to Bom Jesus (5 km, US$0.45). A taxi from the *rodoviária* will cost US$7 one-way, US$12 return including the wait while you visit the sanctuary.

Tourist information Fumcult ⓘ *in the Romarias, T031-3731 1300 ext 114*, acts as the tourist office and is very helpful. On the hill are a tourist kiosk, souvenir shops, the **Hotel Colonial** and **Cova do Daniel** restaurant. There are public toilets on the Alameda das Palmeiras.

O SANTUÁRIO DE BOM JESUS DE MATOSINHOS
ⓘ *Tue-Sun 0700-1900. No direct bus from Congonhas do Campo or Rio to the sanctuary; change at the town of Conselheiro Lafaiete, from where there is a frequent service, US$1.*

The great pilgrimage church and its Via Sacra dominate the town. The idea of building a sanctuary belonged to a prospector, Feliciano Mendes, who promised to erect a cross and chapel in thanks to Bom Jesus after he had been cured of a serious illness. The inspiration for his devotion came from two sources in Portugal, the cult of Bom Jesus at Braga (near where Mendes was born) and the church of Bom Jesus de Matosinhos, near Porto. Work began in 1757, funded by Mendes' own money and alms he raised. The church was finished in 1771, six years after Mendes' death, and the fame that the sanctuary had acquired led to its development by the most famous architects, artists and sculptors of the time as a Sacro Monte. This involved the construction of six linked chapels, or *pasos* (1802-1818), which lead up to a terrace and courtyard before the church.

There is a wide view of the country from the church terrace, below which are six small chapels set in an attractive sloping area with grass, cobblestones and palms. Each chapel shows scenes with life-size Passion figures carved by Aleijadinho and his pupils in cedar wood. In order of ascent they are: the chapel of the Last Supper; the chapel of the Mount of Olives; the chapel of the betrayal of Christ; the chapel of the flagellation and the crowning with thorns; the chapel of Jesus carrying the Cross; and the chapel of Christ being nailed to the Cross.

On the terrace stand the 12 prophets sculpted by Aleijadinho 1800-1805; these are thought of as his masterpieces. Carved in soapstone with a dramatic sense of movement, they constitute one of the finest works of art of their period in the world. Note how Aleijadinho adapted the biblical characters to his own cultural references. The prophets are sculpted wearing leather boots, as all important men in his time would have done. Daniel, who entered the lion's den, is represented with the artist's own conception of a lion, never having seen one himself: a large, maned cat with a face rather like a Brazilian monkey. Similarly, the whale that accompanies Jonah is an idiosyncratic interpretation. Each statue has a prophetic text carved with it. The statues "combine in a kind of sacred ballet whose movements only seem uncoordinated; once these sculptures cease to be considered as isolated units, they take on full significance as part of a huge composition brought to life by an inspired genius." (*Iberian-American Baroque*, edited by Henri Stierlin) The beauty of the whole is enhanced by the combination of church, Via Sacra and landscape over which the prophets preside.

Inside the church, there are paintings by Athayde and the heads of four sainted popes (Gregory, Jerome, Ambrose and Augustine) sculpted by Aleijadinho for the reliquaries on the high altar. Other artists involved were João Nepomuceno Correia e Castro, who painted the scenes of the life and passion of Christ in the nave and around the high altar, João Antunes de Carvalho, who carved the high altar, and Jerônimo Félix and Manuel Coelho, who carved the crossing altars of Santo Antônio and São Francisco de Paula. Despite the ornate carving, the overall effect of the paintwork is almost muted and naturalistic, with much use of blues, greys and pinks. Lamps are suspended on chains from the mouths of black dragons. To the left of the church, through the third door in the building alongside the church, is the Room of Miracles, which contains photographs and thanks for miracles performed.

Up on the hill, the Alameda das Palmeiras sweeps from the **Hotel Colonial** round to the **Romarias**, a large, almost oval area surrounded by buildings. This was the lodging where the pilgrims stayed. It now contains the **Espaço Cultural** and tourist office, as well as workshops, the museums of mineralogy and religious art, and the **Memória da Cidade**. Of the other churches in Congonhas do Campo, the oldest is **Nossa Senhora do Rosário**, Praça do Rosário, built by slaves at the end of the 17th century. The **Igreja Matriz de Nossa Senhora da Conceição**, in Praça 7 de Setembro, dates from 1749; the portal is attributed to Aleijadinho, while parts of the interior are by Manuel Francisco Lisboa. There are also two 18th-century chapels, **Nossa Senhora da Ajuda**, in the district of Alto Maranhão, and the church at **Lobo Leite**, 10 km away.

→OURO PRETO

Ouro Preto, named after the black iron oxide-coated gold that was discovered here by the adventurer Antônio Dias, was one of the first of the Minas gold towns to be founded. As a former state capital, it became the wealthiest and most important town in the region. Although it now has a hinterland of ugly blocks of flats and crumbling favelas, it preserves some of the most significant colonial architecture in Brazil and remains, at heart, an 18th-century city of steep church-crowned hills, cobbled streets, *azulejos*, plazas and fountains. In homage to its historical importance Ouro Preto becomes the capital of Minas Gerais once again every year for one day only, on 24 June. The modern city, with a population of 67,000, bustles with young Brazilians studying and partying at the various local universities and has a thriving café and nightlife scene. Sadly the historic centre, once closed to traffic, is now thick with buses and cars, which is taking its toll on some of the beautiful buildings.

ARRIVING IN OURO PRETO
Getting there and around There are daily bus connections between Congonhas and Ouro Preto, a 55-km journey which takes about two hours. Ouro Preto's **rodoviária** ① *R Padre Rolim 661, T031-3559 3225*, is 1 km north of Praça Tiradentes. A 'circular' bus runs from the *rodoviária* to Praça Tiradentes, US$0.40. Taxis charge exorbitant rates.

Moving on Buses run from the *rodoviária* in Ouro Preto east to the nearby town of Mariana (see page 102) and west to the state capital, Belo Horizonte (see page 105).

Tourist information The **tourist office** ① *Praça Tiradentes 41, T031-3559 3269, www.ouro preto.org.br, 0800-1800*, has details of accommodation in *casas de família*, *repúblicas* and other places. It also has leaflets showing the opening times of sights, which change frequently, and can organize a local guide from the **Associação de Guias de Turismo (AGTOP)** ① *R Padre Rolim s/n, T031-3551 2655, Mon-Fri 0800-1800, Sat and Sun 0800-1700, little English spoken*, which has its own office opposite the bus station. Cássio Antunes is a recommended guide.

PLACES IN OURO PRETO

Praça Tiradentes and around The city has a number of churches and chapels as well as some excellent examples of *chafariz* (public fountains), *passos* (oratories) and stone bridges. The best place to start exploring the city is the central **Praça Tiradentes**, where you'll see a **statue of Tiradentes**, the leader of the Inconfidêntes (see box, page 94). Another Inconfidênte, the poet Tomás Antônio Gonzaga, lived at Rua Cláudio Manoel 61, near the São Francisco de Assis church, and was exiled to Africa. Most Brazilians know his poem based on his forbidden love affair with the girl he called *Marília de Dirceu*. Visitors are shown the bridge and decorative fountain where the lovers held their trysts. The house where she lived, on the Largo Marília de Dirceu, is now a school.

On the north side of Praça Tiradentes is a famous **Escola de Minas (School of Mining)**. It was founded in 1876, is housed in the fortress-like Palácio dos Governadores (1741-1748) and includes the **Museu de Mineralogia e das Pedras** ① *No 20, Mon, Wed-Fri 1200-1645, Sat and Sun 0900-1300, US$1.50*, which has displays of rocks, minerals, semi-precious and

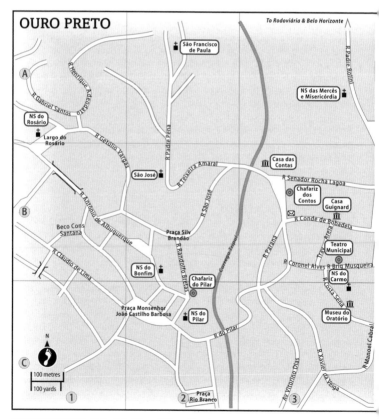

precious stones from all over the world. Just north of the *praça*, towards the *rodoviária*, is the church of **Nossa Senhora das Mercês e Misericórdia** (1773-1793).

On the south side of the *praça*, next to Carmo church, is the **Museu da Inconfidência** ① *No 139, T031-3551 1121, Mon-Fri 0800-1800, US$1.50*, a fine historical and art museum in the former Casa de Câmara e Cadeia, containing drawings by Aleijadinho and the Sala Manoel da Costa Athayde.

West of Praça Tiradentes The church of **Nossa Senhora do Carmo** ① *R Brigadeiro Mosqueira, Tue-Sun 1300-1700, entry is shared with Nossa Senhora do Pilar*, built 1766-1772, was planned by Manoel Francisco Lisboa, and both his son and Mestre Athayde worked on the project. It was a favourite church of the aristocracy. The best of the city's museums is housed in an annexe of the church, the modern and well-appointed **Museu do Oratório** ① *T031-3551 5369, daily 0930-1200, 1330-1730*. Inside is a selection of exquisitely crafted 18th- and 19th-century prayer icons and oratories, many of them with strong indigenous

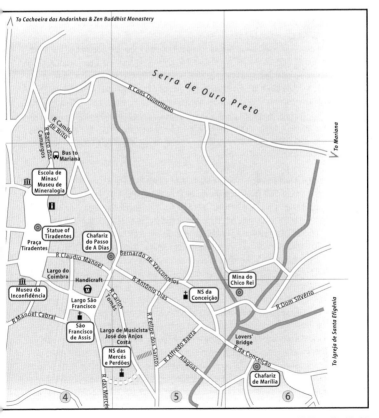

design and some disguised as bullet cases. On the opposite side of the road, the **Teatro Municipal** ① *R Brigadeiro Musqueiro, daily 1230-1800*, is the oldest functioning theatre in Latin America, built in 1769.

A block north of the theatre, **Casa Guignard** ① *R Conde de Bobadela 110, T031-3551 5155, Tue-Fri 1200-1800, Sat, Sun and holidays 0900-1500, free*, displays the paintings of Alberto da Veiga Guignard. Further west, just before the river, the **Casa das Contas** ① *R São José 12, T031-355 1444, Tue-Sat 1230-1730, Sun and holidays 0900-1500, US$0.50*, built 1782-1784, houses a museum of money and finance on its upper storeys. Far more interesting is the damp, dark basement where slaves were formerly housed. In colonial Preto a slave's life was literally worth less than a chicken: swapping an African Brazilian for poultry was considered a good deal.

Following Rua Teixeira Amaral across the river, the church of **São José** was begun in 1752, but not completed until 1811; some of the carving is by Aleijadinho. Up on the hill, **São Francisco de Paula** ① *0900-1700*, was started in 1804, making it the last colonial church in Ouro Preto. Further west, on the Largo do Rosário, the church of **Nossa Senhora do Rosário** dates from 1785, when the present church replaced a chapel on the site. It has a curved façade, which is rare in Brazilian baroque. The interior is more simple than the exterior, but there are interesting side altars.

One of the city's grandest churches, **Nossa Senhora do Pilar** ① *just north of R do Pilar, Tue-Sun 0900-1100 and 1200-1700,* was attended by the Portuguese upper classes. The ceiling painting by João de Carvalhães features a trompe l'oeil effect – as you walk to the front of the church the lamb appears to move from one side of the crucifix to the other – a symbol of the resurrection. Manoel Lisboa, Aleijadinho's father, was responsible for all the carving except the heavily gilded work around the altar, which is by Francisco Xavier de Brito. The **museum** in the church vaults is one of the best in Minas, preserving some stunning gold and silver monstrances and some of Xavier de Brito's finest sculptures, including a wonderful image of Christ.

East of Praça Tiradentes A block southeast of Praça Tiradentes, on the Largo São Francisco is the grand **São Francisco de Assis** ① *Largo de Coimbra, Tue-Sun 0830-1150, 1330-1640, US$2; the ticket also permits entry to NS da Conceição, keep your ticket for admission to the museum*, considered to be one of the masterpieces of Brazilian baroque. Built 1766-1796, Aleijadinho worked on the general design and the sculpture of the façade, the pulpits and many other features. The harmonious lines of the exterior and the beauty of the interior are exceptional; the church feels like a model of Catholic reverence and propriety. It is far from it. Aleijadinho was a mulatto – as were Mestre Athayde's wife and children – and as such they were prohibited from entering white churches like São Francisco, from eating any meat other than offal, ears and trotters and they had no rights in civil society. Mulatto sculptors were not even considered to be artists; they were referred to as artisans or *artistas de sangue sujo* (artists of dirty blood). The church is full of subtle criticisms of the Portuguese encoded in the art by Athayde and Aleijadinho. The model for the Virgin (depicted in the highest heaven, surrounded by cherubs and musicians and saints Augustine, Hieronymous, Gregory and Ambrosius), is said to have been Mestre Athayde's mulatto wife. She has her breasts showing, open legs and her face shows African traces; all of which can only be noticed with careful attention and all of which would have been anathema to the Portuguese. The *Last Supper* painting in the sanctuary replaces the

ON THE ROAD

Milton Nascimento – the voice of Minas

Milton Nascimento is the most influential Brazilian singer and composer not to have come out of Bahia or Rio. He has produced some of Brazil's most haunting music, been nominated for a Grammy and had songs covered by almost as many artists as Paul McCartney.

Milton grew up in rural Minas in a town like many others – lost in a landscape of lush green hills and cattle pasture and where life focused on the *praça* and local church. He was raised by his stepmother who'd once sung in a choir conducted by Villa-Lobos, and who exposed him to religious music from an early age. Catholicism came to underlie both his musical style and lyrical themes, which were expressed most memorably on a string of ground-breaking 1970s albums. The music on these is unique, with rich choral harmonies, jazz interludes and sweetly melancholic melodies interplaying with Afro-Brazilian rhythms and sound effects. Lyrics poetically exalt the day-to-day life of the oppressed. And Milton's golden voice soars over the top.

You'll hear Milton's songs throughout Ouro Preto. If you are tempted to buy one of his records, opt for *Clube de Esquina*, his 1972 classic.

apostles with Portuguese feeding on meat and being attended to by Brazilian servants. And Aleijadinho's *Sacred Heart of Jesus* near the altar has its hands and feet cut into quarters in a reference to the fate that befell Tiradentes at the hands of the Portuguese. A **museum** at the back of the church has a small selection of paintings of serious-looking saints and a fountain by Aleijadinho depicting Blind Faith holding up a banner saying "such is the path to heaven". In the largo outside São Francisco is a handicraft market. South of here, the church of **Nossa Senhora das Mercês e Perdões** ① *R das Mercês, Tue-Sun 1000-1400* (1740-1772), was rebuilt in the 19th century. Some sculpture by Aleijadinho can be seen in the main chapel.

Further east, **Nossa Senhora da Conceição** ① *Tue-Sat 0830-1130, 1330-1700, Sun 1200-1700,* was built in 1722 and is the parish church of Antônio Dias (one of the original settlements that became Vila Rica de Albuquerque). It is heavily gilded and contains Aleijadinho's tomb. It has a **museum** devoted to him but with very few of his pieces. Be sure to see the exquisite miniature crucifixion on the basement floor. Across the river, the **Mina do Chico Rei** ① *R Dom Silvério, 0800-1700, US$1.50,* is not as impressive as some other mines in the area, but is fun to crawl about in and has a restaurant attached. The Chico Rei was supposedly an African king called Francisco, who was enslaved but bought his freedom working in the mine.

On the eastern edge of town, **Santa Efigênia** ① *Ladeira Santa Efigênia and Padre Faria, Tue-Sun 0800-1200,* built 1720-1785, has wonderful panoramic views of the city. This was a church used by black Brazilians only and the gilt that lines the interior is said to have been made from gold dust washed out of slaves' hair. Manuel Francisco Lisboa (Aleijadinho's father) oversaw the construction and much of the carving is by Francisco Xavier de Brito (Aleijadinho's mentor).

Mariana is the oldest of the colonial mining towns in Minas Gerais, founded by *bandeirantes* a few years before Ouro Preto, on 16 July 1696. At first, when it was little more than a collection of huts, it was called Arraial de Nossa Senhora do Carmo. But by 1711 it had become the town of Vila de Nossa Senhora do Carmo, and by the mid-18th century it had grown to be the most important administrative centre in the newly created Capitania de São Paulo e Minas do Ouro. Its name was changed to Mariana in honour of the wife of Dom João V, Dona Maria Ana of Austria. It retains many fine colonial buildings, most of them constructed in the second half of the 18th century. The artist Mestre Athayde was born here, as was the Inconfidênte Cláudio Manuel da Costa. The town was declared a national monument in 1945.

Unlike its more famous neighbour, Ouro Preto, in whose shadow the town tends to sit, Mariana, with a population of 47,000, has remained a working mining centre. For many years the **Companhia do Vale do Rio Doce (CVRD)**, the state mining company, had major operations here and provided a great deal of assistance for the restoration of the colonial heritage. Since CVRD's concentration on its new investments at Carajás, and its subsequent privatization, there have been doubts about its commitment to mining in Mariana and to the town itself.

ARRIVING IN MARIANA
Getting there Buses from Ouro Preto run every 30 minutes (US$0.60), take 20 to 30 minutes and stop at the *rodoviária*, out of town on the main road, then at the **Posto Mariana**, before heading back to the centre at Praça Tancredo Neves. Many buses seem to go only to the *posto* (petrol station) above the town, but it's a long walk from the centre. A bus from the *rodoviária* to the centre via the *posto* and Minas da Passagem costs US$1. **Maria Fumaça** steam trains ① *T031 3551 7705, US$15 return*, run between Ouro Preto and Mariana. They leave Ouro Preto Friday to Sunday at 1100 and 1600, returning from Mariana at 0900 and 1200.

Moving on From the *rodoviária* in Mariana, it's a 2¼-hour bus journey to **Belo Horizone** (see page 105), the capital of Minas Gerais state.

Tourist information The **tourist office** ① *Praça Tancredo Neves, T031-3557 9044, www.mariana.mg.gov.br*, can organize guides and has a map and free monthly booklet, *Mariana Agenda Cultural*, full of information. **Mariana Turismo** ① *R Direita 31*, is also helpful.

PLACES IN MARIANA
The historic centre of the town slopes gently uphill from the river and the **Praça Tancredo Neves**, where buses from Ouro Preto stop. The first street parallel with the Praça Tancredo Neves is Rua Direita, which is lined with beautiful, two-storey 18th-century houses with tall colonial windows and balconies. The **Casa do Barão de Pontal** ① *R Direita 54, Tue 1400-1700*, is unique in Minas Gerais, with its balconies carved from soapstone.

Rua Direita leads to the **Praça da Sé**, on which stands the cathedral, **Basílica de Nossa Senhora da Assunção**. Before Vila de Nossa Senhora do Carmo became a town, a chapel dating from 1703 stood on this spot. In various stages it was expanded and remodelled until its completion in 1760. The portal and the lavabo in the sacristy are by Aleijadinho and the painting in the beautiful interior and side altars is by Manoel Rabello de Sousa. Also in the cathedral is a wooden German organ (1701), made by Arp Schnitger, which was a gift to the first diocese of the Capitania de Minas do Ouro in 1747. It was restored in 1984 after some 50 years of silence. Concerts are held in the cathedral including regular **organ concerts** ① *Fri 1100 and Sun 1200, US$7.50*, see the local press for details.

Turning up Rua Frei Durão, on the right is the **Museu Arquidiocesano** ① *R Frei Durão 49, Tue-Sun 0900-1200, 1300-1700, US$1.50*, which has fine church furniture, a gold and

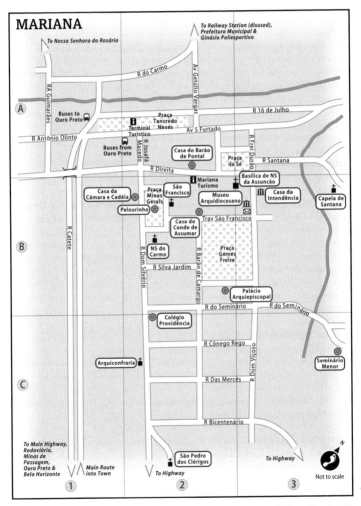

silver collection, Aleijadinho statues and an ivory cross. On the opposite side of the street is the **Casa da Intendência/Casa de Cultura** ① *R Frei Durão 84, 0800-1130, 1330-1700*, which holds exhibitions and has a museum of music. The ceilings in the exhibition rooms are very fine; in other rooms there are *esteiro* (flattened bamboo) ceilings.

The large **Praça Gomes Freire** was where horses would be tied up (there is an old drinking trough on one side) and where festivals were held. Now it has pleasant gardens. On the south side is the **Palácio Arquiepiscopal**, while on the north side is the **Casa do Conde de Assumar**, home of the governor of the capitania from 1717 to 1720; it later became the bishop's palace.

Praça Minas Gerais has one of the finest groups of colonial buildings in Brazil. In the middle is the **Pelourinho**, the stone monument to justice at which slaves used to be beaten. The fine **São Francisco church** ① *daily 0800-1700,* built 1762-1794, has pulpits, a fine sacristy and an altar designed by Aleijadinho, and paintings by Mestre Athayde, who is buried in tomb No 94. The statue of São Roque is most important as he is the patron saint of the city (his day is 16 August). Among Athayde's paintings are the panels showing the life of St Francis, on the ceiling of the right-hand chapel. The church is one of the most simple in Mariana but, in terms of art, one of the richest. There is a small exhibition of the restoration work funded by CVRD.

At right angles to São Francisco is **Nossa Senhora do Carmo** ① *daily 1400-1700,* built 1784, with steatite carvings, Athayde paintings, and chinoiserie panelling. Some consider its exterior to be the most beautiful in Mariana. Unfortunately this church was damaged by fire in 1999. Across Rua Dom Silvério is the **Casa da Cámara e Cadéia** (1768), once the Prefeitura Municipal. It is a superb example of civic colonial construction.

On Rua Dom Silvério the **Colégio Providência** at No 61 was the first college for boarding students in Minas Gerais. Also on this street is the **Igreja da Arquiconfraria** and, near the top of the hill, the **Chafariz de São Pedro**. On Largo de São Pedro is the church of **São Pedro dos Clérigos**, founded by Manuel da Cruz, first bishop of the town (1764), one of the few elliptical churches in Minas Gerais. It is unadorned, although there is a painting by Athayde, *A Entrega do Menino Jesus a Santo Antônio*. The cedar altar was made by José Pedro Aroca. Look for the cockerel, carved in memory of the biblical verses about St Peter betraying Christ before the cock has crowed three times. Ask to see the view from the bell tower.

The **Capela de Santo Antônio**, wonderfully simple and the oldest in town, is some distance from the centre on Rua Rosário Velho. Overlooking the city from the north, with a good viewpoint, is the church of **Nossa Senhora do Rosário** ① *R do Rosário,* dating back to 1752, with work by Athayde and showing Moorish influence.

Outside the centre to the east, but within easy walking distance, is the **Seminário Menor**, now the Instituto de Ciencias Históricas e Sociais of the federal university.

North of the river, Avenida Getúlio Vargas leads to the new **Prefeitura Municipal**. It passes the **Ginásio Poliesportivo** and s**the railway station**. This is a romantic building with a clock tower, but it is rapidly falling into disrepair.

AROUND MARIANA

The small village of **Antônio Pereira**, 24 km north of Mariana, is where imperial topaz is mined. Tours can be made of an interesting cave with stalactites. Local children will show you around for a small fee.

The capital of Minas Gerais, Belo Horizonte, has a population of five million and is the third largest city in Brazil. Although moderately attractive it offers little in the way of sights, beyond a handful of museums and parks. Most travellers come here to change bus on the way to Ouro Preto or Tiradentes, or to find work as an English-language teacher. The bustling modern skyscraper-filled centre sits in a bowl circled by dramatic mountains, which regularly trap pollution as the city strains under ever-increasing tides of rural migration. The city is pocked with hills that rise and fall in waves of red-tiled houses, tall apartment blocks and jacaranda- and ipe-lined streets. These are clogged with cars,

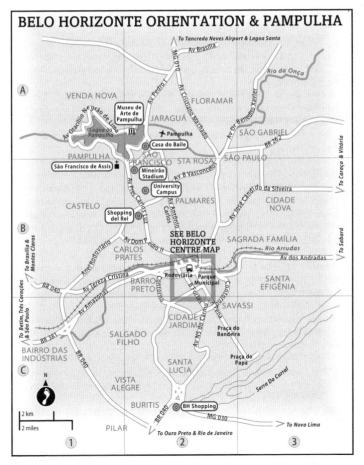

BELO HORIZONTE ORIENTATION & PAMPULHA

particularly during the rush hour, a situation that has led the municipal government to introduce an efficient integrated public transport system linking the bus and metrô networks, in imitation of Curitiba in Paraná.

ARRIVING IN BELO HORIZONTE

Getting there Buses from Ouro Preto and Mariana (US$10) take two and 2¼ hours respectively and arrive at the *rodoviária* next to Praça Rio Branco at the northwest end of Avenida Afonso Pena. The bus station is clean and well organized with toilets, a post office, telephones, left-luggage lockers (US$2, open 0700-2200) and shops.

Moving on If you want to extend the itinerary and fly to Brasília, you could take a 45-minute flight from **Tancredo Neves International Airport**, more commonly referred to as **Confins** ⓘ *39 km north of Belo Horizonte, T031-3689 2700, www.infraero.gov.br*. Flight costs vary hugely according to the day, season, etc, but can be as cheap as US$80. Flights to Diamantina are also available. A taxi from the centre to the airport costs US$50. Buses from the *rodoviária*, either *executivo* (US$15), or the comfortable normal bus (**Unir**, hourly, US$5), go to Confins. From the *rodoviária*, it's a 12-hour bus ride to Brasília or a five-hour journey to Diamantina.

If Belo Horizonte is the end of your trip, there are international flights, also from Tancredo Neves International Airport, to Paris, Lisbon, Buenos Aires, Miami and Panama City. Alternatively, you can fly back to Rio for your return flight home or you can continue your route overland to Parque Nacional Caparaó (see page 110) via Manhuaçu, and from there back to Rio.

Getting around The city has a good public transport system. **Red** buses run on express routes and charge US$1.50; **yellow** buses have circular routes around the Contorno, US$1; **blue** buses run on diagonal routes charging US$1.50. Some buses link up with the regional overground metrô. At present, the metrô is limited to one line and covers a limited portion of the north and west of the city and few areas of interest to tourists. However, there are plans to extend the service to Pampulha airport and the centre, US$0.90.

Orientation Belo Horizonte centres on the large Parque Municipal in the heart of downtown Belo Horizonte and on the broad main avenue of Afonso Pena. This is constantly full of pedestrians and traffic, except on Sunday morning when cars are banned and part of it becomes a huge open-air market. Daytime activity is concentrated on and around the main commercial district on Avenida Afonso Pena, which is the best area for lunch. At night, activity shifts to Savassi, southwest of the centre, which has a wealth of restaurants, bars and clubs.

Best time to visit Central Minas enjoys an excellent climate (16-30°C) except for the rainy season (December to March); the average temperature in Belo Horizonte is 21°C.

Tourist information The municipal office, **Belotur** ⓘ *R Pernambuco 284, Funcionários, T031-3220 1310, www.turismo.mg.gov.br, www.belotur.com.br; also on Parque Municipal, at the airports and rodoviária*, has lots of useful information and maps. The free monthly *Guía Turística* lists events and opening times. The tourism authority for Minas Gerais, **Turminas**

ⓘ *Praça Rio Branco 56, T031-3272 8573, www.turminas.mg.gov.br/intminas.html*, is very helpful, as is its booklet *Gerais Common Ways*. **Instituto Chico Mendes de Conservação da Biodiversidade (ICMBio)** ⓘ *Av do Contorno 8121, Cidade Jardim, T031-3337 2624*, has information on national parks. The website www.belohorizonteturismo.com.br is also useful.

As in any large city, watch out for sneak thieves in the centre and at the bus station. The Parque Municipal is not safe after dark, so it is best not to enter alone.

PLACES IN BELO HORIZONTE

Although dotted with green spaces like the **Parque Municipal** ⓘ *Tue-Sun 0600-1800*, and a few handsome buildings such as the arts complex at the **Palácio das Artes** ⓘ *Afonso Pena 156*, central Belo Horizonte has few sights of interest beyond a handful of small museums. The **Museu Mineiro** ⓘ *Av João Pinheiro 342, T031-3269 1168, Tue-Fri*

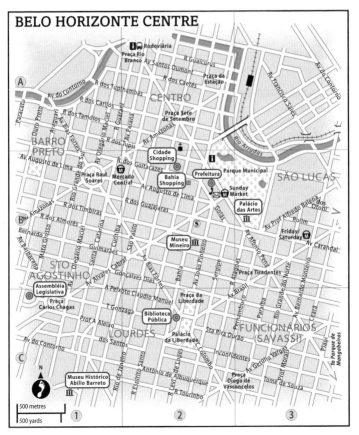

BELO HORIZONTE CENTRE

GOING FURTHER

Diamantina

Diamantina, a UNESCO World Heritage Site and northern Minas's prettiest colonial town, sits nestled in rugged hills 300 km north of Belo Horizonte. The town's colonial buildings are less spectacular than those in Ouro Preto, but Diamantina is better preserved, far less touristy and, with a population of 48,000, retains a sleepy charm all of its own. Regular flights from Belo Horizonte have made visiting Diamantina far easier than it used to be; it is now possible to continue overland from the town to Bahia. Diamantina is easily manageable on foot; the city centre is compact and there are plenty of little streetside cafés and bars. Try and be in the city for the regular Vesperata festivals when groups of musicians serenade passers-by from the city's numerous balconies, especially around the Praça Guerra; a tradition that began in the 17th century.

There are a number of interesting colonial buildings in the city. **Nossa Senhora do Carmo** (Tuesday-Saturday 0800-1200, 1400-1800, Sunday 0800-1200), is most remarkable for its beautiful interior paintings, by José Soares de Araujo, a former bodyguard from Braga in Portugal. Many of the city's churches are painted by him, but this is his finest work. The **Casa de Chica da Silva** (Praça Lobo Mesquita 266, free) is a museum devoted to an extraordinary 18th-century Afro-Brazilian slave who, through sheer force of personality and a marriage to a rich Portuguese man, rose to become the most powerful woman in the city. The church of **Nossa Senhora do Rosário dos Pretos** (Largo Dom Joaquim, Tuesday- Saturday 0800-1200 and 1400-1800, Sunday 0800-1200) is a reminder of the fate of most of her Afro-Brazilian contemporaries. It was designated for the black underclass who were not permitted even to walk in front of the other churches, let alone to attend Mass. President Juscelino Kubitschek, the founder of Brasília, was from Diamantina and his house is now a **museum** on the outskirts of town (Rua São Francisco 241, Tuesday-Sunday 1000-1200 and 1400-1800, US$3).

The cerrado forests that swathe the countryside around Diamantina are home to some of the rarest birds and mammals on the continent. The recently opened **São Gonçalo do Rio Preto** state park, 45 km from Diamantina, is the best base from which to explore them.

Where to stay $$$ Tijuco, R Macau do Melo 211, T038-3531 1022, www.hoteltijuco.com.br. This striking Niemeyer design hotel looks like a building from Thunderbird island. The big wood-panelled 1960s rooms and sweeping staircase are delightfully kitschy. The best are at the front with balconies and glorious views.

1000-1700, Sat and Sun 1000-1600, houses religious and other art in the old senate building, close to the centre. There is a section dedicated specifically to religious art, with six pictures attributed to Mestre Athayde (see pages 99, 100 and 101), exhibitions of modern art, photographs and works by *naïf* painters. Also of interest are the woodcarvings by Geraldo Teles de Oliveira (GTO). The **Museu Histórico Abílio Barreto** ① *Av Prudente de Morais 202, Cidade Jardim, T031-3277 8861, Tue, Wed, Fri, Sun 1000-1700, Thu 1000-1200,* is in an old *fazenda* which has existed since 1883, when Belo Horizonte was a village called Arraial do Curral d'el Rey. The *fazenda* now houses antique furniture and historical exhibits. To get there, take bus No 2902 from Avenida Afonso Pena.

Brazil's capital moved from Rio to wilderness back-land fifty years ago. Brasília was built airplane-shaped, in white concrete and shimmering glass as an architectural articulation of the national motto, 'Order and Progress'. It's a fascinating place – more a monument to the future than a capital city fit for living in – with a plethora of spectacular Oscar Niemeyer buildings offset by vast concrete courts and sweeping avenues, but no pavements, no community spaces, and locals segregated rather than integrated. Tourist blurbs will tell you that the city was built from scratch in five years, but in truth building according to the original plans is still occurring today – with a string of stunning buildings opening on the main Eixo Monumental avenue since the late noughties.

The cathedral remains the most impressive building in Brasília – a concrete crown of thorns coloured with turquoise and indigo stained glass and surrounded by haunting modernist statues. The vast concrete plaza which once engulfed it is now home to the **Museu Nacional** – a space-age dome whose entrance is reached by a sinuous runway, and the **Biblioteca Nacional** – a 400 yard-long white wedge faced with a concrete *Mashrabiya* and watching over a series of inky pools. This complex is crowned by the famous dish and dome **Congress buildings** – and the palatial seats of presidency, justice and diplomacy – the **Palácio da Alvorada** and the **Palácios de Justica** and **Itamarati**. The latter is Niemeyer's masterpiece – a rectangle sitting in lily-filled moat that strikingly mirrors the elegant fluted columns as the blue day turns to twilight. There are sweeping views of the whole city from the Radio Tower at the southern end of the Eixo Monumental.

A visit to Brasília from Minas or Rio de Janeiro will require a short flight or a day-long bus ride, but it's well worth the detour and not just to see Brasília itself. There's some magnificent scenery within easy reach of the city – including two World Heritage sites – the Chapada dos Veadeiros national park and the Portuguese colonial town of **Cidade de Goiás** – an unspoilt and little-visited cousin to Ouro Preto. Brasília can be used as a hub to connect routes – the Pantanal in Mato Grosso is reachable on a long bus journey or a short flight, and the city is well-connected with regular flights to all of Brazil's state capitals, including the cities of the Amazon.

Pampulha The city's most interesting attraction by far is the suburb of Pampulha: a complex of Oscar Niemeyer buildings set around a lake in formal gardens landscaped by Roberto Burle Marx. The project was commissioned by Juscelino Kubitschek in the 1940s, when he was governor of Minas Gerais and a decade before he became president. Some see it as a proto-Brasília, for this was the first time that Niemeyer had designed a series of buildings that work together in geometric harmony. It was in Pampulha that he first experimented with the plasticity of concrete; the highlight of the complex is the **Igreja São Francisco de Assis** ① *Av Otacílio Negrão de Lima, Km 12, T031-3441 9325, daily 0800-1800.* This was one of Niemeyer's first departures from the orthodox rectilinear forms of modernism and one of the first buildings in the world to mould concrete, with its series of parabolic waves running together to form arches. Light pierces the interior through a series of louvres and the curves are offset by a simple free-standing bell tower. The outside walls are covered in *azulejo* tiles by Candido Portinari, Brazil's most respected modernist artist. These were painted in a different style from his previous social realism, as exemplified by pictures such as *O Mestiço*. The building provoked a great deal of outrage because of its modernist design. One mayor proposed its demolition and replacement by a copy of the church of Saint Francis in Ouro Preto.

There are a number of other interesting Niemeyer buildings on the other side of the lake from the church. With its snaking canopy leading up to the main dance hall, the **Casa do Baile** ① *Av Octacílio Negrão de Lima 751, Tue-Sun 0900-1900, free*, is another example of his fascination with the curved line. There are wonderful views out over the lake. People would dance here and then take a boat to the glass and marble **Museu de Arte de Pampulha (MAP)** ① *Av Octacílio Negrão de Lima 16585, T031-3443 4533, www.comarte virtual.com.br, Tue-Sun 0900-1900, free*, which was then a casino set up by Kubitschek. Today it houses a fine collection of Mineira modern art and more than 900 works by national artists.

Just 700 m south of the lake are the twin stadia of **Mineirão** and **Mineirinho**, clear precursors to the Centro de Convenções Ulysses Guimarães in Brasília, which was designed by Niemeyer's office though not the architect himself. Mineirão is the second largest stadium in Brazil after the Maracanã in Rio, seating 92,000 people.

→PARQUE NACIONAL CAPARAÓ

This is one of the most popular parks in Minas, with good walking through strands of Atlantic rainforest, *paramo* and to the summits of three of Brazil's highest peaks, **Pico da Bandeira** (2890 m), **Pico do Cruzeiro** (2861 m) and the **Pico do Cristal** (2798 m). Wildlife is not as plentiful as it is in Caratinga as the park has lost much of its forest and its floral biodiversity. However, there are still a number of Atlantic coast primates here, such as the brown capuchins, together with a recovering bird population.

From the park entrance (small entry fee) it is 6 km on a poorly maintained road to the car park at the base of the waterfall. From the hotel, jeeps (US$20 per jeep) run to the car park at 1970 m (2½ hours' walk), then it's a three- to four-hour walk to the summit of the Pico da Bandeira, marked by yellow arrows. There are plenty of camping possibilities all the way up, the highest being at **Terreirão** (2370 m). It is best to visit during the dry season (April to October), although it can be quite crowded in July and during Carnaval.

ARRIVING IN PARQUE NACIONAL CAPARAÓ
Getting there The park is 49 km by paved road from Manhuaçu on the Belo Horizonte–Vitória road (BR-262). If you have your own transport, drive from Mariana to the BR-262, going through Manhumirim, Presidente Soares and Caparaó village, then 1 km further to the Hotel Caparaó Parque. The only way to reach the park by public transport is via Belo Horizonte, taking a bus from the *rodoviária* to Manhuaçu (six daily, six hours). There are eight daily buses from Manhuaçu to Alto Caparaó village (one hour) where there are hotels including the **Caparaó Parque Hotel** (www.caparaoparquehotel.com.br) and the **Pousada do Bezerra** (www.pousadadobezerra.com.br).

Moving on There are two options for your return to Rio: either return to Belo Horizonte and fly, or else take an 11-hour bus journey from Manhuaçu.

Tourist information To contact the park write to Caixa Postal 17, Alto Jequitibá, or telephone T255, via the operator on 101-PS 1, Alto do Caparaó. **Instituto Chico Mendes de Conservação da Biodiversidade (ICMBio)** ① *T031-291 6588 ext 119/122, www.icmbio. com.br*, also has information.

COLONIAL CITIES OF MINAS GERAIS LISTINGS

WHERE TO STAY

Congonhas do Campo
$$ Colonial, Praça da Basílica 76, opposite Bom Jesus, T031-3731 1834, www.hotel colonialcongonhas.com.br. A roomy converted colonial town house in a superb location right next to the *sanctuário* at the top of the hill. The restaurant downstairs, **Cova do Daniel**, is crammed full of colonial handicrafts and serves good Minas food.

Ouro Preto
$$$ Grande Hotel, R das Flores 164, Centro, T031-3551 1488, www.grandehotelouropreto. com.br. Gorgeous Niemeyer hotel recently renovated and with views over the city.
$$$ Pousada do Mondego, Largo de Coimbra 38, T031-3551 2040, www.Mondego. com.br. A fine colonial house sitting in the city centre near the São Francisco church with rooms of varying size and prices decorated with traditional rural Minas furniture and decor. The hotel runs a *jardineira* bus tour of the city, 2 hrs, minimum 10 passengers, US$18 for non-guests.
$ Pouso Chico Rei, R Brig Musqueira 90, T031-3551 1274, www.pousodochicorei. com.br. A delightful homey old house decorated with bric-a-brac and with faux Portuguese colonial furnishings. Book in advance and try and reserve room No 6.

Tiradentes
$$$ Solar da Ponte, Praça das Mercês, T032-3355 1255, www.solardaponte.com.br. English couple John and Anna Maria Parsons, serve afternoon tea and have decorated this elegant Portuguese colonial country house with romantic colonial fittings. Lovely garden. Tours and excursions (including horse rides) organized.
$$ Pouso das Gerais, R dos Inconfidêntes 109, T032-3355 1234, www.pousodas gerais.com.br. Spotless, fresh, fan-cooled rooms with parquet flooring, desk, TV and marble basins in the bathrooms. Central, quiet, pool and breakfast included.

Belo Horizonte
$$ Mercure, Av Do Contorno 7315 (Santo Antonio), T031-3298 4100, www.mercure. com. The newest of the city's business hotels with a good pool, sauna, gym and rooms decked out in standard business attire. A few kilometres from the centre.

RESTAURANTS

Ouro Preto
$$$ Le Coq D'Or, R Getúlio Vargas 270 (next to Rosário church), T031-3551 5200.
Brazilian-French fusion cooking in a smart dining room with live music. One of the city's best.

WHAT TO DO

Ouro Preto
Grand Tour, T031-3552 1100, www.grandtour.com.br. City tours around Ouro Preto and to Mariana.
Hermes Guia, T031-3551 6783. City tours of the historical sights in Ouro Preto with an accredited Ministry of Tourism guide.

Tiradentes
Caminhos e Trilhas, T032-3355 2477, www.tiradentesgerais.com.br. Walking in the rugged Serra de São José hills around Tiradentes

DREAM TRIP 2:
Salvador→Chapada Diamantina→Abrolhos islands
21 days

Salvador 4 nights, page 115

Parque Nacional Chapada Diamantina
2 nights, page 140
Bus/flight from Salvador to Lençóis
(6 hrs/30 mins)

Morro de São Paulo 3 nights, page 146
Boat/flight from Salvador (2 hrs/20 mins)

Ilha de Boipeba 3 nights (or day trip
from Morro de São Paulo), page 147
Boat from Morro de São Paulo (1 hr)

Itacaré 3 nights, page 147
Bus from Salvador via Ubaitaba (9 hrs);
better from Ilhéus (2 hrs)

Ilhéus Day trip, page 148
Bus/flight from Salvador (8 hrs/40 mins)

Porto Seguro 5 nights (or day trip from
Trancoso), page 150
Bus from Ilhéus via Itabuna (7 hrs)

Trancoso 5 nights (or day trip from Porto
Seguro), page 151
Bus from Porto Seguro (40 mins)

Caravelas 1 night, page 153
Bus from Porto Seguro direct (4 hrs)
or via Eunápolis and Itamarajú

Parque Nacional Marinho dos Abrolhos
Day trip, page 154
Pre-booked tour boats from Caravelas or
tour from Porto Seguro

Salvador 1 night, page 115
Return bus/flight from Porto Seguro
(11 hrs/1 hr)

GOING FURTHER

This route can connect north with the
Recife–São Luís route via the states of
Sergipe and Alagoas (see page 153).

Aracaju (Sergipe) page 153
Bus from Salvador (5 hrs)

Alagoas (Maceió) page 153
Bus from Aracaju (3½ hrs) or flight from
Salvador (45 mins)

Recife page 159
Bus from Alagoas (5½ hrs) flight from
Salvador (1 hr)

DREAM TRIP 2
Salvador→Chapada Diamantina→Abrolhos islands

Bahia is where Brazilians take their holidays. While it remains largely unknown to the rest of the world, this France-sized state is famous throughout Brazil for its Bounty bar beaches, frenetic festivals and captivating Afro-Brazilian culture. This route takes in the highlights of the whole state, beginning in the colonial city of Salvador, Brazil's first capital, whose streets of colourful Portuguese mansions and crumbling, gilt-covered baroque churches are protected as a Unesco World Heritage Site. The acrobatic martial-art dance of capoeira and Afro-Brazilian cult of *candomblé* find their spiritual homes in Salvador, a city with a thriving music scene.

The route then passes inland to the Chapada Diamantina – rugged diamond highlands dripping with waterfalls with some of the best short hiking in Brazil. From here it runs back to the coast to a series of enchanting resort towns surrounded by dozens of deserted beaches lined with coconut palms and washed by warm, tropical seas. These include the laid-back resort of Morro de São Paulo, the surf village of Itacaré, and Porto Seguro, a pretty colonial town built above the beach where modern Brazil began, when the Portuguese arrived here in 1500. The coast south of Porto Seguro gets lonelier and wilder, particularly just beyond the chic boho beach resort of Trancoso. And in the far south of the state, near Caravelas, boats leave for the Abrolhos archipelago, where humpback whales calve in summer and where you can snorkel or dive over pristine coral reefs.

It is possible to connect the Bahia route with the Recife to São Luís route (Dream Trip 3) by passing through the states of Sergipe and Alagoas immediately to the north of Bahia (see page 153 and pages 157-199).

SALVADOR AND THE RECÔNCAVO

Salvador (population 3.2 million) is the capital not just of Bahia but of African Brazil. The country's African heritage is at its strongest here – in the ubiquitous Orixá spirit gods and goddesses, the carnival rhythms of the drum troupe orchestras of Ilê Aiyê and Olodum, the rich spicy cooking, the rituals of candomblé (Brazil's equivalent of santería) and in the martial art ballet of capoeira. You will see the latter being played on Salvador's beaches and in the squares and cobbled streets of the city's historical centre, the Pelourinho. The Pelourinho is also home to one of the most impressive collections of colonial architecture in South America. There are myriad baroque churches here. Some, like the Convento do São Francisco, have interiors covered with tons of gold plate. Others, like Nossa Senhora do Rosário, are decorated with statues of black saints and art that celebrates African Brazilian culture. The city is famous for its frenetic carnival which, unlike Rio's, takes place in the streets to the pounding rhythms of axé music. The crowds are overwhelming and move like a human wave.

The Baía de Todos os Santos, Brazil's largest bay, is dotted with islands; many of them are privately owned by the northeast's wealthy, others serve as weekend resorts for people from Salvador. The best known is Itaparica, a long, thin island lined with palms, with a pretty colonial capital and some reasonable beaches. Many buses run from here, and taking the ferry across from Salvador and then road transport from Itaparica is the quickest way to get to southern Bahia. Behind the bay is the Recôncavo, a fertile hinterland – where agriculture in Brazil was born, and where hundreds of thousands of indigenous Brazilians and enslaved Africans sweated and died to harvest sugar cane, cocoa and coffee. It is dotted with sleepy colonial towns, the most famous of which are Cachoeira and its twin across the Paraguaçu river, São Felix.

→ARRIVING IN SALVADOR AND THE RECÔNCAVO

GETTING THERE

Air Domestic and international flights arrive at the **Luís Eduardo Magalhães airport** ① *32 km northeast of the centre, Praça Gago Coutinho, São Cristóvão, T071-3204 1010, www.infraero.com.br*, previously known as Dois de Julho. ATM machines are tucked away round the corner on the ground floor to the right as you arrive. The tourist information booth (open 24 hours, English spoken), has a list of hotels and a useful map. An air-conditioned *executivo* bus service runs from the airport to the historic centre (every 30 minutes, Monday to Friday 0500-2200, weekends 0600-2200, US$4). This service stops at all the hotels along the coast road en route – a long way round if you are going to the centre. *Ônibus coletivo* (city buses), US$1.20, are more direct but more crowded. Fixed-rate taxis go both to Barra and the centre; tickets can be bought from the desk next to the tourist information booth) for around US$35. Ordinary taxis leave from outside the airport, US$30.

Bus Interstate buses arrive at the **rodoviária** ① *5 km east of the centre, near Iguatemi Shopping Centre*. There are regular bus services to the centre, Campo Grande, Barra and Rio Vermelho (marked Praça da Sé/Centro). An executive bus leaves from outside the shopping centre (reached from the bus station by a walkway; be careful at night) and runs to Praça da Sé or the lower city (Comércio) via the coast road. Taxi to the centre, US$20.

Ferries and catamarans The main ferry dock, principally for car ferries although also for catamarans and passenger boats, is the **Marítimo de São Joaquim** ① *Av Oscar Pontes 1051, T071-3254 1020, www.twbmar.com.br*. It is known colloquially as 'ferry-boat' (pronounced 'fairhee bort)'. The terminal has a bank, cafés and some small shops. Ten car ferries per day arrive here from the little town of Bom Despacho on Itaparica as well as catamarans from Morro de São Paulo (two hours).

Salvador's other boat terminal is smaller and serves only passengers. It lies opposite the Mercado Modelo, five minutes' walk from the historic centre, and is known as the **Terminal Marítimo de Mercado Modelo** or Terminal Marítimo Turistico. Ferries and catamarans run between here and the Baía de Todos os Santos, including the village of Mar Grande on Itaparica (every 30 minutes) and there are catamarans from Morro de São Paulo (five a day in high season; three in low season; the last leaves at 1400).

MOVING ON
There are four flights a day from Luís Eduardo Magalhães airport (see above) to Lençóis for the Parque Nacional da Chapada Diamantina (see page 140). You will need to return to Salvador in order to commence the route south. You can fly or take a catamaran to Morro de São Paulo (see page 146) and thence to Ilha de Boipeba (see page 147), or you can head south along the coast by bus to Itacaré (see page 147) and Ilhéus (see page 148). It is also possible to fly from Salvador to Ilhéus and to visit Itacaré from there.

GETTING AROUND
The city is built on a broad peninsula and is at the mouth of the Baía de Todos os Santos. On the opposite side of the bay's entrance is the Ilha de Itaparica (see page 132). The commercial district of the city and its port are on the sheltered, western side of the peninsula; residential districts and beaches are on the open, Atlantic side. Barra lies at the point of the peninsula.

The centre of the city is divided into two levels, the **Cidade Alta** (Upper City) where the historic centre and Pelourinho lies, and the **Cidade Baixa** (Lower City), which is the commercial and docks district. The two levels are connected by a series of steep hills called *ladeiras*. The easiest way to go from one level to the other is by the *Lacerda* lift, which connects Praça Municipal (Tomé de Sousa) in the Upper City with Praça Cairu and the famous Mercado Modelo market. There is also the *Plano Inclinado Gonçalves*, a funicular railway that leaves from behind the cathedral going down to Comércio, the commercial district. The airport bus (see above) runs between the historic centre, Barra and the beaches and offers the best way to get around.

The **Salvador Bus** ① *T071-8845 9878, www.salvadorbus.com.br*, runs coach tours of the city with commentary in Portuguese and English. Buses are air-conditioned on the lower deck and open-topped above (with a covering for when it rains) and call at Rio Vermelho, the Orla Marítima (esplanade), the Farol da Barra lighthouse and beach, the Forts, the Museu de Arte da Bahia, Praça Castro Alves, the Pelourinho, Elevador Lacerda, The Igreja do Bonfim, the Solar de Unhão and Museu de Arte Moderna, and the Dique do Tororó. They are hop-on, hop-off with a wristband ticket (US$15 adults and US$7 for children under six). Five buses run a day, currently between 0830 and 1900. Tickets can be bought at travel agencies, hotels, commercial centres, Iguatemi Shopping (Salvador) and also on the buses themselves.

Most visitors limit themselves to the centre, Barra, the Atlantic suburbs and the Itapagipe peninsula, which is north of the centre. The roads and avenues between these areas are straightforward to follow and are well served by public transport. Other parts of the city are not as easy to get around, but are of less interest to most visitors. If you go to these areas, a taxi may be advisable until you are familiar with Salvador. The website www.transalvador. salvador.ba.gov.br/transporte has details of bus routes in Salvador with a search facility and prices. Buses are fast and frequent. The main bus stop in the Centro Histórico is at the southern end of Praça Municipal (Tomé de Sousa). Buses from the city centre to Bonfim leave from Avenida da França near the Mercado Modelo.

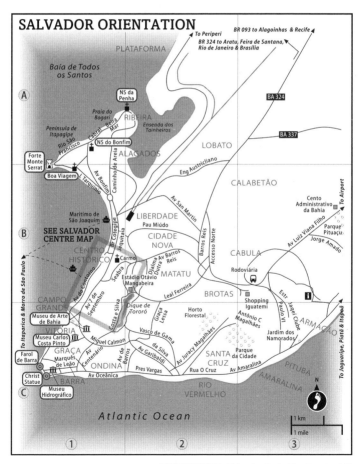

BEST TIME TO VISIT

It can rain at any time of year, but the main rainy season is between May and September. The climate is usually pleasant and the sun is never far away. Temperatures range from 25°C to 32°C, never falling below 19°C in winter.

TOURIST INFORMATION

The main office of **Bahiatursa** ① *Av Simon Bolivar, 650, T071-3117 3000, www.bahia tursa.ba.gov.br, Mon-Fri 0830-1800,* has lists of hotels and accommodation in private homes, can advise on travel throughout the state of Bahia, and has noticeboards for messages. There are also branches at the following locations: **airport** ① *T071-3204 1244, daily 0730-2300;* **Mercado Modelo** ① *Praça Visconde de Cayru 250, T071-3241 0242, Mon-Sat 0900-1800, Sun 0900-1330;* **Pelourinho** ① *R das Laranjeiras 12, Pelourinho, T071-3321 2133/2463, daily 0830-2100;* **Rodoviária** ① *T071-3450 3871, daily 0730-2100;* **Instituto Mauá** ① *Praça Azevedo Fernandes 1, Porto da Barra, T071-3264 4671, Mon-Fri 0900-1800, Sat 1000-1500,* **Shopping Barra** ① *Av Centenário, 2992, Chame-Chame, T071-3264 4566, Mon-Fri 0900-1900, Sat 0900-1400,* **Shopping Iguatemi** ① *Av Tancredo Neves 148, Pituba, T071-3480 5511, Mon-Fri 0900-2130, Sat 0900-1330.* The website www.bahia-online.net lists cultural events and news.

SAFETY

There is a lot of paranoia about safety in Salvador but as long as visitors follow common sense and a few rules they should be fine. The civil police are helpful and resources have been put into policing Barra, the Pelourinho and the old part of the city. All are well lit at night, although police are little in evidence after 2300. The Pelourinho area is generally safe, although there's plenty of begging/touting and pick-pocketing and even occasional muggings do occur. Avoid going to the toilet on the Praça do Reggae and other large communal washrooms on show nights as we have had reports of intimidation by groups of thieves; choose a restaurant loo instead. Be vigilant and wary at all times after dark and avoid carrying credit cards or wads of cash. Buses and the area around the Lacerda lift are unsafe at night. Never venture into the favelas unless on a tour or with a trustworthy local friend. Foreign women often receive unwelcome amounts of attention, especially during Carnaval when levels of physical contact in crowds can be very unpleasant.

→BACKGROUND

On 1 November 1501, All Saints' Day, the navigator Amérigo Vespucci discovered the bay and named it after the day of his arrival – Baía de Todos os Santos. The bay was one of the finest anchorages on the coast, and became a favourite port of call for French, Spanish and Portuguese ships. However, when the Portuguese crown sent Martim Afonso to set up a permanent colony in Brazil, he favoured São Vicente in São Paulo.

It was not until nearly 50 years later that the bay's strategic importance was recognized. When the first governor general, Tomé de Sousa, arrived on 23 March 1549 to build a fortified city to protect Portugal's interest from constant threats of Dutch and French invasion, the bay was chosen as the place from which the new colony of Brazil was to be governed. Salvador was formally founded on 1 November 1549 and, despite a short-lived Dutch invasion in 1624, remained the capital of Brazil until 1763.

The city grew wealthy through the export of sugar and the import of African slaves to work on the plantations. By the 18th century, it was the most important city in the Portuguese empire after Lisbon and ideally situated on the main trade routes of the 'New World'. Its fortunes were further boosted by the discovery of diamonds in the interior. However, as the sugar industry declined, the local economy could not rival the gold and coffee booms of the southeast and this led to the loss of capital status and the rise of Rio de Janeiro as Brazil's principal city. Nevertheless, the city continued to play an influential part in the political and cultural life of the country.

AFRICAN PRESENCE

For three centuries, Salvador was the site of a thriving slave trade, with much of the workforce for the sugar cane and tobacco plantations coming from the west coast of Africa. Even today, Salvador is described as the most African city in the western hemisphere, and the University of Bahia boasts the only choir in the Americas to sing in the Yoruba language. The influence permeates the city: food sold on the street is the same as in Senegal and Nigeria, the music is fused with pulsating African polyrhythms, men and women nonchalantly carry enormous loads on their heads, fishermen paddle dug-out canoes in the bay, and the pace of life is more relaxed than in other parts of the country.

MODERN SALVADOR

Salvador today is a fascinating mixture of old and modern, rich and poor, African and European, religious and profane. The city has 15 forts, 166 Catholic churches and 1000 *candomblé* temples. It remains a major port, exporting tropical fruit, cocoa, sisal, soya beans and petrochemical products. However, its most important industry is tourism, and it is the second largest tourist attraction in the country, after Rio.

Local government has done much to improve the fortunes of this once run-down, poor and dirty city. Major investments are being made in its infrastructure and public health areas. A new comprehensive sewage system has been installed throughout the city, with a view to improving living conditions and dealing with pollution.

The once-forgotten Lower City, Ribeira and the Itapagipe Peninsula districts have received major facelifts. Bahia has become more industrialized, with major investments being made by multinational firms in the automotive and petrochemical industries, principally in the Camaçari complex, 40 km from the city. The Bahian economy is currently the fastest growing in the country.

→CENTRO HISTÓRICO

Most of the interesting sights in Salvador are concentrated in the Centro Histórico in the **Cidade Alta** (Upper City). This is where the Portuguese founded the first capital of Brazil in November 1549. The entire 2-km stretch between the Praça Municipal in the South and the Carmelite churches (Carmo) in the north is a World Heritage Site.

This is the vibrant and colourful heart of Salvador. The colonial houses are painted in pastel colours, and many have been converted into restaurants, small hotels or bars, whose tables spill out onto the patios behind the houses; they host live music several times a week. The entire area proliferates with handicraft shops, artist ateliers and African-Brazilian cultural centres.

Note Most of the churches and museums in the Centro Histórico prohibit the taking of pictures; even without a flash.

PRAÇA MUNICIPAL (TOMÉ DE SOUZA) AND THE PRAÇA DA SÉ

These adjacent squares (connected by the Rua da Misericórdia), link with neighbouring Terreiro de Jesus (Praça 15 de Novembro) to form an almost entirely pedestrianized zone. A decade ago this area was tawdry, but it has been tidied up in recent years. There's arts and crafts, music and souvenir shopping at the many street-side stores and stalls and plenty of places for snacks and refreshments.

The **Praça Municipal** is the oldest part of Salvador – where the first governor Thomé de Souza built the first administrative buildings and churches (after unceremoniously clearing an indigenous Tupinambá village from the site). A statue of the soldier stands on a plinth gazing wistfully out to sea at the southern end of the *praça*. From here the city grew in a bewildering panoply of architectural styles, many of which can be seen around the square. Dominating the view are the neoclassical columns of the former council chamber (1660), now the **Paço Municipal** ① *Praça Municipal s/n, T071-3176 4200, Tue-Sat 0930-1700, free*, and the imposing **Palácio Rio Branco** ① *Praça Municipal s/n, T071-3176 4200, Tue-Sat 0930-1700, free*. Like many of Brazil's opulent buildings, this was built in homage to the French for the state-governor, in 1918. The palace now houses municipal offices. On the western side of the square is the star of many postcards: the huge, art deco **Elevador Lacerda** ① *US$0.05*, which whisks people from the Cidade Alta to the Cidade Baixa, 70 m below, in seconds. It was built in the late 1920s to replace an old hydraulic lift, which in turn replaced the original rope and pulley system first installed by the Jesuits. There are wonderful views over the bay from here.

Heading north from the *praça*, Rua da Misericórdia runs past the church of **Santa Casa da Misericórdia** ① *T071-3322 7666, open by arrangement 0800-1700* (1695), with its high altar and beautiful painted *azulejos* (tiles), to **Praça da Sé**. This is one of central Salvador's most attractive squares, decorated with modernist fountains, shaded by mimosa and flamboyant trees and lined with stately buildings, many of which house smart shops or European-style cafés. Look out for the **Cruz Caída** (Fallen Cross), a sculpture of a fallen and broken crucifix by one of Latin America's foremost sculptors, Mário Cravo Junior (www.cravo.art.br). It is dedicated to the old Igreja da Sé (cathedral), which was pulled down in 1930, together with an entire street of 18th- and early 19th-century townhouses, to make way for the now defunct tramline. Some of the cathedral's foundations have been uncovered and lie bare near the Cruz, covered in wild flowers. Immediately opposite the Cruz Caída is the **Memorial da Baiana do Acarajé** ① *Praça da Sé s/n, Mon-Fri 0900-1200 and 1400-1800;US$5*, a museum and cultural centre telling the story of the *Baianas* – the Bahian women who lead the Lavagem do Bonfim parade and who participate in carnaval throughout Brazil wearing traditional large swirling dresses. There are panels, ritual objects and historic photographs and the café next door serves Bahian snacks and has a small souvenir shop.

TERREIRO DE JESUS (PRAÇA 15 DE NOVEMBRO)

Immediately northeast of Praça da Sé, the Terreiro de Jesus is a large *praça* surrounded by handsome colonial townhouses and the bulk of the city's fabuous baroque churches. The square is the centre of tourist activity and bustles with bars, cafés and a mass of souvenir stalls proffering everything from *acarajé* to *berimbaus*. It's particularly lively on Tuesday

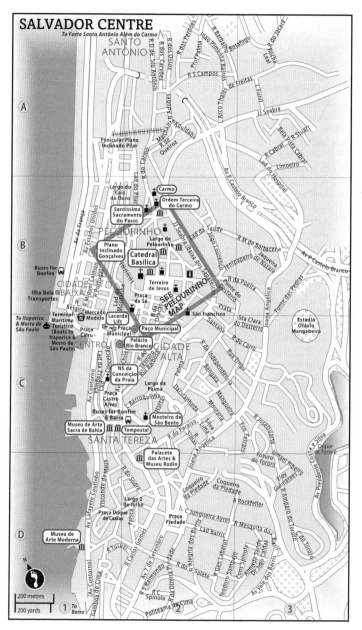

SALVADOR CENTRE

To Forte Santo António Além do Carmo

SANTO ANTÓNIO

Funicular Plano Inclinado Pilar

Largo do Cais do Ouro

Santissimo Sacramento do Passo

Carmo

Ordem Terceira do Carmo

PELOURINHO

Largo de Pelourinho

Plano Inclinado Gonçalves

Catedral Basílica

Terreiro de Jesus

SEE PELOURINHO MAP

Praça da Sé

São Francisco

Buses for Bonfim

Ilha Bela Transportes

CIDADE BAIXA

Mercado Modelo

Lacerda Lift

Paço Municipal

Terminal Marítimo Turístico (Boats to Itaparica & Morro de São Paulo)

To Itaparica & Morro de São Paulo

Praça Cairú

Palácio Rio Branco

CENTRO

CIDADE ALTA

NS da Conceição da Praia

Largo da Palma

Praça Castro Alves

Buses for Bonfim & Barra

Mosteiro de São Bento

Museu de Arte Sacra de Bahia

Tem포stal

SANTA TEREZA

Palacete das Artes & Museu Rodin

Largo 2 de Julho

Praça Duque de Caxias

Praça Piedade

Museu de Arte Moderna

N

200 metres
200 yards

To Barra

nights and at weekends when there are shows or concerts, and there are regular displays of **capoeira** – generally presented without joy and for the tourist dollar; if you stop to watch, you'll be expected to pay. Beware, too, of the persistent *Baianos* offering *fitas* (brightly coloured ribbons given as a good luck present), who swoop down like hawks on new arrivals. The streets that run off the south side of the Terreiro are frequented by drug dealers and beggars – best avoided, especially after dark.

The Terreiro de Jesus takes its name from the 'Church of the Society of Jesus' (ie the Jesuits) that dominates it. It is now **Catedral Basílica** ① *daily 0900-1200, 1400-1800, free*, devolving its ownership to the main body of the Catholic church in 1759, after the Jesuits were expelled from all Portuguese territories. The cathedral, whose construction dates from between 1657 and 1672, is one of the earliest examples of baroque in Brazil – a style that came to dominate in the 18th century and reached its full glory in Minas Gerais. The interior is magnificent: the vast vaulted ceiling and 12 side altars, in baroque and rococo, frame the main altar and are completely leafed in gold. This lavish display is offset by a series of Portuguese *azulejos* on in blue, white and yellow, which swirl together in a tapestry pattern.

The church is said to be built on the site of the original Jesuit chapel built by **Padre Manuel da Nóbrega** in the 16th century. Nóbrega was part of the crew that came from Portugal with Brazil's first governor-general, Tomé de Sousa, arriving in Bahia on 29 March 1549. Together with Padre José de Anchieta, he founded many of the Jesuit seminaries and churches that later became the cities of modern Brazil, including Rio, Recife and São Paulo. **Antônio Vieira**, one of the greatest orators in Portuguese history and a campaigner for the protection of the indigenous Brazilians in the Amazon, preached some of his most famous sermons in the church. He died a sad and disgraced old man of nearly 90 in July 1697, condemned by the Dominican-run Inquisition and prohibited from either preaching or writing after being slanderously accused by his enemies of conniving in the murder of a colonial official. The cathedral also preserves the remains of **Mem de Sá**, the great and brutal Portuguese conquistador and third governor-general of Brazil, who perhaps more than anyone was responsible for the establishment of the Brazilian territories. He ruthlessly crushed the Tupinambá along the Bahian coast and, in liberating Rio from the French, he quelled an insurrection that threatened to overthrow the fledgling Brazilian colony. Note the interesting sculptures, particularly those on the altar of Saint Ursula in a huge chest carved from a trunk of Mata Atlântica *jacarandá*, encrusted with ivory, bone and turtle shell.

Across the square is the church of **São Pedro dos Clérigos** ① *Praca 15 de Novembro, T071-3321 9183, Mon-Fri 0900-1200 and 1400-1800, free*, which is beautifully renovated. Alongside is the church of the early 19th-century **Ordem Terceira de São Domingos** ① *Praca 15 de Novembro, T071-3242 4185 Mon-Fri 0900-1200, 1400-1700, free*, which has a beautiful 18th-century, painted wooden ceiling attributed to **José Joaquim da Rocha**, the father of the Bahian School – perhaps the first Brazilian school of art to adopt the contemporaneous European trompe l'oeil style – which used perspective to create the illusion of three-dimensions.

There are two interesting museums on the square, both housed in the former Jesuit College (and subsequent Bahian School of Medicine building). The **Museu Afro-Brasileiro (MAfro)** ① *Mon-Fri 0900-1800, Sat and Sun 1000-1700, US$3 for a joint ticket with MAE*, charts the history of Africans in Bahia. Between 1440-1640, Portugal monopolized the export of slaves from Africa and they were the last European country to abolish it. Over the

ON THE ROAD

Candomblé

Candomblé is a spiritual tradition that developed from religions brought over by Yoruba slaves from West Africa. It is focused on relationships with primordial spirits or *orixás* who are linked with natural phenomena and the calendar. The *orixas* are invoked in *terreiros* (temples). These can be elaborate, decorated halls, or simply someone's front room with tiny altars. Ceremonies are divided into two distinct parts. The first is when the *orixás* are invoked through different rhythms, songs and dances. Once the dancers have been possessed by the *orixá*, they are led off in a trance-like state to be changed into sacred, often very elaborate costumes, and come back to the ceremonial area in a triumphant procession in which each one dances separately for their deity. Overseeing the proceedings are *mães* or *pães de santo*, priestesses or priests.

Candomblé ceremonies may be seen by tourists, usually on Sundays and religious holidays – although many are just for show and not the real thing. The ceremonies can be very repetitive and usually last several hours, although you are not under pressure to remain for the duration. Appropriate and modest attire should be worn; visitors should not wear shorts, sleeveless vests or T-shirts. White clothing is preferred, black should not be worn especially if it is combined with red. Men and women are separated during the ceremonies, women always on the left, men on the right. No photography or sound recording is allowed. Most temples are closed during Lent, although each one has its own calendar. **Bahiatursa** (see page 118) has information about forthcoming ceremonies, but accurate information on authentic festivals is not always easy to come by.

course of 450 years, they were responsible for transporting more than 4.5 million Africans – some 40% of the total. There are countless exhibits, from both Brazil and the African continent itself, including fascinating ritual objects, musical instruments and textiles. Panels compare West African and Bahian *orixás* (deities) and in a gallery all to themselves are some beautiful wooden carved effigies by the artist Carybé (Hector Julio Páride Bernabó) who lived most of his life in Bahia. Carybé became famous with the *antropofagismo* movement, illustrating Mario de Andrade's *Macunaíma*, and won the prize as the best draughtsman in Brazil in 1955. He was later celebrated for his depictions of *candomblé* rituals and *orixás*. In the basement of the same building, the **Museu de Arqueologia e Etnologia (MAE)** ① *Mon-Fri 0900-18700, Sat and Sun 1000-1700, US$3 for a joint ticket with MAfro*, houses indigenous Brazilian artefacts collected from all over Brazil over the centuries by the Jesuits, alongside archaeological discoveries from Bahia, such as stone tools, clay urns and rock art.

LARGO CRUZEIRO DE SÃO FRANCISCO AND FRANCISCAN CHURCHES

Facing Terreiro de Jesus is the **Largo Cruzeiro de São Francisco**, crowded with souvenir stalls and dominated by a large wooden cross and the church and the modest façade of the convent of **São Francisco** ① *Largo do Cruzeiro de São Francisco, T071-3322 6430; Mon-Sat 0800-1700, Sun 0800-1600, US$2*. The convent is the jewel in Salvador's baroque crown and

ON THE ROAD

Capoeira

Capoeira is the most visually spectacular and gymnastic of all martial arts and the only one to have originated in the Americas. Salvador is the capoeira centre of Brazil and seeing a fight between good Bahian capoeristas is an unforgettable experience. Fighters spin around each other in mock combat, never touching but performing a series of lunges, kicks and punches with dizzying speed and precision. Some wear razor blades on their feet. A ring or *roda* of other capoeristas watches, clapping, singing and beating time on a *berimbau* and hand-held drum. Every now and then they exchange places with the fighters in the centre of the ring.

Although many claim that capoeira derives from an Angolan foot-fighting ritual, this is incorrect. Capoeira originated in Brazil and there is strong evidence to suggest that it was invented by indigenous Brazilians. Padre José de Anchieta a 16th-century ethnologist makes an aside in his 1595 book *The Tupi Guarani Language* that the 'Indians amuse themselves by playing capoiera' and other Portuguese explorers like Martim de Souza recall the same. The word capoeira itself comes from Tupi-Guarani and means 'cleared forest' and the postures, including many of the kicks, spins and the crouching position taken by those in the circle are all Brazilian-Indian. It was in indigenous capoeiras that the fight was passed on to African plantation slaves who modified them, added African chants and rhythms and the *berimbau*; an instrument probably brought to Brazil from West Africa. The art was used as a weapon against the soldiers of the enslaved African king Zumbi who established the Americas' only free slave state just north of Bahia in the 1700s.

one of the finest baroque churches in Latin America. The entrance leads to a sanctuary with another spectacular trompe l'oeil painting by **José Joaquim da Rocha** (1777) and to a set of cloisters decorated with minutely detailed and hand-painted *azulejos*; many are by the celebrated Portuguese artist **Bartolomeu Antunes de Jesus**. Each tile is based on illustrations to epigrams by Horace by the 17th-century Flemish humanist and teacher of Peter Paul Rubens, Otto Venius. 'Quem e Rico? Quem nada ambiciona', proclaims one – 'Who is rich? He who is ambitious for nothing'. The picture shows a man crowned from behind by a bare-breasted woman (representing glory) whilst simultaneously pushing away golden crowns – representing the trappings of aristocracy and establishment. It's hard not to regard this as irony when entering the church itself. It took 64 years to cover the interior with plated gold and iconic art; almost all of it paid for by that same establishment who had grown wealthy on the sugar trade. The irony is compounded by more *azulejos* around the altar showing scenes from St Francis' life – which was remarkable for the saint's Siddhartha-like rejection of his aristocratic birth right, in favour of mendicancy.

Irony aside, only a resolute inverted snob could fail to be transfixed by the artistry inside church. The main body of the church is the most opulent in Brazil – a vast, ornate exuberance of woodcarving in *jacarandá* depicting a riot of angels, animals, floral designs and saints, covered with some 800 kg of solid gold. It's easy to see that the work is by Africans and native Brazilians. Look out for the mask-like faces on the top right- and left-hand corners of the sacristy – an allusion to contemporaneous African art; and the cherubs below the pulpit and encrusted into the walls, whose genitals were hacked off by Portuguese far more prudish than those who carved their church. There are wonderful individual pieces too, including a beautiful sculpture of St Peter of Alcântara (venerated for his mystical visions attained in a state of painful ecstasy), agonisingly captured by the one of the fathers of Bahian baroque sculpture, **Manoel Inácio da Costa**. He was born in Camamu and known as 'Seis Dedos' (six fingers) to his contemporaries. And he chipped the figure from a single hunk of rainforest wood. Other unspecified statues are known to be by Bento dos Reis, born to African slaves and celebrated for the emotion he imparts to his figures.They may include a serene statue of the patron saint of African-Brazilians – the hermit Saint Benedict, born to Ethiopian slaves in Messina in Sicily in 1524 (beatified by Pope Benedict XIV in 1743), and invited to join the Franciscans order after suffering a racist jibe. He carries the Christ child in his arms. The names of the painters of the dozens of magnificent ceiling panels remain unknown.

Next door is the church of the **Ordem Terceira de São Francisco** ⓘ *Ladeira da Ordem Terceira de São Francisco 3, T071-3321 6968, Mon-Sat 0800-1700, Sun 0800-1600, US$2* (1703), with an intricate sandstone façade in the Spanish Churrigueresque style – an elaborate rococo form characterised by exuberant carving. It is one of only two such churches in the country and its carvings were completely covered over with plaster until the early 20th century, probably in protest against associations with Spain. There's a huge and intricately decorated altar piece inside, a chapterhouse covered in striking images of the Order's most celebrated saints and a series of *azulejos* many depicting scenes of Lisbon before the devastating earthquake in 1755.

THE PELOURINHO

The streets north of the Terreiro de Jesus, which run over a series of steep hills to the neighbourhood of Santo Antônio, are referred to as the Pelourinho. The area takes its name from the whipping post where the African slaves were auctioned off or punished by their Brazilian-Portuguese masters. Its steep cobbled streets are lined with brightly painted townhouses leading to little pracas and always thronging with people. The bulk of the restaurants, small hotels and shops in the Centro Histórico are to be found here, and the streets are great for a browse.

The Pelourinho's main thoroughfares run north off the Terreiro de Jesus. **Rua Alfredo Brito** (aka Portas do Carmo) and **Rua João de Deus** and the side streets that run off them are lined with three- or four-storey townhouses occupied by shops, restaurants and boutique hotels. Both descend in steep cobbles to the **Largo de Pelourinho**, a large sunny square watched over by one of Salvador's most important African-Brazilian monuments, the church of **Nossa Senhora do Rosário dos Pretos** ⓘ *Praça Jose Alencar s/n, Largo do Pelourinho, T071-3241 5781, Mon-Fri 0830-1800, Sat-Sun 0830-1500 and with African-Brazilian mass every Tue at 1800, free*, built by former slaves over a period of 100 years, with what little financial resources they had. In colonial times, black Bahians were not even allowed to walk in front of the churches reserved for the white elite, let alone go inside them, and had to worship in their own building.The side altars honour black saints such as São Benedito (see Convento do São Francisco, above) and the painted ceiling and panels are by Jose Joaquim da Rocha (see page 124). The overall effect is of simple tranquillity, in contrast to the busy opulence of the cathedral and the São Francisco church. The church remains a locus for black Bahian culture and has strong connections with *candomblé*. On Tuesdays, following a show by Olodum on the Pelourinho, there is an African-Brazilian mass with singing accompanied by percussion from repiques, tambors and tamborins. Be sure to visit the haunting **slave cemetery** at the back of the building.

At the corner of Alfredo Brito and Largo do Pelourinho is a small museum dedicated to the work of Bahia's most famous author Jorge Amado, **Fundação Casa de Jorge Amado** ⓘ *Largo do Pelourinho s/n, T071-3321 0070, www.jorgeamado.org.br, Mon-Fri 0900-1800, Sat 1000-1600, free.* Amado was born and brought up around Ilhéus but spent much of his life in this house. The people of this part of Salvador provided the inspiration for the larger-than-life characters that populate some of his most famous novels including *Dona*

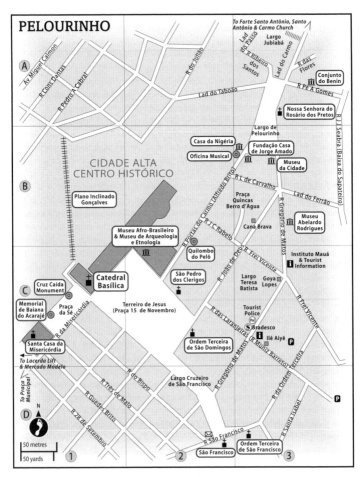

Flor e seus dois maridos (*Dona Flor and Her Two Husbands*, 1966). Information is in Portuguese only, but the walls of the museum café are covered with colourful copies of his book jackets in scores of languages, and all of his work is on sale.

Next door is the **Museu da Cidade** ① *Praça Jose de Alencar 3, Largo do Pelourinho, T071-3321 1967, Tue-Fri 0900-1830, Sat 1300-1700, Sun 0900-1300, free*, in two adjacent 18th-century houses and with exhibitions of arts and crafts, old photographs of the city, many fascinating objects from *candomblé* rituals and effigies of the *orixás*. A further room is devoted to the life and ouvre of the 19th century abolitionist Antônio Frederico de Castro Alves (1847-1871), and from the higher floors there is a good but seldom photographed view of the Pelourinho.

Just around the corner from the Largo do Pelourinho is the **Museu Abelardo Rodrigues** ① *Solar do Ferrão, R Gregório de Matos 45, T071-3320 9383, Tue-Sat 1300-1800, US$2*, preserves one of the most important and impressive collections of religious art outside the São Paulo's Museu de Arte Sacra (see page 215). It is housed in one of the Pelourinho's best-preserved and most stately 18th-century townhouses – once a Jesuit college – and showcases some impressive statuary, engravings, paintings and lavish monstrances from Brazil, all over Latin America and the Far East. All were collected by the Pernambucan who gave the museum its name. There is also a smaller and less illustrious Sacred Art Musuem, the **Museu de Arte Sacra da Bahia**, see page 129.

Below Nossa Senhora do Rosário dos Pretos is the **Conjunto do Benin** ① *R Padre Agostinho Gomes 17, Pelourinho, T071-3241 5679, casadobenin@yahoo.com.br, Mon-Fri 1200-1800*, which has displays of African-Brazilian crafts, photos and a video on Benin and Angola. It hosts exhibitions, dance shows and other artistic events. The **Casa da Nigéria** ① *R Alfredo de Brito 26, Pelourinho, T071-3328 3782*, offers a similar programme orientated more to Yoruba culture and has showcases of African and African Brazilian arts and crafts, photographs and an important library. Yoruba language classes are available here and both cultural centres are important nexuses of African-Brazilian culture and society in Bahia. The **Quilombo do Pelô hotel** ① *Rua Alfredo Brito 13*, also serves as a cultural centre for Jamaican culture. There are occasional shows in the restaurant – where Jamaican food is served – and the hotel receives many Jamaican celebrity guests. There's also Jamaican-Brazilian fusion music played in the **Bar do Reggae**.

MORRO DO CARMO AND SANTO ANTÔNIO

The Ladeira do Carmo climbs up the steep **Morro do Carmo** hill running north from the Largo do Pelourinho, past the **Igreja do Santissimo Sacramento do Passo** and the steps that lead up to it (which were the setting for the city scenes in Anselmo Duarte's award-winning socio-political tragedy, *O Pagador de Promessas*, 'keeper of the promises'), to the **Largo do Carmo**. This little *praça*, at the junction of the Ladeira do Carmo and Rua Ribeiro dos Santos, is watched over by a series of Carmelite buildings. The most impressive is the **Igreja da Ordem Terceira do Carmo** ① *Morro do Carmo s/n, Mon-Sat 0800-1130, 1400-1730, Sun 1000-1200, US$1*, once a piece of striking baroque dating from 1709 but completely gutted in a fire 67 years later and restored in the 19th century. It is in a poor state of repair but houses one of the sacred art treasures of the city, a sculpture of Christ made in 1730 by **Francisco Xavier 'O Cabra' Chagas** ('the Goat'), a slave who had no formal training but who is celebrated by many locals as the Bahian Aleijadinho, who carved *O Cabra*. Two thousand tiny rubies embedded in a mixture of whale oil, ox blood and banana resin give Christ's blood a ghostly, almost transparent appearance and the statue itself is so lifelike it appears almost to move. There is a small museum with a collection of ornate icons and period furniture. The adjacent **Igreja do Carmo** ① *Morro do Carmo s/n, Mon-Sat 0800-1200, 1400-1800, Sun 0800-1200, US$1*, a magnificent painted ceiling by the freed slave, José Teófilo de Jesus, while the **Convento do Carmo**, which served as a barracks for Dutch troops during the 1624 invasion, has been tastefully converted into Salvador's most luxurious hotel (see page 137).

Rua do Carmo continues to climb north from the Morro do Carmo into the neighbourhood of Santo Antonio, where dozens of the pretty colonial houses have been converted into tasteful boutique hotels and *pousadas*, the best of which have gorgeous bay views. The street eventually reaches the Barão do Triunfo (Largo de Santo Antônio), after a little over a kilometre. This handsome square (with barely a tourist in sight), is watched over by the hulking **Forte de Santo Antônio além do Carmo fortress** ① *Barão do Triunfo s/n, Santo Antônio, T071-3117 1488, http://fortesantoantonio.blogspot.com, Mon-Sat 0900-1200 and 1400-1700, US$4*, and another impressive church, the **Igreja de Santo Antônio Além do Carmo** ① *Largo Barão do Triunfo s/n, Santo Antônio, T071-3242 6463, Mon-Sat 0900-1200 and 1400-1730, free*. The fort dates from the last decade of the 17th century and is known locally as the Forte da Capoeira as it is home to half a dozen capoeira schools. It was restored at the turn of the 20th century and there are beautiful views over the bay from its walls.

CIDADE BAIXA AND MERCADO MODELO

Salvador's Cidade Baixa (lower city), which sits at the base of the cliff that runs from Santo Antônio in the north to Praça Municipal and Lacerda lift in the south, was once as delightful and buzzing with life as the Pelourinho. Today, its handsome imperial and early republican 19th-century buildings, many of them covered in *azulejos*, are crumbled and cracked. Others have been pulled down and replaced with ugly concrete warehouses. There are numerous gorgeous baroque churches in a similar state of disrepair, most of them with doors permanently closed. With the exception of the ferry docks, the whole area is dangerous and down at heel – especially at night. However, there are plans for restoration. A big hotel group has apparently bought up one of the old colonial mansions and in 2009 musician Carlinhos Brown opened the **Museu du Ritmo** ① *R Torquato Bahia, 84 Edifício Mercado do Ouro, T071-3353 4333, www.carlinhosbrown.com.br/universo/museu-du-ritmo*, and the **International Centre for Black Music** – a complex built around a 1000-sq-m concert arena housed in a giant courtyard formed from the walls of a former colonial mansion house which once was home to the gold exchange. The museum has plans for over 100 multi-media installations by 2011, a cinema, art gallery, school and recording studio on the site. Shows are advertised in the local press and on Carlinhos Brown's website.

There are few sights of interest. Bahia's best souvenir shopping is in the **Mercado Modelo** ① *Praça Visconde Cayru, Cidade Baixa, Wed-Mon 0900-1900, Sun 0900-1300, closed Tue*. This former customs house is thick with stalls selling everything from musical instruments to life-size sculptures hacked out of hunks of wood. Look out for the colourful handbags, made out of hundreds of can ring-pulls sewn together with fishing twine, and the *orixá* effigies and postcards. There are frequent capoeira shows between 1100 and 1300 on weekdays (you will have to pay to take pictures), occasional live music and numerous cafés and stalls selling Bahian cooking.

Further along the shore to the south is the striking, octaganol church of **Nossa Senhora da Conceição da Praia** ① *R Conceição da Praia at Av Contorno*. The church, which dates from 1736, was built in *lioz* marble in Portugal by Manuel Cardoso de Saldanha, disassembled bit by bit with the stones given numbers, then transported to Salvador and reconstructed. It has an unusual octagonal nave and diagonally set towers, modelled on churches in Portugal such as the Guarda cathedral. Inside it is magnificent, with a stunning ceiling painting of an Italianate panoply of saints gathered around the Madonna in glorious Renaissance perspective – the masterpiece of **José Joaquim da Rocha**.

→SOUTH OF THE CENTRE

The modern city, which is dotted with skyscraper apartment blocks, sits to the south of the old centre towards the mouth of the bay. Rua Chile leads to **Praça Castro Alves**, with its monument to the man who started the campaign that finally led to the abolition of slavery in 1888. Two streets lead out of this square: Avenida 7 de Setembro, busy with shops and street vendors selling everything imaginable; and, parallel to it, Rua Carlos Gomes. **Mosteiro São Bento** ① *Av 7 de Setembro, Mon-Fri 0900-1200 and 1300-1600, T071-3322 4749, www.saobento.org, US$3*, another of Bahia's oldest religious buildings, dates from 1582 but was constructed much later. The cool, colonial spaces and cloistered garden are a welcome quiet space within the bustle of the city. The monastery was used as an arsenal by the Dutch during their occupation in 1624 and narrowly avoided going the way of much of colonial Rio and São Paulo in the 20th century – razed to the ground to make way for ugly modern skyscrapers. It houses a religious art museum with some 2000 priceless antiquities.

Just to the south is the **Palacete das Artes and the Museu Rodin** ① *R da Graça 284, Graça, T071-3117 6986, Tue-Sun 1000-1800, free*, a small museum and cultural centre entirely devoted to Rodin sculptures on loan from France until 2012. Some 62 are exhibited, including *The Thinker* and *The Kiss*.

Museu de Arte Sacra da Bahia ① *R do Sodré 276 off R Carlos Gomes, T071-3243 6511, Mon-Fri 1130-1730, US$2*, is in the 17th-century monastery and church of Santa Teresa d'Avila, at the bottom of the steep Ladeira de Santa Tereza. Many of the 400 carvings are from Europe, but there are some beautiful pieces by the artists who worked on the city's finest churches, such as Frei Agostinho de Piedade and José Joaquim da Rocha. Look out for the hauntingly life-like statue of Christ by the latter, carved from a piece of ivory and crucified on a *jacarandá* cross. Among the reliquaries of silver and gold is one made from gilded wood by Aleijadinho. The views from the patio, out over the Baía de Todos os Santos, are breathtaking and very little photographed. Opposite is **Tempostal** ① *R do Sodré 276, Tue-Fri 0900-1830, Sat and Sun 0900-1800*, a private museum of postcards. Just inland near Campo Belo is the **Dique do Tororo** ① *Av Vasco de Gama*, a lake and leisure area decorated with 3-m-high *orixá* statues by the Bahian sculptor Tatti Moreno. There are large *candomblé* celebrations here at dawn on 2 February before the **Festa da Yemanjá**.

Further south, the **Museu de Arte Moderna and Solar do Unhão** ① *off Av Contorno, T071-3117 6139, Tue-Fri 1300-1900, Sat 1300-2100, free*, is one of the finest modern art museums in northeastern Brazil. The collection includes work by most of Brazil's important artists, including Emiliano di Cavalcanti, the abstract painter Alfredo Volpi, social-expressionist Cândido Portinari and the co-founder of *antropofagismo*, Tarsila do Amaral, alongside pieces by Bahian artists such as Mario Cravo Jr, Carybé and the

Franco-Bahian photographer Pierre Verger, and contemporary artists like Jose Bechara, Siron Franco and the photographer Mario Cravo Neto. The gallery is housed in the Solar do Unhão – itself an important historical monument. It sits right on the waterfront and was built in the 17th century initially as a sugar storage way station. It then became a mansion occupied by a series of influential Bahians over the following centuries, all of whom have left their mark on the building – from little chapels to beautiful painted *azulejos*. The gallery also hosts temporary exhibitions, has an arts cinema (www.saladearte.art.br) and a bar/café with live jazz on Saturdays from 1830. There are many restaurants nearby. The museum is close to a favela and there are occasional muggings particularly after dark; it's best to take a taxi.

Heading towards Porta da Barra, the **Museu de Arte da Bahia** ① *Av 7 de Setembro 2340, Vitória, Tue-Fri 1400-1900, Sat and Sun 1430-1900, US$2*, has interesting paintings by Bahian and Brazilian artists from the 18th to the early 20th century and a collection of 18th- and 19th-century furniture. A kilometre south of here is the **Museu Carlos Costa Pinto** ① *Av 7 de Setembro 2490, Vitória, www.museucostapinto.com.br, Mon and Wed-Fri 1430-1900, Sat and Sun 1500-1800, US$2*, is a modern house with collections of crystal, porcelain, silver and furniture. It ostensibly has the world's only collection of *balangandãs* (slave charms and jewellery). The museum has a pleasant little garden café serving quiches, salads and cakes.

PORTO DA BARRA AND THE ATLANTIC BEACH SUBURBS

Barra is one of the most popular places to stay in Salvador and the best inner-city beaches are in this area. The strip from Porto da Barra as far as the Cristo at the end of the Farol da Barra beach has some of the city's liveliest cafés, restaurants, bars and clubs. A night out here, in nearby Campo Belo and in the exclusive restaurants and bars of the city's most upmarket venue, **Praça dos Tupinambas**, give an idea of how polarized Salvador society is. The clientele is much more middle class than the Pelourhino; the music, food and conversation are more European and American and, in Brazil's African heart, there's hardly a black face in sight.

There are a few sights of moderate interest around Barra. The **Forte de Santo Antônio** and its famous lighthouse are right at the mouth of the bay where Baía de Todos os Santos and the South Atlantic Ocean meet. On the upper floors, the **Museu Hidrográfico** ① *Tue-Sat 1300-1800, US$2*, has fine views of the coast. A promenade leads away from the fort, along the beach to the **Morro do Cristo** at the eastern end, which is crowned with a statue of Christ, arms outstretched over the bay. The statue is unremarkable in itself, but there are good views from the hill.

RIO VERMELHO AND THE OCEAN BEACHES

From Barra the beach road runs east through the beachfront suburbs of **Ondina** and **Rio Vermelho**. Confusingly, the road is known as both Avenida Oceânica and Avenida Presidente Vargas, and both have different numbering, making finding an address a challenge to say the least. **Rio Vermelho** is the only suburb of interest. It has long been the home of many of Salvador's well-to-do artists and musicians and a centre for *candomblé*. Unlike the beachfront neighbourhoods around Barra, the clientele is a healthy mix of middle-class and African-Brazilian. There's a lively market with many little spit-and-sawdust bars, a handful of decent restaurants and small eateries serving some of the city's best *acarajé*. The area is busy at night, especially at weekends, and there are a number of venues playing traditional Bahian music. On 2 February the beach at Rio Vermelho is packed with *candomblé* pilgrims for the **Festa de Yemanjá**. To get here from the city centre, it is a 10-minute taxi ride (US$10-12) or a 20-minute bus journey on the airport–city centre bus. There are some good hotels nearby.

The next beaches along from Rio Vermelho are **Amaralina** and **Pituba**, neither of which are good for swimming but both of which have good surf and small fishing communities. Look out for *Jangadas* – small rafts with sails peculiar to northeast Brazil – on the seashore. Bathing is better at **Jardim de Alah**, **Jaguaripe**, **Piatã** and **Itapoã**, all of which are fairly clean and have fluffy white sand and swaying coconut palms. Any bus from Praça da Sé marked Aeroporto or Itapoã reaches the beaches in about an hour. Near Itapoã is the **Lagoa do Abaeté**, a deep freshwater lake surrounded by brilliant, white sands. This is where local women come to wash their clothes and then lay them out to dry in the sun. The road leading up from the lake offers a panoramic view of the city in the distance with white sands and freshwater less than 1 km from the sea.

Beyond Itapoã are the magnificent ocean beaches of **Stella Maris** and **Flamengo**, both quiet during the week but very busy at the weekends. Beware of strong undercurrents in the sea.

→NORTH OF THE CENTRE: BONFIM, ITAPAGIPE AND RIBEIRA

ⓘ *Take bus S021-00 marked Ribeira-Pituba from the the bus stop on Av da França on the quayside in the Cidade Baixa.*

The most famous sight in the northern suburbs is the church of **Nosso Senhor do Bonfim** ⓘ *Largo do Bomfim 236, Bonfim, T071-3316 2196, www.senhordobonfim.org.br, museum Tue-Fri 0800-1200 and 1400-1700, free* (1745), on the Itapagipe peninsula. It draws extraordinary numbers of supplicants (particularly on Friday and Sunday), making ex-voto offerings to the image of the Crucified Lord set over the high altar. The processions over the water to the church on the third Sunday in January are particularly interesting. The church has some naturalistic interior paintings by Franco Velasco (the modest canvases of the Stations of the Cross) and José Teófilo de Jesus (who painted the ceiling and 34 of the canvases on the church wall). Both almost certainly learnt their techniques from the master José Joaquim da Rocha.

The beach south of the church is far too dirty for swimming and is always busy with touts offering fita ribbons. It is the focus for celebrations during the festival of Nosso Senhor dos Navegantes. The colonial fort of **Monte Serrat** ⓘ *R Santa Rita Durão s/n, T071-3313 7339, Tue-Sun 0900-1700, US$0.50*, has unusual round towers. It is one of the best preserved colonial forts in northeast Brazil and was first constructed in 1583 and altered in the 18th and 19th centuries. It sits next to the pretty Portuguese church of **Nossa Senhora do Monte Serrat** on Monte Serrat – a much photographed local beauty spot overlooking the Baía de Todos os Santos and Bonfim beach.

Further north, at Ribeira, is the church of **Nossa Senhora da Penha** (1743), another beautiful colonial building and important syncretistic pilrgrimage site. The beach here has many restaurants, but is polluted.

Salvador sits on a peninsula which forms the northern head of Brazil's largest bay, the Baía de Todos os Santos. The bay is studded with tropical islands, the largest of which, Itaparica, sits immediately opposite Salvador, forming the bay's southern head. Itaparica is the only island close to Salvador with water clean enough for swimming. It is only 29 km long and 12 km wide and can easily be visited on a day trip.

There are two tiny towns on the island and a cluster of hamlets. **Itaparica** is very picturesque and well worth a visit, with a decent beach and many fine residential buildings from the 19th century. The church of **São Lourenço** is one of the oldest in Brazil, and a stroll through the old town is delightful. In summer the streets are ablaze with the blossoms of the beautiful flamboyant trees. Itaparica town is connected to the main ferry port at **Bom Despacho** via a coastal road run by small buses and *combi* minivans via the hamlets of **Ponta de Areia** (with good beaches and many *barracas*), **Amoureiras** and **Manguinhos**. Bom Despacho itself is little more than a ferry dock shops and restaurants.

The island's principal town is **Mar Grande**, aka Veracruz. There are many *pousadas* and a cluster of restaurants here, as well as at the beaches of **Mar Grande** and **Penha**, to the south. Beaches get better and more deserted the further south you go. They include the **Barra do Gil** (backed with holiday homes), the **Barra do Pote** (with a white-sand beach and calm waters) and **Tairu** (deserted during the week and with fine, white sand).

Arriving on Ilha de Itaparica The island is connected to the mainland by bridge or boat. The main passenger ferry runs from the São Joaquim terminal in Salvador (see page 116) to **Bom Despacho**, every 45 minutes 0540-2230. A one-way ticket for foot passengers during the week costs US$1, US$1.20 at weekends. A catamaran service for Bom Despacho departs twice daily, US$3. **Mar Grande** can be reached by a small ferry (*lancha*) from the Terminal Marítimo, in front of the Mercado Modelo in Salvador. The ferries leave every 45 minutes and takes 20-40 minutes, US$3 return. There is a bridge on the southwest side of the island. Buses from mainland towns such as Nazaré das Farinhas, Valença and Jaguaribe (a small, picturesque colonial port), arrive at Bom Despacho.

From Bom Despacho there are many buses, *combis* and taxis to all parts of the island. There are no banks on the island. *Combis* and taxis can be rented for trips around the island but be prepared to bargain, US$40-50 for a half-day tour.

BAY ISLANDS

There are dozens of other islands in the Baía de Todos os Santos. They include the **Ilha do Frades** and the **Ilha do Maré** (with Mata

Atlântica forest and tiny fishing villages). These can be visited with organized tours with Ilha Bela or **Tatur Turismo** (see page 138).

NAZARÉ DAS FARINHAS

On the mainland, 60 km inland from Itaparica, Nazaré das Farinhas (population 25,000) is reached across a bridge by bus from Bom Despacho. This 18th-century town is celebrated for its market, which specializes in the local ceramic figures, or *caxixis*. There is a large market in Holy Week, particularly on Holy Thursday and Good Friday. From here buses run to southern Bahia. About 12 km from Nazaré (taxi from Salvador US$4.25, bus at 1530) is the village of **Maragojipinha**, which specializes in making the ceramic figures.

→RECÔNCAVO BAIANO

The area around the bay and west of Salvador is known as the Recôncavo Baiano. This was one of the chief centres of sugar and tobacco cultivation in the 16th century and there is some fine colonial architecture here. Places of interest include the sleepy colonial towns of Cachoeira and São Felix, on the banks of the muddy Rio Paraguaçu, which are famous for their festivals and strong connection to *candomblé*. There are also small fishing villages on the bay that are worth exploring, and dotted throughout the countryside are the decaying ruins of once-productive *engenhos* (sugar refineries), some of which can be visited.

SANTO AMARO DA PURIFICAÇÃO AND AROUND

Some 73 km from Salvador, Santo Amaro da Purificação is an old and sadly decaying sugar centre. It is noted for its churches (which are often closed because of robberies), the most famous of which is the **Igreja Matriz Santo Amaro da Purificação** ① *Praça da Purificação, T075-3241 1172, Mon-Fri 0800-1200 and 1400-1700, Sat 0800-1200*, which has a superb painted ceiling by José Joaquim da Rocha. There is also a municipal palace (1769), a fine *praça* and ruined sugar baron mansions including **Araújo Pinto**, the former residence of the Barão de Cotegipe. It is also the birthplace of Caetano Veloso and his sister Maria Bethânia. Other attractions include the splendid beaches of the bay, the falls of Vitória and the grotto of Bom Jesus dos Pobres. There are a number of interesting festivals and craftwork is sold on the town's main bridge. There are no good hotels or restaurants. There are at least 20 buses a day from Salvador to Santo Amaro and onward buses to Cachoeira.

About 3 km beyond Santo Amaro on the BR-420, turn right onto the BA-878 for **Bom Jesus dos Pobres**, a small, traditional fishing village with a 300-year history. There is one good hotel. To get there, take a bus from Salvador's *rodoviária* (four a day, **Camurjipe**, US$3).

CACHOEIRA AND SÃO FELIX

Set deep in the heart of some of the oldest farmland in Brazil, **Cachoeira** and its twin town, São Felix, were once thriving river ports that provided a vital supply link with the farming hinterland and Salvador to the east. The region was the centre of the sugar and tobacco booms, which played such an important role in the early wealth of the colony. The majestic *saveiro* (a gaff-rigged boat) traditionally transported this produce down the Rio Paraguaçu to Salvador across the bay. These boats can still occasionally be seen on the river. The town was twice capital of Bahia: once in 1624-1625 during the Dutch invasion, and once in 1822-1823 while Salvador was still held by the Portuguese.

FESTIVALS
Salvador and Cachoeira

SALAVADOR

January Epiphany (6 Jan) Public holiday with free concerts and events. Beautiful masses in many of the historic churches. **Festa do Nosso Senhor do Bonfim**. Held on the 2nd Sun after Epiphany. On the preceding Thu there is a colourful parade at the church with many penitents and a ceremonial washing of the church itself.

February Carnaval.
Pescadores do Rio Vermelho (2 Feb). Boat processions with gifts for Yemanjá, Goddess of the Sea, accompanied by African Brazilian music.
March/April Holy Week. The week before Easter sees many colourful processions around the old churches in the upper city.

CACHOEIRA

24 June São João, 'Carnival of the Interior'. Celebrations include dangerous games with fireworks, well attended by tourists.

Mid-August Nossa Sehora da Boa Morte.
4 December A famous *candomblé* ceremony at the Fonte de Santa Bárbara.

With the introduction of roads and the decline of river transport and steam, the town stopped in its tracks in the early 20th century and thus maintains its special charm. As in Salvador, *candomblé* plays a very important part in town life (see box, page 123). Easy access by river from Salvador allowed the more traditional *candomblé* temples to move in times of religious repression. Cachoeira was the birthplace of Ana Néri, known as 'Mother of the Brazilians', who organized nursing services during the Paraguayan War (1865-1870).

There are a few interesting sights in Cachoeira. The **Casa da Câmara e Cadeia** ① *Praça de Aclimação, T075-3425 1018, daily 0800-1200 and 1400-1800, US$2* (1698-1712), was, for a brief period when Cachoeira was the state capital in 1822, the seat of the governance of Bahia. Upstairs is the town hall (with stern notices saying no shorts or Havaianas allowed). Downstairs there is a **slavery museum**, housed in the heavy walled dungeon where slaves were imprisoned behind two sets of strong bars. The dungeon has a sad and oppressive atmosphere. The **Museu Regional de Cachoeira** ① *Praça da Aclamação 4, Centro, T075-3425 1123, Mon-Fri 0800-1200 and 1400-1700, Sat 0800-1230, book ahead, US$2*, has a collection of period furniture, sacred images and ecclesiastical items, paintings and documents relating to the history of the town. The dark mark on the walls near the staircase at the entrance show where the river reached during the 1989 flood.

The **Santa Casa de Misericórdia** (1734) was the colonial hospital and has a fine church attached. Other churches include: the 16th-century **Ajuda** chapel (now containing a fine collection of vestments) and the convent of the **Ordem Terceira do Carmo**, whose church has a heavily gilded interior; the **Igreja Matriz** ① *R Ana Nery s/n, Tue-Sat 0900-1200 and 1400-1700, Sun 0900-1200, free*, with 5-m high *azulejos*, and a ceiling painting attributed to José Teolfilo de Jesus (who painted at the Bonfim church in Salvador; and **Nossa Senhora da Conceição do Monte**. All churches are either restored or in the process of restoration.

The **Fundação Hansen Bahia** ① *R 13 de Maio, T075-3425 1453, Tue-Fri 0900-1700, Sat and Sun 0900-1400*, has fine engravings by the German artist **Karl Meinz Hansen**, who

ON THE ROAD

Bahian cuisine

Bahian cooking is spiced and peppery. The main dish is *moqueca* – seafood cooked in a sauce made from coconut milk, tomatoes, red and green peppers, fresh coriander and *dendê* (palm oil). It is traditionally cooked in a wok-like earthenware dish and served piping hot at the table. *Moqueca* is often accompanied by *farofa* (manioc flour) and a hot pepper sauce which you add at your discretion – it's very mild by British or Asian standards. The *dendê* is somewhat heavy and those with delicate stomachs are advised to try the *ensopado*, a sauce with the same ingredients as the *moqueca*, but without the palm oil.

Nearly every street corner has a *Bahiana* selling a wide variety of local snacks, the most famous of which is the *acarajé*, a kidney bean dumpling fried in palm oil, which has its origins in West Africa. To this the *Bahiana* adds *vatapá*, a dried shrimp and coconut milk paté (also delicious on its own), *pimenta* (hot sauce) and fresh salad. For those who prefer not to eat the palm oil, the *abará* is a good substitute. *Abará* is steamed and wrapped in banana leaves.

Bahians usually eat *acarajé* or *abará* with a chilled beer on the way home from work or the beach at sunset. Another popular dish with African origins is *xin-xin de galinha*, chicken on the bone cooked in *dendê*, with dried shrimp, garlic and squash.

Recommended *Baíanas* are: **Chica**, at Ondina beach (in the street behind the Bahia Praia Hotel); **Dinha**, in Rio Vermelho (serves *acarajé* until midnight, extremely popular); **Regina** at Largo da Santana (very lively in the late afternoon); and **Cira** in Largo da Mariquita. Seek local advice on which are the most hygienic stalls to eat from.

---

was born in Hamburg and lived on the Pelourinho in Salvador during the 1950s. In a series of xylographs he documented the miserable lives of the downtrodden women who prostituted themselves for pennies. The museum itself is the former house of **Ana Néri**, Brazil's Florence Nightingale who nursed the injured during the Paraguayan War.

There is a strong **woodcarving** tradition in Cachoeira and many of its artists can be seen at work in their studios.

A 300-m railway bridge built by the British in the 19th century spans the Rio Paraguaçu to **São Felix**, where the **Danneman cigar factory** ① *Av Salvador Pinto 30, 0830-1200 and 1300-1630, T075-3438 3716*, can be visited to see hand-rolling in progress. A trail starting near the **Pousada do Convento** leads to some freshwater bathing pools above Cachoeira. There are beautiful views from above São Félix.

Arriving in Cachoeira and São Felix Cachoeira/São Felix are 116 km from Salvador, and 4 km from the BR-420. There are more than 20 daily buses from Salvador to Cachoeira (2½ hours). The quickest way to get back to Salvador is to take a motorbike taxi from Cachoeira to the BR-420 and wait at the bus stop there; buses pass every 15 minutes and are up to an hour quicker because they have fewer stops than buses that leave from Cachoeira's town centre. There is a Bradesco Bank, Praça Dr Aristides Milton 10, with a Visa ATM.

Cachoeira has a **tourist office** ① *R Ana Néri 4, T075-3425 1123*. It is hard to get lost as there are only a handful of streets, all spreading out from the river. The centre of the city and best point for orientation is the Praça da Aclamação and the Igreja da Ordem Terceira do Carmo.

EXCURSIONS FROM CACHOEIRA

About 6 km from Cachoeira, on the higher ground of the Planalto Baiano, is the small town of **Belém** (the turning is at Km 2.5 on the road to Santo Amaro), which has a healthy climate and is a popular place for summer homes. **Maragojipe**, a tobacco exporting port with a population of 39,000, is 22 km southeast of Cachoeira along a dirt road (BA-123); it can also be reached by boat from Salvador. If you visit, look out for the old houses and the church of São Bartolomeu, with its museum. The main festival is **São Bartolomeu**, in August. Good ceramic craftwork is sold in the town. The tobacco centre of **Cruz das Almas** can also be visited, although transport is poor.

FEIRA DE SANTANA

Located 112 km northwest of Salvador, Feira de Santana (population 450,500) is the centre of a great cattle breeding and trading area. Its Monday market, known as **Feira do Couro** (leather fair), is said to be the largest in Brazil and attracts great crowds to its colourful display of local products. The **artesanato market** in the centre, however, has a bigger selection. The *rodoviária* has an interesting wall of painted tiles (made by **Udo-Ceramista**, whose workshop is in Brotas, Avenida Dom João VI 411, Salvador). The **Micareta**, held in late April, is the biggest out-of-season carnival in Bahia and attracts many popular *axé* music groups from Salvador. Buses run to Salvador every 20 minutes, 1½ hours and there are connections to other towns throughout the state.

SALVADOR LISTINGS

The Centro Histórico is the ideal place to stay – either around the Pelourinho itself or in Santo Antônio, less than 1 km to the north, which has reasonably priced hotels with charm and character. Take a taxi between Santo Antônio and the Pelourinho after dark. The beachside neighbourhood of Barra also has some good apartments with kitchens and, whilst it's far from pristine, the beach is one of the cleaner stretches of sand within 15 mins' bus or cab ride of the Centro Histórico. **Hidden Pousadas Brazil**, www.hidden pousadasbrazil.com, have a network of small hotels in Salvador and throughout Bahia. There are many hostels in Salvador. See www.hostelworld.com.

WHERE TO STAY

Centro Histórico
$$$$ Hotel Villa Bahia, Largo do Cruzeiro de São Francisco 16-18, T071-3322 4271, www.hotelvillabahia.com. This boutique hotel, part of the French **Voyeur** group, is housed in a renovated 18th-century town house right next to the the Convento de São Francisco. It has a series of themed rooms, the airiest and brightest of which is the Goa room, with a huge hardwood bed, 2-m-high shuttered windows and polished wood floors.
$$$$ O Convento do Carmo, R do Carmo 1, T071-3327 8400, www.pestana.com. A range of sumptuous suites and rooms in a beautifully converted baroque convent. Facilities include an excellent restaurant tucked into the 18th-century cloisters, and spa, a small swimming pool and business services.
$$$-$$ Pousada do Boqueirão, R Direita do Santo Antônio 48, Santo Antônio, T071-3241 2262, www.pousadaboqueirao. com.br. The most stylish of all the *pousadas* in Salvador. Lovingly renovated by the Italian interior-designer owner and her brother – a former merchant seaman. There are a variety of themed rooms; the best at the top of the building, with wonderful views out over the Baía de Todos os Santos. Service and breakfast are excellent and the *pousada* sells some fine Brazilian arts and crafts from important artists like Zé Caboclo. Tours organized.
$$-$ Albergue das Laranjeiras, R Inácio Acciolli 13, T/F071-3321 1366, www.laranjeirashostel.com.br. A big, bright and busy HI hostel with a range of white-wall and tile-floor dorms and pricey doubles and triples in a colonial building in the heart of the historic centre. The breakfast area doubles up as a café and crêperie, English spoken and a full range of hostel services.

Barra
$$$ Bahia Flat, Av Oceânica 235, T071-3339 4140, www.bahiaflat.com.br. A range of serviced flats in a building with a pool and a sauna. The best have sea views and are taste-fully decorated and newly refurbished with Miró prints on the walls, patent leather sofas, glass coffee tables, large fridges, sound system and expansive mirror-fronted wardrobes.
$ La Villa Francaise, R Recife 222, Jardim Brasil, T071-3245 6008. This little guesthouse 500 m from the beach behind the Shopping Barra is bright, colourful and well run and attracts a quieter crowd than many of Barra's brasher budget establishments. A/c rooms are well tended, spruce and clean and painted in bright lilacs, lemon yellows and eggshell blues. The helpful and knowledgeable French-Brazilian owners offer a sumptuous breakfast of pastries, fruit and cakes.

Rio Vermelho
$$$$ Zank, Av Almirante Barroso 161, Rio Vermelho, T071-3083 4000, www.zank hotel.com.br. This bonsai boutique hotel sits

in a converted belle époque house 5 mins' cab ride from Rio Vermelho's bars and restaurants. Spacious rooms are decorated in strong monotone blocks, with warm woods offset by cream and white walls; but the stylish open-plan bathrooms are glass-fronted and separated from the rest of the room by a curtain, meaning that whilst they look superb they offer little toilet privacy.

RESTAURANTS

$$$ Amado, Av Lafayete Coutinho 660, Comércio, Campo Grande, T071-3322 3520, www.amadobahia.com.br. The best of Salvador's top-end restaurants, set on a deck overlooking the lapping aquamarine of Todos os Santos bay. The menu from multi award-winning chef Edinho Engel, is strong on seafood with dishes such as squid stuffed with crab and garlic in provençale sauce with a white carrot mousseline.
$$$ Sorriso de Dadá, R Frei Vicente 5, T071-3321 9642, www.dada.com.br. Bahia's most famous chef has cooked for, amongst others, Jorge Amado, Gilberto Gil, Hillary Clinton and most recently Michael Palin, who declared her food the best he'd eaten in Brazil. Her *moqueca* and her *vatapas* are signature dishes. But Dadá is not always the cook in her restaurant and all the stops are seldom pulled for the less high-visibility diners. The quality can be very patchy for so high a price. Check that Dadá is cooking before you order.
$$$-$$ Axego, R João de Deus 1, Centro Histórico, T071-3242 7481. An established restaurant celebrated for its seafood. The *moquecas* are perhaps the best in the Centro Histórico and there is excellent *feijoada* on Sun lunchtime. Meals are served in a pleasant upstairs dining room in a great location less than a 2-min walk from the São Francisco Convent.

WHAT TO DO

Cultural tours and activities
Ben Paris, T071-8812 4576, bt_paris@yahoo.com. A US resident in Salvador who can take you around the sights. Good access to musicians, *candomblé terreiros* and fascinating spots in the Recôncavo.
Casa do Ilê Aiyê, R das Laranjeiras 16, T071-3321 4193, www.ileaiye.org.br. The headquarters of the Ilê Aiyê's drum orchestra and Afro-Brazilian cultural group, where you can find information about their shows and Carnaval events and organize visits to shows at their headquarters in the city suburbs.
Casa do Olodum, R Gregório de Matos 22, T071-3321 5010, www2.uol.com.br/olodum. Olodum's headquarters where they perform every Tue and Sun at 1900 to packed crowds.
Forte de Santo Antônio Alem do Carmo, T071-3117 1488, http://fortesantoantonio.blog spot.com. Salvador is an important centre for the tradition of capoeira (see page 124) and there are a number of schools teaching it – usually in the evenings. They include the **Associação de Capoeira Mestre Bimba**, R das Laranjeiras 1, Pelourinho, T071-3322 0639, and the **Grupo Cultural de Capoeira Angola Moçambique**, R Gregório de Mattos 38, Pelourinho, T071-8113 7455.
Tatur Turismo, Av Tancredo Neves 274, Centro Empresarial Iguatemi, Salas, 222-224, T071-3114 900, www.tatur.com.br. Excellent private tours of the city and the state as well as general travel agency services including flight booking and accommodation. Can organize entire packages prior to arrival or the whole of Brazil. Good English, reliable. Owned by Conor O'Sullivan from Cork.

CHAPADA DIAMANTINA

The beautiful Chapada Diamantina national park comprises a series of escarpments covered in cerrado, caatinga and moist tropical forest, dripping with waterfalls and studded with caves. It is one of the highlights of inland Bahia. Although little of the forest is original, there is still plenty of wildlife including jaguar and maned wolf, and the area is good for birdwatching. Various trails cut through the park offering walks from a few hours to a few days, and many leave from the little colonial mining town of Lençóis, the ideal base for visiting the region.

The road from Salvador to Lençóis and the chapada passes through Feira de Santana, famous for its Micareta, an extremely popular out-of-season carnival.

→LENÇÓIS AND AROUND

Lençóis is the best place from which to explore the *chapada*. It's a pretty little colonial village (population 9000) set on the banks of the fast-flowing Rio Lençóis, in the middle of the park. Many of the sights can be visited on foot from town. Lençóis was established as a mining town in 1844 and takes its name from the tents assembled by the prospectors who first arrived here (*lençóis* means 'white sheets' in Portuguese) set on the brown and green of the hillside. While there are still some *garimpeiros* (gold and diamond prospectors) left, tourism is now the main economic mainstay. Rather than precious metals, visitors are

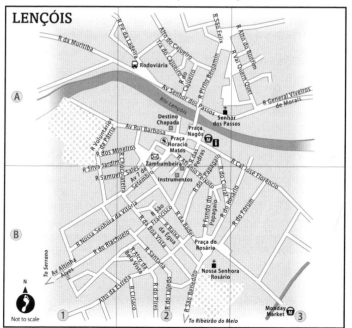

LENÇÓIS

attracted by the cool climate, the relaxed atmosphere and the wonderful trekking in the Diamantina hills. The streets of Lençóis are lined with rustic houses, many of which are now *pousadas*, restaurants or shops selling quirky handicrafts and semi-precious stones.

ARRIVING IN LENÇÓIS

Getting there As the **airport** ① *20 km from town, Km 209, BR-242, T075-3625 8100*, has only one flight a week (on Saturdays, with TRIP, www.voetrip.com.br) to and from São Paulo via Salvador, most tourists either get to or leave from Lençóis and the Chapada by bus. There are four a day from Salvador, the first at 0700 and the last at 2300 (US$30, five hours) which run via Feira de Santana (see page 136). Book in advance, especially at weekends and holidays. There is a tourist office, **Sectur**, inside the market next to the river.

Moving on To reach the coast from Lençóis without making a number of slow local bus connections you will need to return to Salvador.

EXCURSIONS FROM LENÇÓIS

On walking trips from Lençóis it is possible to visit the *serrano* (in the hills above town), which has wonderful natural pools in the river bed, which give a great spring-water massage when you sit under them; or the **Salão de Areia**, where the coloured sands for the bottle paintings come from. **Ribeirão do Meio** is a 45-minute walk from town; here locals slide down a long natural water chute into a big pool (it is best to watch someone else first and take something to slide in). Also near Lençóis are two very pretty waterfalls: the **Cachoeira da Primavera**; and the **Cachoeira Sossego**, a calendar photo cascade plunging into a deep blue pool.

OTHER TOWNS IN THE CHAPADA DIAMANTINA

There is simple accommodation and a few tour operators in **Palmeiras**, some 55 km west of Lençóis. The town makes a far quieter alternative base for exploring the *chapada*. *Combis* run sporadically between Palmeiras and Lençóis. **Mucugê** town in the far south, 134 km from Lençóis is sleepier still, and has a fascinating whitewash cemetery filled with elaborate mausoleums and set against the dark granite of the hillside. There are bus connections with Lençóis and Feira de Santana (see page 136). The adjacent **Parque Municipal de Mucugê** was set-up to protect the *sempre viva* or *chuveirinho* plant – a beautiful globe of white flowers whose popularity with flower arrangers in Brazil almost led to their extinction in the late 20th century. **Igatu** has a population of approximately 350 people, some of them live in the largely abandoned stone houses built into or around Cyclopean boulders that dot the landscape. Wandering around the village and the ruins is a haunting experience. There are two *pousadas* in the village.

→PARQUE NACIONAL DA CHAPADA DIAMANTINA

The Chapada Diamantina national park was founded in 1985 and comprises 1500 sq km of escarpment broken by extensive tracts of *caatinga* scrub forest, *cerrado*, patches of moist Atlantic coast forest and *pântano* (wetlands with permanent plant growth). The diversity of ecosystems have an associated diversity of flora and fauna. There is very little primary forest left, but the area is nonetheless home to rare large mammals such as maned wolf, jaguar and ocelot and birds endemic to all of the ecosystems. Spectaculars include the king vulture, crowned eagle, red-legged seriema and blue-winged macaw. There are birding guides available in Lençóis (see page 144).

CHAPADA DIAMANTINA

Gruta do
Lapa Doce Gruta
Pratinha

To Brasília

Morro do
Pai Inácio
Cachoeira
do Diabo
BR 242
To Salvador
Rio Mucugezinho
Palmeiras
Morrão
Cachoeira
Primavera
Rio Serrano
Valle do
Capão
Cachoeira
da Fumaça
Lençóis
Cachoeira
Sossego
Capão
Rio Roncador
Barra
Parque Nacional da
Chapada Diamantina
Valle do
Paty
Guiné
Andaraí
Rio Prieto
Igatu
Rio Paraguaçu
To Poço Encantado
Parque Municipal
do Mucugê
N
Mucugê
BA 142
10 km
To Baixão & Cachoeira
do Buração (48 km)
10 miles

Trails
.... Morro do Pai Inácio–Capão
.... Lençóis–Capão
.... Lençóis–Cachoeira da Fumaça
.... Igatu– Andaraí
.... Vale do Paty
.... Travessia Diamantina

ARRIVING IN PARQUE NACIONAL DA CHAPADA DIAMANTINA

The **park headquarters** ① *R Barão do Rio Branco 25, T075-3332 2420,* is at Palmeiras, 50 km from Lençóis. However, Lençóis is a much more practical source of information and the numerous agencies make it easy to find out what's what. See also www.infochapada.com.

Roy Funch, an American who used to manage the park and who now offers guided walks (see page 144), has written an excellent book on the *chapada: A Visitor's Guide to the Chapada Diamantina Mountains* (Collection Apoio 45), in English and Portuguese. The book includes history and geology of the region, an itinerary of all the principal sights, with instructions on how to reach them, and a thorough, though not comprehensive checklist of birds and mammals. It is widely available in Lençóis.

BACKGROUND

The *chapada* forms part of the Brazilian shield, one of the oldest geological formations on earth, dating from the when the world was only one land mass. It extends north into the Serra da Capivara and Jalapão, and south into the Serra do Espinhaço and Serra da Canastra in Minas and the mountains of Mato Grosso and northern Bolivia.

Cave paintings and petroglyphs suggest that people have been living in and around the *chapada* for millennia. However, there were no permanent settlers in the hills in recorded history until the arrival of Portuguese prospectors in the 1700s, who discovered gold and diamonds in the extreme south of the *chapada* near Livramento de Nossa Senhora and in the north near Jacobina. The Portuguese kept the findings secret for fear of driving down world gem prices, and ceding the *chapada* to other European powers, notably the Dutch and Spanish, who were invading and occupying Brazilian territory repeatedly during this period.

The *chapada* didn't open up fully to mining until 1844, when Mucugê, Rio de Contas and subsequently Lençóis were founded and settled by miners from neighbouring Minas Gerais and western Bahia, followed by Portuguese noblemen from the Bahian coast. The latter evolved into *coroneis*: robber barons who set-up ruthless local fiefdoms run by gun-toting *jangada* henchmen. The most famous was Horácio de Mattos, a prototype for many modern-day rural Brazilian politicians. De Mattos sucked all the money out of the *chapada* with his personal campaigns. He carried out famous vendettas against two other *coroneis*, Manuel Fabrício de Oliveira and Militão Rodrigues Coelho, to establish patriarchal dominance, overthrew the state government, routed the federal army and chased the infamous communist Prestes column all the way across Brazil and into Bolivia. He was in the back in Salvador in 1930.

VISITING THE CHAPADA DIAMANTINA

The *chapada* is cut by dirt roads, trails and rivers, which lead to waterfalls, viewpoints on table-top mountains, caves and natural swimming holes. There are many different hikes, and many of the routes have been used for centuries by the local farmers and miners, but finding your own way is difficult and it is best to visit on a guided trip.

There are more than 24 tour operators in Lençóis and organizing a trip to even the most distant sights is straightforward. Most tours tend to be car-based and rather sedentary as these are more profitable. But there are plenty of great hikes and sights around Lençóis, so consider all the options before signing up. Brazilian tourists are often more interested in chatting loudly among themselves than in hearing the quiet music of nature, so it can be difficult to see wildlife.

The most impressive sights in the *chapada* are included in the standard packages. Most have an entrance fee. These include: the extensive **Gruta do Lapa Doce** (US$5) and **Pratinha** caves (US$5); the latter of which are cut through by glassy blue water. The table-top mountains at the **Morro do Pai Inácio**, US$2, 30 km from Lençóis, offer the best view of the *chapada*, especially at sunset. The 384 m high **Cachoeira da Fumaça** (Smoke or Glass Waterfall) is the second highest in Brazil and lies deeper within the park 2½ hours hike from the village of **Capão**. The view is astonishing; the updraft of the air currents often makes the water flow back up creating the 'smoke' effect. The **Rio Marimbus** flows through and area of semi-swamp reminiscent of the Pantanal and very rich in birdlife whilst the **Rio Mucugezinho** plunges over the blood-red **Cachoeira do Diabo** in an extensive area of *cerrado* just below the craggy **Roncador** ('snorer') waterfall.

HIKING IN THE CHAPADA DIAMANTINA

It is essential to use a guide for treks as it is easy to get lost. Trail-walking in the park can involve clambering over rocks and stepping stones so bring strong shoes. A reasonable level of physical fitness is advisable. There are a lot of mosquitos in campsites so carry repellent. For overnight trips it is highly advisable to bring a fleece and sleeping bag as nights in the 'winter' months can be cold. Sometimes, guides can arrange these. A tent is useful but optional; although many camps are beside reasonably hospitable caves. Torches (flashlights) and a water bottle are essentials.

The **Morro do Pai Inácio to Capão** trail is a 25-km day-hike that leads from the summit of the Pai Inácio escarpment around other table-top mountains, passing through *cerrado*, *caatinga* and arable areas to the Capão valley. Another day hike is from **Lençóis to Capão**, along a series of rivers (great for swimming) and around the base of the mountains, with a car ride back at the end of the walk.

The **Cachoeira da Fumaça** trail leaves direct from Lençóis and takes two to three days to reach the base of the falls, from where there is a steep hike to the top. If you only have one day, it's possible to drive the 70 km to the **Vale do Capão** and hike the steep 6-km trail to the top of the falls. Both trails are very popular in high season.

A trail runs from **Igatu to Andaraí**, leaving from the central square of the former town past the cemetery and following the Xique-Xique river. The walk takes four hours and offers wonderful views of the mountain landscape. There are plenty of river bank stops for a cooling swim. There are longer treks too.

The **Vale do Paty** hike is a four- to six-day walk running through the heart of the Serra along a valley surrounded by imposing *meseta* table-top mountains. There are many good stopping places with viewpoints, caves, swimming holes and waterfalls. The route usually departs from Capão in the north or from the village of Guiné just west of Andaraí town.

For a full cross-section of the park, hike the 112-km **Travessia Diamantina**, which runs from the Vale do Capão in the north right across the park via the Vale do Paty, to the Cachoeira do Buracão in the far south. Accommodation is in tents and rustic *pousadas* and there are side-trips off to the Cachoeira da Fumaça (near Capão), Igatu, Poço Encantado, and the Marimbus pantanal area and Roncador falls. Establish which of the sights you would like to visit with the tour company before setting off.

CHAPADA DIAMANTINA LISTINGS

WHERE TO STAY

Lençóis

This is by far the best town in which to base yourself in the Chapada, with the bulk of the tour operators, accommodation and places to eat. It also has the best transport links to the rest of Bahia.

$$$$ Canto das Águas, Av Senhor dos Passos, T/F075-3334 1154, www.lencois. com.br. Medium-sized riverside hotel with modest a/c or fan-cooled rooms, a pool and efficient service. The best rooms are in the new wing; others can be musty.

$$$ Hotel de Lençóis, R Altinha Alves 747, T075-3334 1102, www.hoteldelencois. com.br. Plain, dark wood and white-tiled rooms with terracotta roofs set in a handsome colonial house in a grassy garden on the edge of the park. Good breakfast, pool and a restaurant.

$$$ Pousada Vila Serrano, R Alto do Bonfim 8, 3334 1486, www.vilaserrano. com.br. Warm and welcoming mock-colonial *pousada* overlooking a patio and little garden 5 mins' walk from town. Excellent service, breakfast, trips organized. Very friendly and knowledgeable.

$ Casa da Geleia, R Gen Viveiros 187, T075-3334 1151. A handful of smart chalets set in a huge garden at the entrance to the town. English spoken, good breakfast, including sumptuous jams and honeys made or collected by the owner. Zé Carlos is a keen birdwatcher and an authority on the region.

$ HI Lençóis, R Boa Vista 121, T075-3334 1497, www.hostelchapada.com.br. A large, friendly and well-run hostel with an adventure sports agency in one of the town's grand old colonial houses. The building has been completely restored and has singles, en suite doubles and single-sex 4- to 6-bed dorms; shared kitchen and a large, airy garden with hammocks and littered with outdoor chairs.

WHAT TO DO

Lençóis

The only way to visit the Chapada Diamantina is with a guide.

Chapada Adventure, Av 7 de Setembro 7, T075-3334 2037, www.chapada adventure.com. A small operator offering good-value car-based tours and light hiking throughout the chapada.

Edmilson (known as Mil), R Domingos B Souza 70, T075-3334 1319. Knows the region extremely well, knowledgeable and reliable.

Fora da Trilha, R das Pedras 202, www.fora datrilha.com.br. Longer hikes and light adventures, from canyoning to rapelling.

Luiz Krug, contact via Vila Serrano, T075-3334 1102. An independent, English-speaking guide specializing in geology and caving.

Roy Funch, T/F075-3334 1305, www.fcd.org.br. The ex-director of the Chapada Diamantina National Park is an excellent guide and has written a visitors' guidebook to the park in English which has comprehensive information on history, geography and trails of the Chapada Diamantina.

Venturas e Aventuras, Praça Horácio de Matos 20, T075-3334 1304, www.venturas. com.br. Excellent trekking expeditions, up to 6 days.

Zé Carlos, T075-3334 1151, contact through Casa da Geleia or Pousada Vila Serrano. The best guide for birdwatching.

THE COAST OF BAHIA

South of Salvador and the Recôncavo, Bahia descends in a series of glorious beaches, offshore islands and jungly peninsulas, many of them fringed with coral and mangrove or backed by endless kilometres of coconut palms. Sluggish tropical rivers undulate their way across lowland Bahia from the Chapada Diamantina ('diamond mountains') of the interior and interrupt the coastline, while potholed roads connect crumbling colonial towns like Ilhéus and Olivença, which grew fat on the cocoa and dendê oil trade but have since been slowly withering under the tropical sun.

The beaches of the far south of Bahia are among the finest in Brazil – long strands of fine white sand washed by bath-warm sea, or pounded by bottle-green surf and backed by swaying rows of coconut palms. The glorious Cocoa and Dendê Coast is within easy reach of Salvador and every year an increasing number of tourists are discovering its forgotten fishing villages. The surf mecca of Itacaré is gradually turning chic. The expat community of Morro de São Paulo, on the island of Tinharé, is finding its beach haven is getting crowded; the nightlife here is notoriously lively. Those seeking seclusion should head for the Peninsula de Maraú, a little further south, or to the little-explored wild beaches beyond Una. Further south still, the Discovery Coast takes its name from the first landing by the Portuguese. Some beaches here are remote and completely deserted, others are watched over by busy resorts and party towns such as Porto Seguro, or forgotten little villages with only a handful of simple pousadas. Pretty Trancoso is perhaps the most chic beach destination north of Punta del Este in Uruguay, with a ream of gorgeous beach boutiques. Offshore, in the far south, are the Abrolhos: an archipelago of rocky coral islands fringed with reef. The islands form part of one of Brazil's most carefully protected marine reserves and are one of the best places in South America for seeing humpback whales.

ARRIVING ON THE COAST OF BAHIA

The only practical way to reach the Bahian coast from the Chapada Diamantina is through Salvador. While there are connections through Feira de Santana, they involve several changes and rides on slow local buses. Salvador connects directly both to Lençóis and Ilhéus and the other cities along the Bahian coast by bus, has flights to the major hubs (notably Ilhéus and Porto Seguro) and has boats to Morro de São Paulo on Tinharé island.

→TINHARÉ AND MORRO DE SÃO PAULO

Depending on whom you ask, Tinharé is either a single large island separated from the mainland by the estuary of the Rio Una and mangrove swamps, or a mini archipelago divided by estuaries, mangroves and an impossibly turquoise sea. Either way it is stunning: a semi-wild bird-filled *Mata Atlântica* forest fringed with swaying coconut palms and white-sand beaches that until recently were known only to fishermen and a few intrepid Brazilian beach travellers. Before the 1990s the main town here, Morro de São Paulo, on the northern tip of the island, was one of the world's great secret tropical island getaways, together with Ko Phi Phi in Thailand and Zanzibar. Now it is rapidly going the same way as these two former Shangri-Las. It began with the Italians who built a string of small-scale but largely tasteful resorts. By the turn of the millennium, Spanish developers with gold Rolexes and nowhere left to turn into concrete on their own crowded coast, were rubbing their hands in glee. Fishermen's houses and environmental concerns are easily bulldozed out of the way by the power of the euro. Indeed many of the original fishermen who lived on the gorgeous beaches that line Tinharé have already been relocated to ugly makeshift villages in the interior. Every beach for 20 km south of town is now backed by hotels and Morro has become a veritable tourist hotspot.

Morro Town itself sits right at the northern tip of Tinharé and is dominated by a lighthouse and the ruins of an early 17th-century colonial fort, built as a defence against European raiders. However, this did not stop the Dutch and French using the waters around the island as hiding places for attacks on the Portuguese and even establishing bases here for brief periods of time.

Boats from Salvador arrive at a jetty and travellers enter the town through the stone arch that once marked the gateway to the fortress. The battlements are now largely in ruin, perched on top of the craggy hill in front of a series of little streets that branch off a small colonial *praça*. The main thoroughfare runs south to the town's beaches. Another path runs north to the lighthouse and a ruined lookout post complete with cannon (dolphins can be seen in August) and inland to the village of **Gamboa**. From Gamboa it's possible to visit the **Fonte de Ceu** waterfall; make sure you check the tide times, or ask around for a guide. It's possible to take a boat from Gamboa back to Morro (US$10-15).

Morro has five beaches; are all idyllic but are quieter the further from town you go. There is swimming in the sea or in the saltwater coral pools that appear at low tide. The beaches are named prosaically: **Primeira** (first), **Segunda** (second), **Terceira** (third), **Quarta** (fourth) and **Quinta** (fifth). There are boardwalks and a heavy build-up of shacks, beach bars, restaurants and hotels all the way to Terceira. Primeira is barely a beach at all and has the bulk of the hotels. Segunda is a party beach and is very popular with 20-somethings. Quinta is the furthest from town and is the quietest with little noise but the gentle lap of the sea. Before deciding to walk all the way to Quinta (1½ to two hours) check the tide times as the beach gets cut off at high tide. On 7 September there is a big festival at Morro with live music on the beach.

ARRIVING IN TINHARÉ AND MORRO DE SÃO PAULO

Getting there There are direct 20-minute flights from Salvador's airport to the third beach at Morro de São Paulo with **Addey Taxi Aereo** ① *T075-3652 1242, www.addey.com.br*, and **Aerostar Taxi Aereo** ① *T075-3652 1312*. Both fly three times daily and cost around US$90 return. Catamarans run from both of Salvador's ferry terminals (see page 116), taking around two hours US$27. Times vary according to the weather but there are usually several a day 0800-1400; check with the tourist office or **Catamarã Gamboa do Morro** ① *T075-9975 6395*. Part of the trip is on the open sea, which can be rough. There are also numerous water taxis. Modified fishing and speed boats also run from Salvador via Valença and Itaparica. The website www.morrodesaopaulo.com.br is a useful website with the latest boat times and general information in English, Spanish and Italian. There is a port tax of US$4 payable at the *prefeitura* on arrival to Morro and US$0.80 on leaving the island. It is resented by many.

Moving on From Morro, you can either return to Salvador before continuing your journey south by bus or plane, or you can get a boat to Valença, which is connected to southern Bahia by bus.

Getting around Morro is tiny and the first four beaches are easily negotiable on foot. A walk from town to Quarta Praia takes around 40 minutes. Until 2008 all roads were sand or dirt tracks but there is now a partially paved section between the town and the beaches, and this is plied by regular VW buses, motorbikes and beach buggies. These leave from the **Receptivo**, a little café that marks the beginning of the road just behind the second and third beaches; it's not hard to find but if in doubt ask for '*Receptivo*' or '*a estrada*'. There are daily transfers to Boipeba by Toyota at 0930, bookable through hotels or the numerous agencies on the island.

Boat trips around Tinharé island can be organized through hotels or agencies in the village; a full day costs US$20-30. Most of these go in a clockwise direction around Tinharé, visiting Boipeba and the villages to the south (including Moreré), the offshore reef pools for snorkelling, followed by the tiny colonial town of Cairu on the mainland and the shores of the Mangrove-line Rio Cairu, before returning.

Best time to visit Morro is expensive between December and March and gets very crowded during public holidays and prices can more than double. Beware of drug dealers and robbery at the busiest times.

Tourist information There is a tourist booth, Centro de Informações ao Turista (CIT) ⓘ *Praça Aureliano Lima s/n, T075-3652 1083, www.morrosp.com.br*. However, the website www.morrodesaopaulo.com.br is more useful and provides lists of agencies, hotels and other information in several languages.

→ILHA DE BOIPEBA

Ilha de Boipeba, a few hours south of Morro, is a similar but far quieter island and with less infrastructure. Accommodation is grouped in three places: the little town on the banks of the Rio do Inferno where the ferry arrives; the adjacent beach, **Boca da Barra**, which is more idyllic; and the fishing village of **Moreré**, a 30-minute boat ride to the south (only possible at high tide). With just a few simple restaurants and a football field on the beach overlooking a beautiful turquoise bay, life here is tranquil even by Bahian standards. Expect to pay at least US$30 for a boat to Moreré. Walking along the beaches will take about two hours. Have your camera at the ready, bring sunscreen and go at low tide as there is a river to ford.

ARRIVING ON ILHA DE BOIPEBA

Boat trips leave daily from Morro de São Paulo at 0900; book through a travel agent or your hotel. The return journey costs around US$30, and you have to pay this even if you are intending to stay on the island. Tractors and 4WDs leave from Morro's second beach every morning at around 0800 (one hour, US$15), and return at midday; contact Zé Balacha, T075-9148 0343, or ask at your hotel.

→ITACARÉ

Itacaré is a pretty little surfer town at the far end of the Península de Maraú surrounded by glorious forest-fringed beaches. Paulistanos decided it was cool at the turn of the millennium and a handful of beaches are now backed by some of Bahia's most exclusive (and increasingly oversized) resorts, such as **Txai**. Those close to the town itself are more hippy, with an informal surfer-dude feel and a mix of cheaper restaurants and places to stay and more fashionable spots for those swooping in for the evening. Much of the old town remains a simple fishing village whose houses in thick *gouache* shades huddle together under a golden sun around a broad harbour on the banks of the Rio de Contas.

ARRIVING IN ITACARÉ

Getting there and around To travel by bus from **Salvador**, change at Ubaitaba: Salvador–Ubaitaba six hours, US$12, several daily; Ubaitaba–Itacaré three hours, US$3. But most people choose to visit Itacaré from Ilhéus (the nearest town with an airport; 45 minutes, US$7) along the newly paved road . The *rodoviária* is a few minutes' walk from town. Porters are on hand with barrows to help with luggage. For information, contact the **Secretaria de Turismo de Itacaré** ① *T073-3251 2134, www.itacare. com.br. Pousadas* are concentrated on and around **Praia da Concha**, the first beach south of the town centre and the river. More deserted beaches lie along dirt roads to the south and north. To explore the area to the full you will need a car. If you speak some Portuguese, it's worth t aking the time to find your way to one of the smaller places. Itacaré is very busy with Brazilian tourists in high season but receives relatively few international visitors.

Moving on There are bus connections several times a day between Itacaré and Ilhéus (see below).

→ILHÉUS AND AROUND

Whilst it has a few sights of very modest interest and was the birthplace of Jorge Amado, for most visitors Ilhéus (population 242,500) is little more than a necessary transport hub (with fast buses and flights from Salvador) for Itacaré and the beaches of the Peninsula de Maraú.

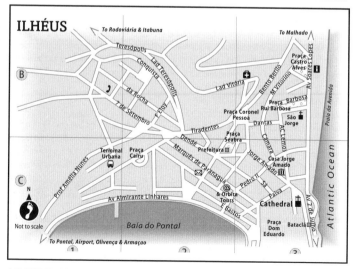

ARRIVING IN ILHÉUS

Getting there The **airport** ① *3 km from the centre, in Pontal on the south bank of the river, is linked to Ilhéus by bridge; taxi into town US$4*, receives flights from Salvador and Porto Seguro, among other cities. The **rodoviária** ① *R Itabuna, 4 km from the centre*, has regular bus connections with Salvador, although the Itabuna–Olivença bus runs through the centre of Ilhéus.

Moving on Ilhéus is connected to Porto Seguro (the transport hub for southern Bahia, see page 150) via the inland city of Itabuna.

Tourist information The **tourist office** ① *on the beach opposite Praça Castro Alves*, is a few minutes' walk from the cathedral. Staff are friendly and can provide maps (US$2, recommended).

AROUND ILHÉUS

The city beach itself is polluted but the beaches around the town are splendid and increasingly deserted the further you go. North of Ilhéus, two good beaches are **Marciano**, with reefs offshore and good surfing, and **Barra**, 1 km further north at the mouth of the Rio Almada. South of the river, the beaches at **Pontal** can be reached by 'Barreira' bus; alight just after the **Hotel Jardim Atlântico**. Between Ilhéus and **Olivença** are a number of fine beaches, including **Cururupe, Batuba** and **Cai n'Água** (in Olivença itself), both popular surf spots. The **Balneário de Tororomba** ① *on the Rio Batuba, 19 km from Ilhéus, bus from São Jorge, Canavieiras or Olivença*, has ferruginous mineral baths.

From Ilhéus, buses run every 30 minutes to **Itabuna** (32 km), the trading centre of the rich cocoa zone; there are also many lumber mills. **Ceplac installations** ① *Km 8, on the Itabuna–Ilhéus road, T073-214 3000, Mon-Fri 0830-1230*, demonstrates the processing of cocoa. Tours of cocoa plantations can be arranged through the **Ilhéus Praia** hotel (www.ilheuspraia.com.br).

Also at Km 8, the Projeto Mico-Leão Baiano at the **Reserva Biológica de Una** ① *www.ecoparque.org.br, book through Orbitá, see page 156*, was founded to protect the golden-faced tamarin. This is the wettest part of Bahia, most notably in October. Jeeps leave from the *rodoviária*. The reserve lies along a dirt road and most easily reached on a tour or by public jeep which leave when full from the *rodoviária*.

ILHEUS TO PORTO SEGURO

To reach Porto Seguro by road from Ilhéus, take a bus to Itabuna and then catch a further bus from there along the main BR-101 interstate highway which runs parallel to the coast some 30 km inland.

The paved coastal road south of Ilhéus continues through Olivença and Una but ends at Canavieiras, a picturesque town which benefited from the cocoa boom. It has several fine beaches worth exploring. The road is broken here by the extensive Rio Jequitinhonha delta, which can only be traversed by hiring a boat at Canavieiras, arriving at Belmonte. There is no infrastructure for tourism and no fixed prices. Allow at least three hours for the crossing. A rough road continues from Belmonte to Porto Seguro.

In AD 1500, Pedro Álvares Cabral became the first European to see Brazil, sighting land at Monte Pascoal south of Porto Seguro. The sea here was too open to offer a safe harbour, so Cabral sailed his fleet north, entering the mouth of the Rio Burnahém to find the harbour he later called 'Porto Seguro' (safe port).

Modern Porto Seguro (population 96,000) is rapidly developing into southern Bahia's largest and most cosmopolitan coastal city, with residents from all over the world. Located on the Rio Buranhém, which separates the city from Arraial d'Ajuda across the water, the attractive dockland area retains a handful of pretty colonial houses.

On the hill above is the higgledy-piggledy **Centro Histórico**, a peaceful place spread out on a grassy slope, with lovely gardens and panoramic views. Brazil began here – on the far side of the grassy square is a block of Cantabrian marble engraved with the Cross Of The Order Of Christ and marking the spot where the conquistador Gonçalo Coelho formally took the Discovery Coast (and by extension the country) from the Tupiniquim people in 1503. Brazil's oldest church sits behind: the **Nossa Senhora da Misericórdia** ① *Praça Pero de Campos Tourinho, T073-3288 5182, Sat-Wed 0930-1330 and 1430-1700, free,* a squat, functional little building in paintbox blue, built in 1526, with heavy fortified walls and a little scrolled Rococo pediment added like a cake decoration. Nearby, and sitting in the ruins of a monastery ransacked by the ancestors of the modern Pataxó, is the Jesuit church of **São Benedito** ① *R Dr Antônio Ricaldi s/n,* built in 1549 with even more heavily fortified walls and the church of **Nossa Senhora da Pena** ① *Praça Pero de Campos Tourinho s/n, T073-3288 6363, daily 0900-1200 and 1400-1700, free,* dating from 1708, but built over another fortified 16th-century structure. Inside is what is said to be the oldest statue in Brazil – an undistinguished effigy of St Francis of Assisi. Next door is the sacred art museum and former jail – the handsome 18th-century **Casa de Câmara e Cadêia** ① *Praça Pero de Campos Tourinho s/n, T073-3288 5182, daily 0900-1700, free.*

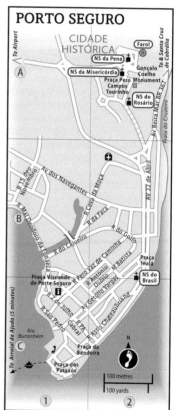

Arriving in Porto Seguro

Getting there Porto Seguro is very well connected to the rest of Brazil by plane, with several daily flights from Salvador and flights connecting with other routes in this book – notably from Rio, São Paulo and Belo Horizonte with **Webjet, Azul, Gol, Trip** and **Tam**. Flights are often very good value if booked in advance or if taken at unsociable hours. The **Aeroporto de Porto Seguro** ⓘ *Estrada do Aeroporto s/n, 2 km north of town, T073-3288 1880*, has banks and a car rental booth in the terminal. A taxi to the centre costs US$8.

There are no longer any direct buses from Itacaré or Ilhéus. To reach Porto Seguro by bus from either, take a local bus to Itabuna on the main BR-101 interstate highway running north–south parallel to the coast (one hour 40 minutes from Ilhéus or two hours 40 minutes from Itacaré), from where there are three daily buses to Porto Seguro (all leaving in the small hours of the morning, 4½ hours, US$25). There is one direct bus daily from Salvador (**Águia Branca**, 11 hours, US$70), or it is possible reach Porto Seguro via Eunápolis (six daily buses from Salvador, 10-11 hours, US$40-100 depending on whether you travel *convencional* or *leito*). From Eunápolis there are half-hourly services to Porto Seguro (45 minutes, US$4). The **rodoviária** ⓘ *2 km west of the centre, on the road to Eunápolis*, has cafés and snack bars. Taxis charge US$6 to the town or ferry (negotiate at quiet times).

Moving on Buses and taxis run from Porto Seguro to Arraial (15 minutes), Trancoso (40 minutes), Espelho (two to three hours) and Caraíva (three to four hours). Buses also run south from Porto Seguro to Caravelas (see page 153) via the inland town of Itamarajú (or via Prado and Cumuruxatiba). One daily bus runs between Porto Seguro and Salvador (11 hours).

Getting around Buses run throughout the city from the waterfront to the old *rodoviária* near the port every 30 minutes, US$0.50. Regular buses run along the seafront from Praça dos Pataxós to the northern beaches, or take a bus to Porto Belo or Santa Cruz Cabrália from the port. For beaches south of the Rio Buranhém, see Arraial d'Ajuda (above) and points further south.

Tourist information The tourist office, **Secretária de Turismo de Porto Seguro** ⓘ *R Pero Vaz de Caminha 475, Centro, T073-3288 3708, www.portosegurotur.com.br*, has information on tours. Alternatively, contact **Portomondo**, *www.portomondo.com*.

→TRANCOSO

In the last five years this once-sleepy little village, 15 km south of the beach-party town of Arraial, has become Bahia's most chic beach destination, beloved of the Brazilian and international jet-set for its combination of low-key atmosphere and high-fashion labels. The coolest São Paulo names fill the tiny shopping centre and the town and beaches are dotted with smart designer boutiques and haute-rural restaurants offering the best food outside Rio de Janeiro and São Paulo. Celebrities come here to be recognized only by those they wish to be recognized by. Despite its status, Trancoso remains a simple little town at heart, and herein lies its charm. It is glossy but intimate, with life focusing on the **Quadrado**, a long grassy square where locals play football in the evening. The square is crowned with the little whitewashed 17th-century church of **São João Batista**, and lined with colourful little *casas*, each housing a bikini boutique, crafts shop, fashionable restaurant, bar or guesthouse. The houses are particularly enchanting at night, when they contrast with the dark indigo canvas of the rainforest, under a dome of stars.

Below the Quadrado are a stretch of beaches extending away to the north and south. The most famous and the closest to town are **Praia do Trancoso** and **Praia dos Nativos**, both washed by gentle waves, with coral far off shore and a cluster of chic-shack *barracas* that host parties for the designer-label brigade during the summer months. **Coquieros** across the little river to the north is quieter, with one simple restaurant and a view. To the south beyond Trancoso beach are **Rio Verde**, with a little river, and beyond it **Itapororoca** a deserted beach with just a few very expensive houses and good clear-water snorkelling.

ARRIVING IN TRANCOSO

In high season, *combis* ply the dirt road along the coast between Arraial and Trancoso, leaving when full. Buses run along the newly paved road between Porto Seguro, Arraial de Ajuda and Trancoso at least once an hour in high season (US$3 from Porto Seguro, US$2 from Arraial). Taxis from Arraial or Porto Seguro cost around US$30. Trancoso can be packed out in high season. Be sure to book ahead. There are no really cheap rooms. Various tour operators around the main square sell *combi*, bus and air tickets for destinations throughout Bahia and organize day trips to Espelho and beyond. The easiest way to get around town is by bike, on foot or motorbike taxi.

→SOUTH FROM TRANCOSO

There is no route south to the rest of the Bahian Coast from Caraíva and you will need to visit the village as an excursion from Porto Seguro. Two daily buses (and an extra bus in high season), connect Porto Seguro with Caraíva and the turn-off to Espelho (from where it's a 5-km walk to the beach).

Boats for the Abrolhos islands leave from Caravelas and, while there are only two weekly buses from Porto Seguro to Caravelas (Thursday and Sunday at 1830, US$15, four hours), the best way to reach this town from Porto Seguro is to travel via the small town of **Itamarajú** (six buses daily from Porto Seguro, U$12, two hours), which lies on the BR-101. There are frequent connections from Itamarajú to Caravelas via **Alcobaça** (seven buses daily, US$7, one hour) and to the other beach towns in the far south, including **Prado** and the tiny, remote resort of **Corumbau** via **Curumuaxatiba** village (where there are pretty sandstone cliffs and a handful of *pousadas*).

GOING FURTHER

Sergipe and Alagoas

It is possible to connect the Bahia route with the Recife to São Luís route by passing through the states of Sergipe and Alagoas immediately to the north of Bahia. Few tourists stop off in these two tiny states whose charm lies in part in their being off the beaten track. Both have fine beaches, easily accessible from the state capitals: Aracaju and Maceió. And both have a series of very pretty Portuguese colonial towns where visitors are still a novelty. Of the capitals, Maceió is by far the more salubrious, with some excellent beaches and lively nightlife. Begin a journey through Sergipe and Alagoas with a visit to Mangue Seco. This tiny fishing village with just a handful of *pousadas* lies in the far north of Bahia and feels lost – both in a shifting sea of sand dunes and in time. It is particularly beautiful at full moon. Continue from here through to Aracaju, stay overnight here – in one of the numerous *pousadas* on Aracaju beach and take a side trip to **São Cristóvão**. This bonsai town of terracotta cottages, crumbling churches and abandoned palaces is the fourth oldest colonial settlement in the country and is Brazil's newest World Heritage Site. Cross into Alagoas via the dusty town of Neópolis – just a couple of hours from Aracaju – which is connected by ferry to another stunning Portuguese colonial town, **Penedo**. Penedo's baroque buildings and stately spires swelter on the banks of the great São Francisco river. Be sure to visit the magnificent church of Nossa Senhora do Corrente whose interior is encrusted with gilt stucco and brilliant blue *azulejo* tiles. From Penedo it's an easy two- to three-hour bus journey to Maceio, perhaps via another sleepy colonial town, **Marechal Deodoro**, which was the birthplace of the founder of the Brazilian Republic. The tiny town is twinned with the adjacent beach of Praia do Frances – a stunning crescent of sugary sand washed by bottle-green Atlantic waves. There are several *pousadas* along the beach. North of Maceió are a string of still more beautiful beaches backed with swaying coconut palms, which stretch to the border of Pernambuco state, some two hours north of the capital. If you have time, consider stopping off at **Praia do Toque** (where there you'll find the pretty **Pousada do Toque**) near **São Miguel dos Milagres**, or at the fishing village turned mini-resort at **Maragogi** right on the Pernambuco state border. Buses from here to Recife where the Recife–São Luís route begins (see page 158) take under three hours.

It is easier to visit southern Bahia with a hire car. Rental cars give you the chance to explore remoter areas, including **Monte Pascoal National Park**, whose strangely shaped triangular peak was the first landmark in Brazil to be sighted by the Portuguese. The best rates are through the agencies at Porto Seguro airport (including www.localiza.com). Expect to pay around US$45 per day for a basic car and bear in mind that it is an offence in Brazil to drive without documents, including personal ID.

CARAVELAS

Continuing south, Caravelas is a charming little town on the banks of the Caravelas estuary, surrounded by mangroves. There are eight fine white-sand beaches nearby. The town is well known for its Catholic festivals, which attract thousands of pilgrims. Caravelas was a major trading port in the 17th and 18th centuries and the town's name was taken from the Portuguese sailing boats whose technology opened up the world to

Lisbon. It is now slowly developing as a resort for Brazilian tourism. The best beaches are about 10 km away at the fishing village of **Barra de Caravelas** (hourly buses). There is a helpful tourist information, **Ibama Centro de Visitantes** ⓘ *Barão do Rio Branco 281*.

Arriving in Caravelas Caravelas is 36 km south of Prado on the BA-001, on the banks of the Rio Caravelas and is served by frequent buses from Eunápolis and Itamaraju from where there are connections to the rest of the state. There are two weekly buses from Porto Seguro and daily connections to Prado to the north. The town is the departure point for the Abrolhos islands.

PARQUE NACIONAL MARINHO DOS ABROLHOS

Abrolhos is an abbreviation of *Abre os olhos*, 'Open your eyes', from Amérigo Vespucci's exclamation when he first sighted the reef in 1503. Established in 1983, the park consists of five small islands: **Redonda**, **Siriba**, **Guarita**, **Sueste** and **Santa Bárbara**, which are volcanic in origin. There are also abundant coral reefs and good diving. Darwin visited the archipelago in 1830 and Jacques Cousteau studied the marine environment here.

The archipelago national park protects the most extensive coral reefs in the south Atlantic with four times as many endemic species than the reefs and atolls in the Caribbean. There are numerous endemic species, including giant brain corals, crustaceans and molluscs, as well as marine turtles and mammals threatened by extinction and huge colonies of nesting seabirds. In addition, the seas around the islands are one of the most important south Atlantic nurseries for humpback whales – which can always be seen in season.

In 2002, the Abrolhos region was declared an area of Extreme Biological Importance by the Brazilian Ministry of Environment, based on the Brazilian commitment to the international Convention on Biodiversity. For more information see **Conservation International**, www.conservation.org. The archipelago is administered by **Ibama** and a navy detachment mans a lighthouse on Santa Bárbara, which is the only island that may be visited. Visitors are not allowed to spend the night on the islands, but may stay overnight on schooners.

Arriving in Parque Nacional Marinho dos Abrolhos The Parque Nacional Marinho dos Abrolhos is 70 km east of Caravelas. The journey to the islands takes three to four hours depending on the sea conditions. Between July and early December, humpback whale sightings are almost guaranteed. Boats leave at 0700 from the Marina Porto Abrolhos some 5 km north of Caravelas town centre (around US$50 depending on numbers) and they return at dusk. It is possible to dive or snorkel at Abrolhos. If you are coming from Porto Seguro everything including transfers and accommodation in Caravelas can be arranged by **Portomondo**, T073-3575 3686, www.portomondo.com. In Caravelas, book with **Abrolhos Turismo**, or **Catamarã Veleiro Sanuk**, see page 156, through any of the hotels listed above; or directly at the Marina Porto Abrolhos. For further information see www.ilhasdeabrolhos.com.br.

THE COAST OF BAHIA LISTINGS

WHERE TO STAY

Tinharé and Morro de São Paulo

$$$-$$ Fazenda Vila Guaiamú, 3rd beach,
T075-3652 1035, www.vilaguaiamu.com.br.
7 tastefully decorated chalets of various sizes
and styles set in tropical gardens. On-site
conservation project for the locally threatened
West-Atlantic land crab (Guaiamú). Guided
rainforest walks available. Excellent food
and a spa/massage service.

$$ Pousada Farol do Morro, 1st beach,
T075-3652 1036, www.faroldomorro.com.br.
A range of small cabins with sea views running
up a steep slope, overlooking a little infinity
pool, and reached by a private funicular railway.

$$-$ Tia Lila, 3rd beach, T075-3652 1532,
www.pousadatialila.com.br. Very simple a/c
rooms with television. Attentive, friendly
service. Check a few rooms as some beds
are spongy. Very good restaurant with
delicious *moqueca de camarão*.

Ilha de Boipeba

$$$-$$ Santa Clara, Boca da Barra beach,
T075-3653 6085, www.santaclaraboipeba.com.
Californian-owned *pousada* with the
island's best restaurant and large, tastefully
decorated duplex cabañas. Very good-value
room for 4 (**$** per person). Superlative
therapeutic massages available.

$$-$ Horizonte Azul, Boca da Barra beach,
T075-3653 6080, www.pousadahorizonte
azul.com. Pretty little *pousada* with a range
of chalets from very comfortable to fairly
simple. The hillside garden is visited by
hundreds of rare birds from the nearby
Atlantic coast rainforest.

Itacaré

$$$ Art Jungle, T073-9996 2167,
www.hiddenpousadasbrazil.com. A modern
sculpture garden with 6 treehouses in the
middle of the forest. All have views out to
the sea and to the Rio de Contas. A favourite
with celebrities.

$ Pedra Bonita, R Lodonio Almeida 120,
T073-3251 3037, www.itacarehostel.com.br.
Pleasant little HI hostel with small doubles
and dorms in an annexe, a small pool, TV
area and friendly staff.

Porto Seguro and Arraial d'Ajuda

$$$$ Toca do Marlin, Estr BA-001, Km 40.5,
Santo André, T073-3671 5041, www.tocado
marlin.com.br. One of the most luxurious
beach resorts in Bahia, with spacious a/c
cabañas next to a ranch overlooking a quiet,
beautiful beach some 50 km north of Porto
Seguro. Excellent food and excursions
including diving and horse riding on the beach.

$$$-$$ Privillage Praia, Estrada da Pitinga
1800, Praia de Pitinga, Arraial d'Ajuda,
T073-3575 1646, www.privillage.com.br.
This tranquil *pousada* sits in secluded forest
overlooking an almost deserted beach 10 mins
from Arraial d'Ajuda town. Rooms – less
beautiful than the setting – are in concrete
chalets and with raw brick walls, tiled floors
and heavy wicker furniture but are well
appointed. Good pool and restaurant.

$$ Victor Hugo, Villa de Santo André,
Km 3, Santa Cruz Cabrália, T073-3671 4064,
www.pousadavictorhugo.com.br. Smart,
tastefully decorated *pousada* right on the
beach on the edge of an environmentally
protected area. Under the palms in a small
garden, the rooms are plain whitewash with
thick oil paint colours, heavy wooden furniture,
lacey bedspreads and dark wood floors.

$$ Pousada do Roballo, Estr do Mucugê,
Arraial d'Ajuda, T073-3575 1053,
www.pousadadoroballo.com.br. Welcoming
pousada with small rooms, each with a tiny

hammock-hung veranda. Set in an attractive garden with a pool.

$$ Pousada Erva Doce, Estr do Mucugê 200, Arraial d'Ajuda, T073-3575 1113, www.ervadoce.com.br. Well-appointed chalets and a decent restaurant, set in a lawned garden and with a pool.

Trancoso and around
$$$$ Pousada Estrela d'Água, Estrada Arraial D'Ajuda, Praia dos Nativos, T073-3668 1030, www.estreladagua.com.br. An infinity pool with waters melding into the turquoise sea leads to a light-flooded living area and a garden with ranks of luxurious faux-fishermen's cottages decorated with minimalist, clean Mediterranean whites and deep blues. Practices sustainable tourism.
$$$$-$$$ Mata N'ativa Pousada, Estr Velha do Arraial s/n (on the way to the beach), Trancoso, T073-3668 1830, www.matanativapousada.com.br. The best in town for nature lovers and those seeking a quiet, relaxed retreat. Elegant and romantic cabins set in a lovingly maintained garden with a pool by the river. Very friendly owners.
$$$ Vila do Mar, R 12 de Outubro s/n, T073-3668 5111, Caraíva, www.pousadavila domar.com.br. The plushest hotel in Caraíva, with spacious, stylish airy, wooden cabañas overlooking the beach set on a lawn around an adult and children's pool.
$$ Marina Porto Abrolhos, R da Baleia, 5 km south of Trancoso, T073-3674 1060, www.marinaportoabrolhos.com.br. One of the most comfortable hotels in the region, with a range of individual and family suites housed in faux-Polynesian chalets and gathered in a palm-tree garden around a large pool. Activities include trips to the Abrolhos.

WHAT TO DO

Ilha de Boipeba
All guesthouses can organize trips on Morro de São Paulo and Boipeba, which include trips around Tinharé, visiting remote beaches and stopping off to snorkel. Numerous agencies offer boat, beach and snorkelling tours around Morro; they include **Zulu**, T075 3652 1599, www.zuluturismo.com.br.

Itacaré
Maris, T073-3255 2348, www.maris.com.br. Boat trips around the Baía de Camamu, trekking along the beaches (including a 2-day walk between the Praia do Pontal and the Rio Piracanga) and trips to small traditional fishing villages such as the boat-building community of Cajaíba.
Orbitá, R Marquês de Paranaguá 270, T073-3634 7700, www.orbitaexpedicoes.com.br. Adventure trips, visits to Maraú and general tours with excellent guide in comfortable Land Rovers. Transfers throughout Bahia as far as the Chapada Diamantina or Porto Seguro.

Trancoso
Ciro Albano, www.nebrazilbirding.com. The best birding guide for the northeast of Brazil offering tips to birding and wildlife sites, including Estação Veracruz, Canudos and the Chapada Diamantina.
Portomondo, Ponta do Apaga Fogo 1, Marina Quinta do Porto Hotel, T073-3575 3686, www.portomondo.com. The best operator in southern Bahia with tours from around Trancoso, Caraíva and Corumbau to Monte Pascoal and Abrolhos. Excellent diving and ecotourism itineraries and car or helicopter transfers.

Parque Nacional Marinho dos Abrolhos
All-inclusive trips from Porto Seguro can be arranged with **Portomondo** (see above). From Caravelas, book with **Abrolhos Turismo**, Praça Dr Emílio Imbassay 8, T073-3297 1149, or **Catamarã Veleiro Sanuk**, T073-3297 1344, www.catamarasanuk.cjb.net.

DREAM TRIP 3:
Recife→Natal→Fortaleza→São Luís 21 days

Recife Day trip, page 159

Olinda 3 nights, page 166
Bus from Recife (20-30 mins)

Fernando de Noronha 2 nights, page 171
Flight from Recife (40 mins) with tour operator

Pipa 3 nights, page 175
From Recife (4 hrs with a change of bus in Goianinha (15 mins away from Pipa), or From Natal (90 mins)

Natal 2 nights, page 175
Bus from Recife (direct 4½ hrs, or via João Pessoa and Pipa) or flight from Fernando de Noronha (40 mins)

Fortaleza 1 night, page 181
Bus/flight from Natal (8 hrs/1 hr)

Jericoacoara 3 nights, page 186
Bus and 4WD from Fortaleza via Jijoca (6 hrs) or minivan direct from Fortaleza

Parnaíba 1 night, page 190
Bus from Fortaleza (8 hrs) or from Jericoacoara via beach buggy, ferry and bus (4 hrs)

Parque Nacional Lençois Maranhenses 4 nights, page 192
Bus from Parnaíba via Barreirinhas or minivan/bus via Tutóia, Paulino Neves and Barreirinhas; otherwise bus or private transfer from São Luís (4 hrs)

São Luís 2 nights, page 193
Bus from Barreirinhas/Parque Nacional Lençois Maranhenses (4 hrs) or bus/flight from Fortaleza (6½ hrs/1 hr)

Alcântara Day trip, page 198
Launch or catamaran tour from São Luís (1 hr)

GOING FURTHER

By flying from São Luís to Belém, this route could link with the Amazon section of Dream Trip 4 (see pages 250-266).

DREAM TRIP 3
Recife→Natal→Fortaleza→São Luís

This hop through Brazil's exhilarating northeast offers an exotic mix of stunning scenery, exuberant colonial cities and vibrant festival culture. It begins in Recife and Olinda, twin cities bristling with Brazilian baroque and reverberating to the staccato dance rhythms of *forró* and *frevo*. The cities vie with Rio and Salvador as the most exciting in the country, hosting a string of traditional festivals including Brazil's most traditional big carnival and the equally colourful *Festas Juninas* in June. Both attract millions of revellers.

The route hugs the coast from here, heading to a series of fabulous beaches. Pipa's sandy coves are backed by crumbling cliffs, coconut groves and rainforest; towering dunes line the long half-moon bay at Ponta Negra in Natal, one of Brazil's most popular small beach resorts; while skyscraper apartment blocks watch over an impossibly aquamarine ocean at lively Fortaleza city, capital of the state Ceará. North of here the coast gets wilder and more windswept. Remote Jericoacoara sitting on the end of a sandy peninsula and surrounded by sweeping dunes is one of the best places to wind- and kitesurf in the world. The dunes are at their most impressive in the Lençóis Maranhenses National Park, where they form a Sahara-like sea of sand, broken between March and September by opal and aquamarine perched dune lakes. The route finishes in sweltering São Luís, set on a broad river estuary where the northeast merges with the Amazon. The city is another of Brazil's colonial gems and, like Salvador, preserves lively Afro-Brazilian culture.

This itinerary could continue north to Belém, Manaus and the Amazon, where it would combine with the latter part of Dream Trip 4 (see pages 250-266).

RECIFE AND OLINDA

Recife has a population of 1.2 million and is one of the most attractive large cities in Brazil. From afar it looks as blighted by skyscrapers as Rio de Janiero or Belo Horizonte, but in the shadows are many fine colonial buildings from the sugar boom, watching over little shady squares or sitting on the edge of the filigree of canals and waterways that divide up the city. The colonial heart is Recife Antigo. This was a no-go area like Rio's Lapa until 15 years ago, but it's now the centre of the city's booming music and alternative culture scene. To the south of the centre are a string of urban beach suburbs – Pina, Boa Viagem and Piedade – which, although frequented by bull sharks, are among the cleanest urban beaches in the country (outside the busy weekends when locals leave rubbish on the sand). The city prides itself on good food and unique fashion and has many fine restaurants and boutiques. Although they retain separate names, Recife and Olinda have long ceased to be two cities. Olinda is now Recife's colonial suburb.

→RECIFE

Recife's architecture is far less celebrated than its pretty neighbour, the former Portuguese capital of Olinda, but it retains some very attractive buildings. Rua da Aurora, which watches over the Capibaribe river, is lined with stately palladian and neoclassical buildings. The islands to the south, over the filigree of bridges, are dotted with imposing churches and surprisingly lavish civic structures, especially around the Praça da República. The city began with the Dutch at the twin forts – the **Forte do Brum** on the island of **Recife Antigo** (Old Recife) which faces the open ocean, and the **Forte das Cinco Pontas** on the neighbouring island of Santo Antonio. Both were built by the Dutch in 1630, seven years before Maurice of Nassau sacked and burned Olinda. The two forts controlled access to the Dutch port of **Mauritsstadt**, as Recife was first known, at the northern and southern entrances.

ARRIVING IN RECIFE
Getting there International (Lisbon and Milan) and domestic flights arrive at **Gilberto Freyre airport** ① *Guararapes, 12 km from the city centre, near the hotel district of Boa Viagem.* The airport is modern and spacious, with a tourist office, banks, shops, post office and car rental and tour agencies. Airport taxis cost US$5 to the seafront; bus No 52 runs to the centre, US$0.40.

Long-distance buses arrive at the **Terminal Integrado dos Passageiros (TIP)** ① *12 km outside the city near the Oficina Brenn and cultural museum at São Lourenço da Mata, T081-3452 1999,* pronounced 'chippy'. To get to the centre from the *rodoviária*, take the metrô to Central station, 30 minutes. If going to Boa Viagem, get off the metrô at Central station (Joana Bezerra station is unsafe) and take a bus or taxi (US$8) from there.

Moving on Recife and Olinda (see page 166) are twin cities with bus connections between them taking about 20 minutes and running throughout the day and night. Flights to Fernando de Noronha (see page 171) will need to be reserved through a tour operator (see **Cariri Ecotours**, page 180) as visitor numbers to the island are controlled. Connections between the coastal cities are fast and frequent. Recife has more than 20 daily buses to João Pessoa (two hours, see page 175) and Natal (4½ hours, see page 175). For a description of the route north from Recife via João Pessoa and Pipa, see page 175.

Getting around City buses cost US$0.90-1.50; they are clearly marked and run frequently until about 2230. Many central bus stops have boards showing routes. On buses, especially at night, look out for landmarks as street names are hard to see. Commuter services, known as the **metrô** but not underground, leave from the Central Station; they have been extended to serve the *rodoviária* (frequent trains, 0500-2300, US$0.40 single). Integrated bus-metrô routes and tickets (US$1) are explained in a leaflet issued by CBTU Metrorec, T081-3251 5256. Trolleybuses run in the city centre. Taxis are plentiful; fares double on Sunday, after 2100 and during holidays.

Orientation The city centre consists of three sections sitting on islands formed by the rivers Capibaribe, Beberibe and Pina: **Recife Antigo**, **Santo Antônio** and **São José**. The inner city neighbourhoods of **Boa Vista** and **Santo Amaro** lie immediately behind to the east. The centre is always very busy by day; the crowds and narrow streets, especially in the Santo Antônio district, can make it a confusing city to walk around. But this adds to its charm. This is one of the few cities in Brazil where it is possible to get lost and chance upon a shady little square or imposing colonial church or mansion. Recife has the main dock area, with the commercial buildings associated with it. South of the centre is the residential and beach district of **Boa Viagem**, reached by bridge across the Bacia do Pina. **Olinda**, the old capital, is only 7 km to the north (see page 166). Although the streets are generally too full to present danger it is wise to be vigilant where the streets are quiet. Always take a taxi after dark if you are walking alone or in a pair.

Tourist information The main office for the Pernambuco tourist board, Setur ① *Centro de Convenções, Complexo Rodoviário de Salgadinho, Av Professor Andrade Bezerra s/n, Salgadinho, Olinda, T081-3182 8300, www.setur.pe.gov.br*, is between Recife and Olinda. There are other branches in Boa Viagem (T081-3463 3621), and at the airport (T081-3224 2361, open 24 hours); they cannot book hotels, but the helpful staff speak English and can offer leaflets and decent maps.

Safety Opportunistic theft is unfortunately common in the streets of Recife and Olinda (especially on the streets up to Alto da Sé). Keep a good hold on bags and cameras, and do not wear a watch. Prostitution is reportedly common in Boa Viagem, so choose nightclubs with care. Should you have any trouble contact the **tourist police** ① *T081-3326 9603/ T081-3464 4088*.

PLACES IN RECIFE
Recife Antigo This 2-km-long island, facing the open ocean on one side and the Rio Beberibe on the other, lays at the heart of old Recife. Until the 1990s its cobbled streets of handsome colonial buildings were a no-go area – frequented only by drug users and prostitutes. However, the area has been almost completely rehabilitated and Recife Antigo is now the spiritual heart of the city. The **Marco Zero** point, sitting in the Praça Rio Branco is the official centre of the city and the locus of activity for Recife's vibrant carnival. The best Pernambucan bands play on the stage here until dawn during carnival week and the streets nearby are busy with bars and little makeshift restaurants most evenings and especially at weekends. The liveliest street is Rua da Moeda.

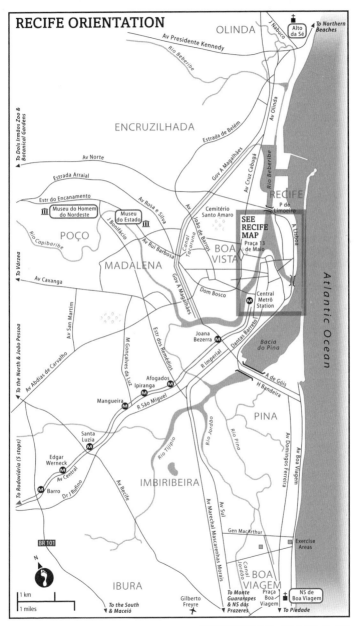

RECIFE ORIENTATION

OLINDA

To Northern Beaches

J Nabuco

Alto da Sé

Av Presidente Kennedy

Rio Beberibe

ENCRUZILHADA

Estrada de Belém

Av Olinda

Av Norte

Av Cruz Cabugá

Rio Beberibe

RECIFE

Estrada Arraial

P de Limoeiro

Estr do Encamento

Av Rosa e Silva

Gov A Magalhães

Museu do Homem do Nordeste

Av João de Barros

SEE RECIFE MAP

A Lisboa

To Dois Irmãos Zoo & Botanical Gardens

Cemitério Santo Amaro

Praça 13 de Maio

Museu do Estado

J Bonifácio

Canal Tacaruna

POÇO

Av Rui Barbosa

BOA VISTA

Rio Capibaribe

MADALENA

Gov A Magalhães

Dom Bosco

Central Metrô Station

Atlantic Ocean

Av Caxanga

To Várzea

Av San Martim

Estr dos Remédios

Joana Bezerra

Dantas Barreto

Bacia do Pina

M Gonçalves da Luz

R Imperial

A de Góis

To the North & João Pessoa

Av Abdias de Carvalho

Afogados

Ipiranga

R São Miguel

H Bandeira

Mangueira

PINA

Santa Luzia

Rio Tijipió

Rio Pina

Av Domingos Ferreira

To Rodoviária (5 stops)

Edgar Werneck

Av Boa Viagem

Av Central

Dr J Rufino

Barro

IMBIRIBEIRA

Av Recife

Av Sul

Av Marechal Mascarenhas Morais

Gen MacArthur

Exercise Areas

BR 101

Canal Jordão

BOA VIAGEM

N

1 km

1 miles

To the South & Maceió

Gilberto Freyre

To Monte Guararapes & NS das Prazeres

Praça Boa Viagem

NS de Boa Viagem

To Piedade

IBURA

The well-preserved whitewashed and terracotta-roofed **Forte do Brum** ① *Praça Comunidade Luso Brasileira s/n, T081-3224 8492, Tue-Fri 0900-1600, Sat and Sun 1300-1700, US$1* (1629), is now an army museum, with huge Dutch and Portuguese canons on its bulwarks, exhibition rooms with photographs and memorabilia from Brazil's Second Word War campaign in Italy and a dusty collection of colonial documents, including some early Dutch maps of Brazil. At the other end of Recife Antigo is the **Kahal Zur Israel Synagogue** ① *R do Bom Jesus 197, T081-3224 2128, Tue-Fri 1000-1200 and 1400-1700, US$2*, an exact replica of the first synagogue to be built in the Americas – in 1637. Under the Dutch, the 'New Christians' (Jews and Muslims forced to convert under the Inquisition), were given freedom to worship. After the city was re-conquered by the Portuguese the synagogue was destroyed and the Jews either fled or were expelled. Many went north to the Dutch colony of Suriname, which retains a large Jewish population to this day.

There are two other sights worth seeing in passing. One of the city's first churches, the elegant, sky-blue **Igreja de Nossa Senhora do Pilar** ① *R de São Jorge s/n*, dating from 1680 is undergoing extensive refurbishment after being badly looted and lying decrepit for decades. The intention is to return the crumbling church to its former glory, complete with its magnificent ceiling paintings. The **Torre** ① *Praça do Arsenal da Marinha, T082-3424 8704, Tue-Sun 1500-2000, free*, is a 19th-century mock-Mudejar tower with a small observatory on its upper floor. It's worth visiting if only for the sweeping view out over the city.

Santo Antônio and São José The bulk of Recife's historical monuments lie in the twin neighbourhoods of Santo Antônio and São José on the island immediately to the south of Recife Antigo (and linked to that neighbourhood by the Buarque de Macedo and Mauricio de Nassau bridges). These neighbourhoods are interesting just to wander around (during the day only) and are replete with magnificent baroque churches. Most impressive of all is the **Capela Dourada da Ordem Terceira do São Francisco** ① *R do Imperador, Santo Antônio, T081-3224 0530, Mon-Fri and Sun 0800-1100 and 1400-1700* (1695-1710 and 19th century), in the church of Santo Antônio of the Convento do São Francisco. This is one of the finest baroque buildings in northeast Brazil and is another national monument. The lavish façade conceals a gorgeous gilt-painted interior with ceiling panels by Recife's Mestre Athayde, **Manuel de Jesus Pinto**. It is his finest work. Pinto was born a slave and bought his freedom after working on a series of Recife's magnificent churches, including the Concatedral de São Pedro dos Clérigos (see below). The chapel was designed and paid for in 1695 by a wealthy Franciscan lay brotherhood, the Ordem Terceira de São Francisco de Assis. The church sits immediately south of the **Praça da República**, one of the city's stateliest civic squares, graced by a fountain, shaded by palms and overlooked by a number of handsome sugar-boom buildings. These include the **Palácio do Campo das Princesas** ① *Praça da República s/n, Mon-Fri 0900-1700, free*, a neoclassical pile with a handsome interior garden by Roberto Burle Marx, which was formerly the Governor's Palace; the pink **Teatro de Santa Isabel** ① *Praça da República s/n, T081-3355 3323, www.teatrosanta isabel.com.br, guided visits Sun 1400 and 1700 in English, and almost nightly performances*, which has a lavish auditorium; and the imposing mock-French **Palácio da Justiça**, topped with a French Renaissance cupola.

Colonial Recife's other great church is the **Concatedral de São Pedro dos Clérigos** ① *Pátio de São Pedro, R Barão da Vitória at Av Dantas Barreto, T081-3224 2954, Mon-Fri 0800-1200 and 1400-1600*, which overlooks one of the city's best-preserved colonial squares, is only a little less impressive. It's a towering baroque building with a beautiful painted and carved octagonal interior with a trompe l'oeuil ceiling (also by Manuel de Jesus Pinto (see Capela Dourada, above). The area has been renovated and is filled with little shops, restaurants and bars. There are sporadic music and poetry shows in the evenings from Wednesday to Sunday. Also worth visiting is the 18th-century **Basílica e Convento de Nossa Senhora do Carmo** ① *Av Dantas Barreto, Santo Antônio, T081-3224 3341, Mon-Fri 0800-1200 and 1400-1900, Sat 0700-1200, Sun 0700-1000*, named after the

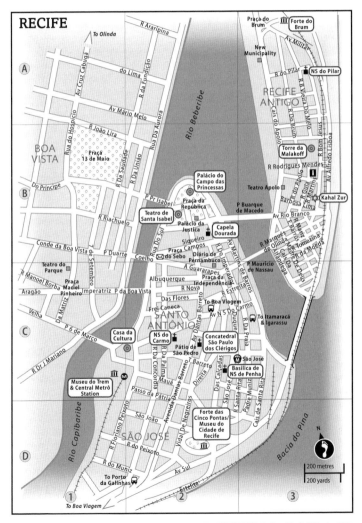

FESTIVALS
Pernambuco

February Carnaval, see box, page 165.

12-15 March Foundation Day, 3 days of music and dancing, night-time only.

March/April Easter, traditional pageants, especially the Passion play at Nova Jerusalem (www.novajerusalem.com.br) near Caruaru and on Fernando de Noronha.

Mid-April Pro-Rock Festival (www.abrilprorock.info), a week-long celebration of rock, hip-hop and *mangue beat* at venues throughout the city.

June Festas Juninas, celebrations which take place throughout Brazil abd have their spiritual home in Pernambuco, Paraíba and Maranhão (where they are celebrated as Bumba-Meu-Boi – see box, page 196). In Pernambuco there are big celebrations throughout the month (in Olinda, Recife and Caruaru, which throws one of the biggest street parties in Brazil). The best days are on and around the eve of St John's Day on 23 Jun when more than one million revellers make the party pilgrimage to Caruaru and to Campina Grande in neighbouring Paraíba and Recife and Olinda come alive. Expect to dance to lively *forró* music, dress up as a *caipira* (yokel) in a tartan shirt and reed hat, eat *canjica* (maize porridge) and drink *quentão* (a Brazilian version of mulled wine). Foreign visitors are still a rare curiosity.

1-8 December Festival of Iemanjá, with foods and drinks, celebrations and offerings to the goddess. Look out for *candomblé* priestesses and devotees dressed in white.

city's patron saint, which has a magnificent painted ceiling and high altar. One of the best places in northeast Brazil to buy arts and crafts lies a stroll to the south, next to the Ponte 6 de Março. The **Casa da Cultura** ① *R Floriano Peixoto s/n, Santo Antônio, T081-3224 0557, www.casada culturape.com.br, Mon-Fri 0900-1900, Sat 0900-1800, Sun 0900-1400*, is a gallery of hundreds of shops and stalls selling clay figurines, leatherwork, lace and ceramics from all over Pernambuco, including the famous arts and crafts town of Caruaru. The building is the former state penitentiary. Immediately west of the Casa da Cultura is Recife's other Dutch fort, the **Forte das Cinco Pontas**. This is now home to the **Museu da Cidade do Recife** ① *Mon-Fri 0900-1800, Sat and Sun 1300-1700, US$1 donation*, which shows a cartographic history of the settlement of Recife.

The **Basílica de Nossa Senhora de Penha** ① *Praça Dom Vital, São José, T081-3424 8500, Tue-Thu 0800-1200 and 1500-1700, Fri 0600-1800, Sat 1500-1700, Sun 0700-0900*, is an Italianate church a few streets north of the fort, which holds a traditional 'blessing of São Felix' on Fridays, attended by hundreds of sick Pernambucans in search of miracles.

SUBURBAN RECIFE

The **Oficina Brennand** ① *Propriedade Santos Cosme e Damião s/n, Várzea, T081-3271 2466, www.brennand.com.br, Mon-Fri 0800-1700, US$3*, is a Dali-esque fantasy garden and museum preserving hundreds of monumental ceramic sculptures by Latin America's most celebrated ceramic artist, Francisco Brennand. Enormous snake penises in hob-nailed boots are set in verdant lawns; surrealist egret heads look out over a Burle Marx garden from 10-m-high tiled walls; haunting chess-piece figures in top hats gaze at tinkling fountains. The museum has a very good air-conditioned restaurant and gift shop. There is no public transport here so take a taxi from Recife (around US$15 including

ON THE ROAD
Carnaval in Pernambuco

The most traditional and least touristy big carnival in Brazil takes place in Recife, its twin city Olinda, and the little towns nearby. Whilst there are few international tourists, Brazilian visitor numbers are as high as those in Bahia or Rio. The music is the most exciting in Brazil, and it is Pernambuco's own. Whilst Salvador pounds to *afoxé* and *axé*, and Rio to samba, Recife and Olinda reverberate to pounding *maracatú*, up-tempo, brassy *frevo* and alternative raucous *mangue beat*. The dancing is some of the best and most acrobatic in the country, with *frevo* dancers leaping, falling into the splits, twirling and throwing tiny, rainbow-hued miniature umbrellas. Unlike Rio but like Salvador, Pernambuco carnival is held in the street. The difference is that in Pernambuco the celebrations are almost all free. The crowds are big but only oppressive at the opening parade.

Recife's carnival takes place in the old city centre, which is dotted with gorgeous Portuguese baroque churches and crumbling mansions. On the Friday, in the streets around the Pátio de São Pedro (Marco Zero) in Recife Antigo, there are spectacular *maracatú* parades with troupes of up to 100 drummers and *blocos* dressed in colourful costumes and swirling white dresses. This square forms the focus of Recife carnival for the following week, with a big stage hosting live acts. Carnival officially opens with the huge Galo da Madrugada (Cock of the Dawn parade), which is said by locals to be the largest street gathering in the world. Despite its name the parade usually begins at around 1000 on Carnival Saturday. Floats with many of the most famous stars – such as Lenine, Alceu Valença and Geraldo Azevedo – pass through the teeming crowds under a baking tropical sun. Try and get a place in one of the shaded bandstands (*camarotes*) at the side of the street as the heat can be oppressive. These can be booked up to a fortnight in advance at the central post office on Avenida Guararapes in Recife – more details from the tourist office or Cariri Ecotours (see page 180). Carnival shows continue until dawn for the next five nights.

In neighbouring Olinda the party is on the steep cobbled streets, between pretty 18th-century houses and opulent churches and overlooking the shimmering Atlantic. Troupes of *frevo* dancers wander through the throng playing and dancing with effortless gymnastic dexterity. Locals join carnival troupes (*blocos*) and parade giant puppets (*bonecos*). Among the best known *blocos* are *O homem da meianoite* (Midnight Man), *A Corda* (a pun on 'the rope' and 'acorda' – wake up!), which parades in the early hours, *Pitombeira* and *Elefantes*. You can join as they pass. Olinda's carnival continues on Ash Wednesday, *a quarta-feira do batata* (Potato Wednesday, named after a waiter who claimed his right to celebrate Carnaval after being on duty during the official celebrations). The streets are very crowded during the height of the celebrations and a little quieter on Ash Wednesday. The local cocktail, *capeta* (guaraná powder, sweet skimmed milk and vodka) is designed to keep you going.

There are parties in other areas throughout both cities. These include the parade of the Virgens do Bairro Novo in Olinda, led by outrageously camp drag queens, and the resolutely Afro-Brazilian Noite dos Tambores Silenciosos, held in a pretty colonial church square in one of the poorest inner-city neighbourhoods of Recife and with celebrations redolent of *candomblé*.

For the street parades be wary of pickpockets and bring only essentials.

The most spectacular of the Carnival celebrations near Recife and well worth a visit are the *maracatu* parades held at Nazaré da Mata and Bezerros.

waiting time; alternatively take a local bus to the *rodoviária* or to Varzea suburb and do a round trip from there, US$10).

The Brennands are one of the wealthiest old-money families in Brazil and Ricardo Brennand – as if not to be outdone by his cousin – has his own museum 10 minutes' taxi ride away. The **Instituto Ricardo Brennand** ⓘ *Alameda Antônio Brennand, Várzea, T081-2121 0352, www.institutoricardo brennand.org.br, Tue-Sun 1300-1700 (last entry 1630), US$3*, is a priceless collection of European and Brazilian art (including the largest conglomeration of Dutch-Brazilian landscapes in the world), books, manuscripts and medieval weapons housed in a fake Norman castle with its own moat and giant swimming pool.

BOA VIAGEM

Recife's beach neighbourhood, and the site of most of the hotels, lies around 6 km south of town in the neighbourhood of Boa Viagem. The 8-km promenade lined with high-rise buildings commands a striking view of the Atlantic, but the beach is backed by a busy road, is crowded at weekends (when it is strewn with rubbish), and is plagued by bull sharks who lost their mangrove homes to the south after a spate of ill-considered coastal development. You can go fishing on *jangadas* at Boa Viagem at low tide. The main *praça* has a good market at weekends.

Arriving in Boa Viagem To get there from the centre, take any bus marked 'Boa Viagem'; from Nossa Senhora do Carmo, take buses marked 'Piedade', 'Candeias' or 'Aeroporto', which run along Avenida Domingos Ferreira, two blocks parallel to the beach, all the way to Praça Boa Viagem (at Avenida Boa Viagem 500). To get to the centre, take the bus marked 'CDU' or 'Setubal' from Avenida Domingos Ferreira. The PE-15 Boa Viagem to Olinda bus runs along the Avenida Boa Viagem and stops at the Praça Boa Viagem. It is fast and frequent.

→OLINDA

About 7 km north of Recife is the old capital, Olinda, founded in 1537 and now a UNESCO World Heritage Site with a population of 350,000. The compact network of cobbled streets is steeped in history and very inviting for a wander. Olinda is a charming spot to spend a few relaxing days, and a much more appealing base than Recife. A programme of restoration, partly financed by the Dutch government, was initiated in order to comply with the recently conferred title of 'national monument', but much is still in desperate need of repair.

ARRIVING IN OLINDA

Getting there and around From Recife, take any bus marked 'Rio Doce', No 981, which has a circular route around the city and beaches; or No 33 from Avenida Nossa Senhora do Carmo, US$1.30; or 'Jardim Atlântico' from the central post office at Siqueira Campos (US$1.30, 30 minutes). From the airport, take the 'Aeroporto' bus to Avenida Domingos Ferreira in Boa Viagem and change to one of the buses mentioned above. From the Recife *rodoviária*, take the metrô to Central station (Joana Bezerra is unsafe) and then change. In all cases, alight in Olinda at Praça do Carmo. The PE-15 Boa Viagem bus runs between Olinda and Boa Viagem every 10-20 minutes (US$1.30, 20 minutes). Taxi drivers between Olinda and Recife often try to put their meters on Rate 2 (only meant for Sundays, holidays and after 2100), but should change it to Rate 1 when queried. A taxi from Boa Viagem should cost around US$14, US$20 at night. From Olinda to the centre of Recife, take a bus marked 'Piedade/Rio Doce' or 'Barra de Jangada/Casa Caiada'.

Tourist information The Secretaria de Turismo ① *Praça do Carmo, T081-3429 9279, daily 0900-2100*, provides a complete list of all historic sites and a useful map, *Sítio Histórico*. Guides with identification cards wait in Praça do Carmo. They are former street children and half the fee for a full tour of the city (about US$12) goes to a home for street children. If you take a guide you will be safe from mugging, which does unfortunately occur.

PLACES IN OLINDA

Whilst Olinda city boasts an ornate church on almost every corner, there are two which rank among the finest in South America – the Igreja e Convento Franciscano de Nossa Senhora das Neves (Brazil's first Franciscan convent) and the Basilica e Mosteiro de São Bento. The **Igreja e Convento Franciscano de Nossa Senhora das Neves** ① *Ladeira de São Francisco 280, T081-3429 0517, Mon-Fri 0700-1200 and 1400-1700, US$2, children free, Mass Tue at 1900, Sat at 1700 and Sun at 0800*, (1585), is one of the oldest religious complexes in South America. It has a modest, weather-beaten exterior, but an interior that preserves one of the

country's most splendid displays of woodcarving, ecclesiastical paintings and gilded stucco. The Franciscans began work on the buildings, which comprise the convent, the church of Nossa Senhora das Neves and the chapels of São Roque and St Anne, in 1585. Even if you are in a rush, be sure to visit the cloisters, the main church and the São Roque chapel, which is covered with beautiful Portuguese *azulejo* tiles.

The **Basilica e Mosteiro de São Bento** ① *R São Bento, T081-3429 3288, Mon-Fri 0830-1130, 1430-1700, Mass Sat 0630 and 1800; Sun 1000, with Gregorian chant; monastery closed except with written permission, free*, is another very early Brazilian church, founded in 1582 by Benedictine monks, burnt by the Dutch in 1631 and restored in 1761. It is the site of Brazil's first law school and was the first place in Brazil to abolish slavery. The vast, cavernous nave is fronted by a towering tropical cedar altarpiece covered in gilt. It is one of the finest pieces of baroque carving in the Americas and was on loan to the Guggenheim museum in New York for much of the first decade of the new millennium. There are fine carvings and paintings throughout the chapels.

It's worth making the short, but very steep, climb up the **Alto da Sé** to the plain and simple **Igreja da Sé** ① *Mon-Fri 0800-1200, 1400-1700* (1537), for the much-photographed views out over Olinda, the palm tree-fringed beaches and the distant skyscrapers of Recife. The chuch was the first to be built in Olinda and has been the city's cathedral since 1677. In the late afternoon and especially at weekends, there are often *repentista* street troubadours playing in the little cathedral square and women selling *tapioca* snacks. The **Igreja da Misericórdia** ① *R Bispo Coutinho, daily 1145-1230, 1800-1830* (1540), a short stroll downhill from the cathedral, has some beautiful *azulejo* tiling and gold work but seemingly random opening hours. The **Igreja do Carmo** (1581), on a small hill overlooking Praça do Carmo, is similarly impressive, but has been closed for years despite assurances that it would be refurbished. Olinda has many handsome civic buildings too, including streets of 17th-century houses with latticed balconies, heavy doors and brightly painted stucco walls. Some, like the mansion housing the **Mourisco** restaurant (Praça João Alfredo 7), are in the Portuguese Manueline style, their façades replete with Moorish architectural motifs.

There's a thriving arts and crafts community in Olinda and this is a good place to stock up on regional souvenirs. Look out for terracotta figurines and woodcarvings. The figurines are often by named artisans (look for their autograph imprinted in the clay on the base) and are becoming collectors' items. You'll find shops selling arts and crafts near the cathedral and in the handicraft shops at the **Mercado da Ribeira** ① *R Bernardo Vieira de Melo*, and the **Mercado Eufrásio Barbosa** ① *Av Segismundo Gonçalves at Santos Dumont, Varadouro*. Every Friday at 2200 there are serenades in Olinda, with a troupe of musicians leaving the Praça João Alfredo (aka Praça da Abolição) and walking throughout the old centre.

The beaches close to Olinda are polluted, but those further north, beyond Casa Caiada, at **Janga**, and **Pau Amarelo**, are beautiful, palm-fringed and usually deserted (although the latter can be dirty at low tide). There are many simple cafés where you can eat *sururu* (clam stew in coconut sauce), *agulha frita* (fried needle-fish), *miúdo de galinha* (chicken giblets in gravy), *casquinha de caranguejo* (seasoned crabmeat) and *farinha de dendê* (served in crab shells). Visit the Dutch fort on Pau Amarelo beach where there is a small craft fair on Saturday nights. To get to the beaches, take either a 'Janga' or 'Pau Amarela' bus; to return to Recife, take a bus marked 'Varodouro'.

Situated 134 km west of Recife, this small town (population 254,000) in the *sertão* is famous for its huge **Festas Juninas**, held throughout June (see box, page 164), and its little clay figures (*figurinhas* or *bonecas de barro*) originated by Mestre Vitalino (1909-1963), and very typical of northeast Brazil. Most of the potters live at **Alto da Moura**, 6 km away, where you can visit the **Casa Museu Mestre Vitalino** ⓘ *buses from Caruaru, a bumpy 30-min ride, US$0.50*, once owned by Vitalino and containing personal objects and photographs, but no examples of his work. UNESCO has recognized the area as the largest centre of figurative art in the Americas. It is also possible to buy the arts and crafts in Caruaru itself. The town hosts a number of markets, which were originally devoted to foodstuffs but which now also sell arts and crafts. The most famous is the **Feira da Sulanca**, held in the city centre on Tuesdays, with some 10,000 stalls and 40,000 visitors.

Arriving in Caruaru The *rodoviária* is 4 km west of town; buses from Recife stop in the town centre. Alight here and look for the **Livraria Estudantil**, on the corner of Vigário Freire and Rua Anna de Albuquerque Galvão; this is a useful landmark. Follow Galvão down hill from the bookshop, turn right on Rua 15 de Novembro to the first junction, 13 de Maio; turn left, and finally cross the river to the Feira do Artesanato (arts and crafts market).

During the **Festas Juninas**, there is a tourist train, **Train do Forró**, from Recife, which is a very spirited affair with bars, and bands playing in the carriages. See www.tremdo forro.com.br and www.caruaru.pe.gov.br for information.

RECIFE AND OLINDA LISTINGS

WHERE TO STAY

$$$ Pousada do Amparo, R do Amparo 199, Olinda, T081-3439 1749, www.pousada doamparo.com.br. Olinda's best hotel is a gorgeous 18th-century house, full of antiques and atmosphere. Rooms have 4-poster beds and each is decorated differently. The public areas include a spacious foyer, a pool and sauna area surrounded by a little flower-filled garden and an excellent, delightfully romantic restaurant.

$$$ Pousada Villa Boa Vista, R Miguel Couto 81, Boa Vista, T081-3223 0666, www.pousadavillaboavista.com.br. The only modern hotel in town, with plain, comfortable a/c rooms (all en suites have bathrooms and powerful showers), around a courtyard. Quiet, safe and a 5-min taxi ride from the centre.

$$ Coqueiral, R Petrolina 43, Boa Viagem, T081-3326 5881, www.hotelcoqueiral.com.br. Dutch-owned (English and French spoken). Simple and plainly decorated small, homely rooms with a/c and a pretty breakfast room.

$$ Pousada dos Quatro Cantos, R Prudente de Morais 441, Olinda, T081-3429 0220, www.pousada4cantos.com.br. A large converted townhouse with a little walled garden and terraces. The maze of bright rooms and suites are decorated with Pernambuco arts and crafts and furnished mostly with antiques. Warm, welcoming and full of character.

$$-$ Olinda Hostel, R do Sol 233, Olinda, T081-3429 1592, www.alberguedeolinda. com.br. HI youth hostel with fan-cooled 8-bed dorms with shared en suites, and doubles. The hostel has a tropical garden, TV room, and a shady area with hammocks next to a pool.

$$-$ Pousada da Praia, Alcides Carneiro Leal 66, Boa Viagem, T081-3326 7085, www.hpraia.com. This ungainly blue block 50 m from the beach has simple tiled rooms, some pocket-sized, others larger suites with space for up to 6. All have a/c and a TV, safe and Wi-Fi and there's a rooftop breakfast and lounge area.

RESTAURANTS

$$$ Leite, Praça Joaquim Nabuco 147/53 near the Casa de Cultura, Santo Antônio. This formal Portuguese-Brazilian fusion restaurant with black tie waiters and a live pianist, is one of the oldest in the country and has been serving Portuguese standards like *bacalhau* (smoked salted cod) for 120 years.

$$ Parraxaxa, Av Fernando Simões Barbosa, 1200, Boa Viagem, T081-3268 4169, www. parraxaxa.com.br. Rustic-style, award-winning buffet of northeastern cuisine, with tapioca breakfasts and a generous spread of dishes at lunch and dinner time. The dining room is decorated with effigies of the sertão bandit Lampião and his consort Maria Bonita.

WHAT TO DO

Cariri Ecotours, T084-9660 1818, www.cariri ecotours.com.br. Tours around Recife and Olinda can be conducted in conjunction with tours throughout the northeast, including to the interior of Pernambuco to Caruaru, to the prehistoric remains at Cariri and Souza and to the beaches of Rio Grande do Norte.

FERNANDO DE NORONHA

This small volcanic island rising from the deep, on the eastern edge of the mid-Atlantic ridge 350 km off the coast, is the St Barts of Brazil and one of the world's great romantic destinations. It is blessed with exceptional natural beauty; rugged like the west of Ireland, covered in maquis like Corsica and fringed by some of the cleanest and most beautiful beaches in the Atlantic. Many of the beaches are exposed to the full force of the ocean and pummelled by a powerful bottle-green surf that has earned the island the nickname 'the Hawaii of the Atlantic'. Surf championships are held on Cacimba do Padre beach. However, there are numerous coves where the sea is kinder and the broad beaches are dotted with deep clear-water rock pools busy with juvenile reef fish. The water changes through shades of aquamarine to deep indigo and is as limpid as any on earth. Diving here is up there with some of the best in the world.

Despite the fact that two-thirds of the island is settled, it is an important nesting ground for turtles and marine birds: both the island itself and the seas around it are a marine park, protected by Instituto Chico Mendes de Conservação da Biodiversidade (ICMBio). All that is needed to make it a sanctuary of international standing is to remove the non-native feral monitor lizards (brought here in the 20th century to kill rats), the goats and the abundant cats and dogs. Tourism, however, is controlled and only limited numbers can visit the island at any time. Book well in advance.

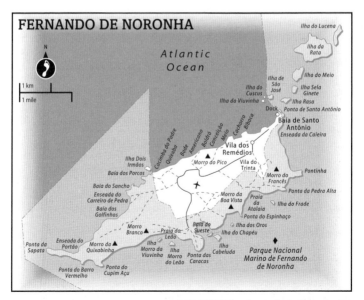

ARRIVING ON FERNANDO DE NORONHA

Getting there and around Flights from Recife to Fernando de Noronha (one hour 20 minutes) and then from the island to Natal (one hour) are run by TRIP, www.voetrip.com.br. CVC, www.cruisevacationcenter.com, operates a small cruise liner, which sails from Recife to Noronha and then back to Recife via Fortaleza and Natal. Buggy hire, motorbike hire and jeep tours are available in town.

Best time to visit The rains are April to July. The vegetation turns brown in the dry season (August to March), but the sun shines all year round. Noronha is one hour later than Brazilian Standard Time. There are far fewer mosquitos here than on the coast but bring repellent.

Tourist information Instituto Chico Mendes de Conservação da Biodiversidade (ICMBio) has imposed rigorous rules to prevent damage to the nature reserve and everything, from development to cultivation of food crops to fishing, is strictly administered. Many locals are now dependent on tourism and most food is brought from the mainland. Entry to the island is limited and there is a tax of US$30 per day for the first week of your stay. In the second week the tax increases each day. Take sufficient reais as it's difficult to change money. For information see www.fernandodenoronha.com.br.

PLACES ON FERNANDO DE NORONHA

The island was discovered in 1503 by Amerigo Vespucci and was for a time a pirate lair. In 1738 the Portuguese built a charming little baroque church, **Nossa Senhora dos Remedios**, some attractive administrative buildings and a fort, **O Forte dos Remédios**, which was used as a prison for political dissidents by the military dictatorship in the late 20th century. The most famous was the communist leader Luis Carlos Prestes, who led the famous long march, the Prestes Column, in 1925-1927. Many people were tortured and murdered here. The islands were occupied by the USA during the Second World War and used as a naval base. US guns sit outside the *prefeitura* in the centre of the main town, **Vila dos Remédios**, which overlooks the coast on the eastern shore.

Some of the best beaches lie immediately south of the town, clustered around an imposing granite pinnacle, the **Morro do Pico**. The most beautiful are **Conceição**, **Boldró**, **Americano**, **Baía do Sancho**, **Cacimba do Padre** and the turquoise cove at **Baía dos Porcos**, which sits on the edge of the beginning of the marine park. Beyond is the **Baía dos Golfinhos**, with a lookout point for watching the spinner dolphins in the bay. On the south, or windward side, there are fewer beaches, higher cliffs and the whole coastline and offshore islands are part of the marine park. As with dive sites, **Instituto Chico Mendes de Conservação da Biodiversidade (ICMBio)** restricts bathing in low-tide pools and other sensitive areas to protect the environment.

There are good possibilities for hiking, horse riding and mountain biking. A guide will take you to the marine park and to beaches such as **Atalaia**, which has the best snorkelling.

WILDLIFE AND CONSERVATION

The island is a UNESCO World Heritage Site. It may look like an ecological paradise but it has been the victim of much degradation. Almost all of the native vegetation was chopped down in the 19th century, when the island was used as a prison, to prevent prisoners from hiding or making rafts. A giant native rodent, recorded by Amerigo

Vespucci was wiped out and linseed, feral cats, dogs, goats, rats, mice, tegu (*teju* in Portuguese) lizards and cavies were introduced in the 16th century. These continue to damage bird and turtle nesting sites and native vegetation. Nonetheless, the island remains an important sanctuary for sea-bird species. Ruddy turnstone, black and brown noddy, sooty tern, fairy tern, masked booby, brown booby and white-tailed tropicbird all nest here. Some endemic bird species still survive: the Noronha vireo (*Vireo gracilirostris*); a tyrant flycatcher, the Noronha elaenia or cucuruta (*Elaenia spectabilis reidleyana*); and the Noronha eared dove or arribaçã (*Zenaida auriculata noronha*). There is an endemic lizard (*Mabuya maculate*) and at least 5% of the fish species are unique to the archipelago. The most spectacular animals are the nesting hawksbill and green turtles, and the spinner dolphins. Good terrestrial wildlife guides are non-existent on Noronha and even **Instituto Chico Mendes de Conservação da Biodiversidade (ICMBio)** spell the species names incorrectly on their information sheets. There are a number of reasonable dive shops; though biological knowledge is minimal.

FERNANDO DE NORONHA LISTINGS

WHERE TO STAY

$$$$ Zé Maria, R Nice Cordeirol, Floresta Velha, T081-3619 1258, www.pousada zemaria.com.br. Spacious bungalows with tiled floors, hardwood ceilings and generous beds. Verandas and hammocks have views out to the Morro do Pico. The highlight is the small deep-blue half-moon pool. The owner, Zé Maria and chef Celso Freire throw frequent banquet parties and run one of the better restaurants on the island.

$$$$-$$$ Solar dos Ventos, T081-3619 1347, www.pousadasolardosventos.com.br. In a very tranquil location with a spectacular bay view, well-appointed wood, brick and tile bungalows and friendly owners.

$$$ Pousada do Vale, T081-3619 1293, www.pousadadovale.com. Friendly, well run *pousada* with comfortable en suite rooms decorated with mosaics. The best are the duplex wooden bungalows. 300 m from Vila dos Remedios town centre.

$$$-$$ Pousada dos Corais, Conj Residencial Floresta Nova, T081-3619 1147, www.pousadacorais.com.br. One of the more economical hotels on the island, with 8 simple a/c rooms, each with a tiny but pretty bathroom decorated with nautically themed mosaics. The hotel has a small pool.

RESTAURANTS

$$$ Ecologiku's, Estr Velha do Sueste, T081-3619 1807. Bahian cooking served in an open-sided, mood-lit restaurant with a little garden.

$ Açai e Raizes, BR-363, Floresta Velha. Roadside sandwich bar with snacks, puddings and delicious cream of *cupuaçu* and *açai*.

WHAT TO DO

Diving
Atlantis Divers, T081-3206 8841, www.atlantisdivers.com.br. All the dive shops in Noronha offer much the same dive locations around Noronha and the offshore islands, as well as dive 'baptism' for complete beginners. Diving costs around US$75 for 2 tanks and is by far the best in Brazil aside from **Atol das Rocas**, 2 days off Bahia.

Tours
Blue Noronha, www.bluenoronha.com.br. One of many companies offering on-land tours and boat trips around the island, bookable through any of the *pousadas*. The best boat excursions leave at lunchtime, catching the late afternoon light on return.

Turtle-watching
It is possible to see hatching turtles in season. For details, contact **Projeto Tamar**, Alameda Boldró, s/n, Caixa Postal 50 - CEP 53.990-000, T081-3619 1171, www.tamar.org.br.

NORTH FROM RECIFE

The coast north from Recife stretches into Paraíba and Rio Grande do Norte states and is lined with idyllic tropical beaches, many of them little visited. They include Praia do Pipa, whose sands are backed with swaying palms, crumbling sandstone cliffs and remnant Atlantic coastal rainforest. Beyond sleepy Natal city things get wilder and more windswept. Coastal Ceará is cooled by prevailing sea winds which have swept the beach sand into huge dunes – around Morro Branco in the south of the state and the tiny resort town of Jericoacoara further north (see page 186).

→RECIFE TO NATAL

It's an easy drive or bus journey from Recife to Natal, taking fewer than four hours on a good road and cutting through the state of **Paraíba**, which most travellers choose to miss. The main sights of interest in the state are the mysterious rock formations and prehistoric art found in the interior around the **Pai Mateus** ranch at **Cariri**. These are most easily visited from Natal or Recife with **Cariri Ecotours** (see page 180). Paraíba has some beautiful beaches, most of which are completely free of foreign tourists. The best run south of the pretty state capital, **João Pessoa** (which has a handful of impressive baroque buildings but little infrastructure), including the city's beachside suburbs at Tambaú and Manaíra (where there are plenty of hotels), the beautiful palm-fringed **Praia de Carapibus** and **Tambada**, the officially designated nudist beach in Brazil's northeast. Tambaba lies near the **Ponta do Seixas**, the most easterly point in the Americas and therefore the first place to see the rising sun.

Over the border from Paraíba, in Rio Grande do Norte, is **Pipa**, an enchanting little tourist town whose mix of local fishermen and settlers from all over Brazil has formed an eclectic alternative community. There are excellent *pousadas* and restaurants in all price ranges and the nightlife is animated. The town is becoming increasingly popular and the number of people can feel overwhelming during Carnaval and New Year. The town beach is somewhat developed, but there are plenty of others nearby. **Praia dos Golfinhos** to the south and **Madeiro** beyond it have only a few hotels and **Praia do Amor** to the north is surrounded by cliffs and has reasonable surf. Access to the shore is down the steps built by the few clifftop hotels or by walking along the beach from Pipa at low tide. There are tours to see dolphins from US$30 per person and also around the mangrove-lined Lagoa Guaraíra at Tibau, particularly beautiful at sunset. Just north of town, on a 70-m-high dune, is the **Santuário Ecológico de Pipa** ① *T084-3211 6070, www.pipa.com.br/santuarioecologico, 0800-1600, US$3*, a 60-ha park created in 1986 to conserve the *Mata Atlântica* forest. There are several trails and lookouts over the cliffs, which afford an excellent view of the ocean and dolphins. Although larger animals like cats and howler monkeys are long gone, this is one of the few areas in the state where important indicator bird species, such as guans, can be found.

NATAL

The state of Rio Grande do Norte is famous for its beaches and dunes, especially around Natal. The coastline begins to change here, becoming gradually drier and less green, as it shifts from running north–south to east–west. The vast sugar cane plantations and few remaining stands of Mata Atlântica (coastal forest) are replaced by the dry caatinga vegetation and caju orchards. The people are known as 'Potiguares', after an indigenous tribe that once resided in the state.

The state capital, located on a peninsula between the Rio Potengi and the Atlantic Ocean, is pleasant enough but has few sights of interest. Most visitors head for the beaches to the north and south. During the Second World War, the city was, somewhat bizarrely, the second largest US base outside the United States and housed 8000 American pilots. Today it has a population of 713,000.

ARRIVING IN NATAL
Getting there Flights arrive from Recife or Fernando de Noronha (among others) at **Augusto Severo International Airport** ① *Parnamirim, 18 km south of centre, 10 km from Ponta Negra, T084-3644 1070.* A taxi to the centre costs US$25; US$20 to Ponta Negra. Buses run every 30 minutes to the old *rodoviária* near the centre, US$1 from where there are connections to Ponta Negra on Route 54 or 56 among others, or take the 'Aeroporto' bus to the city centre and then bus Nos 54 or 46 south to Ponta Negra.

Interstate buses arrive at the new **Rodoviária Cidade do Sol** ① *Av Capitão Mor Gouveia 1237, Cidade da Esperança, 6 km southwest of the centre, T084-3205 4377.* A taxi to Ponta Negra costs around US$18; to the Via Costeira around US$25. Alternatively, take bus No 66 to Ponta Negra. This passes close to the hotel strip whilst not taking Avenida Erivan Franca (the street that runs along the seafront). For Praia do Meio beach and the Via Costeira take bus No 40 and alight at Praia do Meio for an easy walk to any of the hotels on that beach or Praia dos Artistas. Or take any of the Via Costeira buses.

Buses from the south pass Ponta Negra first, where you can ask to alight. The city

buses 'Cidade de Esperança Avenida 9', 'Areia Preta via Petrópolis' or 'Via Tirol' run from the new *rodoviária* to the centre. It is also possible to travel between Natal and Fortaleza by beach buggy, a five- to six-hour ride, bookable through **Cariri Ecotours** (see page 180). It's an exciting trip but not a very environmentally responsible one as buggies have seriously eroded the coast.

Moving on From Natal it's a short flight or an eight-hour bus ride to Fortaleza (see page 181). For a description of the route, see page 179.

Getting around Unlike most Brazilian buses, in Natal you get on the bus at the front and get off at the back. The **Old Rodoviária** ① *Av Junqueira Aires, by Praça Augusto Severo, Ribeira*, is a central point where many bus lines converge. Buses to some of the nearby beaches also leave from here. Taxis are expensive compared to other cities (eg four times the price of Recife); a typical 10-minute journey costs US$15. Buses are the best option. Route 54 and 46 connect Ponta Negra with the city, the former via Via Costeira and the old *rodoviária*.

Tourist information The state tourist office, SETUR ① *Centro de Turismo R Aderbal de Figueiredo 980, Petrópolis, T084-3211 5013 www.setur.rn.gov.brwww.rosaleao.com.br/clientes/setur*, covers the whole of Rio Grande do Norte state, although their information and English is very limited, and the office is not conveniently located. However, there are **tourist information booths** at the airport, the bus station, on Avenida Presidente Café Filho on Praia das Artistas beach and Erivan Franca on Ponta Negra, all open daily 0800-2100. See www.nataltrip.com, www.natal.com.br and www.rn.gov.br for more information.

PLACES IN NATAL

No-one comes to Natal for sightseeing, but the city is not without culture. The oldest part is the **Ribeira** along the riverfront, where a programme of renovation has been started. This can be seen on Rua Chile and in public buildings restored in vivid art deco fashion, such as the **Teatro Alberto Maranhão** ① *Praça Augusto Severo, T/F084-3222 9935*, built 1898-1904, and the **Prefeitura** ① *R Quintino Bocaiuva, Cidade Alta*. The **Cidade Alta**, or Centro, is the main commercial centre and Avenida Rio Branco its principal artery. The main square is made up by the adjoining *praças*, **João Maria**, **André de Albuquerque**, **João Tibúrcio** and **7 de Setembro**. At Praça André de Albuquerque is the old **cathedral** (inaugurated 1599,

restored 1996). The modern cathedral is on Avenida Deodoro. The church of **Santo Antônio** ① *R Santo Antônio 683, Cidade Alta, Tue-Fri 0800-1700, Sat 0800-1400*, dates from 1766, and has a fine, carved wooden altar and a sacred art museum.

The **Museu Câmara Cascudo** ① *Av Hermes de Fonseca 1440, Tirol, T084-3212 2795, www.mcc.ufrn.br, Tue-Fri 0800-1130, 1400-1730, Sat, Sun 1300-1700, US$2.50*, has exhibits on *umbanda* rituals, archaeological digs, the sugar, leather and petroleum industries; there is also a dead whale.

The 16th-century **Forte dos Reis Magos** ① *T084-3202 9006, daily 0800-1630, US$1.50*, is at Praia do Forte, the tip of Natal's peninsula. Between the fort and the city is a military installation. Walk along the beach to the fort for good views (or go on a tour, or by taxi).

At Mãe Luiza is a **lighthouse** with beautiful views of Natal and surrounding beaches (take a city bus marked 'Mãe Luiza' and get the key from the house next door).

SOUTH TO PONTA NEGRA
The urban beaches of **Praia do Meio**, **Praia dos Artistas** and **Praia de Areia Preta** have recently been cleaned up. The first two are sheltered by reefs and good for windsurfing. The beachside promenade, **Via Costeira**, runs south beneath the towering sand dunes of **Parque das Dunas** (access restricted to protect the dunes), joining the city to the neighbourhood of Ponta Negra. A cycle path parallels this road and provides great views of the coastline.

The vibrant and pretty **Ponta Negra**, 12 km south of the centre (20 minutes by bus), is justifiably the most popular beach and has many hotels. The northern end is good for surfing, while the southern end is calmer and suitable for swimming. **Morro do Careca**, a 120-m-high sand dune, surrounded by vegetation, sits at its far end. It is crowded on weekends and holidays. The poorly lit northern reaches can be unsafe after dark.

EXCURSIONS FROM NATAL
The beautiful beaches around Natal – some of which are developed, others are deserted and accessible only by trails – are good all year round for day trips or longer stays. Those north of the city are known as the **Litoral Norte**, where there are extensive cashew plantations; those to the south form the **Litoral Sul**. The areas closest to the city are built-up and get busy during the summer holidays (December to Carnaval), when dune-buggy traffic can become excessive.

Popular tours from Natal include boat trips on the **Rio Potengi**, along the nearby beaches of the Litoral Sul, and to **Barra do Cunhaú**, 86 km south of Natal. The latter goes through mangroves and visits an island and a salt mine, **Passeio Ecológico Cunhaú** ① *T084-9934 0017, www.barradocunhau.com.br*. Other popular pastimes include buggy tours, marlin fishing (11 km from shore, said by some to be the best in Brazil) and microlight flights over the Rio Potengi and sand dunes north of Natal.

The **Centro de Lançamento da Barreira do Inferno** ① *11 km south of Natal on the road to Pirangi, T084-3216 1400, www.clbi.cta.br, visits by appointment on Wed from 1400*, is the launching centre for Brazil's space programme.

The coast between Natal and Fortaleza is known for its many impressive, light-coloured sand dunes, some reaching a staggering 50 m in height and for the string of traditional fishing communities, indigenous villages and small resorts which lie along them. The best of these can be visited through **Rede Tucum** (see page 189) and lie in southern Ceará state.

Northern Rio Grande do Norte begins at **Genipabu**, a weekend resort for the Natal middle classes, is 30 km north of Natal and which has effectively become another beach suburb. Its major attractions are some very scenic dunes and the **Lagoa de Genipabu**, a lake surrounded by cashew trees where tables are set up on a sandbank in the water and drinks are served. There are also many bars and restaurants on the seashore. Buggy rental and microlight flights can be arranged. North of Genipabu, across the Rio Ceará Mirim, are several beaches with coconut groves and dunes, lined with fishing villages and summer homes of people from Natal; access is via the town of Extremoz.

Lovely beaches continue along the state's coastline; as you get further away from Natal the beaches are more distant from the main highways and access is more difficult. Around 83 km north of Natal, in the centre of a region known for its coconuts and lobsters, is the ugly resort town of **Touros**. From here the coastline veers east–west. As it does so, the terrain becomes more dramatic and bleak and the arid *sertão* comes to meet the windswept shore. Sheltered coves are replaced by vast beaches stretching in seemingly interminable broad curves. Behind them are pink, brown and red cliffs, or large expanses of dunes. Highlights are the sleepy little village of **Galinhos**, with its sand streets and beautiful, gentle beach washed by a calm sea, and the Costa Branca near the little fishing towns of **Areia Branca**, **Ponta do Mel** and **Rosadao**, where huge pink and white dunes converge behind magnificent long beaches.

Beaches get gentler again across the border in Ceará, and the scenery becomes even more spectacular, with white, red and orange cliffs and towering pink dunes. The most famous are at **Canoa Quebrada**, where they are blighted by the ungainly barraca beach bars and a long iron walkway, but the resort has the best choice of *pousadas* on this stretch of the route. Far more charming and with even more spectacular *scenery* are the small communities whose accommodation is managed by the **Rede Tucum** ecotourism project (see page 189). These include **Morro Branco**, **Ponta Grossa** and the delightful village of **Prainha do Canto Verde**, where it is possible to learn how to sail a *jangada*. These villages are much the best place to make a break in the journey.

NORTH FROM RECIFE LISTINGS

WHERE TO STAY

Natal and Ponta Negra

$$$$ Manary Praia, R Francisco Gurgel 9067, T084-3204 2900, www.manary.com.br. The best and most tranquil hotel facing the beach and the only one with a trace of style. The rooms, which are decorated in hard wood and pastel colours, have ample bath rooms and secluded private terraces. Good food and an attractive pool. 10 mins' walk from the main restaurant area on Ponta Negra.

$$ Pousada Manga Rosa, R Erivan Franca 240, T084-3219 0508, www.mangarosanatal. com.br. This pretty beachside guesthouse right next to the main restaurant area on Ponta Negra has small, but bright, colourful and contemporary a/c rooms with wooden furniture, flat screen TVs and bonsai bathrooms with electric showers. The best have sea views.

$$-$ Maria Bonita, R Estrela do Mar 2143 at Arabaiana, T084-3236 2941, www.maria bonita2.com.br. A family home turned long-standing *pousada* set back from the beach on the western side of Av Roberto Freire. Simple rooms have tiled floors, marble writing desks and plenty of storage space. Fan-cooled ones have beds with concrete bases; those with a/c are cosier and have flat-screen TVs. There is a tiny pool. Close to restaurants and nightlife.

Pipa

$$$$ Ponta doMadeiro, R da Praia, Estr para Pipa Km 3, T084-3246 4220, www.pontadomadeiro.com.br. Very comfortable spacious a/c chalets, beautiful pool with bar and spectacular views over the Praia do Madeiro. Excellent service and a good pool (set in a pretty tropical garden) and restaurant. Wonderful sweeping views of the beach.

$$$$-$$$ Toca da Coruja, Praia da Pipa, T084-3246 2226, www.tocadacoruja.com.br. One of the best small luxury hotels in northeastern Brazil, with a range of chalets set in forested gardens and decorated with local antiques and art. Beautiful spring-water fed pool and an excellent restaurant.

$$-$ A Conchego, R do Cruzeiro s/n, Praia da Pipa, T084-3246 2439, www.pousada-aconchego.com. Family-run *pousada* with simple chalets with red-tiled roofs and terraces, in a garden filled with cashew and palm trees. Tranquil and central. Good breakfast.

$ Pousada da Pipa, Praia da Pipa, T084-3246 2271, www.pipa.com.br/pousada dapipa. Small rooms in raw stone decorated with a personal touch and with newly renovated bathrooms. The better upstairs rooms have a large shared terrace with glazed terracotta tiles, sitting areas, hammocks and sea views and are some 30% more expensive. Decent restaurant, **Os Golfinhos**.

$ Vera-My house, Praia da Pipa, T084-3246 2295, www.praiadapipa.com/veramyhouse. Good value, friendly and well maintained though simple rooms with bath, cheaper in dormitory, use of kitchen, no breakfast.

WHAT TO DO

Cariri Ecotours, R Francisco Gurgel 9067, Ponta Negra, T084-9993 0027, www.cariri ecotours.com.br. One of the best tour companies in Brazil's northeast, offering excursions throughout the region and especially around Natal, including transfers to and from Recife along the beaches, dune visits, visits to Caruaru, to the prehistoric remains at Cariri and Souza and to the remote beaches of northern Rio Grande do Norte.

FORTALEZA AND JERICOACOARA

The state of Ceará calls itself the 'Terra da Luz' (Land of Light) and much of its 573-km coastline and bone-dry interior is baked under permanent sunshine. It could just as well be called the land of wind: kitesurfers and windsurfers are quickly discovering that there is nowhere better in the world for their sports. Locations such as Jericoacoara are blown by strong winds almost 365 days a year, and the Atlantic Ocean offers varied conditions from glassy flat through to rolling surf. Ceará boasts some beautiful beaches, too – though poor when compared to the rest of Brazil, perhaps – with long, broad stretches of sand backed by ochre cliffs or towering dunes. Sadly they are increasingly populated by expat and profiteering foreigners. Many of the little fishing villages that lay undiscovered for decades are losing their character to ugly condos and concrete hotels. In places like Canoa Quebrada, Jericoacoara and Cumbuco, other European languages are spoken as much as Portuguese. Even the state capital Fortaleza has been affected. Plane-loads of foreign tourists have turned its once-lively nightlife increasingly tawdry; and while the state authorities are cracking down hard on the exploitation, locals in the main tourist towns are often cynical about foreigners.

→FORTALEZA

Brazil's fifth largest city (population 2.1 million) is a stretch of concrete towers along a series of white-sand beaches behind a gloriously misty green and blue Atlantic dotted with rusting wrecks. The water temperature is permanently in the high 20s and there's a constant sea breeze. The sea is surprisingly clean, even in Iracema near the centre, but the best beaches for swimming are further east and west.

Fortaleza has a long history and a number if sights of historic interest. However, most tourists are drawn here by the city's reputation for lively nightlife. The sound of *forró* still reverberates in the streets behind Iracema beach, but nowadays it's hard to find anywhere that isn't overrun with groups of single foreign men and professional local women. Many locals are angry about their city's poor reputation and are wary of tourists. There are signs that this is changing, however – police and local hotel owners have been making concerted efforts to discourage the growth of this kind of tourism and are coming down increasingly hard on any locals and foreigners involved.

ARRIVING IN FORTALEZA

Getting there Eight buses a day travel the 7½-hour journey between Natal and Fortaleza (US$25 *semi-leito*, US$40 *executivo*, US$50 *leito*). The interstate buses arrive at the **Rodoviária São Tomé** ① *Av Borges de Melo 1630, Fátima, 6 km south of the centre, T085-3256 2100*. Information is available from *Disque Turismo* booth, open 0600-1800, which also has lockers for storing luggage.

Opposite the *rodoviária* is **Hotel Amuarama**, which has a bar and restaurant; there's also a *lanchonete*. Many city buses run to the centre (US$1) including No 78, which goes to Iracema via the Centro Dragão do Mar. If in doubt, the tourist information booth will point you in the right direction. A taxi to Praia de Iracema, or Avenida Abolição costs around US$15.

Moving on Rede Tucum (see page 189) will organize transport from Fortaleza to any of their ecotourism projects along the coast. Two daily buses leave from both Fortaleza airport and bus terminal for Jijoca, then connect with 4WD vehicles which take you the remaining short distance to Jericoacoara (see page 186). The journey takes a total of six hours and tickets can be bought at the airport (ask at the Ceará Tourism Information). It's easier and more comfortable to reach Jericoacoara in a minivan (they leave from in front of the Hotel **Casa Blanca**, see page 189). Transfers can be arranged in advance through any of the Jericoacoara *pousadas* or through the tourism counter at the airport. If you decide to skip Jericoacoara there are three daily buses to São Luís (see page 193) from Fortaleza (6½ hours).

International and domestic flights arrive in and depart from **Aeroporto Pinto Martins** ① *Praça Eduardo Gomes, 6 km south of the centre, T085-3392 1200*. There are flights from São Luís for those wanting to fly home from Fortaleza at the end of this trip, and international connections with destinations in Portugal and Italy. The airport has a 24-hour tourist office, T085-3477 1667, car hire, a food hall, internet facilities, bookstore, **Banco do Brasil** for exchange and **Bradesco** and **HSBC** for international ATMs. Bus No 404 runs from Praça José de Alencar in the centre to the airport, US$1.50. **Expresso Guanabara** minibuses run from the *rodoviária* and Beira Mar (US$2). Taxis to/from the centre, Avenida Beira Mar or Praia do Futuro charge a fixed fee of US$25, or US$30 at night (30 minutes, allowing for traffic).

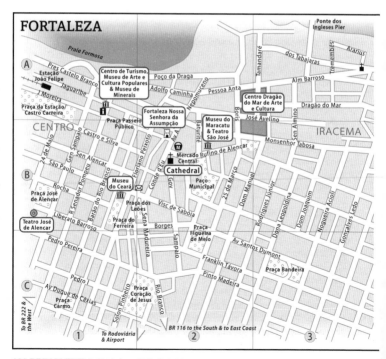

Getting around The city is spread out, with its main attractions in the centre and along the seashore; transport from one to the other can take a long time. The city bus system is efficient if a little rough; buses and vans cost US$1 per journey. The cheapest way to orientate yourself within the city is to take the 'Circular 1' (anti-clockwise) or 'Circular 2' (clockwise) buses which pass Avenida Beira Mar, the Aldeota district, the university (UFC) and cathedral via Meireles, Iracema, Centro Dragão do Mar and the Centre, US$1.50. Alternatively, take the new *Top Bus* run by **Expresso Guanabara** ① *T0800-991992, US$2.50,* an air-conditioned minibus starting at Avenida Abolição.

When driving outside the city, have a good map and be prepared to ask directions frequently as road signs are non-existent or are placed after junctions.

Tourist information The main office of the state tourism agency, **Setur** ① *Secretária do Turismo do Estado do Ceará, Av General Afonso Albuquerque Lima, Fortaleza T085-3101 4688, www.setur.ce.gov.br,* has maps and brochures and can help with hotels and tours. There are also information booths at the airport and *rodoviária,* and at the Farol de Mucuripe (old lighthouse), open 0700-1730. The **Posta Telefônica Beira Mar** ① *Av Beira Mar, almost opposite Praiano Palace Hotel,* provides information, sells *combi* tickets to Jericoacoara, and has postcards, clothes and magazines. If you have problems, contact the **tourist police** ① *R Silva Paulet 505, Aldeota, T085-3433 8171.*

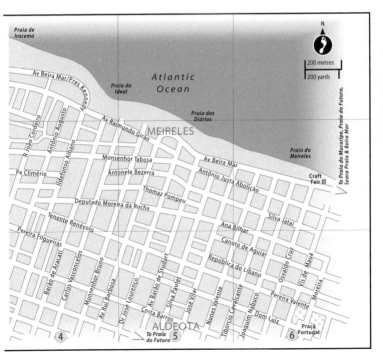

FESTIVALS
Fortaleza

6 January Epiphany.
February Ash Wednesday.
19 March São José.
July Last Sun in Jul is the **Regata Dragão do Mar**, Praia de Mucuripe, with traditional *jangada* (raft) races. During the last week of Jul, the out-of-season Salvador-style carnival, **Fortal**, takes place along Av Almte Barroso, Av Raimundo Giro and Av Beira Mar. In Caucaia, 12 km to the southeast, a **vaquejada**, traditional rodeo and country fair, takes place during the last weekend of Jul.

15 August, the local *umbanda terreiros* (churches) celebrate the **Festival of Iemanjá** on Praia do Futuro, taking over the entire beach from noon till dusk, when offerings are cast into the surf. Well worth attending (members of the public may *'pegar um passo'* – enter into an inspired religious trance – at the hands of a *pai-de-santo*). Beware of pickpockets and purse-snatchers.
Mid-Oct **Ceará Music**, a 4-day festival of Brazilian music, rock and pop in Marina Park.

Safety The city is generally safe for visitors. However, tourists should avoid the following areas: Serviluz favela between the old lighthouse (Avenida Vicente de Castro), Mucuripe and Praia do Futuro; the favela behind the railway station; the Passeio Público at night; and Avenida Abolição at its eastern (Nossa Senhora da Saúde church) and western ends.

PLACES IN FORTALEZA

Walking through the centre of Fortaleza, it is hard to ignore the city's history, which dates back to the 17th century. Pedestrian walkways radiate from the **Praça do Ferreira**, the heart of the commercial centre, and the whole area is dotted with shady green squares. The **Fortaleza Nossa Senhora da Assumpção** ① *Av Alberto Nepomuceno, T085-3255 1600, telephone in advance for permission to visit, daily 0800-1100, 1400-1700*, originally built in 1649 by the Dutch, gave the city its name. Near the fort, on Rua Dr João Moreira, is the 19th-century **Praça Passeio Público** (or Praça dos Mártires), a park with old trees and statues of Greek deities. West of here a neoclassical former prison (1866) houses a fine tourist centre, the **Centro de Turismo do Estado (Emcetur)** ① *Av Senador Pompeu 350, near the waterfront, T0800-991516, closed Sun*, with museums, theatre and craft shops. It houses the renovated **Museu de Arte e Cultura Populares** and the **Museu de Minerais** ① *T085-3212 3566*. Further west along Rua Dr João Moreira, at **Praça Castro Carreira** (commonly known as Praça da Estação), is the nicely refurbished train station, **Estação João Felipe** (1880), which runs commuter services.

The **Teatro José de Alencar** ① *Praça José de Alencar, T085-3229 1989, Mon-Fri 0800-1700, hourly tours, some English-speaking guides, US$1, Wed free*, was inaugurated in 1910 and is worth a visit. It is a magnificent iron structure imported from Scotland and decorated in neoclassical and art nouveau styles. It also houses a library and art gallery. The **Praça dos Leões** or Praça General Tibúrcio on Rua Conde D'Eu has bronze lions imported from France. Around it stand the 18th-century **Palácio da Luz** ① *T085-3231 5699*, former seat of the state government, and the **Igreja Nossa Senhora do Rosário**, built by slaves in the 18th century. Also here is the former provincial legislature, dating from 1871, which houses the **Museu do Ceará** ① *R São Paulo, next to Praça dos Leões, T085-3251 1502, Tue-Fri 0830-1730, Sat*

0830-1400, US$0.80. The museum has displays on history and anthropology. To get there, take bus marked 'Dom Luís'.

The new **cathedral** ① *Praça da Sé*, completed in 1978, in Gothic style but constructed out of concrete with beautiful stained-glass windows, stands beside the new semi-circular **Mercado Central**.

There are several worthwhile museums to visit in and around Fortaleza. The **Museu do Maracatu** ① *Rufino de Alencar 231*, at Teatro São José, has costumes of this ritual dance of African origin. The new and exciting **Centro Dragão do Mar de Arte e Cultura** ① *R Dragão do Mar 81, Praia de Iracema, T085-3488 8600, www.dragaodomar.org.br, Tue-Thu 1000-1730, Fri-Sun 1400-2130, US$0.75 for entry to each museum/gallery, free on Sun*, hosts concerts, dance performances and exhibitions of art and photography. It has various entrances, from Rua Almirante Barroso, Rua Boris, and from the junction of Monsenhor Tabosa, Dom Manuel and Castelo Branco. The latter leads directly to three museums: on street level, the **Memorial da Cultura Cearense**, with changing exhibitions; on the next floor down is an art and cultural exhibition; in the basement is an excellent audio-visual museum of **El Vaqueiro**. Also at street level is the **Livraria Livro Técnico**. There is a **planetarium** with a whispering gallery underneath. The centre also houses the **Museu de Arte Contemporânea do Ceará**. This area is very lively at night.

Some 15 km south of the centre, the **Museu Artur Ramos** ① *in the Casa de José de Alencar, Av Perimetral, Messejana, T085-3229 1898, Mon 1400-1730, Tue-Sun 0800-1200, 1400-1700*, displays artefacts of African and indigenous origin collected by the anthropologist Artur Ramos, as well as documents from the writer José de Alencar.

BEACHES

The urban beaches between Barra do Ceará (west) and Ponta do Mucuripe (east) are polluted and not suitable for swimming. Minibus day tours for other beaches, from US$6, and transfers to Jericoacoara, US$15, leave from along the seafront. The agency CPVTUR ① *Av Monsenhor Tabosa 1001, T085-3219 2511*, also runs trips.

Heading east from the centre, **Praia de Iracema** is one of the older beach suburbs, with some original early 20th-century houses. It is not much of a sunbathing beach as it has little shade or facilities and swimming is unsafe, but at night it is very lively. Of its many bars and restaurants, the **Estoril**, housed in one of the earliest buildings, has become a landmark. The Ponte Metálica or **Ponte dos Ingleses**, nearby, was built by the British Civil engineering firm, Norton Griffiths and Company, in 1921 as a commercial jetty for the port, but was never completed due to lack of funds, and re-opened as a promenade pier in imitation of English seaside piers. It was and is now a very popular spot for watching the sunset and the occasional pod of visiting dolphins.

East of Iracema, the **Avenida Beira Mar** (Avenida Presidente Kennedy) connects **Praia do Meireles** (divided into **Praia do Ideal**, **Praia dos Diários** and Praia do Meireles itself) with Volta da Jurema and Praia do Mucuripe; it is lined with high-rise buildings and most luxury hotels are located here. A *calçado* (walkway), following the palm-lined shore, becomes a night-time playground as locals promenade on foot, roller skates, skateboards and bicycles. Children ride mini-motorbikes, scooters or the 'happiness' train with its Disney characters. Take in the spectacle while sipping an *agua de coco* or *caiprinha* on the beachfront, where there are volleyball courts, bars, open-air shows and a **crafts fair** in front of the Imperial Othon Palace Hotel.

Praia do Mucuripe, 5 km east of the centre, is Fortaleza's main fishing centre, where *jangadas* (traditional rafts with triangular sails) bring in the catch; there are many restaurants serving *peixada* and other fish specialities. The symbol of this beach is the statue of Iracema, the main character of the romance by José de Alencar. From the monument there is a good view of Mucuripe's port and bay. At Mucuripe Point is a **lighthouse** built by slaves in 1846, which houses the **Museu de Fortaleza** (now sadly run down and not a safe area, according to the tourist office). There is a lookout at the new lighthouse, good for viewing the *jangadas*, which return in the late afternoon, and the sunset.

Praia do Futuro, 8 km southeast of the centre, is the most popular bathing beach. It is 8 km long with strong waves, sand dunes and freshwater showers, but no natural shade. Vendors in straw shacks serve local dishes such as crab. On Thursday nights it becomes the centre for the city's nightlife, with people enjoying live music and *forró*. The south end of the beach is known as **Caça e Pesca**; water here is polluted because of the outflow of the Rio Cocó. Praia do Futuro has few hotels or buildings because the salt-spray corrosion is among the strongest in the world.

At **Praia de Sabiaguaba**, 20 km southeast of the centre, is a small fishing village known for its seafood; the area has mangroves and is good for fishing.

Some 29 km southeast of the centre is **Praia Porto das Dunas**, a pleasant beach that is popular for watersports, such as surfing. Buggies and microlight tours can be arranged. The main attraction is **Beach Park** ① *US$20*, the largest water park in South America, with pools, water toboggans, sports fields and restaurants.

→JERICOACOARA

Jericoacoara is another of the northeast's paradise beaches that is getting spoilt. Up until the 1980s it was a magical place: a collection of little fishermen's shacks lost under towering dunes and surrounded by wonderful long, sweeping beaches. São Paulo middle-class hippies used to live here for months, surfing, dancing *forró* and smoking copious amounts of weed. Slowly Jeri began to grow. Then buggies began to race up and down the dunes – including the most delicate, those with fixed vegetation – and local villages started to become tourist attractions. In the 1980s, the Italians discovered Jeri and building began, much of it with braggadocio and little or no environmental considerations; buggies whizzed up and down from dawn to dusk like a plague of motorized flies. Today, few properties or tourism businesses are locally owned and the fishermen and their families are being sidelined and priced out of town.

That said, Jeri remains beautiful and it has a long way to go before it becomes as spoilt as Morro de São Paulo, Canoa Quebrada or Cumbuco. If careful choices are made by tourists (such as supporting local businesses, trying to speak Portuguese, participating in Brazilian culture and avoiding buggy tours and large European-run beachfront resorts), it could turn itself into an inspiring sustainable, small-scale resort. The nearby beaches offer superb conditions for kitesurfing and windsurfing – both practices that do little to damage the environment – and there is excellent walking and cycling along the long flat beaches to beauty spots like the crumbling chocolate-coloured rock arch at **Pedra Furada**. Sandboarding is popular and watching the sunset from the top of the large dune just west of town, followed by a display of capoeira on the beach, is a tradition among visitors.

ARRIVING IN JERICOACOARA

Getting there There are two direct buses a day from Fortaleza to Jijoca from where *jardineiras* (Toyota pickups) do the 45-minute transfer to Jeri. Be sure to take a *VIP* or *executivo* as the journey takes five to six hours (seven to eight hours on other buses). It is far more comfortable to take an air-conditioned minivan; these can be organized through *pousadas* in Jeri. Hotels and tour operators run two- to three-day tours from from Fortaleza. If not on a tour, 'guides' will besiege new arrivals in Jijoca with offers of buggies, or guiding cars through the tracks and dunes to Jeri for US$8. If you don't want to do this, ask if a pickup is going or contact **Francisco Nascimento** ① *O Chicão, at Posta do Dê, or T088-3669 1356*, who charges US$5 per person for the 22-km journey (30 minutes). There are connections with the rest of the state through Sobral. There are no banks in town; most *pousadas* and restaurants accept Visa but it is wise to bring plenty of cash in reais.

Moving on To get to Parnaíba (see page 190) from Jericoacoara, you need to take a Toyota to Camocim, a two-hour journey via the ferry, then an onward two-hour bus to Parnaíba. If you decide to go straight to the Lençóis Maranhenses National Park (see page 192), there are two possible ways: via a private tour running along the beaches and organized through a company, such as Eco Dunas (see page 200), or by taking a beach buggy from Jericoacoara to Camocim (via a ferry) and then a bus to Tutoia, from where there are onward connections to Barreirinhas in the Lençóis Maranhenses.

AROUND JERICOACOARA

Going west along the beach takes you through a succession of sand dunes and coconut groves; the views are beautiful. After 2 km is the beach of **Mangue Seco**, and 2 km beyond this is an arm of the ocean that separates it from **Guriú** (across the bridge), where there is a village on top of a fixed dune. There is good birdwatching here and if you wish to stay hammock space can be found. The village musician sings his own songs in the bar. It's a four-hour walk from Jericoacoara, or take a boat across the bay.

The best surfing, kitesurfing and windsurfing is 10 minutes from town on the pebbly **Praia de Malhada**, reachable either by walking east along the beach or by cutting through town. Top-quality equipment can be rented in Jeri. A 3- to 4-km walk to the east takes you to the **Pedra Furada**, a stone arch sculpted by the sea, one of the landmarks of Jeri, only accessible at low tide (check the tide tables at the **Casa do Turismo**). Swimming

is dangerous here as waves and currents are strong. In the same direction but just inland is **Serrote**, a large hill with a lighthouse on top; it is well worth walking up for the magnificent views.

The best kitesurfing and windsurfing beaches are beyond Jeri, some 15 km east of town (43 km by road via Jijoca and Caiçara), at **Praia do Preá** and **Praia de Guriú**. Both beaches are reachable on day tours for around US$50 if you have your own kitesurf. Tours including equipment (US$60) can be arranged in Jeri through www.kiteclubprea.com. There is accommodation on both beaches. At low tide on Preá, you can visit the **Pedra da Seréia**, a rock pocked with natural swimming pools.

Some of the best scenery in the area is around **Nova Tatajuba**, about 35 km west of Jerí. One Toyota a day passes through the town on the way to the ferry point at Camocim and almost all buggy tours visit. There are simple *pousadas* and restaurants and the village is far smaller and less touristy than Jeri.

Some 10 km beyond Praia do Preá (62 km by road) is the beach of **Barrinha**, with access to the picturesque **Lagoa Azul**. From here it's 10 km inland through the dunes (20 km along the road) to **Lagoa Paraíso** or **Jijoca**, a turquoise, freshwater lake, great for bathing (buggy US$10 per person).

FORTALEZA AND JERICOACOARA LISTINGS

WHERE TO STAY

North to Fortaleza

$$-$ REDE Tucum, R Pinho Pessoa, 86 Joaquim Távora, T085-3226 2476, www.tucum.org. A tourism cooperative with options for homestays and accommodation in small hotels dotted in indigenous and fishing communities, including one near Canoa Quebrada, at the delightful village of Prainha do Canto Verde (where locals still use *jangadas*). Excellent value and a very worthwhile experience.

Fortaleza

$$$$ Beira Mar, Av Beira Mar 3130, T085-4009 2000, Meireles, www.hotelbeira mar.com.br. Newly reformed hotel with some seafront rooms, others have a side view. Comfortable and safe, with a pool, 24-hr business centre with internet and parking. Good value, especially in low season.

$$$-$$ Casa Blanca, R Joaquim Alves 194, T085-3219 0909, www.casablancahoteis. com.br. The best rooms on the upper floors of this tall tower have magnificent ocean views. All are a/c and well appointed (if anony mous) and have international TV. Breakfasts are a feast and there's a tiny rooftop pool, a gym and massage service. Minivans leave from in front of the hotel to Jericoacoara and the hotel can organize transfers.

$$-$ Pousada do Suíço, R Antônio Augusto 141, Iracema, T085-3219 3873, www.pousada dosuico.com.br. A justifiably popular well kept and well run budget hotel in an excellent location near the beach. It is quiet, discreet and on one of the less noisy streets. Some rooms are more spacious than others, some have kitchens, and all have a/c, a TV and fridge. The Swiss owner runs a decent restaurant a few blocks away and can organize tours and give travel advice. Be sure to reserve mid-Oct to Feb.

Jericoacoara

$$$$ Vila Kalango, R do Instituto Chico Mendes de Conservação da Biodiversidade (ICMBio) s/n, T088-3669 2289, www.vila kalango.com.br. The smartest option in town with well-appointed rooms in stilt house cabins in a tree-filled garden set back from the beach. Lovely pool and bar area, decent restaurant and excellent facilities for kite- and windsurfers. There's a sister hotel on Praia da Preá. Shuttle buses to/from Fortaleza.

$$$-$$ Cabana Jericoacoara, R das Dunas s/n, T088-3669 2294, www.pousadacabana. com.br. A/c cabanas with duplex barn doors set in a heliconia-filled tropical garden. Each is bright and spacious with 2 singles or a double bed, boiler-fed showers and they share an attractive hammock-slung lounge area. Wi-Fi and cable TV in all rooms.

$$ Pousada Zé Patinha, R São Francisco s/n, T088-3669 2081, www.pousadaze patinha.com.br. Simple, a/c or fan-cooled tiled and plain white rooms in 2 parallel corridors. No outside windows, just overlooking the corridor. Cool in the heat of the day, quiet, with decent mattresses and locally owned. Sand- and surfboard rental.

WHAT TO DO

Buggy rides Associação dos Bugueiros, Av Principal s/n, T088-3669 2284, www.jerico acoarasite.com.br. Best-value buggy tours to sights around Jeri. Depending on distance, US$30-100 for a buggy seating up to 4 .

Kitesurfing Best beach is Preá, 20 mins south of the town by buggy. Boards are easy to hire in Jeri, either from shops in town or in Preá itself. See also www.velawindsurf.com or contact **Vila Kalango** (see above).

PARNAÍBA TO SÃO LUÍS

The magnificent Delta do Parnaíba, in the state of Piauí, is one of the largest river deltas in the world, replete with mangrove swamps and tiny islands fringed with golden beaches and home to traditional communities who seldom see tourists.

Further north along the coast is the neighbouring state of Maranhão. In the capital, São Luís, which was founded by the French but built by the Portuguese, azulejos and ornate baroque flourishes grace the elegant buildings of the colonial centre. Every Friday and Saturday night its little praças erupt to the riotous rhythms of cacuria, and in June the city becomes the backdrop for one of the most colourful spectacles in the northeast: the Bumba-Meu-Boi pageant.

To the southeast are the Lençóis Maranhenses, a 155,000-ha coastal desert of vast shifting dunes and isolated communities, cut by broad rivers and in the rainy season (between June and September), pocked with lakes, whose clear reflective waters are a vivid sky blue against brilliant white sand.

→PARNAÍBA AND AROUND

Parnaíba (population 133,000) makes a good break in the journey north. It's a relaxed, friendly place, with a pretty colonial centre overlooking the Parnaíba river. If crossing the delta, buy all provisions here. There are beaches at **Luís Correia**, 14 km from Parnaíba, with radioactive sands. About 18 km from Parnaíba is **Pedra do Sal**, with dark blue lagoons and palm trees. At **Lagoa de Portinho**, 12 km from Parnaíba, there are bungalows, a bar, restaurant and canoes for hire; it is possible to camp. **Praia do Coqueiro** is a small fishing village with natural pools formed at low tide. Seafood is good at **Alô Brasil** and **Bar da Cota**.

ARRIVING IN PARNAÍBA
Getting there Parnaíba is an eight-hour bus journey from Fortaleza (US$60). If travelling from Jericoacoara, take a Toyota to Camocim, a two-hour journey via the ferry (US$1 per foot passenger) across the river separating Ceará and Piauí then an onward two-hour bus to Parnaíba (US$12).

Buses marked Praça João Luíz run to the centre from the **rodoviária** ① *5 km south of centre on BR-343, T086-3323 7300*; taxi US$6. About 14 km from the town centre, on the Parnaíba river, is the Porto dos Tatus, where boats leave for the delta (see page 191).

Moving on To get to the Parque Nacional Lençóis Maranhenses (see page 192), take a bus from Parnaíba via Barreirinhas or a minivan or bus via Tutóia, Paulino Neves and Barreirinhas. Alternatively, you can get a bus straight to São Luís (see page 193) and arrange bus or private transfer from there.

Tourist information For tourist information contact **Piemtur** ① *R Dr Oscar Clark 575, T086-3321 1532*; there is another branch at **Porto da Barca**, a pleasant shopping and entertainment complex in the colonial centre, with several good restaurants and an open-air bar on the riverside.

DELTA DO PARNAÍBA

The Delta do Parnaíba, which separates Piauí from Tutóia (see page 193) and the spectacular Lençóis Maranhenses (see page 192) in neighbouring Maranhão, is one of the largest river deltas in the world. It's a watery labyrinth of mangroves, broad rivers and narrow creeks, with unspoilt tropical islands fringed by gorgeous deserted beaches. The interiors of these islands are home to largely unstudied wildlife, including many rare birds, and traditional Caiçara fishing communities, who seldom see tourists. Renting hammock space with them is straightforward and simple makeshift *pousada* accommodation can be arranged. Many people in this region live as they have done for generations, in adobe houses, on a diet of fresh fish cooked in baked-earth ovens. Illiteracy is the norm. There is no mains electricity and the nearest shopping is at Parnaíba or Tutóia.

Arriving at the Delta do Parnaíba Crossing the delta is no longer possible by public ferry, but it's possible to charter a launch (up to 12 people, US$175) in Tutóia or at Porto dos Tatus (also called Porto da Barca), 10 km north of Parnaíba. Recommended boatmen include **Capitão Báu** ① *T086-3323 0145, T086-8831 9581 (mob)*. Alternatively, take a boat from Parnaíba to the crab-fishing village of Morro do Meio on Ilha das Canarias (Monday at high tide, usually in the small hours). It is sometimes possible to hitch a lift from Ilha das Canarias to Tutóia with a crab fisherman. It's more interesting and better value to cross the delta rather than returning to the same place, but allow plenty of time.

Tours can be arranged from Parnaíba for US$30-50 per person (minimum four people) with **Delta do Rio Parnaíba** ① *Porto das Barcas 13, Parnaíba, T086-3321 1969, www.deltadorioparnaiba.com.br*. The company also offers excursions to other locations in Piauí and Maranhão states. The Delta do Parnaiba can be visited as part of a tour between Jericoacoara and the Lençóis Maranhenses, with **Eco Dunas** (see page 200). Day trips also run from Porto dos Tatus, either on a huge boat full of noisy people or a smaller launch. The former include food and drink and cost around US$15 per person. The latter are by charter only (US$250-300 for up to six).

Northeastern Brazil's windswept coast is broken by extensive dunes all the way from Natal to the Amazon. In eastern Maranhão they become so vast that they form a coastal desert stretching for some 140 km between Tutóia on the Delta do Parnaíba and Primeira Cruz, east of São Luís. The Parque Nacional Lençóis Maranhenses, which encloses only a part of the *lençóis*, covers an area of 1550 sq km. The sand extends up to 50 km inland and is advancing by as much as 200 m a year. Dumped by the sea and blown by the wind, it forms ridges 50 m high in long flowing patterns that change constantly. From the air the undulating, talcum powder-white dunes look like giant wrinkled bed sheets ('lençóis' in Portugese). Between December and June the dunes are pocked with freshwater lakes that shine a brilliant blue under the tropical sky and provide a startling contrast with the brilliant white sand.

The coast of the Lençóis Maranhenses provides a refuge for severely endangered species including manatee. Leatherback and green turtles come here to lay their eggs in late summer; while in the forests and scrubland around the Rio Preguiças there are resident puma, jaguar and spectacled caiman. The Lençóis are home to numerous rare species of fish including the South American lungfish, which cocoon themselves in moist mud under the seasonally flooded lake beds in the dry, and shoals of huge game fish like *camurupim* (tarpon) live in the estuaries and rivers. The dunes are a breeding ground for migratory birds such as the lesser yellowlegs, which come all the way from the Arctic to feed here. Recent studies have shown the sparse vegetation to include grasses that are unknown elsewhere.

Excavations begun in 1995 on the supposed site of a Jesuit settlement which, according to local rumour, was buried intact by a sandstorm.

The *lençóis* are not difficult to visit. Travellers who have a few days to spare are rewarded by an amazing panorama of dunes reaching from horizon to horizon, deserted beaches washed by a powerful surf, boat rides on the aptly named **Rio Preguiça** (Lazy River), and tiny, quiet towns and hamlets where strangers are still a relative novelty.

ARRIVING IN PARQUE NACIONAL LENÇÓIS MARANHENSES

Getting there and moving on From the Delta do Parnaíba there is Toyota transport to Paulino Neves via the scruffy port town of Tutóia with further connections west to Barreirinhas – the most scenic and adventurous route, sadly blighted by litter – mainly from wind-blown plastic bags around Tutoia itself. There are also direct buses between Parnaíba town and Barreirinhas.

From Barreirinhas it's easy to reach São Luís (see page 193) by bus (four daily, four hours, US$7); in fact, you could choose to visit the Lençóis Maranhenses as a trip from São Luís by bus or on one of numerous transit combis and Toyotas bookable through São Luís hotels.

VISITING PARQUE NACIONAL LENÇÓIS MARANHENSES

The *lençóis* are divided into two areas. To the west of Rio Preguiça is the park proper and the **Grandes Lençóis**, which stretch between Ponta Verde in the far west and the town of **Barreirinhas** on the banks of the Preguiça. Barreirinhas is the tourist capital for the region and has plenty of *pousadas* and restaurants and tour operators, such as **Eco Dunas**, offering trips into the park. From here it is easy to arrange tours and transfers along the Rio Preguiça both up and downstream and onwards through the Delta do Parnaíba to Jericoacoara.

The dunes east of the Rio Preguiça form the **Pequenos Lençóis**, which extend to **Tutóia**. These are easier to travel through than the Grandes Lençóis but less easy to visit on an organized tour. **Paulino Neves**, a town rather than a hamlet on the Rio Cangata, is just south of a series of large dunes at the eastern end of the *lençóis*.

There are several small, friendly settlements in the Pequenos Lençóis. Most lie on the Rio Preguiça. The two-shack town of **Vassouras** is literally at the feet of the *lençóis*; its make-shift huts are watched over by a spectacular, looming dune whose crest affords wonderful views. Further downstream at **Mandacaru** there is a lighthouse with great views out over the coast and some craft shops selling Buriti palm-weave work and carvings. **Atins** and **Caburé** are miniature beach resorts sandwiched between a rough and windy Atlantic and the lazy blue waters of the Preguiça. Both are surrounded by a bleak sea of sand.

You can walk into parts of the Grandes Lençóis from Atins and into the Pequenos Lençóis from Caburé (see below). Many of the overland tours from Jericoacoara finish in Caburé. Be careful of broken glass – especially in Caburé where rubbish is buried rather than collected.

TRAVERSING THE PEQUENOS LENÇÓIS

It is possible to walk or cycle along the coast in front of the Pequenos Lençóis between **Caburé** and **Tutóia** in either direction; allow about three days. Camping is permitted, but you must take all supplies with you including water, since some dune lakes are salty. The area is very remote and you may not see another person for the duration of the walk. Because of the hot and sandy conditions, this is a punitive trek, only for the very hardy. Do not try the treacherous hike inland across the dunes or a hike into the Grandes Lençóis without a guide. The dunes are disorientating and there have been a number of cases of hikers becoming lost and dying of heat exposure or starvation.

→SÃO LUÍS

The capital and port of Maranhão state, founded in 1612 by the French and named after St Louis of France, stands upon São Luís island between the bays of São Marcos and São José. It's a beautiful city (population 870,000) that rivals Recife and Salvador for colonial charm and, following extensive refurbishment, it is in better condition than both of them. Like those cities, São Luís was a slaving port, initially for indigenous Amazonians who were brought here in huge numbers to grow sugar cane, and subsequently for Africans. São Luís retains an African identity almost as strong as Salvador and Recife. The city is as Amazonian as it is northeastern and is subject to heavy tropical rains. However, a large proportion of the surrounding deep forest has been cut down to be replaced by *babaçu* palms, the nuts and oils of which are the state's most important products.

ARRIVING IN SÃO LUÍS

Getting there From Barreirinhas and the Parque Nacional Lençóis Maranhenses it's a four-hour bus ride on a paved road to São Luís (four daily, US$7). From the **rodoviária** ① *12 km from the centre on the airport road*, the bus marked 'Rodoviária via Alemanha' runs to Praça João Lisboa in the centre (US$1).

Alternatively, you can fly from Parnaíba or from Fortaleza direct to São Luís' **Marechal Cunha Machado airport** ① *13 km from centre, Av Santos Dumont, T098-3217 6100*, and then visit the Lençóis Maranhenses from there. Gol and Tam have offices in the terminal, there is car rental, a tourist office (daily 0800-2200), cyber-café, a **Banco do Brasil** and an office for the Lençóis Maranhenses tour company **Eco Dunas**. *Colectivo* minivans run from outside the terminal to Praça Deodoro in the city centre (every 40 minutes until 2200, US$1, one hour). A taxi to the centre costs US$20 but it's cheaper to call a radio taxi, T098-3232 3232, US$12.

Ferries cross the bay to **Alcântara** (see page 198) from the São Luís docks, **Terminal Hidroviário** ① *Rampa Campos Mello, Cais da Praia Grande, US$4 foot passenger, US$25 car*. To check ferry times call T098-3222 8431.

Moving on If this is the end of your trip São Luís' airport has frequent connecting flights to Fortaleza and Natal for the flight home.

Tourist information Central de Servicos Turísticos ① *Praça Benedito Leite, T098-3212 6211, www.turismo.ma.gov.br*, and São Luís Turismo ① *www.saoluisturismo.com.br*, have useful websites. Also see http://saoluis-ma.com.br. Look out for Corbis photographer Barnabás Bosshart's masterfully photographed map-guides to São Luís and Alcântara.

PLACES IN SÃO LUÍS

The old part of the city, on very hilly ground with many steep streets, has been beautifully restored and is replete with colonial art nouveau and art deco buildings. The damp climate encouraged the use of ceramic *azulejo* tiles for exterior walls. *Azulejos* are a common sight in Portugal but their civic use is relatively rare in Brazil; São Luís displays a greater quantity and variety than anywhere else in the country. Most of the tiles are Portuguese (particularly from Porto), with a handful of print designs from Holland and France.

A good place to start a tour of the centre is **Avenida Dom Pedro II**. This was the heart of the original Tupinambá island village of Upaon Açu. When the French arrived in 1612, captained by Daniel de la Touche, they planted a huge wooden cross in the ground and, with a solemn Mass, decreed the land for France. La Touche renamed the village after Louis XIII, the emperor of France, and declared it the capital of the new land of 'France Equinoxiale' (Equinoctial France). There is a bust of La Touche in the 17th-century **Palácio de la Ravardière** ① *Av Dom Pedro II s/n, T089-3212-0800, Mon-Fri 0800-1800*.

Part of the original wall of the French fort still remains in the bulwarks of the **Palácio dos Leões** ① *Av Dom Pedro II, T089-3214 8638, Mon, Wed and Fri 1500-1800, US$3*, which was extensively embellished by the Portuguese after they re-conquered the city in 1615. When Maranhão became part of the newly independent Brazil in the 19th century, the palace was taken over by the governor. The rooms are furnished with period antiques from Portugal, France and the UK, with a series of paintings by artists including Vitor Meirelles, who was responsible for Imperial Brazil's most famous painting: *A Batalha de Guararapes*. The building is replete with stunning tropcial dark *jacarandá* wood and light *cerejeira* polished floors; visitors are required to use carpet slippers. There are marvellous views from the terrace.

Together with neighbouring Belém, Portuguese São Luís was the centre of a voracious slave trade. *Banderiante* expeditions roamed far into the interior capturing indigenous men, murdering their wives and children and bringing the prisoners to Maranhão to work on the cane fields. Entire Amazon civilizations, including the *Omagua*, were wiped-out this way. The Jesuits were appalled by the cruelty and their most famous politician-priest, Antônio Vieira (see box, page 94), came to São Luís as a missionary to protest against the slave trade in 1653: "At what a different price the devil buys souls today compared with what he used to offer for them! There is no market in the world where the devil can get them more cheaply than in our own land … In Maranhão … what a cheap market! An Indian for a soul! That Indian will be your slave for the few days that he lives; but your soul will be enslaved for eternity… Break the chains of injustice and free those whom you hold captive and oppressed! … It is better to live from your own sweat than from the blood of others". The naves of São Luís's churches once

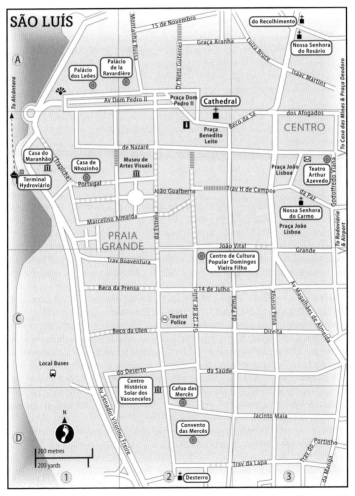

SÃO LUÍS

A
Palácio dos Leões
Palácio de la Ravardière
15 de Novembro
Montanha Russa
Dr Neto Guterres
Graça Aranha
Luiza Bruce
do Recolhimento
Nossa Senhora do Rosário
Isaac Martins

Av Dom Pedro II
Praça Dom Pedro II
Cathedral
Beco da Sé
dos Afogados
CENTRO
To Casa das Minas & Praça Deodoro

To Alcântara

Casa do Maranhão
Terminal Hydroviário
Casa de Nhozinho
Museu de Artes Visuais
de Nazaré
Praça Benedito Leite

Portugal
João Gualberto
Trav H de Campos
Praça João Lisboa
Teatro Arthur Azevedo
da Paz

B
Marcelino Almeida
PRAIA GRANDE
da Estrela
Nossa Senhora do Carmo
Praça João Lisboa

To Rodoviária & Airport

Godolfredo Viana

Trav Boaventura
João Vital
Centro de Cultura Popular Domingos Vieira Filho
Grande
Av Magalhães de Almeida

Beco da Prensa
14 de Julho
da Palma
Afonso Pena

C
Tourist Police
Beco da Ulen
Direita

GZ (28 de Julho)

Local Buses
do Deserto
da Saúde

Centro Histórico Solar dos Vasconcelos
Cafua das Mercês
Av Senador Vitorino Freire

N
Convento das Mercês
Jacinto Maia

D
200 metres
200 yards
Portinho

Trav da Lapa
Trav do Manga

1   2   Desterro   3

ON THE ROAD

Bumba-Meu-Boi

Throughout the month of June the streets of São Luís are alive to the sound of *tambores* and dancers recreating the legend of Catirina, Pai Francisco and his master's bull. Although this mixture of African, indigenous and Portuguese traditions exists throughout the north, it is in Maranhão that it is most developed, with around 100 groups in São Luís alone. Here there are various styles called *sotaques*, which have different costumes, dances, instruments and *toadas*. These are Boi de Matraca da Ilha and Boi de Pindaré, both accompanied by small percussion instruments called *matracas*, Boi de Zabumba marked by the use of a type of drum, and Boi de Orquestra accompanied by string and wind instruments. Although there are presentations throughout June the highlights are the 24th (São João) and the 29th (São Pedro) with the closing ceremony lasting throughout the 30th (São Marçal), particularly in the *bairro* João Paulo. The shows take place in an *arraial*, which are found all over the city, with the ones at Projeto Reviver and Ceprama being more geared towards tourists (however be aware that a livelier more authentic atmosphere is to be found elsewhere in other *bairro*, such as Madre Deus). The Centro de Cultura Popular Domingos Vieira Filho at Rua do Giz 221, Praia Grande is the place to learn more about these variations as well as many other local festivals and traditions such as Tambor de Crioula or Cacuriá, both sensual dances derived from Africa. A good location to see these dances and capoeira practised is *Labouarte*, Rua Jansen Muller, Centro (Cacuriá de Dona Tetê is particularly recommended, with participation encouraged).

---

echoed with his hell fire sermons, including the simple **Catedral da Sé** ① *Praça Dom Pedro II, s/n, T098-3222 7380, daily 0800-1900, free* (1629), with its beautiful 19th-century baroque altarpiece, **Nossa Senhora do Carmo** ① *Praça João Lisboa 350, T098-3222 6104, daily 0700-1115 and 1430-1800, free* (1627), which has an extraordinary, elaborate façade, and the **Igreja do Desterro** ① *Largo do Desterro s/n, daily 0800-1130 and 1500-1830, free*, which was perhaps the first church built in the city. Vieira was eventually driven out of the city and went to Pará where he met with similar failure.

Before he left, Vieira inaugurated the **Convento das Mercês** ① *R da Palma 506, T098-3211 0062, Mon-Fri 0800-1800, Sat 0800-1400*, which houses copies of his 17th-century sermons, along with numerous rare Portuguese and French books (available on request). The main body of the convent is given over to exhibits devoted to Brazilian presidency of Jose Sarney, a former Maranhão senator of dubious repute, whose dynasty continues to rule over Brazil's poorest state with an iron hand, and reap the benefits.

Miraculously some indigenous groups managed to avoid the ravages of the slave trade and still survive in Maranhão. Their cultures are touched upon, from an old-fashioned anthropological perspective, in the **Casa de Nhozinho** ① *R dos Portugueses s/n, T098-3218 9951, 0900-1900, free*. There are also exhibitions devoted to Maranhão *caboclo* life. Nhozinho, who came from Curupuru and gives the house its name, was a famous local wooden toy maker in the mid-20th century.

When the indigenous people died from exhaustion and the slave trade ran dry, Maranhão and the rest of Brazil turned to Africa for their slaves, thus beginning the world's largest skin trade. Like Salvador and Recife, the strong African heritage is celebrated most powerfully in the city's exuberant music and festivals. São Luís is famous for reggae, but this is just the commercial tip of a huge musical iceberg. The exuberance and variety of music can be sampled on any weekend night throughout the year with *cacuriá* dancing and live shows, but becomes most obvious in May and June during the local festivals of **Bumba-Me-Boi** in São Luís, and the syncretistic **Festo do Divino** in Alcântara.

The **Centro de Cultura Popular Domingos Vieira Filho (Casa da Festa)** ① *R do Giz 225, T098-3218 9924, Tue-Sun 0900-1900*, has exhibitions on the **Festa do Divino**, together with the African-Brazilian *Tambor-de-Mina* spirit religion (similar to *candomblé*), and Christmas festivities. The old customs building, **Casa do Maranhão** ① *R do Trapiche s/n, Praia Grande, on the waterfront at the far end of R Portugal*, houses a museum devoted to the **Bumba-Meu-Boi** festival (see box, page 196) and Maranhão music. Downstairs is an exhibition hall with artefacts, costumes and video shows of previous Bumba festivals. Upstairs is a series of rooms devoted to a different Bumba-Meu-Boi African-Brazilian rhythm and instruments associated with the festival.

The centre of the African slave trade in the city was the **Cafua das Mercês** ① *R Jacinto Maia 54, Praia Grande, Mon-Fri 0900-1800*. It is now a museum of African-Brazilian culture with an extensive collection of musical and religious instruments, clothing and cultural artefacts. The **Casa das Minas** ① *R do Sol 302, T098-3221 4537, Tue-Sun 0900-1800*, is one of the oldest sacred spaces in Brazil for African-Brazilian religions and is an important centre of black culture in São Luís.

There are numerous other buildings of interest. Although the prettiest and liveliest colonial streets are **Rua Portugal** and **Rua do Giz** (28 de Julho), it is Caixa Econômica Federal in the 19th-century **Edifício São Luís** ① *R da Nazare at R do Egíto*, that preserves what is probably the largest *azulejo*-fronted building in the Americas. It now houses a bank. The **Teatro Arthur de Azevedo** ① *R do Sol 180, T089-3232 0299, daily 1500-2000 or when there are shows*, is a very handsome 19th-century theatre restored to its original spendour in the 1990s. Some of the city's best performances are held here. The **Centro Histórico Solar dos Vasconcelos** ① *R da Estrela 462, Praia Grande, T098-3231 9075, Mon-Fri 0800-1900, Sat and Sun 0900-1900, free*, is a fine colonial town house devoted to the history of the city with many interesting paintings, photographs and exhibits. The first floor of the **Museu de Artes Visuais** ① *R Portugal 293, Praia Grande, T098-3231 6766, Tue-Fri 0900-1900, Sat and Sun 0900-1800*, has a collection of some of the city's most precious and intricate European *azulejos*, mostly from Portugal but with some pieces from England, Holland and Belgium. Upstairs is a collection of important Brazilian art including pieces by Tarsila do Amaral, Cícero Dias and Alfredo Volpi.

→AROUND SÃO LUÍS

Calhau is a huge beach, 10 km away. **Ponta D'Areia** is nearer to São Luís but more crowded. **Raposa**, a fishing village built on stilts, is a good place to buy handicrafts; there are a few places to stay on Avenida Principal. To get there, take a bus from the Mercado Central in São Luís (one hour with Viação Santa Maria, every 30 minutes). Another fishing village, **São José de Ribamar**, has a church dedicated to the patron saint and is a centre for *romeiros* in September. Many bars on the seafront serve local specialities such as fried stonefish. It is a 30-minute bus ride with **Maranhense** from the market in São Luís.

ALCÂNTARA

The former state capital, Alcântara (population 22,000), is on the muddy mainland bay of São Marcos, 22 km by boat from São Luís across the turbid Rio Bacanga. It's a sleepy, but beautifully preserved colonial town with one of the largest and least modified groups of 17th- and 18th-century colonial buildings in Brazil, whose terracotta roofs and brightly painted façades sit under a baking sun. The town is another of Maranhão's World Heritage sites. During the sugar boom, Alcântara was the preferred retreat of Portuguese plantation owners. The crop was initially harvested by enslaved Indians captured from the Amazon. Most were wiped out by cruelty and disease in the 17th century, and it is the descendants of the African slaves brought in to replace their numbers who give contemporary Alcântara its distinctive Afro-Brazilian culture and cuisine. The town is reknowned for its *cacuriá* dancing (from which lambada is derived), its spicy food and the practice of the *candomblé* spirit religion.

Arriving in Alcântara Launches run to Alcântara from the **Terminal Hidroviário** ⓘ *Rampa Campos Mello, Cais da Praia Grande, São Luís*, at around 0700 and 0930 (US$20), returning to São Luís at about 1630, depending on the tide. The journey takes about an hour. The sea can be very rough between September and December. Catamaran tours can be booked in São Luís (see page 200).

Places in Alcântara The town clusters around a pretty grassy square called the **Praça da Matriz**, which retains a pillory at its centre. Some 50 of the city's few hundred houses, civic buildings and churches are protected by the federal heritage bureau, IPHAN, and many have been restored. The **Museu Histórico** ⓘ *Praça da Matriz, s/n, daily 0900-1400*, houses some fine *azulejos* and colonial miscellanea, including a bed which was built especially for a

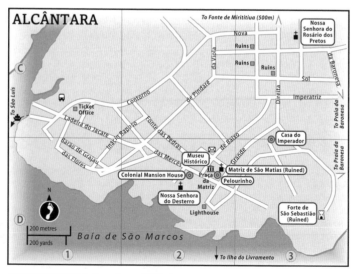

scheduled, but cancelled, visit by the Emperor Dom Pedro. It has never been slept in. Another small museum, the **Casa Histórica** ① *Praça da Matriz, Mon-Fri 1000-1600*, has some 18th-century English furniture and porcelain imported by the Alcântara aristocracy. There is a ruined fort on the southern edges of town and a number of crumbling churches and mansions, These include the 17th-century **Igreja de Nossa Senhora do Carmo** ① *Praça da Matriz, Mon-Fri 0800-1300, 1400-1800, Sat-Sun 0900-1400, free*, with a finely carved rococo interior, the ruined **Matriz de São Matias** (1648), and colonial mansions, such as the **Casa** and **Segunda Casa do Imperador**. These sit alongside numerous old plantation aristocracy mansions with blue, Portuguese-tile façades.

Canoe trips go to **Ilha do Livramento**, where there are good beaches and walks around the coast. It can be muddy after rain, and watch out for mosquitoes after dark. A rocket-launching site has been built nearby.

PARNAÍBA TO SÃO LUÍS LISTINGS

WHERE TO STAY

Parnaíba
\$\$ Pousada Chalé Suiço, Av Padre R J
Vieira 448, Fátima, T086-3321 3026,
www.chale suico.com.br. Cheaper without
a/c or breakfast, bar, laundry, pool, tours
arranged on the Delta do Parnaíba, windsurfing, sand-boarding, buggies and bikes.

Lençóis Maranhenses
\$\$\$ Buriti, R Inácio Lins s/n, Barreirinhas,
T098-3349 1800, www.pousadadoburiti.
com.br. Corridors of large, plain rooms with
concrete terraces near a pool and breakfast
area. Simple but the best in the centre of town.
\$\$ Belo Horizonte, R Joaquim Soeiro de
Carvalho 245, T098-3499 0054, www.bhmirante.
com.br. Well-kept tiled and whitewashed
rooms near the central square. The quietest are
at the front. Good service from the welcoming
owner, Albino and a pleasant rooftop breakfast
area. Sister *pousada* in Caburé.

\$ Pousada do Paulo (aka **Pousada Lençóis
de Areia**), Praia do Caburé, T098-9143 4668.
Well-kept rooms for up to 4. The owner was
the first to settle here and named the town
after a local bird. Best food in the village.
Inky black and full of stars at night. Vast,
sweeping Atlantic beach (watch out for glass).
There are other options in town and rooms
are always available outside peak season.

São Luís
\$\$\$ Quality São Luís Hotel, Praça Dom
Pedro II 299, T098-2109 3500, www.atlantica
hotels.com.br. A newly refurbished 1960s
grand dame with plain rooms, the best of
which have sea views. Business facilities,
pool and gym.
\$\$ Portas da Amazônia, R do Giz 129,
T098-3222 9937, www.portasdaamazonia.
com.br. Tastefully converted wood-floor
rooms in a colonial building in the centre.

WHAT TO DO

Visiting the Lençóis Maranhenses
Eco Dunas, T098-3349 0545, R Inácio Lins
164, Bareirinhas, www.ecodunas.tur.br.
The best option for tours of Lençóis
Maranhenses, the delta and tours all the
way from São Luís to Jericoacoara or vice
versa. Excellent guides, infrastructure and
organization. English spoken and flights
organized. Can arrange wonderful scenic
flights over the Lençóis with pilot Amirton
for around US$150. The company also run
1-day tours around São Luis, trips to the
Parque Nacional das Sete Cidades and visits
to Alcântara. Organized and professional.

Visiting Alcântâra
It's worth taking a half day to visit Alcântâra,
the former state capital of Maranhão just

across the estuary. It's a sleepy but, beautifully preserved colonial town with some
impressive 17th- and 18th-century buildings
sitting next to crumbling mansions and
churches, neglected after the town lost its
fortunes with the collapse of the sugar trade
in the 19th century. The vegetation is
notably more exuberant and lush, feeling
more Amazonian than northeast Brazilian.
Phylipi, T098-8118 1710, phylipi@hot
mail.com. Very good guide for São Luís
and Alcântara. Fluent English and French.
US$35 for a 2- to 3-hr city centre tour.
Around US$100/day for groups of up to 10.
Excellent guided tours of the Bumba-Meu-
Boi celebrations. Trips also run to the Lençóis
Maranhenses; also offers transfers to the
Delta do Parnaíba and Jericoacoara.

DREAM TRIP 4:
São Paulo→Iguaçu→Pantanal→Amazon 21 days

São Paulo 2 nights, page 203

Iguaçu Falls 2 nights, page 225
Bus/flight from São Paulo (16-20 hrs/
1 hr 20 mins) to Foz do Iguaçu

SOUTHERN PANTANAL

Campo Grande Transfer, page 237
Bus from Foz do Iguaçu via Cascaval
(12 hrs) or flight via São Paulo (2 flights
1 hr 20 mins each)

Bonito 3 nights, page 238
Bus from Campo Grande (3½ hrs), or
bus/private transfer from Miranda (3½ hrs)

Miranda 3 nights, page 240
Bus from Campo Grande (2½ hrs), or
bus/private transfer from Bonito (3½ hrs)

NORTHERN PANTANAL

Cuiabá 3 nights, page 242
Flight from Foz do Iguaçu (2 hrs) or bus
from Campo Grande (at least 12 hrs)

Chapada dos Guimarães Day trip,
page 245
Bus from Cuiabá (1½ hrs), self-drive or
organized tour

Nobres and Bom Jardim 2 nights,
page 246
Organized tour or bus from Cuiabá (2½ hrs)

Cristalino Rainforest Reserve 2 nights,
page 247
Flight (80 mins) or bus (12 hrs) from Cuiabá
to Alta Floresta

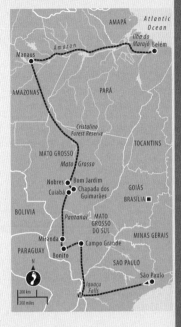

AMAZON

Manaus 3 nights, page 253
Flight from Campo Grande (4-5 hrs
depending on plane change) or Cuiabá (2 hrs)

Belém 1 night, page 262
Boat from Manaus via Santarém (4 days)

GOING FURTHER

There are flights from Manaus and Belém
to Fortaleza, Rio, São Paulo and other state
capitals for your flight home. A possible
extension to this itinerary would be to
spend a few days relaxing on a beach near
Fortaleza (page 185) before flying home.

DREAM TRIP 4
São Paulo→Iguaçu→Pantanal→Amazon

Following in the footsteps of wildlife film crews and intrepid explorers, this route takes you into the heart of Brazil's wild interior, where sketchy transport infrastructure is more than made up for by spectacular scenery and the chance to see rare wildlife. It begins in the concrete jungles of São Paulo, South America's largest city, where you will find the best restaurants, shopping and upmarket nightlife in Brazil.

It's a short flight or a long bus ride from here to the Iguaçu Falls, a sheet of water twice as high and many times wider than Niagara set in a vast rainforest national park. From here the route heads northwest to the Pantanal, the world's largest wetland and the best place in the Americas to see wildlife. Dozens of caiman bask on the banks of the Pantanal's rivers, the air is filled with a bewildering array of birds and the open savannahs and low forests offer the best chance of seeing jaguars in South America. Head to the southern Pantanal to stay in a traditional ranch house, meet indigenous Brazilians and snorkel in clear-water rivers in Bonito; make your way to the northern Pantanal if you're determined to see a jaguar at all costs.

It's another flight from the Pantanal to the Amazon and the land-locked city of Manaus, where tour companies run trips into the rainforest – based on cruise boats or in jungle lodges. Boats leave from the city for Belém, a Portuguese colonial city set in the mouth of the great river and offering access to the wilds of Marajó island where the police patrol the rainforest-backed beaches on water buffaloes.

From Belém, Fortaleza is a relatively short hop and there are onward connections to Europe through Lisbon or Italy. Americans can fly to destinations throughout the USA from Fortaleza with Delta via Atlanta.

SÃO PAULO

São Paulo is as famous for its ugliness as Rio is for its beauty. But while Rio looks marvellous from a distance and less than perfect close to, São Paulo is the opposite. Restaurants, shops, hotels and nightlife here are infinitely better than in Rio. And, while wandering and browsing in plush neighbourhoods such as Jardins, it is even possible to forget that few cities in the world have quite so much relentless concrete punctuated with quite so few green spaces; or have rivers quite so disgracefully polluted as the Tietê. Marlene Dietrich perhaps summed it up when she said – "Rio is a beauty – but São Paulo; ah … São Paulo is a city."

São Paulo is vast (population 18-20 million) and can feel intimidating on first arrival. But this is a city of separate neighbourhoods, only a few of which are interesting for visitors, and once you have your base it is easy to navigate. São Paulo is the intellectual capital of Brazil. Those who don't flinch at the city's size and leave, who are instead prepared to spend time (and money) here, and who get to know Paulistanos, are seldom disappointed and often end up preferring the city to Rio. Nowhere in Brazil is better for concerts, clubs, theatre, ballet, classical music, all-round nightlife, restaurants and beautifully designed hotels. You will not be seen as a gringo in São Paulo, and the city is safer than Rio if you avoid the centre after dark and the outlying favelas (which are impossible to stumble across).

ARRIVING IN SÃO PAULO

GETTING THERE

Air São Paulo is Brazil's main international entry point and its domestic transport hub. There are three airports, the main international airport at Guarulhos in the suburbs, Congonhas airport near the city centre (which is principally domestic) and Campinas airport in the commuter town of Campinas some 95 km from São Paulo.

Nearly all international flights and many of the cheapest internal flights arrive at **Guarulhos airport** ① *Guarulhos, 25 km northeast of the city, T011-2445 2945, www.infraero.gov.br*, officially known as **Cumbica**. There are plenty of banks and money changers in the arrivals hall, open daily 0800-2200, and cafés, restaurants and gift shops on the second floor and arrivals lobby. There is a post office on the third floor of Asa A. Tourist information, including city and regional city maps and copies of the entertainment section from the Folha de São Paulo newspaper with current listings, is available from **Secretaria de Esportes e Turismo (SET)** ① *ground floor of both terminals, Mon-Fri 0730-2200, Sat, Sun and holidays 0900-2100.*

Airport taxis charge US$65 to the centre and operate on a ticket system: go to the second booth on leaving the terminal and book a co-op taxi at the Taxi Comum counter; these are the best value. **Guarucoop** ① *T011-6440 7070, 24 hrs, www.aeroportoguarulhos.net*, is a leading, safe radio taxi company operating from the airport. The following **Emtu buses** ① *www.emtu.sp.gov.br/aeroporto*, run every 30-45 minutes (depending on the bus line) from Guarulhos between 0545 and 2215, to the following locations: **Nos 257 and 299** – Guarulhos to Metrô Tatuape (for the red line and connections to the centre), US$2; **No 258** for Congonhas airport via Avenida 23 de Maio and Avenida Rubem Berta, US$15; **No 259** for the Praça da República via Luz and Avenida Tiradentes, US$15; **No 316** for the principal hotels around Paulista and Jardins via Avenida Paulista, Rua Haddock Lobo and Rua Augusta, US$15; **No 437** for Itaím and Avenida Brigadeiro Faria Lima in the new business district, via Avenida Nove de Julho and Avenida Presidente Juscelino Kubitschek; and No 472 for the Barra Funda Rodoviária and metrô station via the Rodoviária Tiete. A full timetable for each line with precise leaving times is listed on the website. **Airport Bus Service Pássaro Marron** ① *T0800-285 3047, www.airportbusservice.com.br*, also run buses between the airport, the city centre, *rodoviária*, Congonhas airport, Avenida Paulista and Jardins hotels, Avenida Faria Lima, metrô Tatuape, *rodoviária* Tietê and the Praca da República. Buses leave every 10 minutes from 0500-0200 costing US$12.50, children under five free. All are air conditioned and a free paper and bottle of water is provided for the journey. They also run a service directly from the airport to Ubatuba and São Sebastião (for Ilhabela). Full details of this and other services are listed on their website. The company have waiting rooms in terminals 1 and 2 at Guarulhos – look for their distinctive red and blue logo or ask at the tour information desk if you can't find the lounge.

Flights with the Brazilian franchise of the US budget airline, **Azul** ① *www.voeazul. com.br*, have begun to run from **Viracopos airport** in the city of **Campinas** just under 100 km from São Paulo, which the company cheekily calls São Paulo Campinas airport. Fares are very competitive and the company runs a bus connection between Campinas and São Paulo which connects with the flights. Azul buses leave from Terminal Barra Funda and Shopping Eldorado (Estação CPTM Hebraica Rebouças) around every 30 minutes – details on website.

The domestic airport, **Congonhas** ① *Av Washington Luiz, 7 km south of the centre, 5 km from Jardins, T011-5090 9000, www.aeroportocongonhas.net*, is used for the Rio–São Paulo shuttle and other domestic services. A taxi to the city centre or Jardins costs about US$30.

MOVING ON

If you are just passing through São Paulo on a connecting flight, try to ensure that your arrival and departure leave from the same airport as transferring from one to the other will take two to three hours. After São Paulo, the first stop on this itinerary is the Iguaçu Falls (see page 225). There are many daily flights to Foz de Iguaçu (80 minutes) from both Congonhas and Guarulhos airports (with more flights from the latter). Congonhas is better if you're staying in São Paulo; Guarulhos is better if you are just changing plane and the flight you're connecting from arrives in Guarulhos. There are also flights via Campinas. If after the Iguaçu Falls you return to São Paulo to catch a connecting flight to Campo Grande in the Pantanal (see page 237), you can fly from either Congonhas or Guarulhos; the airport you choose will depend on which airport your Foz do Iguaçu flight arrives at.

If you are travelling by bus to Foz de Iguaçu, it will leave from the main terminal, **Rodoviária do Tietê** ① *5 km north of the centre, T011-2223 7152, www.passagem-em-domicilio.com.br (with details of bus times and prices in Portuguese)*, the largest bus terminal in Latin America. Left luggage costs US$6 per day per item. You can sleep in the bus station after 2200 when the guards have gone; showers US$6. There is a metrô with connections throughout the city, US$1.20, and buses to the centre (less safe), US$0.80. Taxis to Jardins cost US$25, US$30 at weekends.

GETTING AROUND

Bus Buses in São Paulo are operated by **SP Trans** ① *www.sptrans.com.br*, who have an excellent bus route planner on their website. The system is fairly self-explanatory even for non-Portuguese speakers – with boxes allowing you to select a point of departure (*de*) and destination (*para*). It also enables you to plan using a combination of bus, metrô and urban light railway (*trem*). Google maps mark São Paulo bus stops and numbers. Right clicking on the number shows the bus route and time and there is a search facility for planning routes. There is a flat fee of US$1.20 for any bus ride – payable to a conductor sitting behind a turnstile in the bus. The conductors are helpful in indicating where to hop on and off. Buses are marked with street names indicating their routes, but these routes can be confusing for visitors and services slow due to frequent traffic jams. However, buses are safe, clean and only crowded at peak hours (0700-0900 and 1700-1830). Maps of the bus and metrô system are available at depots, eg Anhangabaú.

Metrô and the CPTM Urban light railway The best and cheapest way to get around São Paulo is on the excellent **metrô system** ⓘ *daily 0500-2400, www.metro.sp.gov.br, with a clear journey planner and information in Portuguese and English*, which is clean, safe, cheap and efficient. It is integrated with the overground CPTM light railway. São Paulo's was the first metrô in Brazil, beginning operations in 1975. It now has five main lines.

The CPTM (Companhia Paulista de Trens Metropolitanos) ⓘ *www.cptm.sp.gov.br*, is an urban light railway which serves to extend the metrô along the margins of the Tietê and Pinheiros rivers and to the outer city suburbs. There are six lines, which are colour-coded like the metrô.

Taxi Taxis in São Paulo are white with a green light on the roof. They display their tariffs in the window (starting at US$5) and have meters. Ordinary taxis are hailed on the street or more safely at taxi stations (*postos*), which are never more than five minutes' walk away anywhere in the city. Hotels, restaurants and some venues will call a taxi on request – either from a *posto* or a taxi driver himself. Radio taxis are more expensive but less hassle.

ORIENTATION

At the heart of the city, the **Centro Histórico** is a place to visit but not to stay. Most of the historical buildings and former beauty are long gone, but its pedestrianized streets are fascinating and gritty, with lively markets and a cluster of interesting sights lost in the concrete and cobbles. For a bird's eye view of the city, head to the lookout platform at the top of the **Edifício Italia** tower, preferably at dusk. The commercial district, containing banks, offices and shops, is known as the **Triângulo**, bounded by Ruas Direita, 15 de Novembro, São Bento and Praça Antônio Prado, but it is rapidly spreading towards the Praça da República.

Immediately southwest of the Centro Histórico is the city's grandest and most photographed skyscraper-lined street, **Avenida Paulista**. The Museo de Arte de São Paulo (MASP), the best art gallery in the southern hemisphere, is here. North of Avenida Paulista is the neighbourhood of **Consolação**, centred on tawdry Rua Augusta but undergoing a Renaissance at the cutting edge of the city's underground live music and nightlife scene. South of Avenida Paulista is the neighbourhood of **Jardins**. This is the city's most affluent inner neighbourhood with elegant little streets hiding Latin America's best restaurants and designer clothing boutiques. There are plenty of luxurious hotels and some budget options.

Next to Jardins, 5 km south of the centre, the **Parque do Ibirapuera** is the inner city's largest green space, with running tracks, a lake and live concerts. Like Brasília, it is a repository of historically important Oscar Niemeyer buildings, many of which are home to

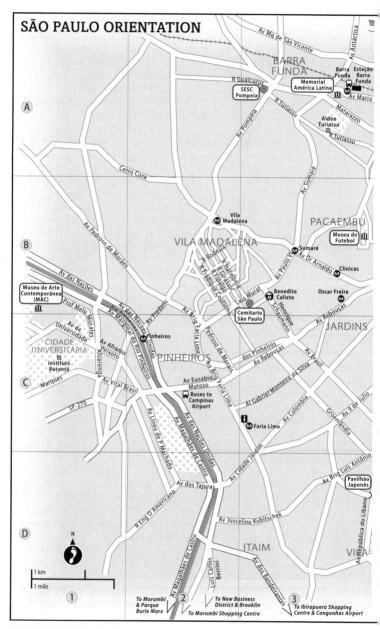

SÃO PAULO ORIENTATION

Av Mq de São Vicente

Av Antártica

BARRA FUNDA

Barra Funda

Estação Barra Funda

R Guaicurus

SESC Pompeia

Memorial América Latina

Av Mario

Av Pompéia

R Turiassu

Matarazzo

Aldea Turiassu

R Turiassu

Cerro Cora

Av Sumaré

PACAEMBU

Vila Madalena

Museu do Futebol

VILA MADALENA

Sumaré

Av Paulo VI

Av Dr Arnaldo

Clínicas

R Rodésia

Av Pedroso de Morales

R Girassol

R Fradique Coutinho

R Harmonia

Av das Nações

Av Brig Faria Lima

Luis Murat

Benedito Calixto

Oscar Freire

Museu de Arte Contemporânea (MAC)

Prof Melo Morales

Av das Nações Unidas

Av Marginal do Rio Pinheiros

Av Fradeic

Cemitario São Paulo

Henrique Schaumann

Av Reboucas

JARDINS

Av da Universidade

Pinheiros

dos Pinheiros

Av Brasil

CIDADE UNIVERSITÁRIA

Av Afranio Peixoto

Av Alvarenga

PINHEIROS

Pedroso de Morales

Av Reboucas

Instituto Butantã

Av Vital Brasil

Av Eusabio Matoso

Buses to Campinas Airport

Al Gabriel Monteiro da Silva

Av Colombia

Groenlândia

Av 9 de Julio

Marques

SP-270

Av Lineu de P Machado

Av Magalhães de Castro

Faria Lima

Av Cidade Jardim

Av Brig Luis Antônio

Pavilhão Japonês

Av dos Tajuras

Av Juscelino Kubitschek

ITAIM

Av dos Bandeirantes

Av República do Líbano

VILA

R Eng O'Americano

Luis Carlos Berrini

N

1 km
1 mile

① To Morumbi & Parque Burle Marx ② To New Business District & Brooklin / To Morumbi Shopping Centre ③ To Ibirapuera Shopping Centre & Congonhas Airport

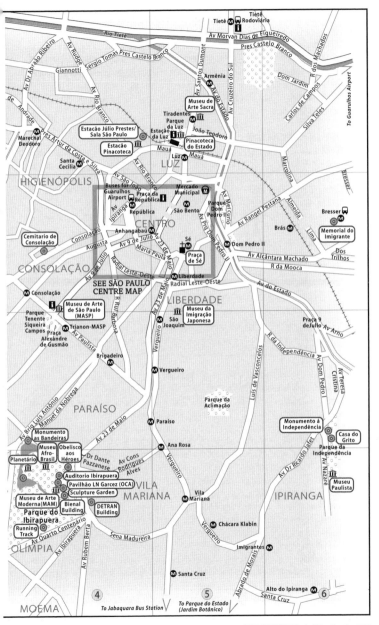

Tietê Rodoviária
Tietê

Av Morvan Dias de Figueiredo
Pres Castelo Branco

To Guarulhos Airport

Rio Tietê

Av Santos Dumont
Av Cruzeiro do Sul
Armênia

Dom Jardim
Carlos de Campos
Silva Teles
R dos Machados

Giannotti

Sérgio Tomás Pres Castelo Branco
Av Rudge
Av Rio Branco
de Andrade
Dr Abraão Ribeiro

Marcolina
Dom Pedro II
Bresser

Museu de Arte Sacra

João Teodoro

Estação Júlio Prestes/
Sala São Paulo
Pres Artur da Costa e Silva
Marechal Deodoro

Tiradentes
Parque da Luz
Estação da Luz
Pinacoteca do Estado

Estação Pinacoteca
Santa Cecília

Maúa
Luz
Maúa
LUZ

Av São João
Av Rio Branco
HIGIENÓPOLIS

Buses to Guarulhos Airport
Praça da República
República
Av Ipiranga

Mercado Municipal
São Bento
Parque Dom Pedro II

Av Rangel Pestana
Brás
Lima
Bresser

Memorial do Imigrante

CENTRO

Anhangabaú
Sé
Praça de Sé
Dom Pedro II

Av Piq Dom Pedro II

Av Alcântara Machado
R da Mooca
Dos Trilhos

Cemitério de Consolação
Consolação
Augusta
Av 9 de Julio
Maria Paula
Av 23 de Maio

CONSOLAÇÃO

SEE SÃO PAULO
CENTRE MAP

Liberdade
Radial Leste-Oeste
Av do Estado

Consolação

Museu de Arte de São Paulo (MASP)
Trianon-MASP
Av Paulista

LIBERDADE
Museu da Imigração Japonesa
São Joaquim

Praça 9 de Julho
Av Arno

Parque Tenente Siqueira Campos
Praça Alexandre de Gusmão

Brigadeiro

R da Independência

Av Teresa Cristina

Verguiero

PARAÍSO
Av 23 de Maio

Parque da Aclimação

Luís de Vasconcelos

R Dom Pedro

Monumento as Bandeiras
Museu Afro-Brasil
Planetário
Obelisco aos Héroes
Dr Dante Pazzanese
Av Cons Rodrigues Alves

Paraíso
Ana Rosa

Monumento á Independência
Casa do Grito
Parque da Independência
Av Dr Ricardo Jafet
Av Nazaré
Museu Paulista

Auditorio Ibirapuera
Pavilhão LN Garcez (OCA)
Sculpture Garden
Museu de Arte Moderna (MAM)
Bienal Building
DETRAN Building
Parque do Ibirapuera
Running Track

VILA MARIANA
Vila Mariana

IPIRANGA

Av Brig Luís Antônio
Manuel da Nóbrega

Chácara Klabin

Av Quarto Centenário
Av Ibirapuera

Sena Madureira
Verguiero

Imigrantes

OLIMPIA
Av Rubem Berta

Santa Cruz

Abraão de Morais
Santa Cruz
Alto do Ipiranga

MOEMA

4
To Jabaquara Bus Station

5
To Parque do Estado
(Jardim Botânico)

6

interesting museums. The adjoining neighbourhoods of **Vila Mariana** and **Paraíso** have a few hotel options and great live music at SESC Vila Mariana.

Situated between Ibirapuera and the river, **Itaim**, **Moema** and **Vila Olímpia** are among the nightlife centres of São Paulo with a wealth of streetside bars, ultra-chic designer restaurants and European-style dance clubs. Hotels tend to be expensive as these areas border the new business centre on Avenida Brigadeiro Faria Lima and Avenida Luís Carlos Berrini, in the suburb of **Brooklin**. **Pinheiros and Vila Madalena** are less chic, but equally lively at night and with the funkiest shops.

TOURIST INFORMATION

There are tourist information booths with English-speaking staff in international and domestic arrivals (ground floor) at **Cumbica airport** (Guarulhos). There are also tourist information booths in the **bus station** and in the following locations throughout the city: **Praça da Luz** ① *in front of the Pinacoteca cafe, daily 0900-1800*; **Avenida São João** ① *Av São João 473, Mon-Fri 0900-1800*; **Avenida Paulista** ① *Parque Trianon, T011-3251 0970, Sun-Fri 0900-1800*; and **Avenida Brig Faria Lima** ① *opposite the Iguatemi shopping centre, T011-3211 1277, Mon-Fri 0900-1800*. An excellent map is available free at these offices.

Editora Abril publishes maps and the excellent *Guia de São Paulo – Sampa* guide (in Portuguese only). For cheap travel, *Viajar Bem e Barato*, is available at news-stands and bookshops throughout the city.

The best website in English is www.brazilmax.com. www.guiasp.com.br has comprehensive entertainment listings in Portuguese, but is readily understandable. Also see http://vejasaopaulo.abril.com.br for entertainment, restaurants and general information in Portuguese.

BACKGROUND

The history of São Paulo state and São Paulo city were much the same from the arrival of the Europeans until the coffee boom transformed the region's economic and political landscape. According to John Hemming (*Red Gold*), there were approximately 196,000 indigenous inhabitants living in what is now São Paulo state at the time of conquest. Today their numbers have been vastly diminished and of the few who survived, some live in villages within São Paulo itself and can be seen selling handicrafts in the centre.

The first official settlement in the state was at São Vicente on the coast, near today's port of Santos. It was founded in 1532 by Martim Afonso de Sousa, who had been sent by King João III to drive the French from Brazilian waters, explore the coast and lay claim to all the lands apportioned to Portugal under the Treaty of Tordesillas.

In 1554, two Jesuit priests from São Vicente founded São Paulo as a *colégio* (a combined mission and school) on the site of the present Pátio de Colégio in the Centro Histórico. The Jesuits chose to settle inland because they wanted to distance themselves from the civil authority, which was based in Bahia and along the coast. Moreover, the plateau provided better access to the indigenous population who they hoped to convert to Catholicism. Pioneers seeking to found farms followed in the Jesuits' wake and as the need for workers on these farms grew, expeditions were sent into the interior of the country to capture and enslave the indigenous people. These marauders were known as *bandeirantes* after the flag wielder who ostensibly walked at their head to claim territory.

Most of their number were the culturally disenfranchised offspring of the indigenous Brazilians and the Portuguese – spurned by both communities. São Paulo rose to become the centre of *bandeirante* activity in the 17th century and the *bandeirantes'* ignominious expeditions were responsible for the opening up of the country's interior and supplying the indigenous slave trade. A statue by one of Brazil's foremost modernist sculptors, Victor Brecheret, sits on the edge of Ibirapuera in homage to the *bandeirantes*. Yet whilst São Paulo was their headquarters, the *bandeirantes'* success in discovering gold led to the economic demise of the city in the 18th century. The inhabitants rushed to the gold fields in the *sertão*, leaving São Paulo to fall to ruin and fall under the influence of Rio de Janeiro. The relative backwardness of the region lasted until the late 19th century when the coffee trade spread west from Rio de Janeiro. Landowners became immensely rich. São Paulo changed from a small town into a financial and residential centre. Exports and imports flowed through Santos and the industrial powerhouse of the country was born. As the city boomed, industries and agriculture fanned outwards to the far reaches of the state.

Between 1885 and the end of the century the boom in coffee and the arrival of large numbers of Europeans transformed the state beyond recognition. By the end of the 1930s more than a million Italians, 500,000 Portuguese, nearly 400,000 Spaniards and 200,000 Japanese had arrived in São Paulo state. São Paulo now has the world's largest Japanese community outside Japan. Their main contribution to the economy has been in horticulture, raising poultry and cotton farming, especially around cities such as Marília. Nowadays, increasing numbers of Japanese-Brazilians work in the professions and the music industry. Significant numbers of Syrian-Lebanese arrived too, adding an extra dimension to the cultural diversity of the city. Many of the city's wealthiest dynasties are of Middle Eastern descent. São Paulo also has a large and successful Jewish community.

Much of the immigrant labour that flooded in during the early years of the 20th century was destined for the coffee *fazendas* and farms. Others went to work in the industries that were opening up in the city. By 1941 there were 14,000 factories and today the city covers more than 1500 sq km – three times the size of Paris – and greater São Paulo has a population of around 20 million.

CENTRO HISTÓRICO

São Paulo's city centre was once one of the most attractive in South America. English visitors in the 19th century described it as being spacious, green and dominated by terracotta-tiled buildings. There were even macaws and sloths in the trees. Today they are long gone and the centre is dominated by towering (and rather ugly) buildings, broken by a handful of interesting churches and cultural centres, and criss-crossed by narrow pedestrian streets. These are lined with stalls selling everything from shoes to electronics, second-hand goods and bric-a-brac, throughout the week. The best way to explore the area is by metrô and on foot, but don't stay after dark as the area is unsalubrious.

PRAÇA DA SÉ AND AROUND
① *Metrô Sé.*
The best place to begin a tour is at the **Praça da Sé**, an expansive square shaded by tropical trees and dominated by the hulking Catholic **Catedral Metropolitana** ① *Praça da Sé, T011-3107 6832, Mon-Sat 0800-1800, Sun 0830-1800, free, Metrô Sé.* This is the heart of

the old city and has been the site of Brazil's largest public protests. Crowds gathered here in the late 1980s to demand the end to military rule. And in 1992, they demanded the impeachment and resignation of the new Republic's second elected president, Fernando Collor – the first in a seemingly never-ending series of corrupt leaders who in 1990 had frozen the country's savings accounts and personally pocketed millions. The *praça* is always busy with hawkers, beggars, shoeshiners and business men rushing between meetings. Evangelists with megaphones proselytize on the steps of the cathedral – a symbol of the war between Christians for the souls of the poor that dominates contemporary urban Brazil. The *praça* is a great spot for street photography though be discreet with your camera and check that you aren't followed after taking your shots. Like São Paulo itself, the cathedral is more remarkable for its size than its beauty and is an unconvincing mish-mash of neo-Gothic and Renaissance. A narrow nave is squeezed

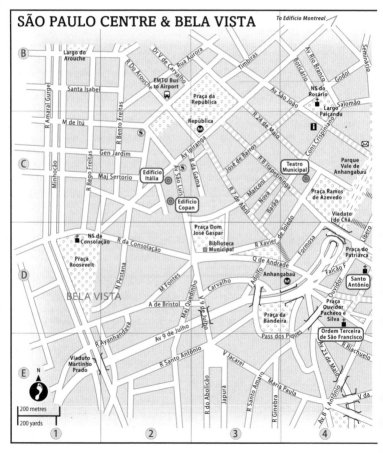

SÃO PAULO CENTRE & BELA VISTA

uncomfortably between two monstrous 97-m-high spires beneath a bulbous copper cupola. It was designed in 1912 by the inappropriately named engineer Maximiliano Hell, inaugurated in the 1950s and fitted with its full complement of 14 towers only in 2002. The interior is bare but for a few stained-glass windows designed in Germany and capitals decorated with floral motifs. In the basement there is a vast, pseudo-Gothic crypt.

There are a few other sights of interest around the *praça*. Next door to the cathedral itself and housed in a 1930s art deco building is the **Conjunto Cultural da Caixa** ① *Praça da Sé 111, T011-3321 4400, www.caixacultural.com.br, Tue-Sun 0900-2100, US$2, Metrô Sé,* a gallery that hosts excellent small international art and photography exhibitions by day, and, in the evenings, a boutique theatre. It also has a small banking museum with colonial furniture, on one of its upper floors. Two minutes' walk immediately to the west of the cathedral, squeezed between ugly modern buildings at the end of Rua Senador Feijó, is the

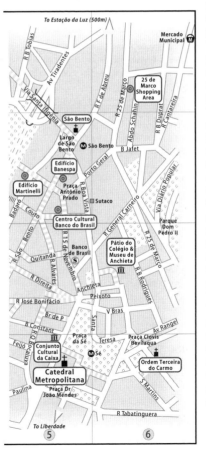

Igreja da Ordem Terceira de São Francisco ① *Largo de São Francisco 133, T011-3106 0081, closed at time of publication, Metrô Sé.* This is one of the city's oldest churches, preserving a modest baroque interior (parts of which date to the 17th century) painted in celestial blue. It is quiet and meditative inside. The exterior is largely an 18th-century excrescence. The church is often referred to as 'O Convento de São Francisco' after a beautiful baroque convent that stood here until the 1930s. This was demolished along with vast swathes of the old colonial centre and sadly the Igreja da Ordem Terceira is in danger of undergoing the same fate – it was condemned in 2008 and remains closed pending donations for a restoration project. There are now only two churches in the centre of one of Brazil's oldest cities which retain any baroque remnants – the Igreja de Santo Antônio (see page 213) and the **Igreja da Ordem Terceira do Carmo** ① *R Rangel Pestana 230, Tue-Sun 0900-2100, free, Metrô Sé.* This church sits just off the far northeastern corner of the Praça da Sé, dates from 1632 and preserves its original gilt baroque altarpiece together with some other stucco work, religious paintings and artefacts. It is a peaceful little place in all the heat, hustle and bustle, and has with few visitors.

PÁTIO DO COLÉGIO AND AROUND
ⓘ *Metrô Sé.*

The site of the founding of São Paulo can be reached by walking north from the bottom of the Praça da Sé (farthest from the cathedral) along Rua Santa Teresa and to the Praça Pátio do Colégio. Here lies the **Pátio do Colégio and Museu de Anchieta** ⓘ *Praça Pátio do Colégio, T011-3105 6899, www.pateodocollegio.com.br, museum: Tue-Fri 0840-1630, US$3, free on the last Sun of the month, Metrô Sé.* Jesuit priests, led by 18-year-old Padre José de Anchieta arrived here in 1554, when the area was a tiny clearing on a hill in the midst of a vast forest. They made camp and instructed their domicile indigenous Guarani to construct a simple wattle and daub hut. They inaugurated the building with a celebration of Mass on 25 January 1554, the feast of the conversion of São Paulo. Their simple hut took the saint's name, the 'Colégio de São Paulo de Piratinga'. The hut became a school for converted indigenous Brazilians seduced from the forests around. The school became a church and the church gave its name – São Paulo – to a settlement for *bandeirante* slaving raids into the Brazilian interior. In 1760, the Jesuits were expelled from the city they founded, for opposing the *bandeirantes* and their indigenous slave trade. But the Pátio do Colégio (as the complex of buildings came to be known) remained, becoming the palace of the fledgling province's Portuguese colonial captains general, and then of its Brazilian imperial governors. The church's tower fell down in 1886, and shortly after the whole building, but for one piece of wattle and daub wall, was demolished. The Jesuits didn't return to São Paulo until 1954 but they had long memories and immediately set about building an exact replica of their original church and college, which is what stands today. Most of the buildings are occupied by the **Museu Padre Anchieta**. This preserves, amongst other items, a modernist and not altogether sympathetic painting of the priest, by Italian Albino Menghini, bits of his corpse (which is now that of a saint after Anchieta was canonized by Pope John Paul II), a 17th-century font used to baptize the indigenous Brazilians and a collection of Guaraní art and artefacts from the colonial era. The Pátio has a great little al fresco café with a view, serving good snacks and light meals.

The exhibition spaces, cultural centres and concert halls of the **Centro Cultural Banco do Brasil** ⓘ *R Álvares Penteado 112, T011-3113 3651, www.bb.com.br, Mon-Fri 0900-1800, free except for exhibitions, Metrô Sé or São Bento,* can be reached by turning immediately west from the front of the Pátio do Colégio along Rua do Tesouro and then right for a block along Rua Álvares Penteado. These are housed in an attractive art deco building with a pretty glass ceiling. Many of the galleries are contained within the banks original vaults, some of which retain their massive iron doors. The cultural centre has a diverse programme of art and photography shows, cultural events and, in the evenings, theatre, music and cinema. It is always worth a visit in passing.

MOSTEIRO DO SÃO BENTO AND AROUND
ⓘ *Metrô São Bento. Largo São Bento, T011-3228 3633, www.mosteiro.org.br, Mon-Fri 0600-1800, Sat and Sun 0600-1200 and 1600-1800, Latin Mass with Gregorian chant Sun 1000; Latin vespers Mon-Fri 1725, Sat 1700, free.*

The most beautiful of all the churches in São Paulo is the Benedictine Basilica de Nossa Senhora de Assunção, known as the Mosteiro do São Bento. Benedictines arrived on this site in 1598, shortly after the Jesuits and, like them, proceeded to proselytize the indigenous people. Despite their long history in the city the monastery is a modern church dating from 1914. It was designed by Munich-based architect Richard Bernl in homage to the English Norman style. Its façade is strikingly similar to Southwell cathedral in Nottinghamshire, though with added Rhineland roofs and baroque revival flourishes. But few visit São Bento for the exterior. The church preserves a striking Beuronese interior painted by Dom Adelbert Gresnicht, a Dutch Benedictine monk. The style is named after techniques developed by Benedictines in the monastery of Beuron in southwest Germany in the late 19th and early 20th centuries. It finds much inspiration in Byzantine art and is characterized by compressed perspective and iconic, almost exaggerated colours. São Bento is one of the finest Beuronese churches in the world. The stained glass (and much of the statuary) is also by Dom Adelbert. Most of the windows show scenes from the life of St Benedict with the most beautiful, at the far end of the nave, showing Our Lady ascending to heaven guided by the Holy Spirit in the form of a dove. The church has Brazil's finest organ which is given its own festival in November and December every year. And with this being a Benedictine monastery, there is of course a temple to commerce: the shop sells delicious sweets home-made by the monks in their bakery.

Immediately in front of the monastery, at the corner of Avenida São João and Rua Libero Badaró, is the **Edifício Martinelli (Martinelli Building)** ① *Av São João 35, not open to the public, Metrô São Bento*. This was the city's first skyscraper and, when it was built, looked out over a sea of terracotta roofs and handsome tree-lined avenues. The building is reminiscent of New York's upper east side but is by no means as distinguished: while colonial São Paulo was unique and beautiful, the buildings that replaced it looked tawdry and crowded next to the New York it longed to imitate.

Around the corner is another architectural pastiche, the **Edifício Altino Arantes** (aka **Edifício Banespa/Santander Cultural**) ① *R João Bricola 24 (Metrô São Bento), T011-3249 7466, Mon-Fri 1000-1500, free, passport ID is required, visits limited to 10 mins (dusk visits are limited to those with prior appointments), daypacks must be left in reception, no tripods or bags can be taken to the viewing deck*, looking a bit like a wan Empire State Building, small enough to collapse under the weight of King Kong. The view of the city from the observatory is awe-inspiring. On its fringes are the vast favelas and new distant neighbourhoods with infant skyscraper flats and hundreds of helicopters whirling busily overhead like giant buzzing flies.

Less than 50 m from the Edifício Altino Arantes is the oldest church in São Paulo's city centre, the **Igreja de Santo Antônio** ① *Praça do Patriarca s/n, Mon-Fri 0900-1600, free, Metrô São Bento*, with parts dating from 1592. It was fully restored in 2005 and together with the Igreja do Carmo is the only church in the city centre with a baroque interior – although much of what you see today is from reforms in 1899. It's a tranquil spot in the middle of one of the world's busiest city centres.

The streets between São Bento and Luz are some of the busiest shopping districts in the city. The partially covered **Rua 25 de Março** ① *daily 0700-1800, Metrô São Bento shopping complex*, runs north to Rua Paula Sousa and Luz Metrô station. Two blocks to the east of 25 de Marco along Rua Comendador Afonso Kherlakian is the beautiful art deco **Mercado Municipal** ① *R da Cantareira 306, Centro, T011-3326 3401, www.mercado municipal.com.br, Mon-Sat 0600-1800, Sun 0600-1600, free, Metrô São Bento or Luz*. The area offers some of the best people-watching and shopping adventures in the city. It's an easy walk from the market or Rua 25 de Março to Luz, though caution should be observed at all times. The streets to the west, between the centre and Júlio Prestes station, should be avoided. This is a notorious area for crack dealing.

PRAÇA DA REPÚBLICA

① *Metrô República.*

There are a few interesting sites here. Most notable is the **Edifício and Terraço Itália** ① *Av Ipiranga 344, T011-2189 2990 and T011-2189 2929, www.edificioitalia.com.br, restaurant: www.terracoitalia.com.br, US$8, Metrô República,* a rather unremarkable restaurant in the city's tallest building with a truly remarkable view from the observation deck. Arrive half an hour before sunset for the best balance of natural and artificial light, and bring a tripod. The skyscraper immediately in front of the *terraço* is Oscar Niemeyer's **Edifício Copan** ① *Av Ipiranga 200, not open to the public though some visitors are allowed to go to the terraço at the discretion of security, Metrô República,* built in 1951 in a spate of design by the architect, which also included the nearby **Edifício Montreal** ① *Av Ipiranga at Cásper Líbero,* and the **Edifício Califórnia** ① *R Barão de Itapetininga.* Edifício Copan was the setting for a series of memorable short stories, diseecting daily life and class in São Paulo written by the Paulistano writer Regina Rheda, and published in English as *First World, Third Class and Other Tales of the Global Mix* in 2005.

From the corner of Praça da República, a 10-minute walk southeast along Rua 24 de Maio brings you back into the main part of the city centre and Metrô Anhangabaú, via the **Teatro Municipal Opera House** ① *Praça Ramos de Azevedo s/n, T011-3397 0300, www.prefeitura.sp.gov.br/cidade/secretarias/cultura/teatromunicipal/, box office Mon-Fri 1000-1900, Sat 1000-1700, tickets from US$5, Metrô Anhangabaú, República or São Bento,* based on the 1874 Beaux-Arts, Palais Garnier, but stunted in comparison, in dull stone and with huge baroque flourishes on the roof which make it look rather ridiculous. Maria Callas, Nureyev and Fonteyn and Duke Ellington have all graced the concert hall and the venue continues to host a slice of the better classical music, theatre and ballet performances in the city. Next to the theatre is the **Viaduto do Chá,** a steel bridge riding over the attractive but scruffy Vale de Anhangabaú park and the traffic-heavy Avenida 23 de Maio and 9 de Julho urban highways.

NORTH OF THE CENTRE

LUZ

① *Metrô Luz or Metrô Tiradentes, CPTM Luz or Júlio Prestes.*

Some of São Paulo's finest museums are to be found a few kilometres north of the city centre in the neighbourhood of Luz. The area is dominated by two striking 19th- and early 20th-century railway stations, both in use today: the **Estação da Luz** ① *Praça da Luz 1, T0800-550121 for information on suburban trains,* and **Estação Júlio Prestes** ① *Praça Júlio Prestes 51, www.estacoesferroviarias.com.br/j/jprestes.htm.* The former marked the realization of a dream for O Ireneu Evangelista de Sousa, the Visconde de Mauá, who was Brazil's first industrial magnate. A visit to London in the 1840s convinced de Sousa that Brazil's future lay in rapid industrialization – a path he followed with the founding of an ironworks employing some 300 workers from England and Scotland. It made him a millionaire and in 1854 he opened his first railway, designed and run by the British. It linked Jundiaí, in the heart of the São Paulo coffee region, with Santos on the coast via what was then the relatively small city of São Paulo. The line is still extant; though passenger trains only run on the Jundiaí to São Paulo section. The grandness of the Estação de Luz station, which was completed in 1900, attests to the fact that the city quickly grew wealthy by exploiting its position at the railway junction. By the time the Estação Júlio Prestes was built, Britannia no longer ruled the railways. This next station was modelled on Grand Central and Penn in New York. In 1999 the enormous 1000-sq-m grand hall was converted into the magnificent, cathedral-like **Sala São Paulo concert hall** ① *Praça Júlio Prestes 51, T011-3337 9573, www.salasaopaulo.art.br, guided visits Mon-Fri 1300-1630, Sat 1330, Sun 1400 (when there is an evening performance) or 1230 (when there is an afternoon performance), US$2.50, free on weekends, foreigners should book ahead through the website as English-speaking guides must be arranged, box office T011-3223 3966, Mon-Fri 1000-1800, Sat 1000-1630, concerts from US$10, Metrô Luz, CPTM Luz or Júlio Prestes*, Brazil's most prestigious classical music venue.

The city's finest collection of Brazilian art lies 100 m from the Estação da Luz in the **Pinacoteca do Estado** ① *Praça da Luz 2, T011-3324 0933, www.pinacoteca.org.br, Tue-Sun 1000-1800 (last entry at 1730), Sat 1000-1730, US$3, free on Sat, Metrô Luz, CPTM Luz, excellent museum shop and café*. Here you will find works by Brazilian artists from the colonial and imperial eras, together with paintings by the founders of Brazilian modernism, such as Lasar Segall, Tarsila do Amaral, Candido Portinari and Alfredo Volpi. The gallery also contains sculpture by Rodin, Victor Brecheret and contemporary works by artists such as the Nipo-Brazilian painter Tomie Ohtake. The excellent photography gallery in the basement displays some of the world's greatest black-and-white photographers, many of whom are from Brazil. The museum overlooks the **Parque da Luz**, a lovely shady green space dotted with modernist sculpture and shaded by large tropical figs and palms. Take care in this area after dark.

The Pinacoteca's sister gallery, the **Estação Pinacoteca and Memorial da Resistência museum** ① *Largo General Osório 66, T011-3337 0185, daily 1000-1730, US$2, free for the Memorial da Resistência and for the galleries on Sat, very good café restaurant, Metrô Luz, CPTM Luz and Júlio Prestes*, is just over 500 m west of the Pinacoteca along Rua Mauá, next to the Estação Júlio Prestes and Sala São Paulo. It houses 200 of the country's finest modernist paintings from the archive of fthe Fundação José e Paulina Nemirovsky, including further key pieces by Tarsila do Amaral, Emiliano Di Cavalcanti, Portinari Anita Malfatti, Victor Brecheret and Lasar Segall. International art includes Chagall, Picasso and Braque. The building was once the headquarters of the Departamento Estadual de Ordem Politica e Social do Estado de São Paulo (DEOPS/SP) – the counter-insurgency wing of the Policia Militar police force. Thousands of Paulistanos were tortured and killed here between 1940 and 1983, during the Vargas years and the military dictatorship. The Memorial da Resistência de São Paulo museum on the ground floor tells their story in grisly detail – through panels, documents and photographs – and shows how the CIA supported the oppression.

Luz's other excellent museum is the **Museu de Arte Sacra** ① *Av Tiradentes 676, 400 m north of the Pinacoteca, T011-3227 7687, www.museuartesacra.org.br, Mon-Fri 1000-1700, Sat and Sun 1000-1900, US$2, Metrô Tiradentes, CPTM Luz*. This superb little museum is often overlooked by visitors, yet it is one of the finest of its kind in the Americas and lies almost immediately opposite the Pinacoteca. The collection is housed in a large wing of one of the city's most distinguished colonial buildings, the early 19th-century Mosteiro da Luz. Parts of the monastery are still home to Conceptionist sisters and the entire complex is imbued with a restful sense of serenity. Even those who are not interested in church art will find the galleries a delightfully peaceful haven from the frenetic chaos of São Paulo. The collection, however, is priceless and of international importance. Rooms house various objects and artefacts – from lavish monstrances and ecclesiastical jewellery to church altarpieces. Of particular note is the statuary, with pieces by many of the most important Brazilian baroque masters. Amongst objects by Aleijadinho, Mestre Valentim and Frei Agostinho da Piedade is a wonderful Mary Magdalene by Francisco Xavier de Brito, displaying an effortless unity of motion and melancholy contemplation. There are sculptures by (anonymous) Brazilian indigenous artists, a majestic African-Brazilian São Bento (with blue eyes) and an extraordinarily detailed 18th-century Neapolitan nativity crib comprising almost 2000 pieces, which is the most important of its kind outside Naples.

BARRA FUNDA AND HIGIENÓPOLIS
① *Metrô Palmeiras-Barra Funda, CPTM Barra Funda.*
The monumentalist group of modernist concrete buildings making up the **Memorial da América Latina** ① *Av Mário de Andrade 664, next to Metrô Barra Funda, T011-3823 4600, www.memorial.org.br, Tue-Fri 0900-2100, Sat 0900-1800, Sun 1000-1800, free*, were designed by **Oscar Niemeyer** and built in March 1989. They comprise a monumental 85,000-sq-m-complex of curvi-linear galleries, conference spaces, walkways, bridges and squares, broken by an ugly, urban highway and dotted with imposing sculptures. The largest of these is in the shape of an outstretched hand. The complex was built with the grand aim of integrating Latin American nations, culturally and politically, but it is sorely underused. Occasional shows (details on the website) include the annual Latin American art exhibition in the Pavilhão de Criatividade.

A few kilometres west of Barra Funda – and a quick hop along the CPTM's Linha Rubi, in the emerging nightlife district of **Água Branca**, is **SESC Pompeia** ① *R Clélia 93, T011-3871 7700, www.sescsp.org.br, CPTM Água Branca, 10 mins' walk southeast or US$3 in a taxi*, an arts complex housed in a striking post-industrial building designed by Lina Bo Bardi, which together with SESC Vila Mariana (see page 220) showcases some of the best medium-sized musical acts in the city – names like João Bosco, CéU and Otto. It is a vibrant place, with a theatre, exhibitions, workshops, restaurant and café, as well as a gym and areas for sunbathing and watching television.

The upper middle-class neighbourhood of **Higienópolis** lies between Barra Funda and Consolação. It is a favourite haunt of artists and musicians; particularly the **Bretagne building** ① *Av Higienópolis 938, T011-3667 2516*, one of a handful of delightful mid-20th-century blocks of flats whose curved lines, brilliant mosaics and polished stone looks like a film set for an arty 1960s picture. Higienópolis also boasts one of the city's plushest shopping malls, the **Patio Higienópolis** ① *Av Higienópolis 618, T011-3823 2300, www.patiohigienopolis.com.br.*

WEST OF THE CENTRE

AVENIDA PAULISTA
① *Metrô Vergueiro or Paraíso for the southeastern end of Paulista.*
Southwest of the Centro Histórico, Avenida Paulista, is lined by skyscrapers and is thick with six lanes of cars. It is one of São Paulo's classic postcard shots and locals like to compare it to Fifth Avenue in New York. In truth, it's more commercial and lined with functional buildings, most of which are unremarkable individually and awe-inspiring as a whole.

The avenue was founded in 1891 by the Uruguayan engineer Joaquim Eugênio de Lima, who wanted to build a Paulistano Champs-Élysées. After he built a mansion on Avenida Paulista, many coffee barons followed suit and by the early 20th century, Paulista had become the city's most fashionable promenade. The mansions and the rows of stately trees that sat in front of them were almost all demolished in the 1940s and 1950s to make way for ugly office buildings, and in the 1980s these were in turn demolished as banks and multinationals established their headquarters here.

The highlight of Avenida Paulista is the **Museu de Arte de São Paulo (MASP)** ⓘ *Av Paulista 1578, T011-3251 5644, www.masp.art.br, Tue-Wed and Fri-Sun 1100-1800, Thu 1100-1900, US$5, Metrô Trianon-MASP*. This is the most important gallery in the southern hemisphere, preserving some of Europe's greatest paintings. If it were in the US or Europe it would be as busy as the Prado or the Guggenheim, but here, aside from the occasional noisy group of schoolchildren, the gallery is invariably deserted. Even at weekends, visitors can stop and stare at a Rembrandt or a Velazquez at their leisure. The museum has a far larger collection than it is able to display and only a tiny fraction reaches the walls of the modest-sized international gallery. France gets star-billing, with 11 Renoirs, 70 Degas, and a stream of works by Monet, Manet, Cezanne, Toulouse-Lautrec and Gauguin. Renaissance Italy is represented by a Raphael Resurrection, an impeccable Bellini and a series of exquisite late 15th-century icons. The remaining walls are adorned with paintings by Bosch, Goya, Van Dyck, Turner, Constable and many others, cherry-picked from post-War Europe. A gallery downstairs, the Galeria Clemente de Faria, houses temporary exhibitions, mostly by contemporary Brazilian artists and photographers, and the museum has a decent and good-value restaurant serving buffet lunches and a small gift shop. On Sunday, an antiques fair is held in the open space beneath the museum.

Opposite MASP is the **Parque Tenente Siqueira Campos** ⓘ *R Peixoto Gomide 949 and Av Paulista, daily 0700-1830*, also known as Parque Trianon, covering two blocks on either side of Alameda Santos. It is a welcome, luxuriant, green area located in what is now the busiest part of the city. The vegetation includes native plants typical of the *Mata Atlântica*.

CONSOLAÇÃO AND THE PACAEMBU MUSEU DO FUTEBOL
ⓘ *Metrô Consolação.*
Consolação, which lies between the northeastern end of Avenida Paulista and the Edifício Italia and Praça República in the city centre, is emerging as the edgiest and most exciting nocturnal neighbourhood in São Paulo. Until a few years it was home to little more than rats, sleazy strip bars, street-walkers and curb-crawlers, but now it harbours a thriving alternative weekend scene. Its untidy streets are lined with grafitti-scrawled shop fronts, the deep velvet-red of open bar doors, go-go clubs with heavy-set bouncers outside and makeshift street bars. On Fridays and Saturdays from 2200 a jostle of hundreds of young Paulistanos down bottles of cooler-fresh Bohemia beer at rickety metal tables, and lines of sharply dressed and well-toned 20- and 30-somethings queue to enter a gamut of fashionable bars, clubs and pounding gay venues, including one of Brazil's most exciting underground venues: **Studio SP**.

Just north of Consolação, on the other side of the Sacramento Cemetery and rushing Avenida Doutour Arnaldo, is the beautiful art deco **Estádio Pacaembu** which hosts domestic games and big international rock concerts. It sits in a square named after Charles Miller, the Englishman who brought football to Brazil. Inside is the **Museu do Futebol**

① *Metrô Clinicas, Estádio do Pacaembu, Praça Charles Miller, T011-3663 3848, www.museudofutebol.org.br, Tue-Sun 1000-1700, US$3, free on Thu, children under 7 go free, restaurants next to the museum in the stadium, Metrô Sumaré (20-min walk)*, which cost US$15 million and which was inaugurated by Pelé in September 2008. The World Cup, which Brazil have won more often than any other team, is the principal focus. One gallery is devoted to the tournament, profiling the games and what was happening in the world at the time, and telling both stories through video footage, photographs, memorabilia and newspaper cuttings. Music from the likes of Ary Barroso and Jorge Ben forms the soundtrack, along with recordings of cheering fans. A second gallery showcases Brazil's greatest stars, including Garrincha, Falcão, Zico, Bebeto, Didi, Romário, Ronaldo, Gilmar, Gérson, Sócrates, Rivelino, Ronaldo (who is known as Ronaldinho or Ronaldinho Fenomeno in Brazil) and, of course, Pelé. The shirt he wore during the 1970 World Cup final – a game frequently cited as the greatest ever played when Brazil beat Italy 4-1 to take the title for the third time – receives pride of place. A third gallery is more interactive, offering visitors the chance to dribble and shoot at goals and test their knowledge on football facts and figures.

JARDINS

① *Metrô Consolação or Oscar Freire (Linha Amarela from 2014).*
West of Avenida Paulista, a 10-minute walk from Consolação Metrô along Rua Haddock Lobo, is the plush neighbourhood of Jardins. This is by far the most pleasant area to stay in São Paulo; it has the best restaurants, shops and cafés and is a tranquil spot for a strong coffee and people-watching, or an urban boutique browse. Jardins is in reality a series of neighbourhoods – each with its own name – the stretches closest to Paulista are known as **Cerqueira César** (to the northwest) and **Jardim Paulista** (to the southeast). These two areas have the bulk of the boutique shops, swanky hotels and chic restaurants. The most self-consciously chic of all is the cross section between Rua Oscar Freire, Rua Bela Cintra and Rua Haddock Lobo, where even the poodles wear collars with designer labels and everyone, from the shop owner to the doorman, addresses people as *'Querida'* (Darling).

Immediately west of Jardim Paulista and Cerqueira César, and separated from those neighbourhoods by a stately city highway preserving a handful of coffee Baron mansions (Avenida Brasil), are three more Jardins. **Jardim Paulistano** is dominated by Avenida Gabriel Monteiro da Silva, which is lined by very expensive, internationally reknowned home decor and furniture stores. Between Jardim Paulistano and Ibirapuera Park are **Jardim America** and **Jardim Europa**, both made up of leafy streets lined with vast mansion houses, almost completely hidden behind towering walls topped with razor wire and formidable electric fencing. Their idyllic seclusion is spoilt only by the stench of raw favela sewage from the nearby River Pinheiros.

The **Museu Brasileiro da Escultura** (**MUBE**) ① *Av Europa 218, T011-2594 2601, www.mube.art.br, Tue-Sun 1000-1900, free*, showcases contemporary Brazilian sculpture through visiting exhibitions. Most are rather lacklustre and the museum merits a visit more for the building itself, which is by Brazil's Prtizker prize-winning architect Paulo Mendes da Rocha. Like many Brazilian architects Espírito Santo-born Rocha is celebrated for his inventive, minimalist use of concrete. The museum is made up of a series of massive, grey, bunker-like concrete blocks which contrast starkly with the surrounding gardens (by Burle Marx), but which integrate them with the underground exhibition spaces. To get there from Metrô Consolação, take bus 702P-42, marked 'Butantã', from the corner of Rua Augusta and Avenida Paulista.

The **Museu da Casa Brasileira** ① *Av Brigadeiro Faria Lima 2705, T011-3032 3727, Tue-Sun 1000-1800, US$2*, preserves a collection of antique (mostly baroque) Brazilian and Portuguese and contemporary international furniture in one of the few remaining coffee baron mansions. The museum also hosts the annual Prêmio Design MCB design awards, which has become one of the most celebrated in Brazil. Temporary exhibition spaces showcase the winners and the museum has a pleasant garden (with live music on Sundays) and a good café-restaurant. From CPTM Cidade Jardim it's 10 minutes' walk; from Pinheiros head east along Rua Professor Artur Ramos to Avenida Brigadeiro Faria Lima.

VILA MADALENA AND PINHEIROS
① *Metrô Madalena.*

If Jardins is São Paulo's upper East Side or Bond Street, Vila Madalena and neighbouring Pinheiros are its East Village or Notting Hill – still fashionable, but younger, less ostentatiously moneyed and with more of a skip in their step. Streets are crammed with bars, restaurants and an array of the city's freshest designer labels, clambering over the steep hills and buzzing with young and arty middle-class Paulistanos. Younger boutique brands have set up shop in Vila Madalena. Galleries such as **Choque Cultural** ① *R João Moura 197, T011-3061 4051, Mon-Fri 1000-1700, Sat 1100-1700, www.choquecultural.co.uk*, sell work by the newest wave of the city's increasingly famous street artists (as well as prints available online through their UK website).

There's music on every corner in both neighbourhoods – from spit-and-sawdust samba bars to mock-Bahian *forró* clubs and well-established live music venues. The area attracts the artistically rich and famous: Seu Jorge lives and drinks in Vila Madalena, as does leading avant garde musician, Max de Castro. The only sight of any consequence is the **Instituto Tomie Ohtake** ① *R dos Coropés 88, T011-3814 0705, www.instituto tomieohtake.org.br, Tue-Fri 1000-1800, US$3*, a monolithic, rather ungainly red and purple tower by Unique Hotel architect Ruy Ohtake. It has galleries inside devoted to the work of his Japanese-Brazilian artist mother, Tomie, and a series of other exhibition halls with work by up-and-coming artists. To get there, go to Metrô Vila Madalena, then take bus 701-10 southwest along Rua Purpurina and Rua Fradique Coutinho, getting off at the stop at Fradique Coutinho 1331. Leave the stop and turn right onto Rua Wisard. After 200 m continue onto Rua dos Miranhas. After 400 m continue onto Rua dos Tamanás and after 150 m turn right into Rua dos Coropés.

SOUTH OF THE CENTRE

LIBERDADE
① *Metrô Liberdade.*

Liberdade was the first centre for the Japanese community in São Paulo; a city with more ethnic Japanese than any other outside Japan. It lies directly south of the Praça da Sé and can easily be reached on foot in under 10 minutes. There are all manner of Asian shops selling everything from woks to *manga* and the streets are illuminated by lights designed to resemble Japanese lanterns. A market selling Asian produce and food is held every Sunday in the Praça da Liberdade and there are many excellent Japanese restaurants.

The **Museu da Imigração Japonesa** ① *R São Joaquim 381, 3rd floor, T011-3209 5465, www.nihonsite.com/muse, Tue-Sun 1330-1730, US$3, Metrô Liberdade*, in the Japanese-Brazilian cultural centre, is a modern, well-kept little museum with exhibitions telling the story of the Japanese migration to Brazil, a replica of the first ship that brought the Japanese to Brazil, reconstructions of early Japanese Brazilian houses, artefacts.

BELA VISTA

Bela Vista lies immediately west of Liberdade and east of Consolação between the city centre and Avenida Paulista. In the late 19th and early 20th century the neighbourhood was a centre of Italian immigration. It is a higgledy-piggledy mass of small streets lined with residential houses. There are few sights of interest but the area is a pleasant place for a wander – especially at weekends. On Sunday there is an antiques market, the **Feira das Antiguidades** ① *Praça Dom Orione, Bixiga, Bela Vista, Sun 1000-1500*, sometimes with live *chorinho*. There are Italianate houses nearby on Rua dos Ingleses, and a number of little cafés and bars. During carnival the **Vai Vai samba school** ① *R São Vicente 276, T011-3266 2581, www.vaivai.com.br, US$6 for the carnival party*, opens its doors to as many as 4000 visitors who come to dance samba and process through the nearby streets. They often throw a smaller *feijoada* party at weekends. **Rua Avanhandava**, which runs off Rua Martins Fontes in the north of Bela Vista, was closed to traffic in 2007, and has since become one of the prettiest streets in the neighbourhood, lined with some traditional Italian restaurants.

PARAÍSO AND VILA MARIANA

Southwest of Liberdade and beginning where Avenida Paulista becomes Rua Vergueiro, are the neighbourhoods of Paraíso and Vila Mariana. Paraíso is dominated by the hulking dome of the the the **Catedral Ortodoxa** ① *R Vergueiro 1515, Paraíso, T011-5579 3835, www.catedralortodoxa.com.br, Mon-Fri 0900-1300 and 1500-1800, Sat 1000-1300, Mass at 1015 on Sun, Metrô Paraíso*. The church is modelled on the Hagia Sofia in Istanbul and is one of the largest Antiochian Orthodox churches in the world. Most of the worshippers are Brazilians of Syrian and Lebanese descent. The church of Antioch is one of the five original churches and was founded in Antioch, Turkey by the apostles Peter and Paul. It's seat is in Damascus, Syria and the current patriarch is His Beatitude Patriarch Ignatius IV (Hazim) of Antioch and all the East. Vila Mariana is principally a residential neighbourhood abutting Ibirapuera park. The **SESC Vila Mariana** ① *R Pelotas 141, Vila Mariana, T011-5080 3000, www.sescsp.org.br, daily 1000-2000*, is a cultural centre with a swimming pool, internet, a gym and a concert hall which hosts some of the best small acts in São Paulo. From Metrô Ana Rosa, it's 10 minutes' walk south of Ana Rosa, east along Avenida Cnso Rodrigues Alves, right onto Rua Humberto I (after 500 m) and left onto Pelotas (after 200 m).

PARQUE DO IBIRAPUERA

① *Entrance on Av Pedro Álvares Cabral, daily 0500-2400, T011-5573 4180, www.parquedo ibirapuera.com, free, unsafe after dark, www.parquedoibirapuera.com. Metrô Ana Rosa is a 15-min walk east of the park: turn right out of the station and walk due west along Av Conselheiro Rodrigo Alves, continue onto Av Dante Pazzanese which comes to the Av 23 de Maio urban freeway, the park sits in front of you on the other side of the road and can be reached via a footbridge 200 m to the right in front of the DETRAN building; alternatively bus 5164-21 (marked Cidade Leonor, direção Parque do Ibirapuera) leaves every 30 mins from Metrô Santa*

Cruz for Ibirapuera; any bus to DETRAN (the Driver and Vehicle licensing building, labelled in huge letters) stops opposite Ibirapuera. Lines include 175T-10, 477U-10 and 675N-10.

The park was designed by architect Oscar Niemeyer and landscape artist Roberto Burle Marx for the city's fourth centenary in 1954. It is the largest of the very few green spaces in central São Paulo and its shady woodlands, lawns and lakes offer a breath of fresher air in a city that has only 4.6 sq m of vegetation per inhabitant. The park is home to a number of museums and monuments and some striking Oscar Niemeyer buildings that were designed in the 1950s but have only been constructed in the last five years. These include the Pavilhão Lucas Nogueira Garcez, most commonly referred to as the **Oca** ① *Portão 3, open for exhibitions*, a brilliant white, polished concrete dome, built in homage to an indigenous Brazilian roundhouse. It stages major international art exhibitions (see website, above, for what's on). Next to it is the **Auditório Ibirapuera** ① *Portão 3, www.auditorio ibirapuera.com.br*, a concert hall shaped like a giant wedge. The **Fundação Bienal** ① *Portão 3, http://bienalsaopaulo.globo.com, open for exhibitions*, are also by Niemeyer and house the city's flagship fashion and art events: the twice yearly São Paulo fashion week and the Art Biennial, the most important events of their kind in the southern hemisphere.

A **sculpture garden** separates the Bienal from the Oca; this garden is watched over by the **Museu de Arte Moderna (MAM)** ① *Portão 3, T011-5085 1300, www.mam.org.br, Tue-Sun 1000-1800 (ticket office closes at 1730), US$2.50*. This small museum, with a giant mural outside by Os Gêmeos, showcases the best Brazilian contemporary art in temporary exhibitions. There is always something worth seeing and the gallery has an excellent buffet restaurant and gift shop. MAM is linked by a covered walkway to the **Museu Afro-Brasil** ① *Portão 10, T011-4004 5006, www.museuafro brasil.com.br, Tue-Sun 1000-1800, US$4*, which lies inside Niemeyer's spectacular, stilted **Pavilhão Manoel da Nobrega** building and devotes more than 12,000 sq m to a celebration of black Brazilian culture with regular films, music, dance, and theatrical events and an archive of over 5000 photographs, paintings, ritual objects and artefacts which include the bisected hull of a slaving ship showing the conditions under which Africans were brought to Brazil.

A few hundred metres to the west of here, on the shores of the artificial lake, the **Planetário e Museu de Astronomia Professor Aristóteles Orsini** ① *Portão 10, T011-5575 5206, www.prefeitura.sp.gov.br/astronomia, Sat and Sun 1200-1800, US$5*, was restored in 2006 with a new projection ceiling and state-of-the-art Star Master projection equipment by Carl Zeiss, and is now one of the most impressive in Latin America. Shows are in Portuguese.

Less than 100 m to the south, is the **Pavilhão Japonês** ① *Portão 10, T011-5081 7296, Wed, Sat, Sun and holidays 1300-1700, free except for exhibitions*. The building is a reproduction of the Palácio Katsura, in Tokyo, built in Japan in strict adherence to Japanese aesthetic principles and re-assembled next to the park's largest lake (which has illuminated fountain displays on weekday evenings). The pavilion on the lower floor has an exhibition space devoted to Japanese-Brazilian and Japanese culture and a traditional Japanese tearoom upstairs.

The park also has a **running track** (with pit stops for exercise with pull-up bars, weight machines and chunky wooden dumbells), football pitches and hosts regular open-air concerts on Sundays. Those seeking something quieter on a Sunday can borrow a book from the portable library and read it in the shade of the **Bosque da Leitura** or 'reading wood'. Bicycles can be hired in the park (US$3 per hour) and there are dozens of small snack vendors and café-restaurants.

FESTIVALS

São Paulo

Throughout the year there are countless anniversaries, religious feasts, fairs and exhibitions. To see what's on, check the local press or the monthly tourist magazines. Fashion week is in the **Bienal Centre** (Bienal do Ibirapuera) in Ibirapuera Park, Parque do Ibirapuera, T011-5576 7600.

25 January Foundation of the city.

February Carnaval. *Escolas de samba* parade in the Anhembi Sambódromo.

During Carnaval most museums and attractions are closed.

June Festas Juninas and the **Festa de São** Vito, the patron saint of the Italian immigrants.

September Festa da Primavera.

October Formula One Grand Prix at Interlagos.

December Christmas and New Year.

Ibirapuera also has a few monuments of note. **O Monumento as Bandeiras**, which sits on the northern edge of the park, is a brutalist tribute to the marauding and bloodthirsty slave traders, or *bandeirantes*, who opened up the interior of Brazil. It was created by Brazil's foremost 20th-century sculptor, Victor Brecheret. The **Obelisco aos Héroes de 32**, on the eastern edge of the park, is a monumental Cleopatra's needle built in honour of the Paulistano rebels who died in 1932 when the dictator Getúlio Vargas crushed resistance to his Estado Novo regime. Above the rushing Sena Madureira urban highway – where it thunders into the tunnel which passes beneath the park – is **Velocidade, Alma e Emoção** (Speed, Soul and Emotion), a bronze tribute to one of São Paulo's favourite sons, the Formula One driver **Ayrton Senna**, by local artist Melinda Garcia.

A bridge leads across the 16-lane Avenida 23 de Maio urban highway in the southeast corner of the park near Portao 4 to the former DETRAN building, which is a giant oblong on stilts by Oscar Niemeyer. Until 2007 it was home to the state transit authority. In late 2012 it opened as a new permanent exhibition space for **Museu de Arte Contemporanea Universidade de São Paulo (MAC USP)** ① *T011-5573 9932, www.mac.usp.br, Tue-Sun 1000-1800, free*, who have their principal gallery on the USP campus (see page 225). MAC USP Ibirapuera showcases paintings from the MAC collection (which include works by Picasso, Chagall and Modigliani as well as Brazlian artists) together with temporary exhibitions.

ITAIM BIBI, VILA OLÍMPIA AND MOEMA

① *Metrô Faria Lima (from 2013), CPTM Vila Olímpia and Cidade Jardim.*

Business mixes with pleasure in these plush neighbourhoods south of Jardins and near Ibirapuera park. By day they are filled with office workers; by night, especially at weekends, hundreds of bars and clubs are busy with partying Paulistano professionals. There are also glamorous shops, including the city's notorious temple to excess, **Daslu**, a shop so exclusive that it sits behind its own security gate, shirks changing rooms in favour of women- and men-only shopping galleries, and which boasts a roof covered in helipads for its preferred clientele. It is possible to spend a fortune and an entire day in Daslu, which is dotted with exclusive cafés and restaurants and even has its own private party area on the upper floor.

SÃO PAULO LISTINGS

WHERE TO STAY

A booming business sector and general lack of rooms has seen accommodation costs soar in São Paulo over the last 5 years. Room prices are not good value when compared to other world cities of similar stature. The best rates are always found over the internet.

$$$$ Emiliano, R Oscar Freire 384, T011-3069 4369, www.emiliano.com.br. Together with the **Fasano** (fasano.com.br) and slickly designed **Unique** (www.hotel unique.com), these are best suites in the city: bright, light and beautifully designed with attention to every detail. No pool but a relaxing small spa. Excellent Italian restaurant, location and service and lovely details like Campana brother cable chairs in the lobby.

$$$$-$$$ Park Plaza, Alameda Lorena 360, T011-2627 6000, www.goldentulippark plaza.com. A spacious lobby with a café-bar, leads to a range of well-appointed, newly renovated rooms, all of which mean business – functional, bright (with white walls, modest decor and wood-slat floors), free of clutter and with decent-sized work-spaces. Basic Wi-Fi is free and there is a spa, pool, business centre and with Av Paulista and a string of good restaurants and boutiquey shops in easy walking distance.

$$ Ibis São Paulo Paulista, Av Paulista 2355, T011-3523 3000, www.accorhotels. com.br. Modern, business-standard rooms with a/c and Wi-Fi, in a tower right on Av Paulista. Cheaper at weekends. Online reservations give the best rates.

$$ Pousada Dona Zilah, Alameda Franca 1621, Jardins, T011-3062 1444, www.zilah.com. A small *pousada* in a renovated faux-colonial house with plain but well-maintained rooms and common areas. Excellent location in upmarket Jardins, bike rental and generous breakfast included. Triple rooms available.

$$-$ Paradiso Hostel, R Chui 195, Paraiso, T011-9758 70747. Vague staff and sketchy service are more than made up for by a superb location (just off Av Paulista at Paraiso tube), and spacious, homey rooms furnished with a soupçon of design taste. The price doesn't include breakfast but there's an excellent bakery just around the corner. Lowest rates are for dorm accommodation.

RESTAURANTS

Together with Lima, São Paulo has the best restaurants in South America and is *the* place in Brazil for a gourmet splurge.

$$$ 348 Parrilla Porteña, R Comendador Miguel Calfat, 348, Vila Olímpia, T011-3849 0348, www.restaurante348.com.br. Brazil is famous for its meat grill restaurants. But for the best steak in the country come to this Argentinian restaurant whose owner boasts that he has the choicest cuts of meat in South America available only on export from Buenos Aires. The *ojo del bife* cuts like brie and collapses in the mouth like wafered chocolate. The accompanying wines are equally superb, especially the 2002 **Cheval dos Andes**. Great, unpretentious atmosphere.

$$$ D.O.M., R Barão de Capanema 549, Jardins, T011-3088 0761. Listed as the fourth best restaurant in the world in 2012 by prestigious *Restaurant* magazine, Alex Attala's chic upmarket eatery renders traditional Brazilian ingredients like manioc and palm hearts gourmet. Dishes include *salada de tomate pêra, água demelancia, salsinha lisa, beldroega e mini mussarela*

de búfala (plum tomato salad with watermelon juice, parsley, purslane and miniature buffalo mozzarella) and *arroz negro levemente tostado com legumes verdes e leite de castanha do Pará* (black rice lightly toasted and served with green vegetables and Brazil nut milk). Book ahead.
$$$ Dui, Alameda Franca 1590, T011-2649 7952, www.duirestaurante.com.br. Paulistano star chef Bel Coelho apprenticed with Laurent Suaudeau, worked at the **Fasano** and **D.O.M.**, for Gordon Ramsay and the two-star Michelin **Celler de Can Roca** in Girona. This is her first solo venture

serving sumptuous light Brazilian-Asian-Mediterranean fusion. Great cocktails in the downstairs bar.
$$$ Jun Sakamoto, R Lisboa 55, Pinheiros, T011-3088 6019. With the largest number of ethnic Japanese outside Japan, São Paulo boasts as many Japanese restaurants as traditional Brazilian *churrascaria* meat grills. This is one of the finest – serving Japanese cuisine with a French twist and utilizing superb fresh ingredients, some flown in especially from Asia and the USA. The dishes of choice are the degustation menu and the duck breast teppaniyaki.

WHAT TO DO

Nightlife
São Paulo has superb nightlife – with a bar on every corner and far too many samba bars, live music venues and dance clubs to list here. A comprehensive choice is available from the Footprint São Paulo book, which can be downloaded through the Footprinttravelguides.com website.
Grazie a Dio, R Girassol, 67, Vila Madelena, T011-3031 6568, www.grazieadio.com.br. The best bar in Vila Madalena to hear live music – there's a different band every night with samba on Sun. Great for dancing, always packed, respectable restaurant.
Ó do Borogodó , R Horácio Lane 21, Vila Madalena, T011 3814 4087. It can be hard to track down this down-at-heel, intimate club opposite the cemetery and in an unmarked house next to a hairdressers on the edge of Vila Madalena. But it's well worth the effort. The tiny dance hall is always packed with people between Wed and Sat. On Wed there's classic *samba canção* from retired cleaner Dona Inah who sings material from the likes of Cartola and Ataulfo Alves. And on other nights there's a varied programme of choro, forró and MPB from some of the best samba players in São Paulo.

Tours
SPin Brazil Tours, T011-5904 2269 / T011-9185 2623 (mob), www.spintours.com.br. Tailor-made services and private tours of São Paulo with options on destinations further afield. These include bilingual 3- and 4-hr tours of the city (including key sights such as the Football Museum, Edifício Italia and MASP, US$50), and coordinated visits to football matches and the Brazilian Grand Prix. **SPin** can also help to organize accommodation for a surcharge and offer a driver/guide service for business trips. Comfortable cars. Excellent organization.
Trip on Jeep, R Arizona 623, Brooklin, T011 5543 5281, www.triponjeep.com. Wonderful day or weekend trips away from the heat and the dust of São Paulo city to the lush and bird- and wildlife-filled forests nearby, to the caves in PETAR and other destinations in the state of São Paulo. Tours are in comfortable Land Rovers and are conducted by English- speaking zoologists and botanists. The Parelheiros trip includes organic lunch at the Centro Paulus (which also offers accommodation – www.centropaulus.com.br), a delightful haven in secondary forest.

IGUAÇU FALLS

Foz do Iguaçu (www.fozdoiguaçu.pr.gov.br), or Las Cataratas del Iguazú as they are known in Spanish, are the most overwhelming and spectacular waterfalls in the world. Situated on the Río Iguaçu (meaning 'big water' in Guaraní), which forms the border between Argentina and Brazil, they are made up of no less than 275 separate waterfalls. The Paraguayan city of Ciudad del Este is just a few kilometres away but Paraguay does not own territory at the falls themselves.

The most spectacular part is the Garganta do Diabo (Devil's Throat), the mouth of a 28-km-long gorge that stretches downstream to the Alto Río Paraná. It is best visited from the Argentine side (see Arriving at Iguaçu Falls, below, and page 230).

Viewed from below, the water tumbles and roars over the craggy brown cliffs, framed by verdant rainforest encrusted with bromeliads, orchids, begonias and dripping ferns. A seemingly perpetual rainbow hovers over the scene and toco toucans, flocks of parakeets, caciques and great dusky swifts dodge in and out of the vapour whilst a vast number of butterflies dance over the forest walkways and lookouts.

ARRIVING AT IGUAÇU FALLS

The town nearest the falls is also, confusingly, called Iguaçu – or to give it its full name – Foz do Iguaçu. For information on getting from São Paulo to Foz do Iguaçu, see page 232.

Around 80% of the falls lie in Argentina, which offers the most spectacular views and the best infrastructure. Tickets costs about US$22 on both sides (discount for Mercosur members). The Argentine side only accept Argentine pesos (ATMs at the entrance); dollars and euro can be used as well as reais on the Brazilian side. There are national parks protecting extensive rainforest on both sides. Transport between the two parks is via the Ponte Tancredo Neves, as there is no crossing at the falls themselves.

The **Brazilian park** offers a superb panoramic view of the whole falls and is best visited in the morning (four hours is enough for the highlights) when the light is better for photography. The **Argentine park** (which requires at least half a day) includes a railway trip in the entrance fee as well as offering closer views of the individual falls. To fully appreciate the forest, with its wildlife and butterflies, you need to spend a full day and get well away from the visitor areas. Both parks can, if necessary, be visited in a day, starting at about 0700. However, in the heat, the brisk pace needed for a rapid tour is exhausting. Sunset is best from the Brazilian side.

The busiest times are holiday periods and on Sunday, when helicopter tours are particularly popular. Both parks have visitor centres, though the information provided by the Argentine centre is far superior to that in the Brazilian centre. Tourist facilities on both sides are constantly being improved.

There are many advantages to staying in Foz do Iguaçu town and commuting to the Argentine side; it has, for example a much bigger choice of hotels and restaurants. Whichever side you decide to stay on, most establishments will accept reais, pesos or dollars. Cross-border transport usually accepts guaraníes as well.

A useful guidebook is *Iguazú, The Laws of the Jungle* by Santiago G de la Vega, Contacto Silvestre Ediciones (1999), available from the visitor centre.

GETTING TO THE FALLS FROM FOZ DO IGUAÇU

Buses leave Foz do Iguaçu town from the **Rodoviária Terminal Urbana** ① *Av Juscelino Kubitschek, 1 block from the infantry barracks*. The grey or red **Transbalan** service runs to the falls every half an hour 0530-2330, past the airport and **Hotel Tropical das Cataratas** (40 minutes, US$1.25 one way, payable in reais only). Return buses run 0800-1900. The bus terminates at the visitor centre, where you must pay the entrance fee and transfer to the free park shuttle bus, which leaves every five minutes 0830-1900. If driving, cars must be left in the visitor centre car park. Taxis from Foz do Iguaçu charge US$20 one way. You can negotiate in advance the return trip, including waiting and pay separately for each journey. Many hotels organize tours to the falls, which have been recommended in preference to taxi rides. Be wary of transfer offers from Iguaçu's travel agencies – they are often even more expensive than taking your own taxi.

CLOTHING

In the rainy season when water levels are high, waterproof coats or swimming costumes are advisable for some of the lower catwalks and for boat trips. Cameras should be carried in a plastic bag. Wear shoes with good soles, as the rocks can be very slippery in places.

IGUAÇU FALLS ORIENTATION

BACKGROUND

The Caiagangue people originally inhabited the region, but the first European visitor to the falls was the Spaniard Alvaro Núñez Cabeza de Vaca in 1541. He nearly fell off one of the waterfalls on his search for a connection between the Brazilian coast and the Río de la Plata, and named them the Saltos de Santa María (Santa Maria waterfalls). Though the falls were well known to the Jesuit missionaries, they were largely forgotten until the area was explored by a Brazilian expedition sent out by the Paraguayan president, Solano López, in 1863.

PARQUE NACIONAL FOZ DO IGUAÇU (BRAZIL)

The Brazilian national park was founded in 1939 and designated a World Heritage Site by UNESCO in 1986. The park covers 185,262 ha on the Brazilian side and 67,000 ha on the Argentinian side, extending along the north bank of the Rio Iguaçu, then sweeping northwards to Santa Tereza do Oeste on the BR-277. The subtropical rainforest benefits from the added humidity in the proximity of the falls, creating an environment rich in flora and fauna. Given the massive popularity of the falls, the national parks on either side of the frontier are surprisingly little visited.

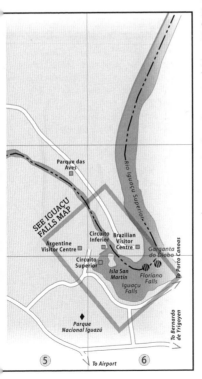

FAUNA

The parks on both sides of the falls are replete with wildlife and are a haven for birders. The most common mammals seen are coatis, which look like long-nosed racoons and squeakily demand food from visitors; do not be tempted as these small animals can be aggressive. There are other mammals here too, including jaguar, puma, ocelot and margay, which can occasionally be seen along the park roads just before and after dawn. They are wary of humans, although in 2003 a jaguar broke into the Parque das Aves (see page 231) and ate the zoo's prize caiman. Most frequently encountered are little and red brocket deer, white-eared opossum, *paca* (which look like large dappled guinea pigs) and a subspecies of the brown capuchin monkey. Other mammals include white-lipped peccary, bush dog and southern river otter. The endangered tegu lizard is common. Over 100 species of butterflies have been identified, among them the electric blue morpho, the poisonous red and black heliconius and species of papilionidae and pieridae.

The birdlife is especially rewarding. Five members of the toucan family can be seen: toco and red-breasted toucans, chestnut- eared araçari, saffron and spot-billed toucanets. From the bamboo stands you may see spotted bamboo wren, grey-bellied spinetail, several antshrikes and short-tailed ant-thrush. In the forest you might see rufous-thighed kite, black-and-white hawk-eagle, black-fronted piping-guan, blue ground dove, dark-billed cuckoo, black-capped screech-owl, surucua trogon, rufous-winged antwren, black-crowned tityra, red-ruffed fruitcrow, white-winged swallow, plush-crested jay, cream-bellied gnatcatcher, black-goggled and magpie tanagers, green-chinned euphonia, black-throated and utlra-marine grosbeaks, yellow-billed cardinal, red-crested finch. (Bird and mammal information supplied by Douglas Trent, **Focus Tours**. www.focustours.com.)

THE FALLS

All cars and public buses stop at the visitor centre, where there are souvenir shops, a **Banco do Brasil** ATM and *câmbio* (1300-1700), a small café and car park. If possible, visit on a weekday when the walks are less crowded. The centre is open daily in winter 0900-1700 and in summer 0900-1800. There is a R$12 (US$6.80) car-parking fee, payable only in Brazilian currency. This includes a transfer to the free park shuttle bus.

The first stop on the shuttle bus is the overpriced **Macuco Safari** ① *US$90 (bookable through most agencies, which may charge a premium for transfers)*. The safari takes one hour 45 minutes, leaving every 15 minutes, and visits the forest near the falls on an electric jeep and with a short trail walk climbing down to to a beach on the Garganta do Diabo. From here there are great views of the falls from below and the option to take a boat to the falls themselves; trips dunk visitors under one of the smaller cascades. Be sure to bring a fully waterproof, sealable plastic or rubber bag. Despite what guides say to the contrary, you and all your belongings will get completely soaked on this boat trip, which is the only part of the safari that can't be done solo. Visitors to Iguaçu will see as much wildlife and forest walking their own trails and boardwalks as they will with Macuco.

Iguazu Explorer ① *Sheraton Hotel, www.iguazujungle.com*, offer a 'Great Jungle Adventure' for US$45 – a shorter trip modelled than Macuco's, but inferior. It involves bombing through the jungle in a noisy truck followed by a short walk and a boat trip up the Garganto do Diabo to the falls. A better deal is the 12-minute solo boat trip up the Garganta for US$20, without the truck and trail walk.

The second stop is the **Cataratas Trail** (starting from the hotel of the same name, non-residents can eat at the hotel, midday and evening buffets). This 1.5-km paved walk runs part of the way down the cliff near the rim of the falls, giving a stupendous view of the whole Argentine side of the falls. It ends up almost under the powerful **Floriano Falls**; from here there is a lift to the top of the Floriano Falls; a path adjacent to the lift leads to Porto Canoa. A catwalk at the foot of the Floriano Falls gives a good view of the **Garganta do Diabo**.

The **Porto Canoas** complex, with its snack bar, toilets, souvenir shops and terraces with views of the falls, was completed in 2000 after some controversy. Its restaurant serves a US$22.50 buffet, which is good for a memorable meal.

IGUAÇU FALLS

Entrance to Brazilian Park

Central Station

Visitor Centre

Entrance to Argentinian Park

Sendero Verde

Waterfall Station

Circuito Inferior

Circuito Superior

Three Marie's Port

Isla San Martín

ARGENTINA

Rio Iguaçu Inferior

Rio Iguaçu Inferior

Rio Iguaçu Superior

Rio Iguaçu Inferior

Parque Nacional Foz do Iguaçu

Macuco Safari

BRAZIL

Rod das Cataratas

Visitor Centre

Garganta do Diabo

Boardwalk

Ruta 12

Devil's Canyon Station

To Porto Canoas

N

400 metres
400 yards

Waterfalls 〰
Duas Irmãs (Two Sisters) **1**
Pequena (Small) **2**
Ramírez **3**
Bossetti **4**
Bernabé Méndez **5**
Mbiguá **6**
Adão e Eva (Adam & Eve) **7**
San Martín **8**
Escondido **9**
Rivadavia **10**
Lanousse **11**
Alvar Núñes **12**
Dois Mosqueteiros
 (two Musketeers) **13**
Belgrano **14**
Três Mosqueteiros
 (three Musketeers) **15**
Mitre **16**
Peñón **17**
Santa Maria **18**
Floriano **19**
Deodoro **20**
Benjamin Constant **21**
Unión **22**

PARQUE NACIONAL IGUAZÚ (ARGENTINA)

Created in 1934, the park extends over an area of 67,620 ha, most of which is covered by the same subtropical rainforest as on the Brazilian side. It is crossed by Route 101, a dirt road that runs southeast to Bernardo de Yrigoyen on the Brazilian frontier. Buses operate along this route in dry weather, offering a view of the park.

FAUNA

You would have to be very lucky to see jaguars, tapirs, brown capuchin monkeys, collared anteaters and coatimundi. As in Brazil, very little of the fauna in the park can be seen around the falls; even on the nature trails described below you need to go in the early morning and have luck on your side. Of the 400 species of birds, you are most likely to spot the black-crowned night heron, plumed kite, white-eyed parakeet, blue-winged parrolet, great dusky swift, scale-throated hermit, suruca trogon, Amazon kingfisher, toco toucan, tropical kingbird, boat-billed flycatcher, red-rumped cacique, and the colourful purple-throated euphonia.

THE FALLS

The park is open daily 0800-1800 in summer and 0800-1700 in winter. Entry costs US$22, cash payment in Argentine pesos only. There are two cash machines by entrance. Guests at **Hotel Sheraton** should pay and get tickets stamped at the hotel to avoid paying again. The visitor centre includes a museum of local fauna and an auditorium for slide shows (available on request, minimum of eight people). It also sells a good guide book on Argentine birds. Food and drinks are available in the park but are expensive, so it is best to take your own. There is a **Telecom** kiosk at the bus stop.

A free train service leaves every 30 minutes from the visitor centre, departing for the start of two sets of walkways, both taking about an hour. The 'Circuito Inferior' or **Lower Trail**, leads down very steep steps to the lower falls and the start of the boat trip to Isla San Martin (see below). The easy 'Circuito Superior', **Upper Trail**, follows the top of the falls, giving panoramic views. The **Sendero Verde** path, taking about 20 minutes from near the visitor centre, leads to the start of the Upper and Lower trails. A second train route takes visitors to the start of an easy walkway that leads just over 1 km to the **Garganta del Diablo** (Devil's Throat). A visit here is particularly recommended in the evening when the light is best and the swifts are returning to roost on the cliffs, some behind the water.

Below the falls, a free ferry leaves regularly, subject to demand, and connects the Lower Trail with **Isla San Martín**. A steep path on the island leads to the top of the hill, where there are trails to some of the less-visited falls and rocky pools (take bathing gear in summer).

WHAT TO DO

A number of activities are offered, both from the visitor centre and through agencies in Puerto Iguazú (Argentina). On clear nights the moon casts a blue halo over the falls. During the full moon, there are sometimes night-time walking tours between the **Hotel Sheraton** and the falls (or from the **Hotel Tropical das Cataratas** on the Brazilian side. For serious birdwatching and nature walks with an English-speaking guide, contact the **Pantanal Bird Club** (www.pantanalbirdclub.org).

The proximity of the falls have made Foz (population 260,000) the third most visited town in Brazil. It has no attractions of its own but is only 28 km from the falls and although there are some upmarket hotel options, the town has a greater range of cheap accommodation and restaurants.

From the town it is possible to visit a number of beaches on the shores of **Lake Itaipu** (see Itaipu Dam); the closest are at **Bairro de Três Lagoas** (Km 723 on BR-277), and in the municipality of **Santa Terezinha do Itaipu** (US$1.70), 34 km from Foz. The leisure parks have grassy areas with kiosks, barbecue sites and offer fishing as well as bathing. It is also possible to take boat trips on the lake.

The bird park, **Parque das Aves** ① *Rodovia das Cataratas Km 16, www.parquedasaves.com.br, US$12,* is well worth visiting. It contains rare South American (and foreign) birds including various currasows, guans, parrots, macaws and toucans. These are housed in large aviaries through which you can walk, with the birds flying and hopping around you. There is also a butterfly house. The bird park is within walking

FOZ DO IGUAÇU

distance of the **Hotel San Martín**. The **HI Paudimar Falls Hostel** (see page 233) offers a discount for its guests. The national park bus stops here, 100 m before the entrance to the falls.

ARRIVING IN FOZ DO IGUAÇU

Getting there   Flights from São Paulo arrive at Foz do Iguaçu's **Aeroporto Internacional Cataratas** ① *Rodovia BR-469, Km 16.5, T045-3521 4200*, which is 12 km from the town centre. The airport has a Banco do Brasil, a Bradesco and a *câmbio*, car rental offices, a tourist office and an official taxi stand. Taxis cost US$25 to the town centre and vice versa. Transbalan (Aeroporto/ Parque Nacional, http://onibusbrasil.com/empresa/transbalan) buses run to town, US$1.50, but don't permit large amounts of luggage (backpacks are fine); they run every 20 minutes 0545-2400. The buses go to the Terminal de Transporte Urbano in the centre. There are two terminals in Iguaçu so sometimes you have to change buses, but you only pay once so the system acts a bit like a metro – it's an integrated transport system. Many hotels run minibus services for a small charge. From the airport buses run to cities throughout southeastern Brazil and to Asunción in Paraguay.

Buses from São Paulo take 16 hours (Pluma US$50, *executivo* six a day, plus one more comfortable and more expensive *leito*). They arrive at the **Foz do Iguaçu Rodoviária** ① *Av Costa e Silva, 4 km from centre on road to Curitiba, T045-3522 3633*. There is a tourist office, Cetreme desk for tourists who have lost their documents, *guarda municipal* (police) and luggage store. Buses to the centre cost US$1.50. Buy onward tickets on arrival if possible as seats get booked up well in advance. There is also a local bus station, **Terminal Urbana**, in the centre of town.

Moving on   The next step will depend on whether you plan to visit the southern or the northern Pantanal (see pages 236 and 241). Travel from Foz do Iguaçu to Campo Grande in the southern Pantanal requires a change of bus in Cascavel (12 hours total journey time). To fly to Campo Grande you'll need to go via São Paulo. There are direct flights from Foz do Iguaçu to Cuiabá in the northern Pantanal, whereas buses will take 23 hours and go via Campo Grande.

Tourist information   The Secretaria Municipal de Turismo ① *Praça Getulio Vargas 69, Centro, T0800-451516, www.fozdoiguacu.pr.gov.br, daily 0700-2300*. There are tourist booths at the *rodoviária*, T045-3901 3575, daily 0630-1800, and the airport, T045-3521 4276, open for all arriving flights, with a free map and bus information, and Terminal de Transporte Urbano, T045-3523 7901, daily 0700-1800.

IGUAÇU FALLS LISTINGS

WHERE TO STAY

Aside from the Hotel das Cataratas, the best hotels are on the Argentinean side of the falls. Brazilian tour companies such as **Guayi** (see below) can move freely between the countries and you will have no difficulties if you choose to stay in Argentina.

$$$$ Hotel das Cataratas, directly overlooking the falls, 28 km from Foz, T045-2102 7000, www.hoteldascataratas. com.br. This hotel in the **Orient Express** group is the only establishment within the park on the Brazilian side. Housed in a mock-belle époque building it has generous rooms, grand public areas and a poolside garden visited by numerous birds, butterflies and, at dawn, small mammals. The hotel is right next to the falls offering the easiest access and the best chance to beat the crowds. The restaurant overlooking the falls has excellent Brazilian-Mediterranean cooking and there is a grill restaurant next to the pool. The only other restaurant options are a pricey cab ride away in Foz do Iguaçu town. Non-resident evening diners will be in the park after it closes and must take a taxi back to town.

$$$$ La Aldea de la Selva, Puerto Iguazu, Misiones, Argentina, T+54 3757-493010, www.laaldeadelaselva.com. Attractive hardwood and brick cabins set in rainforest rich in bird and small mammal life on the edge of a protected area near the falls. Cabins are linked by low-lit boardwalks, which also connect to a swimming pool, and which give a real sense of immersion in the forest. Decent restaurant and free Wi-Fi throughout.

$$ Pousada Cataratas, R Parigot de Sousa, 180, T045-3523 7841, www.pousada cataratas.com.br. Well-maintained modern rooms with modest furniture, tiled floors and en suite bathrooms with decent hot showers. These are gathered around a small pool. Good value with regular discounts and promotions through the website. 8-km from the park. The hotel can organize tours and transfers to and from the airport and *rodoviária*. Triple, quad and quintuple rooms available.

$$-$ HI Paudimar Campestre, Rodovia das Cataratas Km 12.5, Remanso Grande, near airport, T045-3529 6061, www.paudimar. com.br. Youth hostel with spotless single-sex dorms, pool, communal kitchen, football pitch, camping. The gardens are visited by birds and small mammals. Transfers and good-value tours arranged. Breakfast included. There's a Paudimar desk at the *rodoviária*. Only HI members in high season when the hostel gets very busy. Low prices are per person.

WHAT TO DO

Guayi Travel, R Irian Kalichewiski 265, Vila Yolanda, T-045 3027 0043, www.guayi travel.com. Excellent tours to both sides of the falls, Ciudad del Este, Itaipu and around, including options for birders and wildlife enthusiasts. English and Spanish.

Macuco Safari, Rodovia das Cataratas, Km 25, Parque Nacional do Iguaçu T045-3529 7976, www.macucosafari.com.br. This company offer a range of excursions, from canyoning to canopy tours, rappelling and rafting. Tours include the Macuco Safari itself, a much tourist-tramped 2-hr walk, with an electric car ride and boat trip, from US$75. The trails gets up close to the base of the falls themselves. The tour is only worth taking for the boat trip (there's better walking for free on the Argentinean side). Bring your own waterproof bag, strong enough to withstand total immersion (for cameras and clothes). You will get soaked to the bone and the bags provided by the company are inadequate.

THE PANTANAL

The Pantanal UNESCO Biosphere Reserve is the world's largest freshwater wetland and is the best place in the Americas for spotting wild animals, and one of the best places in the world to see birds. Capybara, anaconda, peccary, giant otter, metre-long macaws and ocelots are common sights and it is even possible to see that most elusive of South American mammals, the jaguar. At the end of the dry season, between June and August, the number of waterbirds, raptors and parrots has to be seen to be believed. Visiting the wetlands is easy with a large choice of camping tours from Campo Grande, Cuiabá, Corumbá or Miranda; or there's the more comfortable option of staying at one of the fazenda ranch houses that are increasingly opening their doors to tourists. Families with children will enjoy the little resort town of Bonito, which is famous for its clear-water rivers and caves, and makes a good base for visiting the Pantanal.

Within Brazil the Pantanal comprises a plain of around 21,000 sq km divided between two states, Mato Grosso do Sul and Mato Grosso; but it extends beyond Brazil into Bolivia, Paraguay and Argentina to form an area totalling 100,000 sq km. The plain slopes 1 cm in every kilometre north to south and west to east to the basin of the Rio Paraguai and is rimmed by low mountains. From these, 175 rivers flow into the Pantanal and after the heavy summer rains they burst their banks, as does the Paraguai itself, to create vast shallow lakes broken by patches of high ground and stands of cerrado forest. Plankton then swarm in the water to form a biological soup that contains as many as 500 million micro algae per litre. Millions of amphibians and fish spawn or migrate to consume them. And these in turn are preyed upon by waterbirds and reptiles. Herbivorous mammals graze on the stands of water hyacinth, sedge and savannah grass and at the top of the food chain lie South America's great predators – the jaguar, ocelot, maned wolf and yellow anaconda. In June, at the end of the wet season, when the sheets of water have reduced, wildlife concentrates around the small lakes or canals and then there is nowhere else on earth that you will see such vast numbers of birds or so many crocodilians. Only the plains of Africa can compete for mammals and your chances of seeing a jaguar or one of Brazil's seven other species of wild cat are greater here than anywhere on the continent.

These days, even the Pantanal is grazed by cattle, and the great Amazonian forests of northern Mato Grosso state are steadily giving way to soya beans. However, substantial pockets of forest still remain for now, particularly around the Rio Cristalino near the town of Alta Floresta, where one of the best jungle lodges in the Americas can be found.

ARRIVING IN THE PANTANAL

GETTING THERE AND AROUND
The Pantanal can be reached from two 'gateway cities', in Mato Grosso do Sul and Mato Grosso states. In Mato Grosso do Sul, access is from the state capital, Campo Grande, from where there are road connections to the little cattle ranching town of Miranda and from Corumbá on the border with Bolivia. In Mato Grosso access is from the capital city, Cuiabá.

There are direct flights between Foz do Iguaçu and Cuiabá (for the northern Pantanal). There are no direct flights between Foz do Iguaçu and Campo Grande (for the southern Pantanal) although Trip has flights between Cuiabá and Campo Grande; alternatively, you could fly from Foz do Iguaçu to Campo Grande via another hub city (for example with GOL via São Paulo).

Reaching the Pantanal from Foz do Iguaçu overland is arduous. For Campo Grande you need to go via Cascavel (two hours from Foz and 10 hours from Campo Grande). Services are frequent. For Cuiabá travellers must change bus in Campo Grande for another 12-hour bus journey. There is nowhere of any interest to break the journey.

Once in one of the gateway cities, there are three ways to visit the Pantanal. The easiest way is on an **organized tours**, which is increasingly popular. The best tours are with experienced guiding companies who use excellent guides – like **Pantanal Nature** in Cuiabá (who are specialists in jaguar safaris) and **Explore Pantanal** (see page 249), based out of Miranda (with pick-ups from Campo Grande), who offer immersion in the Pantanal way of life, including the indigenous culture, alongside safaris. There are also cheaper backpacker options where guiding is generally poorer and corners are cut on accommodation, transport (which can be very uncomfortable) and organization. Most tours generally involve camping or sleeping on a boat and/or stays in a *fazenda* (ranch house), with a range of activities, including hiking, canoeing and wildlife and birdwatching.

Another option is to organize a tour directly through a *fazenda*, which are generally comfortable with air-conditioning and good home cooking. Many can organize decent wildlife guides who know English and scientific names for birds and animals.

It is also possible to visit the Pantanal on a self-drive tour, by hiring a 4WD in Cuiabá or Campo Grande. Those considering this option should speak good Portuguese and stick to the two principal dirt roads that enter the Pantanal: the **Transpantaneira** in Mato Grosso and the **Estrada Parque** in Mato Grosso do Sul. For further information on the Pantanal, consult www.visitbrasil.com, www.turismo.ms.gov.br and www.sedtur.mt.gov.br.

BEST TIME TO VISIT

The Pantanal is worth visiting at any time of year. However, the dry season from June to October is the ideal time to see wildlife as animals and birds congregate at the few remaining areas of water. This is also the breeding season, when birds form vast nesting areas, with thousands crowding the trees, creating an almost deafening cacophony of sounds. The white-sand river beaches are exposed, *jacarés* bask in the sun, and capybara frolic in the grass. It is during these months you are most likely to see jaguars, however, July sees lots of Brazilian visitors and the increased activity decreases the chances of sightings. From the end of November to the end of March (wettest in February), most of the area, which is crossed by many rivers, is subject to flooding. At this time mosquitoes abound and cattle crowd onto the few islands remaining above water. In the southern part of the Pantanal, many wild animals leave the area, but in the northern Pantanal, which is slightly higher, the animals remain.

MATO GROSSO DO SUL AND THE SOUTHERN PANTANAL

Mato Grosso do Sul is dominated by the Pantanal wetlands in the north and by the low Serra da Bodoquena mountains in the south, which surround the family-orientated ecotourism town of Bonito. The mountains are honeycombed by caves and cut by numerous glassy clear streams. There are only a few towns of any size and the state is a centre of soya plantations and cattle ranching. Many of the designated backpacker tours of the Pantanal leave from the state capital, Campo Grande, which is a prosperous, modern city with lively nightlife. However, they take half a day to reach the Pantanal itself, which begins in earnest east of Campo Grande, near the cattle-ranching town of Miranda. Many of the best *fazenda* ranch houses are in the area surrounding Miranda, as well as a handful of small, upmarket tour operators. The town also has one of the Pantanal's liveliest festivals, O Festa do Homen Pantaneiro, in November. Corumbá, on the banks of the Rio Paraguai, is another popular departure point for the Pantanal, and lies close to the Estrada Parque dirt road (which runs through the wetlands) and to Nhecolândia, a wilderness area visited by most of the Campo Grande backpacker tours.

VISITING THE SOUTHERN PANTANAL

Campo Grande offers most of the tours. Touts are ready and waiting for buses arriving from destinations in eastern Brazil like Foz do Iguaçu and at the airport. Not all offer a good deal and it's advisable to book ahead. The better agencies will meet you at either the airport or rodoviária and will include such transfers in the price. Most of the tours visiting the southern Pantanal involve a transfer from Campo Grande to the **Estrada Parque** dirt road (which begins halfway between Miranda and Corumbá at a turn-off called Buraco da Piranha). Varous *fazendas* (ranch house safari hotels) line this road, which cuts through the heart of the Pantanal to **Nhecolândia**, a region particularly rich in wildlife. Four-wheel drives run by the tour operators or the *fazendeiros* wait at the Buraco da Piranha to meet tour buses arriving from Campo Grande. They then take visitors either to *fazendas* or to campsites in Nhecolândia.

    Corumbá at the end of the Estrada Parque was once the capital of backpacker tourism in the Pantanal but is now used more as a departure point for boat trips. **Miranda**, which lies halfway between Campo Grande and the Estrada Parque at the turn-off to Bonito, is a small Pantanal ranching town free of touts, with a large indigenous Terena community and the best of the Pantanal *fazendas* are situated close by. The best tour company in the southern Pantanal, **Explore Pantanal** (see page 249), is based here.

CAMPO GRANDE

A major gateway to the Pantanal, Campo Grande (population 665,000) is a pleasant, modern city on a grid system, with wide avenues. It was founded in 1899 and became the state capital in 1979. Because of the *terra roxa* (red earth), it is known as the 'Cidade Morena'.

In the centre is a shady park, the **Praça República**, commonly called the Praça do Rádio after the Rádio Clube on one of its corners. Three blocks west is **Praça Ari Coelho**. Linking the two squares, and running east–west through the city, is the broad Avenida Afonso Pena; much of its central reservation is planted with yellow *ypé* trees. In spring, their blossom covers the avenue, and much of the city besides. The avenue's eastern reaches are the centre of a burgeoning restaurant and nightlife scene. City tours are on offer everywhere but they are generally expensive and there are few obvious sights.

Arriving in Campo Grande The airport ① *Av Duque de Caxias, 7 km, T067-3368 6000,* receives flights from Cuiabá and São Paulo (among other cities). A bus leaves every 10 minutes from outside the airport terminal for the city centre and bus station. A taxi costs US$10 (10 minutes). It is safe to spend the night at the airport if you arrive late. **Banco do Brasil** at the airport exchanges dollars; the **Bradesco** just outside has a Visa ATM. The airport also has a tourist information booth (little English, many pamphlets), a post office, car rental and airline offices.

There are frequent buses from Foz do Iguaçu involving a change of bus in Cascavel, a 12- to 14-hour journey (US$45) and on to Miranda (from where buses run to Bonito). Buses leave and arrive from the new **rodoviária** ① *15 km outside the city centre on Av Gury Marques (BR-163) 1215, T067-3026 6789; bus 087 leaves every 20 mins from Praça Ari Coelho in the centre, US$1.50, shuttle bus to the airport US$5, taxi to the centre US$17.* The terminal has cafés, internet, a handful of shops and left luggage. Most Pantanal tour operators will meet clients off the bus and organize transfers to destinations further afield.

The **Trem do Pantanal** train connects Campo Grande with Miranda at weekends but takes three times as long as the bus and is more expensive.

Moving on Bonito (see page 238) and Miranda (see page 240) can both be accessed by bus from Campo Grande. For the next stage of your trip, flights to Manaus go via Brasília or Cuiabá.

Tourist information There are Centro de Atendimento ao Turista ① *www.prefeiturade campogrande.com.br, Mon-Fri 0900-1800,* tourist booths throughout the city: at the airport, T067-3363 3116; in the rodoviária, T067-3382 2350; and in the Mercado Municipal, T067-3314 9949.

Places in Campo Grande Just north of the Praça República, is the **Museu Dom Bosco** ① *Av Alfonso Pena, Parque Naçoes Indígenas, T067-3312 6491, www.museu.ucdb.br, usually Tue-Sat 0800-1800, Sun 0800-1200 and 1400-1700, US$1.50, but with a temporary restriction on* visits in early 2009, contact Professor Dirceu or Señor Juliano on T067-3326 9788, which contains relics of the tribes who suffered at the hands of aggressive Salesian missionaries in the early and mid-20th century. The largest collections are from the Tukano and Bororo people from the upper Rio Negro and Mato Grosso respectively, both of whose cultures the Salesians were responsible for almost completely wiping out. Traditional practices such as sleeping in *malocas* or wearing indigenous clothing were banned, and the *indígenas* were indoctrinated in rigorous, literalistic pre-Vatican II Catholicism. These exhibits sit alongside a rather depressing display of stuffed endangered species (mostly from the Pantanal), as well as peculiarities such as a two-headed calf, and seashells from around the world.

Next to the railway line, the **Museu do Arte Contemporâneo** ① *Marechal Rondón and Av Calógeras, Mon-Fri 1300-1800, free*, displays modern art from the region.

The **Parque dos Poderes**, a long way from the centre, covers several hectares. As well as the Palácio do Governo and state secretariats, there is a small zoo for rehabilitating animals from the Pantanal. Contact the **Centro de Reabilitação de Animais Silvestres (CRAS)** ① *T067-3326 1370*, to arrange a visit. There are many lovely trees in the park, along with cycling and jogging tracks. Plenty of capybara live in the lakes.

BONITO AND AROUND

The designated tourist town of Bonito (population 17,000) lies just south of the Pantanal in the **Serra da Bodoquena** hills. It is surrounded by beautiful *cerrado* forest cut by clear-water rivers rich with fish and dotted with plunging waterfalls and deep caves. The town was 'discovered' by *Globo* television in the 1980s and has since grown to become Brazil's foremost ecotourism destination. There are plenty of opportunities for gentle adventure activities such as caving, rafting and snorkelling, all with proper safety measures and great even for very small children. Those looking to see animals and contemplate nature should opt for the forest walks of the Sucuri river. Despite the heavy influx of visitors, plenty of wildlife appear on and around the trails when it is quiet. **Paca** and **agouti** (large, tailless foraging rodents), **brown capuchin** monkeys and **toco toucans** are abundant, as are endangered species like the tiny and aggressive **bush dog** and cats such as **ocelot** and **jaguarundi**. **Bare-faced currasows** (magnificent turkey-sized forest floor birds) can often be seen strutting around the pathways. Rarely seen small toucans such as the **chestnut-eared aracari** are relatively easy to spot here, flitting in and out of the trees.

For all its attractiveness, many of Bonito's prices are becoming almost offensively steep and many of the attractions would simply not be worth the entry ticket at half the price.

Arriving in Bonito The *rodoviária* is on the edge of town. Several buses daily run to/from Campo Grande (five hours), and still more to Miranda (two to three hours) from where there are frequent connections to Campo Grande and Corumbá and the Bolivian border. There is also a shuttle service to Campo Grande which will pick up from your hotel and which can be booked through Bonito hotels or through **Explore Pantanal** (see page 249). Bonito town is a grid layout based around one principal street, Rua Coronel Pilad Rebuá, which extends for about 2 km. The town is easily negotiated on foot.

Tourist information The tourist office: **Conselho Municipal de Turismo (COMTUR)** ① *Rodovia Bonio, Guia Lopes da Laguna km1, T067-3255 2160, www.bonito-ms.com.br*, has limited information and staff do not speak English. The private website www.portal bonito.com.br is a more useful source of information. Prices in Bonito have risen sharply over the years, making the area prohibitively expensive for those on a budget. Local attractions can only be visited with prior booking through one of the town's numerous travel agents. With the exception of specialist activities like cave diving, all agents offer exactly the same products at exactly the same price, but only a few offer transport. Taxis to the sights are exorbitantly expensive; an alternative would be to hire a car.

Best time to visit The number of visitors to Bonito is limited so pre-booking is essential during December and January, Carnaval, Easter and July; prices during these times are also very high. The wet season is in January and February; December to February are the hottest months; July and August coolest.

Places in Bonito There are scores of different sights in Bonito and those sketched out below are a mere representative selection. The website www.bonito-ms.com.br has a full list, with pictures and links to each individual attraction's website.

Gruta Lagoa Azul ① *Rodovia para Tres Moros 22 km, daily 0700-1700, US$20*, is a cave with a lake 50 m long and 110 m wide, 75 m below ground level. The water's temperature is 20°C, and it is a jewel-like blue, as light from the opening is refracted through limestone and magnesium. Prehistoric animal bones have been found in the lake. The light is at its best in January and February, from 0700 to 0900, but is fine at other times. A 25-ha park surrounds the cave. The cave is filled with stalactites and stalagmites. It is reached via a very steep 294-step staircase which can be slippery in the rain and is completely unilluminated.

Nossa Senhora Aparecida cave has superb stalactites and stalagmites and can be visited, although there is no tourism infrastructure.

On the banks of the Rio Formoso, the **Balneário Municipal** ① *7 km on road to Jardim, US$4*, has changing rooms, toilets, camping, swimming in clear water and plenty of colourful fish to see. Strenuous efforts are made to keep the water and shore clean. The Horminio waterfalls ① *US$1*, consist of eight falls, which are suitable for swimming. There's a bar and camping is possible. **Rafting** is also a popular activity. The 2½-hour trip combines floating peacefully downriver, swimming and shooting down the four waterfalls.

The **Aquário Natural** ① *Estrada para Jardim 8 km and then 5.5 km of dirt road, daily 0900-1800, US$70 including lunch*, is a 600-m-long clear-water river lagoon filled with dourado and other fish and is formed by one of the springs of the Rio Formoso. This is the most child-friendly snorkelling in Bonito – easy and with almost no current.

It is possible to snorkel further along the **Rio Formoso** ① *Estrada para Ilha do Padre 12 km, daily 0800-1700, US$28*, or float on rubber dinghies over gentle rapids.

One of the better value, and more peaceful tours involves birding and swimming or snorkelling in crystal-clear water from the springs of the **Rio Sucuri** ① *Rodovia Bonito, Fazenda São Geraldo, Km 18, T067-3255 1030, daily 0900-1800, US$75 with lunch*, to its meeting with the Formoso, followed by horse riding or trail walking. Other tours include **Rio da Prata** (US$40), a beautiful spring with underground snorkelling for 2 km. There are also plenty of chances for walking along ecological trails, horse riding and fishing trips. The **fishing** season is from 1 March to 31 October. In late October and early November is the *piracema* (fish run). The fish return to the spawning grounds and hundreds can be seen jumping the falls.

Abismo Anhumas ① *Fazenda Anhumas, Estrada para Campo dos Indios s/n, T067-3225 3313, US$210 (for abseiling and snorkelling) or US$310 (for rapelling and scuba diving)*, is another of Bonito's spectacular caves, filled with a glassy pool. The ticket gives visitors an abseil (of just a few metres) into the cave, followed by three to four hours snorkelling or scuba diving.

Bonito Aventura ① *Estrada para Jardim 8 km, daily 0900-1800, US$28, including lunch*. This little reserve comprises a stand of pretty cerrado forest with many rodents like paca and agouti as well as capuchin monkeys and toco toucans in the trees. Trails cut through it to a clear-water river filled with fish.

JARDIM

Jardim, reached by paved road (60 km from Bonito) could be an alternative base to Bonito for trips on clear-water rivers and visits to caves. There is far less infrastructure and consequently far fewer tourists and cheaper accommodation, restaurant and taxi prices. The town itself has a wide, tree-lined main street, a handful of hotels and basic café-restaurants. The official town website, www.jardim.ms.gov.br, has information and photos of what to see and do. The *rodoviária* has regular bus connections with Campo Grande and other towns. From Bonito a road leads to Porto Murtinho, where a boat crosses to Isla Margarita in Paraguay (entry stamp available on the island).

MIRANDA

This little farming town built around a now disused mill and a railway station lies some 200 km west of Campo Grande at the turn-off to Bonito. It has long been overlooked as a gateway to the Pantanal and Bonito, but is actually far closer to both than either Corumbá or Campo Grande. Many of the best of the southern Pantanal *fazendas* are found here: **San Francisco** has an impressive big cat project and almost guaranteed ocelot or jaguar sightings, while **Refúgio Ecológico Caiman** would sit comfortably within the pages of *Condé Nast Traveller*. Miranda is also a real town (population 23,000), preoccupied more with its own local economy and culture than with tourism. It lies in the heart of indigenous Terena land and the communities have a large **cultural and arts centre** ① *at the entrance to town, Mon-Fri 0700-2200, Sat and Sun 0800-2200, free*, with panels on Terena history and arts and crafts for sale. Every October Miranda throws the spectacular **Festa do Homem Pantaneiro**: four days of rodeos, lassoing and general revelry that

combine well with the water festival in Corumbá. For dates ask tour operators (see page 249). The crystal-clear river Salobrinho just outside town has great birdlife and a community of giant otters. There is a wonderful British girder bridge just west of town given as a gift to Brazil by King George V.

Arriving in Miranda The Campo Grande–Corumbá road crosses the Rio Miranda bridge (two service stations before it), then continues paved all the way to cross the Rio Paraguai. Miranda is served by numerous daily buses from Corumbá, Campo Grande and Bonito. There is a tourist booth just outside the *rodoviária*, opposite the **Zero Hora** bakery and supermarket. The **Trem do Pantanal** tourist train (see below) runs to and from Campo Grande at weekends, taking 10 to 11 hours and costing US$75. There is no tourist office but **Explore Pantanal** can provide information in English, see also www.miranda.ms.gov.br. The town is tiny and can be walked from end to end in less than 10 minutes.

TREM DO PANTANAL

ⓘ *Estação Ferroviaria s/n, T067-3384 6755, http://serraverdeexpress.com.br, Sat-Sun 1 departure, US$75 or US$400 for a private cabin for up to 8 people, bookable only through tour operators.*

Miranda is the terminus for the Trem do Pantanal. This is a tourist-designated diesel train which takes 11 hours to make the 220-km trip across the southwestern Pantanal from Campo Grande. The journey includes a two-hour stop for lunch in the tiny town of Aquidauana (lunch costs extra) and breaks at stations to buy indigenous arts and crafts. There's little wildlife to see along the way– the occasional rhea striding across the pasture, distant lakes filled with birds – but the journey is more comfortable and leisurely than on the bus; and many times more expensive.

MATO GROSSO AND THE NORTHERN PANTANAL

Mato Grosso, immediately to the north of Mato Grosso do Sul, shares the Pantanal with that state and has equally well-developed tourism facilities. Although there are just as many opportunities for seeing wildlife, trips to the Pantanal near the state capital, Cuiabá, tend to be more upmarket than those leaving from Corumbá in Mato Grosso do Sul. The state also has abundant though rapidly depleting areas of Amazon forest; Alta Floresta, in the north, has an excellent birdwatching and wildlife lodge and one of the Amazon's most comfortable lodges, the Jardim da Amazônia, lies in the middle of vast fields of soya to Alta Floresta's southwest. The much-vaunted Chapada dos Guimarães hills, near Cuiabá, afford good light walking and birdwatching, although the natural landscape has been greatly damaged by farming and development.

Background The area that is now Mato Grosso and Mato Grosso do Sul was first demarcated as Spanish territory, but it was the Portuguese Aleixo Garcia who was the first to explore it in 1525. Jesuits and then *bandeirantes* entered the Mato Grosso for their different ends during the 17th and early 18th centuries, and, when gold was discovered near Cuiabá, a new influx of explorers began. Mato Grosso became a captaincy in 1748 and the borders between Portuguese and Spanish territories were decided in the following years. Throughout the 19th century, after the decline in gold extraction, the province's economy stagnated and its population dwindled. This trend was reversed when the rubber boom brought immigrants in the early 20th century to the north of the region. Getúlio Vargas's 'March to the West' in the 1940s brought added development, accompanied first by the splitting off of Rondônia and by the formation of Mato Grosso do Sul in 1977.

VISITING THE NORTHERN PANTANAL

There are two main access points to the northern Pantanal: the **Transpantaneira road**, which cuts through the wetland and is lined with *fazendas*; and the town of **Barão de Melgaço**, which is surrounded by large lakes and rivers and is not as good for wildlife. Both are reached from Cuiabá in Mato Grosso (see below).

The Transpantaneira was built in 1976 and was originally planned to connect Cuiabá with Corumbá, but it currently goes only as far as the border at Porto Jofre on the Rio Cuiabá. Work has been suspended indefinitely – ostensibly because of the division of the two Mato Grosso states – and is a superb spot for wildlife watching. Hundreds of thousands of birds congregate here, particularly between June and September, to wade through the shallow wetlands to either side of the road. And at any time of year there seems to be a raptor on every other fence post. Mammals and reptiles can often be spotted crossing the road or even sitting on it, particularly at dawn and dusk. Most of the northern Pantanal's tourist-orientated *fazendas* are here. The road is unpaved, potholed and punctuated by numerous rickety wooden bridges and, although it can be driven in a standard hire car, progress is slow. It is probably better to see the Transpantaneira as part of a tour as most of the guides have access to the *fazendas* along the way. If you choose to go alone, be sure to book in advance; private individuals who turn up unannounced may or may not be welcome at some *fazendas*.

The easiest access is in the dry season (July to September). In the wet, especially January and February, there is no guarantee that you will get all the way to Porto Jofre. Bring plenty of water and some extra fuel as petrol stations often run out. If you choose not to take a tour or hire a car you can hitch a ride along the Transpantaneira from Poconé. Do not travel alone and be prepared for a bumpy ride in the back of a truck. There are several excellent companies based in Cuiabá who offer trips along the Transpantaneira to Porto Jofre, often combining them with visits to the Chapada dos Guimarães (see page 245), Nobres or the Mato Grosso Amazon. They include **Pantanal Nature** and the **Pantanal Bird Club** (www.pantanalbirdclub.org).

CUIABÁ

An important starting point for trips into the Pantanal, Cuiabá, a state capital (population 470,000), is an ordered and increasingly wealthy city; rich on soya from the vast plantations to the north. There are few sights of more than a passing interest, but the city has a number of leafy *praças* leading it to be called the 'Cidade Verde' (green city) by Matogrossenses. Cuiabá is in reality two twinned cities – separated by the sluggish Rio Cuiabá, an upper tributary of the Rio Paraguai – **Cuiabá** on the east bank of the river, and **Várzea Grande** on the west. They vie with Teresina in Piauí and Corumbá in Matto Grosso do Sul as the hottest cities in Brazil, with temperatures pushing up to the high 40s in the Antipodean summer months. The coolest months are June, July and August in the dry season.

Arriving in Cuiabá

Getting there There are flights to Cuiabá straight from Foz de Iguaçu or from Campo Grande if you have decided to visit the southern Pantanal first. Flights arrive at **Marechal Rondon airport** ① *Av João Ponce de Arruda, s/n, Várzea Grande, T065-3614 2500, 10 km from the centre*. There are ATMs outside the airport, as well as a post office, car hire booths and Sedtur office. To get to the centre, take any white **Tuiuiú** bus (the name will be written on the side), from in front of the airport to Avenida Tenente Coronel Duarte. Taxis cost US$20. It's also possible to take a bus from Foz do Iguaçu, a journey which in total takes 23 hours (US$100-115). It's worth breaking it halfway in Campo Grande where you will have to change bus (you could stop off here in either the southern Pantanal or Bonito). There are several buses daily from Campo Grande, which take 12 hours (US$55-65). These interstate buses arrive at the rodoviária ① *north of the centre at R Jules Rimet, Bairro Alvorada*. Town buses stop at the entrance of the *rodoviária*.

Many local bus routes have stops in the vicinity of Praça Ipiranga. Bus Nos 501 or 505 ('Universidade') to the university museums and zoo (ask for 'Teatro') leave from Avenida Tenente Coronel Duarte by Praça Bispo Dom José, a triangular park just east of Praça Ipiranga.

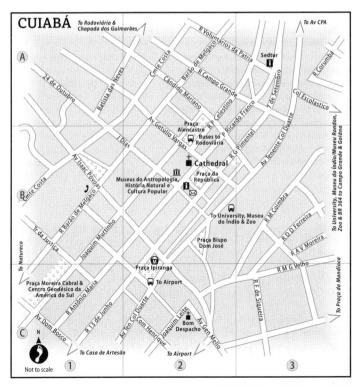

Moving on From Cuiabá there are buses to Chapada dos Guimarães (see page 245), Nobres and Bom Jardim (see page 246) and Alta Floresta for the Cristalino Rainforest Reserve (see page 247). There are also flights to Alta Floresta as well as to Manaus and the Amazon (see page 250) for the next stage of this itinerary.

Tourist information Sedtur ① *R Marechal Rondon, Jardim Aeroporto, Várzea Grande and with a smaller office at R Ricardo Franca at Voluntarios da Patria, T065-3613 9300, Mon-Fri 0900-1800, www.sedtur.mt.gov.br*, provides maps and general information on hotels and car hire and has a website in English. Staff are friendly and speak English and Spanish. They are very helpful in settling disputes with local tour companies.

Places in Cuiabá The most pleasant public space in Cuiabá is the lush **Praça da República** which is surrounded by a cluster of imposing buildings and dotted with sculptures and shady trees. Other pedestrian shopping streets and further squares lead off the *praça*. The brutalist façade of the **cathedral**, flanked by two functionalist clock towers, dominates the square. Until the late 1960s a beautiful 18th-century baroque church stood here but this was demolished to make way for the current building in a sweep of modernization that saw almost all the city's colonial charm destroyed.

On **Praça Ipiranga**, at the junction of avenidas Isaac Póvoas and Tenente Coronel Duarte, a few blocks southwest of the central squares, there are market stalls and an iron bandstand from Huddersfield in the UK, or Hamburg in Germany, depending on which story you believe. There is live acoustic music on Thursday and Friday on the **Praça da Mandioca**, a small square just east of the centre.

On a hill beyond the square is the extraordinary church of **Bom Despacho**, built in the style of Notre Dame. It is best viewed from afar as it is sadly run down and not open to visitors. In front of the Assembléia Legislativa on Praça Moreira Cabral, is a point marking the **Geodesic Centre of South America** (see also under Chapada dos Guimarães, below).

The rather dusty **Museus de Antropologia, História Natural e Cultura Popular** ① *Fundação Cultural de Mato Grosso, Praça da República 151, Mon-Fri 0800-1730, US$0.50*, are worth a look. There are interesting historical photos, a contemporary art gallery, indigenous weapons, archaeological finds and pottery. The section of stuffed wildlife from the Pantanal is disturbingly compelling.

At the entrance to the Universidade de Mato Grosso by the swimming pool, 10 minutes by bus from the centre, is the small **Museu do Índio/Museu Rondon** ① *T065-3615 8489, www.ufmt.br/ichs/museu_rondon/museu_rondon.html, Tue-Sun 0800-1100, 1330-1700, US$1*, with artefacts from tribes mostly from the state of Mato Grosso. Particularly beautiful are the **Bororo** and **Rikbaktsa** headdresses made from macaw and currasow feathers, and the **Kadiwéu** pottery (from Mato Grosso do Sul). Continuing along the road through the campus, signed on the left before a right turn in the road, is the **Zoológico** ① *Tue-Sun 0800-1100, 1330-1700, free*. The jacaré, capybara, tortoise and tapir pen can be seen at any time, but are best in the early morning or late afternoon. It also has coatis, otters, rhea, various monkeys and peccaries and a few, birds.

The **Águas Quentes** hot springs are 86 km away (9 km south of the BR-163, 77 km east of Cuiabá) and can be visited as a day trip

THE CHAPADA DOS GUIMARÃES AND NOBRES

Although consumed by agriculture and blighted by ill-considered careless tourism development, the craggy, cave-pocked escarpments of the Chapada dos Guimarães (www.chapadadosguimaraes.com.br) constitute one of the oldest plateaux on earth and one of the most scenic areas in Mato Grosso. They are very easy to visit in a day trip from Cuiabá. They begin to rise from the hot plains around Cuiabá some 50 km from the city, forming a series of vertiginous stone walls washed by waterfalls and cut by canyons. A dramatic, winding road, the MT-020, ascends through one to an area of open savannah standing at around 700 m, broken by patches of *cerrado* forest and extensive areas of farmland, dotted with curiously eroded rocks, perforated by dripping caves and grottoes, and leading to whole series of viewpoints out over the dusty Mato Grosso plains. There is one small settlement, the tranquil and semi-colonial village of **Chapada dos Guimarães**, where life focuses on a single *praça* and people snooze through the week until the crowds rush in from Cuiabá on Fridays and Saturdays.

The Chapada is said to be the geodesic heart of the South American continent and, about 8 km east of Chapada dos Guimarães town, at the **Mirante do Ponto Geodésico**, there is a monument officially marking this. It overlooks a great canyon with views of the surrounding plains, the Pantanal and Cuiabá's skyline on the horizon.

As the geodesic centre, the highlands are rich with **New Age folklore**. Crystals tinkle in the shops in Chapada dos Guimarães village, and peyote people in tie-dye clothing gather in cafés to murmur about apocalypse and a new human evolution, over hot chocolate and soggy cake. The Chapada's rocks are said to have peculiar energizing properties; a fact more solidly grounded in truth than you may suspect – a local magnetic force that reduces the speed of cars has been documented here by the police.

The Chapada is pocked with caves. These include the **Caverna Arroe-jari** ① *43 km of Chapada dos Guimarães village, daily 0900-1800, US$5, allow 3-4 hrs for the walk to and from the cave*, whose name means the 'home of souls' in a local Brazilian language. It's a haunting place – an 800-m-long cavern coursed by a little mountain stream running into a deep aqua blue lake, set in boulder-strewn grassland. It's best visited early in the day during the week, to ensure the fewest numbers of visitors possible, and to soak up the atmosphere. The walk to the cave cuts through waterfall-filled rainforest before emerging in open cerrado. Birdlife is rich.

The Chapada is a popular destination for birders, who often combine it with the Pantanal and Alta Floresta to up their species count. **Birdwatching** here is fruitful, in open country and with grassland and *cerrado* species not found in Alta Floresta and the Pantanal. Guides listed under the northern Pantanal (see page 249) can organize one- or two-day trips here and many are even based in the little town of Chapada dos Guimarães. Mammals, such as puma, jaguarundi, giant river otter and black-tailed marmoset can also be seen with time and patience.

Chapada dos Guimarães village The colourful village of Chapada dos Guimarães, 68 km northeast of Cuiabá, is the most convenient and comfortable base for excursions. It's a pretty little place, with a series of simple, brightly painted buildings clustered around a small *praça* graced with the oldest church in the Mato Grosso, **Nossa Senhora de Santana**, dating from 1779 and with a simple whitewashed façade. It is open intermittently. Just outside the town, there's a big **piscina publica** ① *R Dr Pem Gomes*, a spring-water fed, public swimming pool.

Frequent, regular buses run between Cuiabá and Chapada dos Guimarães town (about 1½ hours, US$5). The *chapada* can be visited in a long day trip either by self-drive (although access is via rough dirt roads that may deteriorate in the rainy season), bus or most easily through agencies such as **Pantanal Nature** (see page 249). The **tourist office** ① *R Quinco Caldas 100, 4 blocks from the praça*, near the entrance to the town, provides a useful map of the region and can help organize tours. The **Festival de Inverno** is held in the last week of July; during this time, and around **Carnaval**, the town is very busy and accommodation is scarce and expensive.

Parque Nacional da Chapada dos Guimarães This begins just west of Chapada dos Guimarães town, near where the Salgadeira tourist centre offers bathing, camping and an unsightly restaurant right beneath the **Salgadeira waterfall**. The beautiful 85-m **Véu da Noiva waterfall** (Bridal Veil), 12 km from the town, near Buriti (well signposted; take a bus to Cuiabá and ask to be dropped you off), is less blighted and can be reached by either a short route or a longer one through forest. Other sights include: the **Mutuca** beauty spot, named after a vicious horsefly that preys on tourists there; the viewpoints over the breathtaking 80-m-deep **Portão do Inferno** gorge off the MT-020 road; and the **Cachoeirinha falls**, where there is another small, inappropriately situated restaurant.

About 60 km from town are the archaeological sites at **Pingador** and **Bom Jardim**, which include caverns with petroglyphs dating back some 4000 years.

Nobres and Bom Jardim Some 100 km north of the Chapada is the little town of **Nobres**, which, like Bonito in Mato Grosso do Sul (see page 238), is surrounded by clear water rivers full of dourado fish and many beautiful caves. Unlike Bonito, there are few tourists and, whilst over-priced, the attractions are a good deal cheaper and far less spoilt. Nobres is the name for the area, but the main village, with a couple of small *pousadas* and a single restaurant, is called **Bom Jardim**. The town sits 2 km from the **Lago das Araras** ① *Bom Jardim, US$5*, a shallow lake surrounded by stands of buriti palm where hundreds of blue and yellow macaws roost overnight. Come at dawn for a wonderfully raucous dawn chorus. The restaurant **Estivado** ① *Rodovia MT-241, Km 66, 500 m northeast of Bom Jardim on the ponte Rio Estivado, US$4 for swimming (bring your own snorkel), US$7 for lunch*, offers

ON THE ROAD

Cristalino Rainforest Reserve

Much of the great forest of northern Mato Grosso and southern Pará is now a sea of soya, whose crop is destined for the post-BSE cattlefeed markets of Europe and the burgeoning Chinese market.

For now there are patches of forest intact, notably near the Rio Cristalino, which is home to the Cristalino Rainforest Reserve (Alta Floresta, T066-3512 7100, www.cristalino lodge.com.br). This is one of the best locations in the Amazon for wildlife enthusiasts, with superb guided visits to pristine rainforest, comfortable accommodation and wildlife-watching facilities as good as the best in Costa Rica or Ecuador. Cristalino is a private reserve the size of Manhattan contiguous with the 184,940-ha Cristalino State Park. This is itself connected to other protected Amazon areas, forming an important large conservation corridor in the southern Amazon. Ecotourism at Cristalino is a model of best practice. The management fulfil all four of the key conservational tourism criteria: conserving natural resources and biodiversity; conducting environmental education activities with the local community (leading to employment); practising responsible ecotourism (with recycling, water treatment, small group sizes and excellent guiding); and funding a research foundation. Wildlife is abundant. Cristalino has so far recorded 600 bird species, with new ones added almost monthly.

All the spectacular large mammals are found here alongside very rare or endemic species such as bush dogs, the red-nosed bearded saki monkey and the recently discovered white-whiskered spider monkey. And the reserve offers some of the best facilities for seeing wildlife in the Americas – on trail walks, boat trips on the river or from the lodge's enormous canopy-lookout tower. There is also a hide next to a clay lick for seeing tapir, peccary and big cats, and harpy eagles nest in the grounds of the reserve's twin hotel, the Floresta Amazônica in Alta Floresta town. Cristalino is reachable from Alta Floresta town, whose airport, Aeroporto Deputado Benedito Santiago (4 km from the city centre, Avenida Ariosto da Rivas s/n, T066-3521 2159), has connections with both Cuiabá and Brasília with two of Brazil's larger airlines. There are also daily overnight buses from Cuiabá, 12 hours.

a taste of what Nobres has to offer. It sits over the slow-flow of the Rio Esitvado, which forms a wide pool next to the restaurant and is filled with fish.

Nobres' other attractions dot the countryside around Bom Jardim, and as in Bonito they are on private ranch land. There is good snorkelling at the **Reino Encantado** ① *18 km from Bom Jardim at Alto Bela Vista, T065-9237 4471, US$50 for full day use including lunch, guide and equipment, US40 per night for a double room in the adjacent pousada*; the **Recanto Ecológico Lagoa Azul** ① *14 km from Bom Jardim at Alto Bela Vista, US$25 for entry, guide and equipment, US$8 extra for lunch*; and at the **Rio Triste** ① *18 km from Bom Jardim village, US$30 for a 2-hr float with guide and equipment rental*. The former two are 500-m floats down the Rio Salobra, which is filled with piraputanga (*Brycon microlepis*), piova (*Schizodon Borelli*) and piauçu (*Leporinus macrocephalus*) fish. The Rio Triste is filled with these species as well as fierce, salmon-like dourado (*Salminus maxillosus*) and spectacular mottled fresh-water stingrays, which should be treated with caution as they will inflict a painful wound if stepped on or handled. The most spectacular cave is the **Gruta do Lagoa Azul**, which was closed as this book went to press, and is set open according to the whims of **Ibama**, Brazil's environmental protection agency.

Bom Jardim town is served by a single daily bus from Cuiabá. However, there are at least four buses daily from Cuiabá (as well as services from Sinop and Alta Floresta) to Nobres town, from where there are regular connections to Bom Jardim. Taxis can be booked through the Pousada Bom Jardim to take visitors to the various attractions – there is no public transport. This can prove expensive (up to US$45 for a round trip to any single attraction, with waiting time), and the most practical way of visiting Nobres is with a tour agency in Cuiabá, such as **Pantanal Nature** (see page 249). The former can include the trip in conjunction with the Chapada dos Guimarães or Jardim da Amazônia and is better for wildlife.

THE PANTANAL LISTINGS

WHERE TO STAY

Southern Pantanal

$$$ Fazenda 23 deMarço, T067-3321 4737, www.fazenda23demarco.com.br. Simple rustic *fazenda* with a pool, and a handful of rooms near Miranda in Aquidauna. The *fazenda* is a Centrapan centre for the preservation of Pantanal culture, where visitors can learn to lasso, ride a bronco and turn their hand to other Pantanal cowboy activities and it is set in beautiful woody cerrado rich with animals.

$$$ Fazenda Baia Grande, Estr La Lima, Km 19, T067-3382 4223, www.fazendabaia grande.com.br. Very comfortable a/c rooms set around a pool in a bougainvillea- and *ipê*-filled garden. The *fazenda* is surrounded by savannah and stands of *cerrado* broken by large lakes. The owner, Alex, is very friendly, enthusiastic and eager to please.

$$$ Pousada Olho d'Água, Rod Três Morros, Km 1, Bonito, T067-3255 1430, www. pousadaolhodagua.com.br. Comfortable accommodation in fan-cooled cabins set in an orchard next to a small lake. Horse riding, bike rental, solar-powered hot water and great food from the vegetable garden.

$$ Pantanal Ranch Mandovi, BR 262 Km 554 Miranda, T067-9686 9064, www.pantanal ranchmandovi.com. Rustic guesthouse set in forested gardens and run by a Kadiweu indigenous Pantaneiro and his Swiss wife. Great food, lovely atmosphere, many birds and some of the best tours in the Pantanal. Full board available and camping area (**$**).

Northern Pantanal

$$$$ Araras Lodge, Km 32, T065-3682 2800, www.araraslodge.com.br. Book direct or through **Pantanal Nature** or any of the other opertors in Cuiabá as part of a tour. One of the most comfortable places to stay with 14 a/c rooms. Excellent tours and food, home-made *cachaça*, a pool and a walkway over a private patch of wetland filled with capybara and caiman. Very popular with small tour groups from Europe. Book ahead.

$$$$ Pousada Rio Claro, Km 42, www. pousadarioclaro.com.br, book through **Pantanal Nature**. Comfortable *fazenda* with a pool and simple a/c rooms on the banks of the Rio Claro, which has a resident colony of giant otters. The child-friendly *pousada* is popular with Brazilian families; however, few Brazilians who visit here are as interested in foreigners in seeing wildlife, or in the silent contemplation of pristine nature.

WHAT TO DO

Southern Pantanal

Explore Pantanal, Pantanal Ranch Mandovi (see above), T067-9292 3342, www.explore pantanal.com. Run by a Kadiweu indigenous guide and his Swiss partner, with many years of experience. Excellent tours throughout the Pantanal including contact with indigenous people. Great for small groups who want to get off the beaten track. Trips to Bonito (including pre-arranged transport), camping tours, hotel booking and day tours.

Northern Pantanal

Pantanal Nature, R Campo Grande 487, Cuiabá, T065-3322 0203, www.pantanal nature. com.br. Great trips to the northern Pantanal – both to the *fazendas* along the Transpantaneira and to Porto Jofre, from where the company runs the best designated jaguar safari in the Pantanal, and to Nobres, the Chapada dos Guimarães and **Pousada Jardim da Amazônia**. Guiding is excellent and service professional.

THE AMAZON

The Amazon is far more than a river. It is a continent of forests, savannahs and mountains, coursed by myriad veins of flowing water, pocked with lakes, overflowing with flooded forests and home to several million people. The wildlife is spectacular but the forests are dense and animals are far easier to spot in the Pantanal or cerrado. What is magical about the Amazon are its vast landscapes – its oceanic rivers, shimmering skies and labyrinthine backwaters – and the unique human drama which is played out here day after day.

The Amazon offers great diveristy. In the north, along the border with Venezuela and Colombia, are the forests and savannahs of the Guiana Shield where vegetation grows like a giant filigree over white sand and recycles 99.9% of its water and nutrients. West of here, the magnificent Rio Negro, black as coffee and fringed with pearly beaches, gushes past giant boulders the size of mountains before winding through the world's largest river archipelago, the Anavilhanas, and spreading out over several kilometres as it reaches the teeming port of Manaus.

In the east, the Amazon is joined by a series of rivers which are in their own right some of the largest in the world: the glassy blue Tapajos, the inky Xingu and, just as the river reaches its mouth, the Tocantins. Here the Amazon divides around an island the size of Denmark, the Ilha de Marajó, before spilling into the Atlantic, turning it fresh 100 miles offshore. Two cities lie on its banks: sleepy Macapá, with road connections to the Guianas; and bustling Belém, a historic colonial city with some of the best nightlife and cuisine in Brazil.

VISITING THE FOREST

WHAT TO VISIT

The scenery is at its best on the **Rio Negro**, especially around the **Anavilhanas** archipelago, and further upstream where the mountains of the Guiana Shield punctuate the forest like giant worn crocodile teeth. However, the Rio Negro is an acidic, black-water river and consequently has a lower level of biodiversity than the more PH-neutral brown-water rivers like the Solimões (Amazon). So if you are intent on seeing wildlife, you will see far more in the regions south of Manaus, on the smaller river tributaries, creeks (*igarapés*) and flooded forest areas (*varzea* and *igapós*), especially those that are farthest from people. The **Lago Mamori**, **Lago Piranha** and the **Rio Urubu** are popular destinations for operators in Manaus. These are semi-protected areas which mix wild forests, rivers, creeks, igapo lakes and riverine communities living within nature at minimum impact. Only the farther reaches of either have prolific wildlife, but all offer a taste of the forest, and there are fascinating community tourism projects at Mamori (see **Amazon Gero Tours**, page 268). The best area for wildlife and genuine, accessible wilderness is the **Mamirauá Ecological Reserve** near Tefé, 30-40 minutes by plane from Manaus or 11-12 hours by fast boat (see page 261). Some of the lodges very close to Manaus have their own reserves, which have been populated with rescued primates and birds.

WHEN TO VISIT

There is no best time to visit the forest; it depends what you want to see. The Amazon around Manaus is far more than a big river; think of it rather as an inland sea. Water is everywhere, especially during the **wet season**, which lasts from November to May.

During the floods, the water rises by 5-10 m and the forests around the main rivers form areas known as *varzea* (on brown-water rivers) and *igapós* (on black-water rivers). Trees are submerged almost to their canopies and it is possible to canoe between their trunks in search of wildlife. In the morning you can often hear the booming call of huge black caiman and the snort of dolphins. And as the boats pass through the trees, startled hatchet fish jump into the bows. It is possible to canoe for tens of kilometres away from the main river flow, as *varzea* and *igapós* often connect one river to another, often via oxbow lakes covered in giant lilies. The lakes are formed when a meandering river changes course and leaves part of its previous flow cut off from the stream. In the **dry season** the rivers retreat into their main flow, exposing broad mudflats (on the brown-water rivers) or long beaches of fine white sand. Caiman and giant river turtles can often be seen basking on these in the evening sun, and wildlife spotting is generally a little easier at this time of year. Trees in the Amazon bear fruit at different times throughout the year; whenever a particular tree is in fruit it attracts large parrots, macaws and primates.

CHOOSING A TOUR OR LODGE

Once you have decided on when and where to go, the next decision is to choose a lodge or an operator. Those used to the quality of wildlife information supplied by rainforest tour operators in Costa Rica, Peru, Ecuador or Bolivia will be disappointed by the lack of professional wildlife knowledge and ecotourism services offered by many of the operators in Manaus. If you are interested first and foremost in wildlife and want accurate information, be sure to request a specialist wildlife guide (see page 268) and question your tour company carefully to test their knowledge. A good way of doing this is to ask whether they can supply a species list for the area around their lodge or for the forests they visit during their tours. Few can. Serious wildlife enthusiasts and birders looking to visit the Brazilian Amazon should think about heading for **Mamirauá Ecological Reserve** near Tefé (see page 261) or **Cristalino Jungle Lodge** (see page 247) in Mato Grosso.

That said, the better Manaus tours offer a fascinating glimpse of the forest and filigree of rivers, and insights into river people's lives. And they are far cheaper than either Mamirauá or Cristalino. **Standard tours** involve a walk through the forest looking at plants and their usage, caiman spotting at night (many guides drag caiman out of the water, which has negative long-term effects and should be discouraged), piranha fishing and boat trips through the *igapós* (flooded forests) or the *igarapés* (creeks). They may also visit a *caboclo* (river village) or one of the newly established indigenous villages around the city. Other trips involve light adventure such as rainforest survival, which involves learning how to find water and food in the forest, and how to make a shelter and string up a hammock for a secure night's sleep.

Trips vary in length. A half-day or a day trip will usually involve a visit to the 'meeting of the waters' and the Lago de Janauri nature reserve, where you are likely to see plenty of birds, some primates and river dolphins. The reserve was set up to receive large numbers of tourists so there are captive parrots on display and numerous tourist shops. Yet ecologists agree that the reserve helps relieve pressure on other parts of the river. Boats for day trippers leave the harbour in Manaus constantly throughout the day, but are best booked at one of the larger operators. Those with more time can take the longer cruises with a company like **Amazon Clipper** (see page 268) or stay in one of the rainforest lodges. To see virgin rainforest, a five-day trip by boat is needed.

ON THE ROAD
The Amazon and the theory of evolution

While the Spanish and Portuguese came to the Amazon to plunder, pillage and enslave, the Europeans who followed them in the 18th and 19th centuries were more interested in beetles and botany than gold. Among the first was the Frenchman Charles Marie de la Condamine, who came to the Andes in the mid-1700s to ascertain whether the earth was a perfect sphere. He narrowly escaped being stoned by a superstitious mob in Cuenca, Ecuador, and fled to Cayenne. In doing so he was obliged to cross the Amazon, producing the first accurate map of the basin along the way and bringing rubber back to Europe. De la Condamine inspired other Enlightenment scientists to follow him. The greatest was Alexander von Humboldt, today known for the Humboldt Current (which he did not discover) and the Humboldt River (which he never saw), but who, in his time, was considered the pre-eminent scientist in Europe. During his stay on the upper Rio Negro, this great German collected some 12,000 specimens and survived shocks by electric eels, *curaré* poison and bathing with piranhas. He captured and dissected a 7-m caiman and established the region as the best in the world for the study of natural sciences. The English followed him: Henry Bates, Richard Spruce and, in 1848, Alfred Russel Wallace, who wrote: "I'd be an Indian here, and live content, to fish and hunt, and paddle my canoe, and see my children grow, like wild young fawns, In health of body and peace of mind, rich without wealth, and happy without gold! "

The seemingly infinite variety of plants and animals in the Amazon caused Wallace to reflect on how all this variety had come about: "so alike in design yet so changeable in detail? "Places not more than fifty or a hundred miles apart have species of insects and birds at the one which are not found at the other. There must be some boundary which determines the range of each species, some external peculiarity to mark the line which each one does not pass."

Charles Darwin had the same thought two years earlier after his return from Brazil and while reading an essay by Thomas Malthus on population. In his essay the economist argued that the realization of a happy society will always be hindered by its tendencies to expand more quickly than its means of subsistence. If this is true of animals, thought Darwin, then they must compete to survive and Nature must act as a selective force, killing off the weak, and species must evolve each from another through this process. Darwin was terrified by the implications of his thought and did not commit it to paper for six years, then sealing it and handing it to his wife with instructions to publish it after his death.

Alfred Russel Wallace was younger and less timid. While in a high fever on a field trip in Indonesia he was pondering over the thoughts that had haunted him since his days on the Amazon, and he too recalled the same essays by Malthus. The same thought which had struck Darwin, flashed into his own mind: "I saw at once that the ever-present variability of all living things would furnish the material from which, by the mere weeding out of those less adapted to the actual conditions, the fittest alone would survive the race." Wallace wrote to Darwin who was, at that time, the most famous natural scientist in Britain, explaining his theory and asking for his advice. Darwin's hand was forced and, after papers written by both scientists were presented at the Linnean Society on the same day, the theory of evolution was born.

Prices vary but usually include lodging, guide, transport, meals (but not drinks) and activities. The recommended companies charge around US$110-125 per person for a day trip, or US$300-350 for three days.

BEWARE OF THE TOUTS

There are many hustlers at the airport in Manaus and on the street (particularly around the hotels and bars on Joaquim Nabuco and Miranda Leão), and even at hotel receptions. It is not wise to go on a tour with the first friendly face you meet. All go-betweens earn a commission so recommendations cannot be taken at face value and employing a freelance guide not attached to a company is potentially dangerous as they may not be qualified; check their credentials. Tourist offices are not allowed by law to recommend guides, but can provide you with a list of registered companies. Unfortunately, disreputable companies are rarely dealt with in any satisfactory manner, and most continue to operate. Book direct with the company and ask for a detailed, written contract if you have any doubts. Above all avoid the cheapest tours. They are almost invariably the worst.

WHAT TO TAKE

Leave luggage with your tour operator/hotel in Manaus and only take what is necessary. Long-sleeved shirts and long trousers, walking boots, insect repellent and a hammock and/or mosquito net, if not provided by the local operator, are advisable for treks in the jungle, where insects can be voracious. A hat offers protection from the sun on boat trips. Powerful binoculars are essential for spotting wildlife (at least 7x magnification is recommended, with the ability to focus at between 2.5 m and infinity). Buying bottled water at the local villages can be expensive in the lodges and it produces a great deal of waste plastic. Bring iodine, purification tablets or a modern water filter like (best with iodine for Amazon river water).

ECOTOURISM BEST PRACTICE IN MANAUS

Most of the lodges around Manaus do not adhere to proper ecotourism practices; this guide lists the exceptions. Good practice includes integration and employment for the local community, education support, recycling and proper rubbish disposal, and trained guides with good wildlife lodges. Ecotourism in Brazil is often a badge for adventure tourism in a natural setting and few operators conform to the best practices of the **International Ecotourism Society**, www.ecotourism.org. In Manaus, a relatively small number of communities have benefited from a boom which has seen the total number of beds rise from just six in 1979 to more than 1000 today. Only 27% of labour derives from local communities and very few of the lodges are locally owned. We would love to receive feedback about lodges and operators you feel are (or aren't) making a difference.

MANAUS

Manaus, the state capital, sits at 32 m above sea level some 1600 km from the Atlantic and has a population of 1.4 million. The city sprawls over a series of eroded and gently sloping hills divided by numerous creeks, and stands at the junction of the liquorice-black Rio Negro and the toffee-coloured Solimões, whose waters flow side by side in two distinct streams within the same river. The city is the commercial hub for a vast area including parts of Peru, Bolivia and Colombia, and ocean-going container vessels often dock here.

ON THE ROAD

The number of animals facing extinction in Brazil has tripled since the early 1990s. In 2009 federal authorities caught one trafficking ring that was responsible for poaching an estimated 500,000 animals from the wild every year.

Poaching of wild animals is big business in Brazil. The Brazilian government estimates that as many as 12 million animals are poached every year. Despite there being posters all over every airport denouncing animal trafficking, between 1998 to 2009 the legislation against trafficking weakened and prosecutions became weak and confused. Large-scale trafficking is undertaken by gangs, yet Brazilian law does not distinguish between large-scale poaching for the trafficking industry and individuals poaching a single animal from the wild as a pet.

New-found wealth has turned Manaus from tawdry to tourist-friendly in the last 10 years and the city will be one of the host cities for the 2014 World Cup. The **Centro Histórico** (old rubber boom city centre), which huddles around the green and gold mock-Byzantine dome of the **Teatro Amazonas** opera house, has been tastefully refurbished and now forms an elegant pedestrian area with cafés, galleries, shops and musuems. The area is a pleasant place to stroll around and sip a cool juice or a strong coffee, and many of the best hotels and guesthouses are found here. There are plenty of restaurants, bars and clubs, which support a lively, colourful nightlife.

Despite the city's size, the forest is ever present on the horizon and always feels just a short boat trip away. Beaches fringe its western extremities at Ponta Negra, whose sands are backed by towering blocks of flats, making it feel like a kind of Amazonian Ipanema.

There are plenty of sights near Manaus. The most vaunted are generally the least interesting. However, the **Anavilhanas** – the largest river archipelago in the world, comprising a beautiful labyrinth of forested islands, some fringed with white-sand beaches lapped by the jet-black waters of the Rio Negro – should not be missed. Try to be there for sunset when thousands of swifts descend to roost and the light is a deep, rich gold.

Manaus is also the main departure point for rainforest tours. There are many lodges around the city, from 20 minutes to four hours away. And although animals here are not as easy to see as in Tefé or on the **Rio Cristalino**, the scenery is breathtaking.

ARRIVING IN MANAUS

Getting there Visitors almost invariably arrive in Manaus by plane or boat. It is not possible to travel by bus from the Pantanal to Manaus. You can fly from both the southern Pantanal (Campo Grande – via Brasília or Cuiabá) and the northern Pantanal (Cuiabá via Porto Velho and Rio Branco). The modern **Eduardo Gomes airport** ① *10 km north of the city centre, T092-3652 1120*, also has international connections. Airport buses run to the Praça da Matriz restaurant (aka Marques da Santa Cruz), next to the cathedral in the centre of town (every 30 minutes 0500-2300, US$1.50). A taxi to the centre costs around US$30 on the meter. Taxi drivers often tell arrivals that no bus to town is available – be warned.

Moving on You can either fly or take a boat from Manaus to Belém (it is not possible to travel by bus). The Manaus–Belém boat trip on the lower Amazon takes four days, including an 18-hour stop in Santarém (suite US$250, double berth US$150, hammock space US$65). *Nélio Correa* is best on this route; *Defard Vieira*, very good and clean; *São Francisco* is the largest, new and modern, but the toilets are smelly; *Cisne Branco* of similar quality; *Cidade de Bairreirinha* is the newest on the route, a/c berths. *Lider II* has good food and pleasant atmosphere; *Santarém* is clean, well organized and recommended; *João Pessoa Lopes* is also recommended. The route is very busy. Try to get a cabin if you can.

Boat passengers leave from the newly renovated **floating docks** ① *in the city centre, a couple of blocks south of Praça da Matriz*, with direct access to the main artery of Avenida Eduardo Ribeiro, and 10 minutes' walk from the opera house and main hotel area. The docks are open to the public 24 hours a day. Bookings can be made up to two weeks in advance at the ticket sales area by the port's pedestrian entrance, bear left on entry and walk past the cafés. The names and itineraries of departing vessels are displayed here.

Boats for **São Gabriel da Cachoeira**, **Novo Airão**, and **Caracaraí** go from São Raimundo, upriver from the main port. Take bus No 101 'São Raimundo', No 112 'Santo Antônio' or No 110, 40 minutes; there are two docking areas separated by a hill, the São Raimundo *balsa*, where the ferry to Novo Airão, on the Rio Negro, leaves every afternoon (US$10); and the Porto Beira Mar de São Raimundo, where the São Gabriel da Cachoeira boats dock (most departures are on Friday).

Many boat captains will allow you to sleep on the hammock deck of the boat for a day before departure or after arrival. Be careful of people who wander around boats after they've arrived at a port; they are almost certainly looking for something to steal. Agencies in town can book boat tickets for a small surcharge.

Getting around The Centro Histórico and dock areas are easily explored on foot. All city bus routes start on Marquês de Santa Cruz next to the Praça da Matriz and almost all then pass along the Avenida Getúlio Vargas (two blocks east of the Opera House). Taxis can be found near the opera house, at the *rodoviária*, airport and in Ponta Negra. Many of the upmarket hotels are in Ponta Negra, which is 13 km from the city centre and can feel somewhat isolated.

Tourist information There are several Centros de Atendimento ao Turista (CAT) ① *main office: 50 m south of the opera house, Av Eduardo Ribeiro 666, T092-3622 0767, Mon-Fri 0800-1700, Sat 0800-1200*, throughout the city. There are also offices in **Amazonas Shopping** ① *Av Djalma Batist 482, Chapada, T096-3236 5154, Mon-Sat 0900-2200, Sun 1500-2100*; at the **airport** ① *T096-3652 1120 or T0800-280 8820, daily 0700-2300*; at the **port** ① *regional terminal, R Marquês de Santa Cruz, armazém 07, Mon-Fri 0800-1700*, and ① *international terminal, R Marquês de Santa Cruz, armazém 10*, which opens only when cruise liners dock. There is a **CAT** trailer in the **rodoviária** ① *R Recife s/n, Flores, Mon-Sat 0800-1200*.

The **Amazon Bus** ① *T092-2324 5071, www.tucunareturismo.com.br, departures from CAT next to Teatro Amazonas, Mon-Sat 0900 and 1430, US$35, US$17 for children under 12*, is a double decker bus (air-conditioned ground floor and open-top upper deck), which visits the principal attractions in Manaus on a three-hour, principally drive-by tour with guided commentary in Portuguese. It doesn't represent very good value for time or money. Many of the more interesting sights are not included (notably the Palacete Principal, the floating docks and INPA), there are some bizarre inclusions (like the football stadium, the Olympic village and the Federal University) and there's only one proper stop – at Ponta Negra beach (where the bus breaks for snacks and a breath of warm air).

The website for tourism in the Amazon, www.amazonastur.am.gov.br, has extensive information on accommodation throughout the state in Portuguese and English. *A Crítica* newspaper lists local events.

CENTRO HISTÓRICO

The colonial streets that spread out from Teatro Amazonas and Praça São Sebastião are a reminder of Manaus's brief dalliance with wealth and luxury. Eduardo Ribeiro, the state governor who presided over these golden years, was determined to make 19th-century Manaus the envy of the world: a fine European city in which the nouveau riche could parade their linen and lace. He spared no expense. Trams were running in Manaus before they were in Manchester or Boston and its roads were lit by the first electric street lights in the world. The city's confidence grew with its majesty. Champagne flowed under the crystal chandeliers and prices rose to four times those of contemporaneous New York.

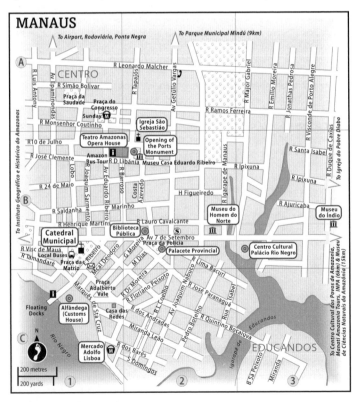

Extravagance begot extravagance and rubber barons eager to compete in statements of affluent vulgarity fed their horses vintage wine or bought lions as guard cats.

In the 1890s, Ribeiro decided to put the icing on his cake, commissioning the Gabinete Português de Engenharia e Arquitetura to build an Italianate opera house, the **Teatro Amazonas** ① *Praça São Sebastião, T096-622 1880, Mon-Sat 0900-1600, 20-min tour US$6, students US$2.50*, and to surround it with stone-cobbled streets lined with elegant houses, plazas, and gardens replete with ornate fountains and gilded cherubs. Masks adorning the theatre walls were made in homage to great European artists, including Shakespeare, Mozart, Verdi and Molière and the driveway was paved in rubber to prevent the sound of carriage wheels spoiling performances. For the lavish interior, Ribeiro turned to the Roman painter Domenico de Angelis (who had painted the Opera House in Belém in 1883) and Giovanni Capranesi (an Italian colleague who had worked with Angelis on the Igreja de São Sebastião near the Teatro). Their grandiose decorations are magnificent both in their pomp and their execution. They include a series of trompe l'oeuil ceilings – showing the legs of the Eiffel Tower from beneath (in the auditorium) and the muse of the arts ascending to heaven surrounded by putti in the Salão Nobre reception room. Ribeiro also commissioned a Brazilian artist to paint a stage curtain depicting *Iara*, the spirit of the river Amazon at the centre of the meeting of the waters, and a series of scenes of idealized indigenous Brazilian life based on Paulistano Carlos Gomes' opera, *O Guarany*, in the ballrooms. The steel for the building was moulded in Glasgow, the mirrors made in Venice and priceless porcelains from France, China and Japan were purchased to grace mantelpieces, stairwells and alcoves. After the theatre doors were opened in 1896, Caruso sang here and Pavlova danced.

But for all its beauty and expense the theatre was used for little more than a decade. In the early 20th century the rubber economy collapsed. Seeds smuggled by Englishman Henry Wickham, to the Imperial Gardens at Kew and thence to Malaysia, were producing a higher yield. The wild-rubber economy dwindled and the doors to the opera house closed. Over the decades, the French tiles on the dome began to crack, the Italian marble darkened and the fine French furniture and English china slowly began to decay. What you see today is the product of careful restoration, which has returned the *Teatro* to its original glory. There are regular performances, which sell out very quickly, and an arts festival every April.

The Teatro Amazonas sits at the head of a handsome square, the **Praça São Sebastião**, paved with black and white dragon's tooth stones and surrounded by attractive, freshly painted late 19th- and early 20th-century houses. Many are little cafés, galleries or souvenir shops and the area is a safe and pleasant place to while away an hour or two. There are often free concerts on weekend evenings. In the middle of the square is another grand rubber boom construction, the bronze monument to the **Opening of the Ports**. It depicts *Iara* (see Teatro Amazonas, above), embraced by Mercury – representing commerce and standing over five ships, representing the continents of Europe, Africa, America, Oceania and Antarctica. In front of the monument is the modest **Igreja de São Sebastião** ① *R 10 de Julho 567, T092-3232 4572*, whose interior is filled with more brilliantly coloured romantic paintings by Domenico de Angelis, Giancarlo Capranesi (who painted in the Teatro Amazonas and in Belém) and canvases by Bellerini and Francisco Campanella, both also Italian.

Eduardo Ribeiro's house sits on the southwestern edge of the *praça*, opening in late 2010 as a museum, the **Museu Casa de Eduardo Ribeiro** ① *R José Clemente s/n, Centro, Mon-Fri 0900-1700, Sun 1600-2100, free guided tours (in Portuguese)*. The house is a tall town mansion built in a typically late-Victorian, eclectic style – with a neoclassical façade topped with balcony finished with a Baroque flourish. The two floors of the three-storey interior are devoted to Ribeiro. They are sober when you consider his excesses, bringing together items known to have belonged to the ex-state governor along with photographs, letters and memorabilia, and furniture and decorations from the rubber boom period.

ON THE WATERFRONT

The city's other sights are huddled around the waterfront. The **Mercado Adolfo Lisboa** ① *R dos Barés 46*, was built in 1882 as a miniature copy of the now-demolished Parisian Les Halles. The wrought ironwork, which forms much of the structure, was imported from Europe and is said to have been designed by Eiffel.

The remarkable harbour installations, completed in 1902, were designed and built by a Scottish engineer to cope with the Rio Negro's annual rise and fall of up to 14 m. The large **floating dock** is connected to street level by a 150-m-long floating ramp, at the end of which, on the harbour wall, can be seen the high-water mark for each year since it was built. The highest so far recorded was in 2009. When the river is high, the roadway floats on a series of large iron tanks measuring 2.5 m in diameter. The large beige **Alfândega (Customs House)** ① *R Marquês de Santa Cruz, Mon-Fri 0800-1300*, stands at the entrance to the city when arriving by boat. Said to be have been modelled on the one in Delhi, it was entirely prefabricated in England, and the tower once acted as a lighthouse.

Dominating the streets between the opera house and the waterfront; and right next to the local bus station, is the **Catedral Municipal**, on Praça Osvaldo Cruz, built in simple Jesuit style and very plain inside and out. Originally constructed in 1695 in wood and straw, it was burnt down in 1850. Nearby is the main shopping and business area, the tree-lined **Avenida Eduardo Ribeiro**, crossed by Avenida 7 de Setembro and bordered by ficus trees.

Some 200 m east of the cathedral is the **Biblioteca Pública (Public Library)** ① *R Barroso 57, T096-3234 0588, Mon-Fri 0730-1730*, inaugurated in 1871, is part of the city's architectural heritage. Featuring an ornate European cast-iron staircase, it is well stocked with 19th-century newspapers, rare books and old photographs, and is worth a visit. Nearby, on the leafy, fountain-filled Praça Heliodoro Balbi (aka Praça da Policia) is a new museum complex, the **Palacete Provincial** ① *Praça Heliodoro Balbi s/n, Centro, T092-3635 5832, Tue-Fri 0900-1700, Sat 1000-1900, Sun 1600-2100, free*. The Palacete is a stately late-19th-century civic palace which was once the police headquarters. It is now home to six small museums: the Museu de Numismática (with a collection on Brazilian and international coins and notes), the Museu Tiradentes (profiling the history of the Amazon police and assorted Brazilian military campaigns), the Museu da Imagem e do Som (with free internet, cinema showings and a DVD library), the Museu de Arqueologia (preserving a handful of Amazon relics), a restoration atelier and the Pinacoteca do Estado – one of the best art galleries in northern Brazil, with work by important painters such as Oscar Ramos, Moacir Andrade and Roberto Burle Marx. The Palacete is a very pleasant place to while away a few hours and has decent air-conditioned café serving tasty coffee, cakes and savouries.

OTHER MUSEUMS AND CULTURAL CENTRES

The **Museu do Homem do Norte** ① *Av 7 de Setembro 1385, near Av Joaquim Nabuco, T096-3232 5373, Mon-Thu 0900-1200, 1300-1700, Fri 1300-1700, US$1*, is an interesting review of the way of life of the Amazonian population, or 'men of the north', although it has deteriorated in recent years and is now gathering dust. Social, cultural and economic aspects are displayed with photographs, models and other exhibits.

The **Palácio Rio Negro** ① *Av 7 de Setembro 1546, T096-3232 4450, Mon-Fri 0900-1400, free*, was the residence of a German rubber merchant until 1917 whereupon it became the state government palace. It underwent a major refurbishment in 2010 and now has an assortment of rooms presenting potted hagiographies of Amazonas state governors, exhibition spaces and a little café.

The **Museu do Índio** ① *R Duque de Caxias 296, near Av 7 Setembro, T096-234 1422, Tue-Fri 0930-1730, Sat, Sun and holidays 1300-1700, US$1.70, free on Sun*, is managed by the Salesian missionaries who have been responsible for the ravaging of much of the indigenous culture of the upper Rio Negro. It is rather run down and betrays a Victorian view of indigenous culture. The displays are dusty and poorly displayed, but there are plenty of artefacts, including handicrafts, ceramics, clothing, utensils and ritual objects from the various indigenous tribes of the upper Rio Negro. There is also a small craft shop.

WEST OF THE CENTRE

The **Instituto Geográfico e Histórico do Amazonas** ① *R Frei José dos Inocentes 132, Manaus, T092-3622 1260, Mon-Fri 0900-1200 and 1300-1600, US$1.50*, is located in the oldest part of Manaus – a cluster of streets of tiny cottages dotted with grand, rubber boom buildings. It houses a museum and library of over 10,000 books, which thoroughly document Amazonian life through the ages.

The **Zoo** ① *Estrada Ponta Negra 750, T096-625 2044, Tue-Sun 0900-1630, US$3, free on Sun, take bus No 120 from R Tamandaré by the cathedral, US$0.70, every 30 mins, get off 400 m past the 1st infantry barracks*, a big white building, is run by CIGS, the Brazilian Army Unit specializing in jungle survival. It has recently been expanded and improved. About 300 Amazonian animals are kept in the gardens, including anacondas in a huge pit.

FURTHER AFIELD

The **Bosque da Ciência INPA** is maintained by the **Instituto Nacional de Pesquisas da Amazônia (INPA)** ① *R Otavio Cabral, Petropolis, T092-3643 3293, US$3, Tue-Fri 0900-1130, 1400-1630, Sat and Sun 0900-1630, take bus No 519 from the Praça da Matriz*, which conducts research into all aspects of the Amazon. There is a small park that is good for a taste of rainforest flora and fauna before you head out to the forest. Paca (*Agouti paca*), agouti (*Myoprocta exilis*), squirrel monkeys (*Saimiri scicureus*) and tamarins (*Saguinus sp*) roam free, and among the other animals on display are Amazonian manatee (*Trichechus inunguis*) and giant otter (*Pternura brasiliensis*). A small museum within the park has displays on indigenous peoples' use of the forest, medicinal plants and bottles of pickled poisonous snakes. INPA also manages what is probably the largest urban rainforest reserve in the world, on the northeastern edge of Manaus. Pedro Fernandes Neto (T092-9090 9983, pedroffneto@hotmail.com) takes guided tours and other activities in and around the city. This is far more interesting than the Jardim Botânico Chico Mendes – which isn't really worth visiting.

The **Centro Cultural dos Povos da Amazônia** ① *Praça Francisco Pereira da Silva s/n, Bola da Suframa, Centro, T092-2125 5300, www.ccpa.am.gov.br,* is a large cultural complex devoted to the indigenous peoples of the Amazon. Outside the building there are Desano and a Yanomami *maloca* (traditional buildings), and the large, modern and well-curated museum in the main building preserves many artefacts, including splendid headdresses, ritual clothing and weapons. Explanatory displays are in Portuguese and passable English. It's a far better museum than the old-fashioned Museu do Indio. There are also play areas for the kids, a library and internet.

There is a curious little church, **Igreja do Pobre Diabo**, at the corner of Avenida Borba and Avenida Ipixuna, in the suburb of Cachoeirinha. It is only 4 m wide by 5 m long, and was built by a local trader, the 'poor devil' of the name. To get there, take the 'Circular 7 de Setembro Cachoeirinha' bus from the cathedral to Hospital Militar.

The **Museu de Ciências Naturais da Amazônia (Natural Science Museum)** ① *Av Cosme Ferreira, Cachoeira Grande suburb, 15 km from centre, T092-3644 2799, Mon-Sat 0900-1200 and 1400-1700, US$6, best to combine with a visit to INPA, and take a taxi from there (see above),* is one of the city's little-known treasures. The remote museum is run by Japanese, with characteristic efficiency, and the exhibits are beautifully displayed and clearly labelled in Japanese, Portuguese and English. The main building houses hundreds of preserved Amazon insects and butterflies, together with stuffed specimens of a selection of the river's bizarre fish. You can also see live versions, including the endangered pirarucu (*Arapaima gigas*), which can grow up to 3.5 m, and a primitive osteoglottid fish that breathes air.

BEACHES
Manaus has two sandy beaches on the outskirts of the city. The **Praia da Ponta Negra**, which lies upstream of the city's pollution, is the most popular and the most heavily developed. It is backed by high-rise flats and lined with open-air restaurants, bars and areas for beach volleyball and football. Nightlife here is lively, especially at weekends. However, on most nights at least one of the bars (such as **O Laranjinha**) will have Boi Bumba dance shows. Many of the better hotels are situated here. To get here take any bus marked 'Ponta Negra' (eg No 120) from the local bus station next to the cathedral. Boats also leave from here for other beaches on the Rio Negro.

AROUND MANAUS

THE MEETING OF THE WATERS
About 15 km from Manaus is the confluence of the coffee-coloured **Rio Solimões** (Amazon) and the black-tea coloured **Rio Negro**, which is itself some 8 km wide. The two rivers run side by side for about 6 km without their waters mingling. This phenomenon is caused by differences in the temperature, density and velocity of the two rivers. Tourist agencies run boat trips to this spot (US$60-160). The simplest route is to take a taxi, or bus No 713 'Vila Buriti', to the Porto de CEASA dock, and take the car ferry across to Careiro. Ferries leave all the time when full and there are many other smaller boats too. The last departure from CEASA is at 1800 and the last return to CEASA from Careiro is 2000. Motor boats for the meeting of the water charge US$15 per person or US$80 per boat (up to five people). Boats also leave from the hotel **Tropical** (US$90 per boat, up to five people). You should see dolphins, especially in the early morning. Alternatively, hire a motorized canoe from near the market in the city

ON THE ROAD

Mamirauá Ecological Reserve

ⓘ *T097-3343 4160, www.mamiraua.org.br and www.uakarilodge.com.br.*

Tefé is a scruffy town roughly halfway between Manaus and the Colombian border. The local airport authorities confiscated all of the city's rubbish lorries in a dispute over the municipal dump, and now it is piled up willy-nilly. But few come here for the town itself, for this is the access point to one of the world's most important primate and waterfowl reserves, the Mamirauá Ecological Reserve. This is a **Ramsar**, www.ramsar.org, site set up with British support to protect huge areas of terra firme, gallery, *varzea* and *igapó* forest at the confluence of the Solimões and Japurá rivers, and to manage them sustainably with the local riverine people. There are abundant birds including numerous rare trogons, cotingas, currasows, hoatzin, harpy eagle and five species of macaw. There are black caiman (one of which lives under the floating lodge), both species of Amazon dolphin, and numerous rare primates – the most spectacular of which are the endemic black-headed squirrel monkey and the endangered white uakari, known locally as the 'macaco Ingles' because of its red complexion and its genitalia. A visit is unforgettable.

The reserve has a small floating lodge, the **Pousada Uacari** on the Mamirauá river and visitors stay here in simple but elegant wooden rooms. Trips include walks in terra firme forest, boat and canoe trips to *igarpe* creeks, *varzea* and *igapó* forest and the vast Mamirauá lake. Visits must be booked in advance.

Tefé is connected to Manaus by air daily on **Trip** (www.voetrip.com.br), with onward flights to Tabatinga. There are regular slow boats (at least one a day) from Manaus or from Tabatinga and fast speed boats from Manaus (see page 255). The town is small enough to negotiate on foot.

centre (about US$30; per person or US$180 per boat for up to eight people). Allow three to four hours to experience the meeting properly. A 2-km walk along the Porto Velho road from the CEASA ferry terminal leads to some ponds, some way from the road, in which huge Victoria Regia water lilies can be seen from April to September.

MUSEU SERINGAL

ⓘ *Igarapé São João, 15 km north of Manaus up the Rio Negro, Tue-Sun 0800-1600, T092-3234 8755, US$3 and US$15 round trip on a private launch.*

This museum sitting at the end of a pretty *igarapé* (creek) off the Rio Negro is a full-scale reproduction of an early 20th-century rubber-tapping mansion house, with serf quarters, a factory and a shop complete with authentic products. It was built as a film set for the 2002 Portuguese feature film, *A Selva*. A guided tour – especially from one of the former rubber tappers – brings home the full horror of the system of debt peonage that enslaved Brazilians up until the 1970s. The museum can be visited with **Amazon Gero Tours**.

ARQUIPÉLAGO DE ANAVILHANAS

This filigree of more than 350 brilliant-green islands in the jet-black Rio Negro – some fringed with white-sand beaches, others anchored only by their roots – is one of the area's must-see sights. The scene is particularly beautiful at the end of the day when the

ON THE ROAD

As a percentage of population Brazil has few indigenous people. But total numbers are large, with estimates varying between 450,000 and almost a million; in some 227 tribal nations. These are scattered throughout the country from the far south to the Amazon; with the greatest numbers in that region. In addition some 30% of Brazilians are part indigenous, many being *caboclo* (a word in the interior or north and northeast) or *caiçara* (used on the south and southeast coast) peoples leading traditional semi-indigenous largely self-sufficient lives. There are also traditional communities founded by African fugitives from slavery – or *quilombos*. It is possible to visit all of these communities. This should always be organized beforehand (see page 250). Visitors who arrive unannounced will not be welcome and in some areas may be putting themselves at considerable risk.

sky looks vast and warm and the light on the trunks of the partially submerged trees is a thick orange-yellow. Birds fly into the Anavilhanas to roost and millions of bats leave for their night hunt. The air is silent but for bird calls, the lapping of the river and the bluster of river dolphins surfacing for air. The islands are 80 km upstream of Manaus. Several companies arrange visits to the archipelago (US$195-285, per person, one day – it takes four hours to reach the islands), as can most of the Rio Negro lodges. Rio Negro safari cruises almost all visit the Anavilhanas.

It is possible to see *botos* (pink river dolphins) being fed, and even to swim with them at the **Boto Cor-de-Rosa restaurant** in the Anavilhanas village of Novo Airão. Visits should be booked through a Manaus tour operator in as small a group as possible.

BELÉM

Belém do Pará is the great port of the eastern Amazon. The city received an extensive facelift in the new millennium and is now a very pleasant capital (population 1.3 million) with much of cultural interest – with streets of freshly painted, impressive 19th-century buildings from the rubber boom era and one of Latin America's liveliest contemporary music scenes. The reforms included opening up the waterfront and converting the derelict docks into a breezy promenade, which leads to one of Brazil's more colourful markets – Ver-o-Peso. Belém is a good base for boat trips along the river – either as cruises or public transport to Santarém, Manaus and beyond. An archipelago of beautiful, unspoilt tropical river islands lies a short boat trip offshore. The largest, Marajó, is as big as Denmark. With mean temperatures of 26°C, Belém is hot, but frequent showers and a prevailing breeze freshen the streets. The city has its fair share of crime and is prone to gang violence. Take sensible precautions, especially at night.

ARRIVING IN BELÉM
Getting there There are **boats** to Belém from locations throughout the Amazon. Prices vary according to the season and the boat. Expect to pay around US$80-100 for a three-day journey from Manaus including food (cooked in river water). The return journey takes five

days as it is upstream. Bring a hammock. Information on the latest prices and on sailings can be obtained from **Paratur** ① *Praça Maestro Waldemar Henrique S/N, T091-3212 0669, www.paraturismo.pa.gov.br*, or from the public boat terminal in Manaus. Amazon Star also run sailings between Manaus and Belém. All boats stop at Santarém along the way. Other destinations connecting to Belém on Amazon boats include Macapá, Parintins and the Ilha de Marajo (see box, page 265). Boats berth at the **Companhia das Docas** (aka Docas do Pará) ① *Av Marechal Hermes, s/n, at Armazém 10 (warehouse 10, entrance on Av Marechal Hermes, corner of Av Visconde de Souza Franco) or a few blocks to the south Armazém 3 at the foot of Av Pres Vargas*.

Boats to Marajó run from Armazém 10 on the docks in town and from the port at Icoaraci (20 km north of Belém, 30 minutes by bus from the *rodoviária* or from the Ver-oPeso market, taxi US$25), Monday to Friday 0630, 0730, Saturday 1600, 1700, Sunday 1600, 1700 and 1800.

Moving on Val-de-Cans international airport ① *Av Júlio César s/n, 12 km from the city, T091-3210 6000*, receives flights from Manaus and has onward flights to Fortaleza, Rio, São Paulo and other state capitals for your flight home (it is also connected internationally to Paramaribo in Suriname). The airport bus 'Perpétuo Socorro–Telégrafo' or 'Icoaraci' runs every 15 minutes to the Prefeitura on Praça Felipe Patroni (US$1.50, allow 40 minutes). A taxi from the airport into town costs US$25. Ordinary taxis are cheaper than co-operatives, buy ticket in advance in the Departures side of the airport. There are ATMs in the terminal, tourist information, cafés and car rental.

From Belém there is also a three-day bus link back to São Paulo via Brasília. São Luís is a 12-hour bus ride, Fortaleza 16 hours. Interstate buses leave from the **rodoviária** ① *end of Av Gov José Malcher, 3 km from the centre*. There are restaurants and agencies with information and tickets for riverboats. Buses from the centre cost US$0.50; taxis charge US$5-7.

Getting around The city centre is easily explored on foot. City buses and taxis run to all the sites of interest and to transport hubs away from the centre.

Tourist information Paratur ① *Praça Waldemar Henrique, Reduto, on the waterfront, T091-3224 9493, www.paraturismo.pa.gov.br*, has information on the state and city. Some staff speak English and can book hotels and tours to Marajó island. For information on national parks contact the **Instituto Chico Mendes de Conservação da Biodiversidade (ICMBio)** ① *www.icmbio.gov.br*. The website www.belemonline.com.br is also useful.

BACKGROUND

Established in 1616 because of its strategic position, Belém soon became the centre for slaving expeditions into the Amazon Basin. The Portuguese of Pará, together with those of Maranhão, treated the indigenous Brazilians abominably. Their isolation from the longer-established colonies allowed both places to become relatively lawless. In 1655, the Jesuits, under Antônio Vieira, attempted to lessen the abuses, while enticing the indigenous Brazilians to descend to the *aldeias* around Belém. This unfortunately led to further misery when smallpox spread from the south, striking the Pará *aldeias* in the 1660s.

Soon after Brazil's Independence, the Revolta da Cabanagem, a rebellion by the poor blacks, indigenous Brazilians and mixed-race *cabanos*, was led against the

Portuguese-born class that dominated the economy. The movement came to an end in 1840 when the *cabanos* finally surrendered, but the worst years of violence were 1835-1836. Some estimates say 30,000 were killed. The state's strategic location once again became important during the Second World War, when Belém was used as an airbase by the Americans to hunt German submarines in the Atlantic.

PLACES IN BELÉM

Belém used to be called the 'city of mango trees' and there are still many such trees remaining. There are some fine squares and restored historic buildings set along broad avenues. The largest square is the **Praça da República**, where there are free afternoon concerts; the main business and shopping area is along the wide Avenida Presidente Vargas, leading to the river, and the narrow streets which parallel it.

The recently restored neoclassical **Teatro da Paz** ① *R da Paz, T091-4009 8750, www.theatrodapaz.com.br, Mon-Fri 0900-1700, Sat 0900-1200, tours US$3* (1878), is one of the largest theatres in Brazil and its handsome ballrooms, polished floors, extensive murals and paintings and overall opulence are every bit as impressive as those of the theatre's more famous counterpart in Manaus. It was inspired by the Scala in Milan and is

ON THE ROAD

Marajó is an island the size of Denmark in the mouth of the Amazon confluence where the federal police patrol on buffaloes and the river feels as vast as an ocean. A visit here is an unforgettable experience. Much of the island is wild varzea, gallery and mangrove forest and is completely inaccessible to tourists. But there are a handful of settlements, notably Salvaterra and Soure (three hours boat ride from Belém), which were founded as buffalo and cattle ranches. There are *pousadas* in each town and superb beaches backed by swaying coconut palms near Soure. Boats to the Porto Camara port on Marajó leave from the Terminal Hidroviário at Armazem 10 at the Companhia das Docas Monday to Saturday 0630 and 1430, Sunday 1000. From Porto Camara it is a 25-km or 30-km bus ride to Salvaterra and Soure respectively. Buses meet the boats.

stuffed with imported materials from Europe – an iron frame built in England, Italian marble, French bronzes and a Portuguese mosaic stone floor. The auditorium once featured a magnificent ceiling painting by Domenico de Angelis (see page 266) who also worked in the Teatro Amazonas in Manaus, which crumbled and fell to the floor only decades after it was painted. The theatre stages performances by national and international stars, and offers free concerts and shows.

West of here, at the **Estação das Docas**, the abandoned warehouses and quays of the port have been restored into a waterfront complex with an air-conditioned interior with a gallery of cafés, restaurants and boutiques. It's a great place to come in the late afternoon when the sun is golden over the Baía do Guajará and locals promenade along the cobbles under the towering 19th-century cranes. There are three converted warehouses in the Estação das Docas – each a 'boulevard'. The Boulevard das Artes contains the **Cervejaria Amazon** (brewery), with good beer and simple meals, an archaeological museum and arts and crafts shops. The Boulevard de Gastronomia has smart restaurants and the five-star **Cairu** ice cream parlour (try açaí or the *pavê de capuaçu*). In the Boulevard das Feiras there are trade fairs. Live music is transported between the boulevards on a moving stage. There are also ATMs and an internet café within the complex.

Heading south, the 17th-century **Mercês church** (1640) is the oldest in Belém. It forms part of an architectural group known as the Mercedário, the rest of which was heavily damaged by fire in 1978 and has now been restored.

Near the church, the Belém market, known as **Ver-o-Peso** ① *Blvd Castilhos França 27, T091-3212 0549*, was the Portuguese Posto Fiscal, where goods were weighed to gauge taxes due, hence the name: 'see the weight'. Inside are a flurry of stalls selling all manner of items – herbal remedies, Brazil nuts, açaí, bead jewellery, African-Brazilian religious charms, incense and, in the main gallery, scores of tiled slabs covered with bizarre river fish – from piraiba as big as a man to foot-long armour-plated cat fish. You can see them being unloaded at around 0530, together with hundreds of baskets of açaí. A colourful, if dirty, dock for fishing boats lies immediately upriver from the market and whole area swarms with people, including armed thieves and pickpockets.

Around Praça Dom Pedro II is a cluster of interesting buildings. The **Palácio Lauro Sodré** and **Museu do Estado do Pará** ① *Praça Dom Pedro II, T091-3225 3853, Mon-Fri 0900-1800,*

Sat 1000-1800, is a gracious 18th-century Italianate building. It contains Brazil's largest framed painting, *The Conquest of Amazônia*, by Domenico de Angelis. The building was the work of the Italian architect Antônio Landi, who also designed the cathedral, and was the administrative seat of the colonial government. During the rubber boom many new decorative features were added. Also on Praça Dom Pedro II is the **Palácio Antônio Lemos**, which houses the **Museu de Arte de Belém** as well as the **Prefeitura** ① *Tue-Fri 0900-1200, 1400-1800, Sat and Sun 0900-1300*. It was originally built as the Palácio Municipal between 1868 and 1883, and is a fine example of the Imperial neoclassical style. In the downstairs rooms there are old views of Belém; upstairs, the historic rooms, beautifully renovated, contain furniture and paintings, which are all well explained.

The **cathedral** ① *Praça Frei Caetano Brandão, Mon 1500-1800, Tue-Fri 0800-1100, 1530-1800* (1748), is also neoclassical, and contains a series of brilliantly coloured paintings by the Italian artist Domenico de Angelis – famous for his work on the Teatro Amazonas in Manaus, but whose first visit to the Amazon was to Belém in 1884 at the invitation of the bishop to paint this cathedral and the Teatro da Paz. Directly opposite is the restored 18th-century **Santo Alexandre church** ① *Praça Frei Caetano Brandão s/n, Mon 1500-1800, Tue-Fri 0800-1100, 1530-1800*, with a fabulous rococo pediment and fine woodcarving. This was once the Jesuit headquarters in Belém – where Father Antonio Vieira (see box, page 94) would have preached his hellfire sermons denouncing the indigenous slave trade; inciting the wrath of the locals, Pombal and eventually contributing to the disestablishment of the order.

Also in the old town is the **Forte do Castelo** ① *Praça Frei Caetano Brandão 117, T091-3223 0041, daily 0800-2300*, which was rebuilt in 1878. The fort overlooks the confluence of the Rio Guamá and the Baía do Guajará and was where the Portuguese first set up their defences. There is a good restaurant, the **Boteco Onze**, where you can watch the sunset (entry US$1, drinks and *salgadinhos* served on the ramparts from 1800). At the square on the waterfront, the açaí berries are landed nightly at 2300, after being picked in the jungle. Açaí berries, ground up with sugar and mixed with manioc, are a staple food in the region.

East of the centre, the **Basílica de Nossa Senhora de Nazaré** ① *Praça Justo Chermont, Av Magalhães Barata, Mon-Sat 0500-1130, 1400-2000, Sun 0545-1130, 1430-2000*, was built in 1909 from rubber wealth. It is romanesque in style and has marble and stained-glass windows. The *basílica* feels very tranquil and sacred, especially when empty. A museum here showcases one of the largest and most colourful festivals in the north of Brazil, the **Círio de Nazaré**. The Nossa Senhora de Nazaré sits illuminated in a shrine in the sacristy.

The botanic gardens, **Bosque Rodrigues Alves** ① *Av Almirante Barroso 2305, T091-3226 2308, Tue-Sun 0800-1700*, is a 16-ha public garden (really a preserved area of original flora), with a small animal collection. To get there, take the yellow bus marked 'Souza' or 'Cidade Nova' (any number), 30 minutes from Ver-o-Peso market, or from the cathedral. The **Museu Emílio Goeldi** ① *Av Magalhães Barata 376, Tue-Thu 0900-1200, 1400-1700, Fri 0900-1200, Sat and Sun 0900-1700, US$1*, takes up an entire city block and consists of the museum proper (with a fine collection of indigenous Marajó pottery and an excellent exhibition of Mebengokre tribal lifestyle), a rather sad zoo and botanical exhibits including Victoria Régia lilies. Buses run from the cathedral.

The Murucutu ruins, an old Jesuit foundation, are reached by the Ceará bus from Praça da República; entry is via an unmarked door on the right of the Ceará bus station.

THE AMAZON LISTINGS

WHERE TO STAY

Hotels
Manaus

$$$$ Park Suites, Av Coronel Teixeira, 1320 A, Ponta Negra, T092-3306 4500, www.atlanticahotels.com.br. The best appointed and most modern hotel in the city – in the upmarket river beach suburb of Ponta Negra. Suites are modern and well appointed, housed in a large tower block with great views out over the river from the upper floors. The hotel has the best business facilities in the city and has a lovely infinity pool set in gardens overlooking the beach.

$$$ Go Inn, R Monsenhor Coutinho 560, Centro Histórico, T092-3306 2600, www.atlanticahotels.com.br. This recent opening is one of the very few decent, modern a/c accommodation options in the city centre – with undistinguished but no-nonsense corporate-designed rooms with tiny work desks, queen-sized beds and wall-mounted TVs which look like they could be in a **Premier** Inn. Facilities include a café, disabled rooms, gym and paid Wi-Fi in all rooms.

$ Hostel Manaus, R Lauro Cavalcante 231, Centro, T092-3233 4545, www.hostel manaus.com. HI hostel in one of the city's original houses. Good-value dorms and private rooms. Reasonably central with views of the city from the rooftop patio and quiet. Australian-run. Great place to join a jungle tour – with a good tour operator in the lobby. Not to be confused with a non-HI hostel in the city using a similar name.

Belém

$$ Le Massilia, R Henrique Gurjão 236, T091-3224 2834, www.massilia.com.br. An intimate, French-owned boutique hotel with chic little duplexes and more ordinary doubles. Excellent French restaurant and a tasty French breakfast.

Rainforest lodges

$$$$ Acajatuba Jungle Lodge, Lago Acajatuba, 4 hrs up the Rio Negro from Manaus. Office at Av 7 de Setembro 1899, Manaus, T092-3234 3199, www.acajatuba. com.br. This Rio Negro lodge sits in a beautiful location on the edge of Acajatuba lake – a large *igarapé* visited by *boto* dolphins, at the far southern end of the Anavilhanas islands. 40 apartments, a bar and a restaurant. Accommodation is in simple round, thatched-roof bungalows with mosquito screens (but bring your own net). The lodge does not conform to best ecotourism practice – guides handle wild animals.

$$$$ Anavilhanas Lodge, Edifício Manaus Shopping Centre, Av Eduardo Ribeiro 520, sala 304, T092-3622 8996, www.anavilhanas lodge.com. This is the nearest jungle lodges in Brazil get to boutique hotels. Minimalist rooms with high-quality cotton sheets on the beds, low-lighting, flat-screen TVs and tasteful rustic chic hangings and decor sit in thatch-roofed cabins whose front wall is entirely glass fronted – giving spectacular views out over the Rio Negro and the adjacent Anavilhanas archipelago. Each is fronted with a broad wooden hammock deck. There's a lodge bar and a range of comfortable lounging areas. But bring a mosquito net. The large menu of activities includes the standard piranha fishing, community visits, hikes and dolphin spotting alongside more meditative kayaking and sunset tours of the Anavilhanas.

$$$ Ararinha Lodge, Paraná do Araçá, exclusively through **Amazon Gero Tours** (see below). One of the more comfortable in the Mamori area, this lodge sits on a river bank overlooking the Paraná do Araça – a little-visited and unspoilt river running off the Lago do Mamori. Accommodation is in smart wooden chalets housing suites of individual rooms which come complete with double or single beds with mosquito nets. The area is one of the best for wildlife in the Mamori region.

$$$ Juma, Lago da Juma, T092-3232 2707, www.jumalodge.com. A newly refurbished lodge in a beautiful location on the further reaches of Lago Mamori at Juma. Accommodation is in comfortable wooden and palm-thatch huts on stilts right on the river bank, with rooms and a big round dining room sitting right over the water. The owners have a burgeoning interest in birdwatching and proper wildlife tours.

$$$-$$ Amazon Antônio Lodge, through **Antônio Jungle Tours**, www.antonio-jungle tours.com. A thatched-roof wooden lodge with plain, fan-cooled rooms and an observation tower. Set in a beautiful location overlooking a broad curve in the river Urubu some 200 km from Manaus.

$$$-$$ Aldeia dos Lagos Lodge, near Silves, run by the **Silves Project**, T092-3248 9988, through **Viverde** tours (see below), www.aldeiadoslagos.com. A community-based eco-project run in conjunction with an NGO. Accommodation is in a simple floating lodge set in a system of lakes near the tiny town of Silves and with high environmental diversity. Profits are fed back into local communities.

$$ Zequinha, through **Amazon Gero Tours**, www.amazongerotours.com. Very simple wooden fan-cooled rooms and one a/c suite in a round maloca building 100 m from a large oxbow lake.

WHAT TO DO

Águia Amazomas Turismo, R 24 de Maio 440 CA-H sala 1, Vila Baipendi, T092-3231 1449, www.aguiaamazonas.com.br. Bespoke trips, lodge stays and cruises conducted by Samuel Basilio, an experienced guide from the upper Rio Negro specializing in long expeditions (he has worked as a location finder on many BBC documentaries).

Amazon Antônio Jungle Tours, office located inside the **Hostel Manaus**, R Lauro Cavalcante 231, T092-3234 1294 and 092-9961 8314, www.antonio-jungletours.com. Jungle stays on the Rio Urubu, a black-water river 200 km northeast of Manaus with some of the best-value packages for backpackers and a reliable, well-run service with English speaking, locally sourced guides.

Amazon Gero Tours, R10 de Julho 695, T092-3232 4755 or T092-9983 6273, www.amazongerotours.com. Excellent tours south of the Solimões – to a series of lodges around Lago Mamori, day trips to Presidente Figueiredo and around the city of Manaus (including meeting of the waters), and bookings made for lodges everywhere.

Gero, the owner is very friendly and dedicated and one of the few operators in Manaus genuinely to contribute shares of his profits to the local riverine communities.

Viverde, R das Guariúbas 47, Parque Acariquar, T092-3248 9988, www.viverde. com.br. A family-run agency acting as a broker for a broad range of Amazon cruises and lodges (including the beautiful Aldeia dos Lagos Lodge near Silves) and running their own city tours and local excursions.

Cruises
Amazon Clipper, T092-3656 1246, www.amazonclipper.com.br. The leading small boat cruise operator. Excellent trips along the Rio Negro with knowledgeable wildlife guides, including wildlife cruises, sports fishing and bespoke tours.

Amazon Star, R Henrique Gurjão 236, Belém, T091-3241 8624, T091-3982 7911 (mob), www.amazonstar.com.br. Cruises along the Amazon from Belém to Manaus and trips to Marajó. Also offers 3-hr city tours and river tours of Belém.

PRACTICALITIES

INS AND OUTS

→BEST TIME TO VISIT BRAZIL

The best time for a visit is from April to June and from August to October. Business visitors should avoid mid-December to the end of February, when it is hot and people are on holiday. In these months, hotels, beaches and transport tend to be very crowded. July is a school holiday month. If visiting tourist centres such as Salvador, Rio and the colonial cities in Minas Gerais in the low season, be aware that some tourist sights may be closed.

In Rio de Janeiro conditions during the winter (May to September) are like those of a north European summer, including periods of rain and overcast skies, with temperatures from 14°C to the high 20s. It is more like a Mediterranean autumn in São Paulo and the southern states and it can get very cold in the far south; warm clothing is required as temperatures can change dramatically and it can get cold on high ground anywhere in Brazil, particularly at night. The heaviest rain is from November to March in Rio and São Paulo, and from April to August around Recife (although irregular rainfall causes severe droughts here). The rainy season in the north and Amazônia can begin in December and is heaviest from March to May, but it is getting steadily shorter, possibly as a result of deforestation. Few places get more than 2 m (the coast north of Belém, some of the Amazon Basin, and a small area of the Serra do Mar between Santos and São Paulo). Summer conditions all over the country are tropical, although temperatures rarely reach 40°C.

The average annual temperature increases steadily from south to north, but even on the equator, in the Amazon Basin, the average temperature is not more than 27°C. The highest recorded was 42°C, in the dry northeastern states. From the latitude of Recife south to Rio, the mean temperature is 23-27°C along the coast, and 18-21°C in the highlands. South of Rio, towards the boundary with Uruguay, the mean temperature is 17-19°C. Humidity is relatively high in Brazil, particularly along the coast. The luminosity is also very high, and sunglasses are advisable.

→GETTING TO BRAZIL

AIR

Flights into Brazil generally land in São Paulo, which has direct connections with the rest of **South and Central America**, the **USA**, **Canada**, **Mexico** and **Europe** and **Asia** and indirect connections with **Australasia** via Buenos Aires, Santiago or Los Angeles.

Rio de Janeiro, Brasília, Salvador, Belo Horizonte, Fortaleza, Manaus and Recife have connections to the USA and Europe. Many other Brazilian cities have connections to Europe, mostly through Lisbon.

Brazil is connected to Spanish-speaking **Latin America** principally through Rio de Janeiro, São Paulo, Manaus, Porto Alegre and Brasília. It is connected to the **Guianas** through Belém, Fortaleza, Boa Vista and Macapá. Belém also receives flights from the **Caribbean**.

Charter flights, often at very attractive prices, are available from the USA and Europe. For details see www.netflights.com, www.dialaflight.com, www.charterflights.co.uk, www.edreams.co.uk, www.edreams.pt or www.edreams.it.

Prices are cheapest in October, November and after Carnaval and at their highest in the European summer and the Brazilian high seasons (generally 15 December to 15 January, the Thursday before Carnaval to the Saturday after Carnaval, and 15 June to 15 August).

Airport information For most visitors the point of arrival will be **Cumbica International Airport** at Guarulhos (which is often used as an alternative name) in São Paulo (see page 203) or **Tom Jobim International Airport** (also known as **Galeão**) on the Ilha do Governador, 16 km from the centre of Rio de Janeiro (see page 35). Make sure you arrive two hours before international flights. It is wise to reconfirm your flight as departure times may have changed. For airport tax, see page 282.

SEA

Travelling as a passenger on a cargo ship to South America is not a cheap way to go, but if you have the time and want a bit of luxury, it makes a great alternative to flying. The passage is often only available for round trips.

→TRANSPORT IN BRAZIL

Public transport in Brazil is very efficient, but distances are huge. Most visitors will find themselves travelling by buses and planes, except in the Amazon when a boat is often the only way to get around. Train routes are practically non-existent, car hire is expensive and hitchhiking not advisable. Taxis vary widely in quality and price but are easy to come by and safe when taken from a *posto de taxis* (taxi rank).

AIR

Because of the size of the country, flying is often the most practical option and internal air services are highly developed. All state capitals and larger cities are linked with each other with services several times a day, and all national airlines offer excellent service. Recent deregulation of the airlines has greatly reduced prices on some routes and low-cost airlines offer fares that can often be as cheap as travelling by bus (when booked through the internet). Paying with an international credit card is not always possible online; but it is usually possible to buy an online ticket through a hotel, agency or willing friend without surcharge. GOL (www.voegol.com.br), TAM (www.tam.com.br), TRIP/Total (www.voetrip.com.br, www.total.com.br), Varig (www.varig.com.br) and Webjet (www.webjet.com.br) operate the most extensive routes. Most of their websites provide full information, including a booking service, although not all are in English.

Air passes TAM and GOL offer a 21-day **Brazil Airpass**, which is valid on any TAM destination within Brazil. The price varies according to the number of flights taken and the international airline used to arrive in Brazil. They can only be bought outside Brazil. One to four flights start at around US$540, five flights start at US$680, six flights start at US$795, seven flights start at US$915, eight flights start at US$1035, and nine flights start at US$1155. The baggage allowance is the same as that permitted on their international flights. Children pay a discounted rate, and under-threes pay 10% of the adult rate. Some of the carriers operate a blackout period between 15 December and 15 January.

RAIL

There are 30,379 km of railways, which are not combined into a unified system; almost all run goods trains only. Brazil has two gauges and there is little transfer between them. Two more gauges exist for the isolated **Amapá** railway (used to transport manganese from the Serra do Navio) and the tourist-only **São João del Rei** and **Ouro Preto–Mariana** lines. There is also the **Trem do Pantanal** – a tourist-designated train running between Campo Grande and Miranda in the Pantanal.

RIVER

The only area where travel by boat is not merely practical, but often necessary is the Amazon region. There are also some limited transport services along the São Francisco River and through the Pantanal.

ROAD

The best paved highways are heavily concentrated in the southeast, but roads serving the interior are being improved to all-weather status and many are paved. Most main roads between principal cities are paved. Some are narrow and therefore dangerous; many are in poor condition.

Bus There are three standards of bus: *Comum*, or *Convencional*, are quite slow, not very comfortable and fill up quickly; *Executivo* are more expensive, comfortable (many have reclining seats), and don't stop en route to pick up passengers so are safer; *Leito* (literally 'bed') run at night between the main centres, offering reclining seats with leg rests, toilets, and sometimes refreshments, at double the normal fare. For journeys over 100 km, most buses have chemical toilets (bring toilet paper). Air conditioning can make buses cold at night, so take a jumper; on some services blankets are supplied.

Buses stop fairly frequently (every two to four hours) at *postos* for snacks. Bus stations for interstate services and other long-distance routes are called *rodoviárias*. They are frequently outside the city centres and offer snack bars, lavatories, left luggage, local bus services and information centres. Buy bus tickets at *rodoviárias* (most now take credit cards), not from travel agents who add on surcharges. Reliable bus information is hard to come by, other than from companies themselves. Buses usually arrive and depart in very good time. Many town buses have turnstiles, which can be inconvenient if you are carrying a large pack. Urban buses normally serve local airports.

Car Renting a car in Brazil is expensive: the cheapest rate for unlimited mileage for a small car is about US$65 per day. These costs can be more than halved by reserving a car over the internet through one of the larger international companies such as **Europcar** (www.europcar.co.uk) or **Avis** (www.avis.co.uk). Minimum age for renting a car is 21 and it's essential to have a credit card. To drive in Brazil you need an international licence. A national driving licence is acceptable if your home country is a signatory to the Vienna and Geneva conventions. Companies operate under the terms *aluguel de automóveis* or *auto-locadores*. Check exactly what the company's insurance policy covers. In many cases it will not cover major accidents or 'natural' damage (eg flooding). Ask if extra cover is available. Sometimes using a credit card automatically includes insurance. Beware of being billed for scratches that were on the vehicle before you hired it.

Fuel prices vary weekly and between regions. *Gasolina común* is about US$1.65 per litre with *gasolina aditivada* a few cents more. *Alcool* is around US$1. Unleaded fuel is known as *sem chumbo*. *Comun* (and sometimes in the smaller petrol stations, *aditivada*) is often diluted with acetone as a means of making more profit. Buy from the larger stations to avoid trouble. With alcohol fuel you need about 50% more than regular gasoline as fuel consumption is heavier. Many cars operate a **Flex system** whereby it is possible to put both alcohol and petrol in the same tank.

Insurance against accident and theft is very expensive. If the car is stolen or written off you will be required to pay very high import duty on its value. The legally required minimum cover for third party insurance is not expensive.

Try to never leave your car unattended except in a locked garage or guarded parking area. Remove all belongings and leave the empty glove compartment open. Also lock the clutch or accelerator to the steering wheel with a heavy, obvious chain or lock. Adult minders or street children will usually protect your car fiercely in exchange for a tip.

Taxi Rates vary from city to city, but are consistent within each city. At the outset, make sure the meter is cleared and shows 'tariff 1', except (usually) from 2300-0600, Sunday, and in December when '2' is permitted. Check that the meter is working; if not, fix the price in advance. The **radio taxi** service costs about 50% more but cheating is less likely. Taxis outside larger hotels usually cost more. If you are seriously cheated, note the number of the taxi and insist on a signed bill; threatening to take it to the police can work. **Mototaxis** are much more economical, but many are unlicensed and there have been a number of robberies of passengers.

→WHERE TO STAY IN BRAZIL

There is a good range of accommodation options in Brazil. An *albergue* or hostel offers the cheapest option. These have dormitory beds and single and double rooms. Many are part of the IYHA, www.iyha.org. **Hostel world**, www.hostelworld.com; **Hostel Bookers**, www.hostelbookers.com; and **Hostel.com**, www.hostel.com, are useful portals. **Hostel Trail Latin America** – T0131-208 0007 (UK), www.hosteltrail.com – managed from their hostel in Popayan, is an online network of hotels and tour companies in South America. A *pensão* is either a cheap guesthouse or a household that rents out some rooms.

A *pousada* is either a bed-and-breakfast, often small and family-run, or a sophisticated and often charming small hotel. A *hotel* is as it is anywhere else in the world, operating according to the international star system, although five-star hotels are not price controlled and hotels in any category are not always of the standard of their star equivalent in the USA, Canada or Europe. Many of the older hotels can be cheaper than hostels. Usually accommodation prices include a breakfast of rolls, ham, cheese, cakes and fruit with coffee and juice; there is no reduction if you don't eat it. Rooms vary too. Normally an *apartamento* is a room with separate living and sleeping areas and sometimes cooking facilities. A *quarto* is a standard room; *com banheiro* is en suite; and *sem banheiro* is with shared bathroom. Finally there are the *motels*. These should not be confused with their US counterpart: motels are used by guests not intending to sleep; there is no stigma attached and they usually offer good value (the rate for a full night is called the '*pernoite*'), however the decor can be a little garish.

It's a good idea to book accommodation in advance in small towns that are popular at weekends with city dwellers (eg near São Paulo and Rio de Janeiro), and it's essential to book at peak times.

LUXURY ACCOMMODATION

Much of the luxury private accommodation sector can be booked through operators. **Angatu**, www.angatu.com, offers the best private homes along the Costa Verde, together with bespoke trips. **Dehouche**, www.dehouche.com, offers upmarket accommodation and trips in Bahia and Rio. **Brazilian Beach House**, www.brazilianbeachhouse.com, has some of the finest houses in Búzios and Trancoso but is not so great at organizing transfers and pick-ups. **Matuete**, www.matuete.com, has a range of luxurious properties and tours throughout Brazil.

HOMESTAYS

Staying with a local family is an excellent way to become integrated quickly into a city and companies try to match guests to their hosts. **Cama e Café**, www.camaecafe.com.br, organizes homestays in Rio de Janeiro, Olinda and a number of other cities around Brazil.

QUALITY HOTEL ASSOCIATIONS

The better international hotel associations have members in Brazil. These include: **Small Luxury Hotels of the World**, www.slh.com; the **Leading Hotels of the World**, www.lhw.com; the **Leading Small Hotels of the World**, www.leadingsmallhotels oftheworld.com; **Great Small Hotels**, www.greatsmallhotels.com; and the **French Relais et Chateaux group**, www.relaischateaux.com, which also includes restaurants.

The Brazilian equivalent of these associations is the **Roteiros de Charme**, www.roteiros decharme.com.br, with some 30 locations in the southeast and northeast. Whilst membership of these groups pretty much guarantees quality, it is by no means comprehensive. There are many fine hotels and charming *pousadas* listed in our text that are not included in these associations.

→FOOD AND DRINK IN BRAZIL

FOOD

Brazilians consider their cuisine to be up there with the world's best. Visitors may disagree. Mains are generally heavy, meaty and unspiced. Deserts are often very sweet. That said, the best cooking south of the Rio Grande is in São Paulo and Rio, where a heady mix of international immigrants has resulted in some unusual fusion cooking and exquisite variations on French, Japanese, Portuguese, Arabic and Italian traditional techniques and dishes. The regional cooking in Pará is also a delight – utilizing unusual fruits and vegetables from the Amazon and the sumptuous Amazonian river fish.

PRICE CODES

WHERE TO STAY

$$$$	over US$150	**$$$**	US$66-150
$$	US$30-65	**$**	under US$30

Prices include taxes and service charge, but not meals. They are based on a double room, except in the **$** range, where prices are almost always per person.

RESTAURANTS

$$$	over US$20	**$$**	US$8-20	**$**	under US$8

Prices refer to the cost of a two-course meal, not including drinks.

Outside the more sophisticated cities it can be a struggle to find interesting food. The Brazilian staple meal generally consists of a cut of fried or barbecued meat, chicken or fish accompanied by rice, black or South American broad beans and an unseasoned salad of lettuce, grated carrot, tomato and beetroot. Condiments are weak chilli sauce, olive oil, salt and pepper and vinegar.

The national dish is a greasy campfire stew called *feijoada*, made by throwing jerked beef, smoked sausage, tongue and salt pork into a pot with lots of fat and beans and stewing it for hours. The resulting stew is sprinkled with fried *farofa* (manioc flour) and served with *couve* (kale) and slices of orange. The meal is washed down with *cachaça* (sugarcane rum). Most restaurants serve the *feijoada completa* for Saturday lunch (up until about 1630). Come with a very empty stomach.

Brazil's other national dish is mixed grilled meat or *churrasco*, served in vast portions off the spit by legions of rushing waiters, and accompanied by a buffet of salads, beans and mashed vegetables. *Churrascos* are served in *churrascarias* or *rodízios*. The meat is generally excellent, especially in the best *churascarias*, and the portions are unlimited, offering good value for camel-stomached carnivores able to eat one meal a day.

In remembrance of Portugal, but bizarrely for a tropical country replete with fish, Brazil is also the world's largest consumer of **cod**, pulled from the cold north Atlantic, salted and served in watery slabs or little balls as *bacalhau* (an appetizer/bar snack) or *petisco*. Other national *petiscos* include *kibe* (a deep-fried or baked mince with onion, mint and flour), *coxinha* (deep-fried chicken or meat in dough), *empadas* (baked puff-pastry patties with prawns, chicken, heart of palm or meat), and *tortas* (little pies with the same ingredients). When served in bakeries, *padarias* or snack bars these are collectively referred to as *salgadinhos* (savouries).

The best cooking in Brazil is not national but regional. **Bahia** offers an African-infused, welcome break from meat, rice and beans further south, with a variety of seafood dishes. Unlike most Brazilians, Bahians have discovered sauces, pepper and chilli. The most famous Bahian dish is *moqueca*, fresh fish cooked slowly with prawns in *dendê* palm oil, coconut milk, garlic, tomatoes, cilantro and chili pepper. A variety served in Espírito Santo, the state south of Bahia, is seasoned with blood-red *urucum* berry and served in a clay pot. Other Bahian dishes include *vatapá* and *Caruaru*, pastes made from prawns, nuts, bread, coconut milk and *dendê* oil, *xinxim de galinha*, a rich, spicy chicken stew, best without *dendê* oil, and *acarajé*, black-eyed peas or beans squashed into a ball, deep-fried in *dendê* oil and served split in half, stuffed with *vatapá* or *Caruaru* and seasoned with chilli.

Minas Gerais and **Goiás** are famous for their buffets of stews served over a wood-fired stove and made from a variety of meats and *cerrado* fruits and vegetables like the *pequi*, which is sucked and never bitten; its flesh covers thousands of tiny, razor sharp spines. Minas specialities include *tutu á mineira* made with bacon, egg, refried beans in a paste, and *feijão tropeiro*, herb-infused beans served with *farofa*. A watery, white soft and almost entirely flavourless cheese, *queijo minas* is often served for dessert with ultra-sweet *guava* paste.

Some of the most interesting cooking comes from the **Amazon**. The river fish here are delicious, especially the firm flesh of the *pacu* and *tambaqui*. The *piracururu* is an endangered species and should only be eaten where it is farmed or fished sustainably, from reserves such as **Mamirauá** (see page 261). The most celebrated regional dish in the Amazon is *tacacá no tucupi*, prawn broth cooked in manioc juice and *jambu* leaf. The soup is infused with an alkaloid from the *jambu* that numbs the mouth and produces an energetic rush to the head.

There are many unusual and delicious fruits in the Amazon and in Brazil as a whole. They include the pungent, sweet *cupuaçu*, which makes delicious cakes, the tart *camu-camu*, a large glass of which holds a gram of vitamin C, and *açai* – a dark and highly nutritious berry from a varzea (seasonally flooded forest) palm tree, common in the Amazon. *Açai* berries are often served as a frozen paste, garnished with *xarope* (syrup) and sprinkled with *guaraná* (a ground seed, also from the Amazon, which has stimulant effects similar to caffeine). The *cerrado* gives Brazil fruits such as the delicious *umbu*, *seriguela* and *mangaba*; small pulpy fruits which produce refreshing juices. Brazil also produces some of the world's best mangoes, papayas, bananas and custard apples, all of which come in a variety of flavours and sizes.

The cheapest dish is the *prato feito* or *sortido*, an excellent-value set menu usually comprising meat/chicken/fish, beans, rice, chips and salad. The *prato comercial* is similar but rather better and a bit more expensive. Portions are usually large enough for two and come with two plates. If you are on your own, you could ask for an *embalagem* (doggy bag) or a *marmita* (takeaway) and offer it to a person with no food (many Brazilians do). Many restaurants serve *comida por kilo* buffets where you serve yourself and pay for the weight of food on your plate. This is generally good value and is a decent option for vegetarians. *Lanchonetes* and *padarias* (diners and bakeries) are good for cheap eats; usually serving *prato feitos*, *salgadinhos*, excellent juices and other snacks.

The main meal is usually taken in the middle of the day; cheap restaurants tend not to be open in the evening.

DRINK

The national liquor is *cachaça* (also known as *pinga*), which is made from sugar-cane, and ranging from cheap supermarket and service-station fire-water, to boutique distillery and connoisseur labels from the interior of Minas Gerais. Mixed with fruit juice, sugar and crushed ice, *cachaça* becomes the principal element in a *batida*, a refreshing but deceptively powerful drink. Served with pulped lime or other fruit, mountains of sugar and smashed ice it becomes the world's favourite party cocktail, caipirinha. A less potent caipirinha made with vodka is called a *caipiroska* and with sake a *saikirinha* or *caipisake*.

Some genuine Scotch whisky brands are bottled in Brazil. They are far cheaper even than duty free; Teacher's is the best. Locally made and cheap gin, vermouth and campari are pretty much as good as their US and European counterparts.

Wine is becoming increasingly popular, with good-value Portuguese and Argentinean bottles and some reasonable national table wines such as Château d'Argent, Château Duvalier, Almadén, Dreher, Preciosa and more respectable Bernard Taillan, Marjolet from Cabernet grapes, and the Moselle-type white Zahringer. A new *adega* tends to start off well, but the quality gradually deteriorates with time; many vintners have switched to American Concorde grapes, producing a rougher wine. Greville Brut champagne-style sparkling wine is inexpensive and very drinkable.

Brazil is the third most important wine producer in South America. The wine industry is mainly concentrated in the south of the country where the conditions are most suitable, with over 90% of wine produced in Rio Grande do Sul. There are also vineyards in Pernambuco. There are some interesting sparkling wines in the Italian spumante style (the best is Casa Valduga Brut Premium Sparkling Wine), and Brazil produces still wines using many international and imported varieties. None are distinguished – these are drinkable table wines at best. At worst they are plonk of the Blue Nun variety. The best bottle of red is probably the Boscato Reserva Cabernet Sauvignon. But it's expensive (at around US$20 a bottle); you'll get far higher quality and better value buying Portuguese, Argentine or Chilean wines in Brazil.

Brazilian beer is generally lager, served ice-cold. Draught beer is called *chope* or *chopp* (after the German Schoppen, and pronounced 'shoppi'). There are various national brands of bottled beers, which include Brahma, Skol, Cerpa, Antartica and the best Itaipava and Bohemia. There are black beers too, notably Xingu. They tend to be sweet. The best beer is from the German breweries in Rio Grande do Sul and is available only there.

Brazil's many fruits are used to make fruit juices or *sucos*, which come in a delicious variety, unrivalled anywhere in the world. *Açaí*, *acerola*, *caju* (cashew), *pitanga*, *goiaba* (guava), *genipapo*, *graviola* (*chirimoya*), *maracujá* (passion fruit), *sapoti*, *umbu* and *tamarindo* are a few of the best. *Vitaminas* are thick fruit or vegetable drinks with milk. *Caldo de cana* is sugar-cane juice, sometimes mixed with ice. *Água de côco* or *côco verde* is coconut water served straight from a chilled, fresh, green coconut. The best known of many local soft drinks is *guaraná*, which is a very popular carbonated fruit drink, completely unrelated to the Amazon nut. The best variety is *guaraná Antarctica*. Coffee is ubiquitous and good tea entirely absent.

ESSENTIALS A-Z

Accident and emergency
Ambulance T192. **Police** T190. If robbed or attacked, contact the tourist police. If you need to claim on insurance, make sure you get a police report.

Electricity
Generally 110 V 60 cycles AC, but in some cities and areas 220 V 60 cycles AC is used. European and U.S 2-pin plugs and sockets.

Embassies and consulates
For embassies and consulates of Brazil, see www.embassiesabroad.com.

Health
See your GP or travel clinic at least 6 weeks before departure for general advice on travel risks and vaccinations. Try phoning a specialist travel clinic if your own doctor is unfamiliar with health in the region. Make sure you have sufficient medical travel insurance, get a dental check, know your own blood group and, if you suffer a long-term condition such as diabetes or epilepsy, obtain a **Medic Alert** bracelet (www.medicalalert.co.uk).

Vaccinations and anti-malarials
Confirm that your primary courses and boosters are up to date. It is advisable to vaccinate against polio, tetanus, typhoid, hepatitis A and, for more remote areas, rabies. Yellow fever vaccination is obligatory for most areas. Cholera, diptheria and hepatitis B vaccinations are sometimes advised. Specialist advice should be taken on the best antimalarials to take before you leave.

Health risks
The major risks posed in the region are those caused by insect disease carriers such as mosquitoes and sandflies. The key parasitic and viral diseases are malaria, South American trypanosomiasis (Chagas disease) and dengue fever. Be aware that you are always at risk from these diseases.

Malaria is a danger throughout the lowland tropics and coastal regions. **Dengue fever** (which is currently rife in Rio de Janeiro state) is particularly hard to protect against as the mosquitoes can bite throughout the day as well as night (unlike those that carry malaria); try to wear clothes that cover arms and legs and also use effective mosquito repellent. Mosquito nets dipped in permethrin provide a good physical and chemical barrier at night. **Chagas disease** is spread by faeces of the triatomine, or assassin bugs, whereas sandflies spread a disease of the skin called **leishmaniasis**.

Some form of **diarrhoea** or intestinal upset is almost inevitable, the standard advice is always to wash your hands before eating and to be careful with drinking water and ice; if you have any doubts about the water then boil it or filter and treat it. In a restaurant buy bottled water or ask where the water has come from. Food can also pose a problem, be wary of salads if you don't know whether they have been washed or not.

There is a constant threat of **tuberculosis** (TB) and although the BCG vaccine is available, it is still not guaranteed protection. It is best to avoid unpasteurized dairy products and try not to let people cough and splutter all over you.

Another risk, especially to campers and people with small children, is that of the **hanta virus**, which is carried by some forest and riverine rodents. Symptoms are a flu-like illness which can lead to complications. Try as far as possible to avoid rodent-infested areas, especially close contact with rodent droppings.

Language

Brazilians speak Portuguese, and very few speak anything else. Spanish may help you to be understood a little, but spoken Portuguese will remain undecipherable even to fluent Spanish speakers. To get the best out of Brazil, learn some Portuguese before arriving. Brazilians are the best thing about the country and without Portuguese you will not be able to interact beyond stereotypes and second guesses. Language classes are available in the larger cities. **Cactus** (www.cactuslanguage.com), **Languages abroad** (www.languagesabroad.co.uk) and **Travellers Worldwide** (www.travellersworld wide.com) are among the companies that can organize language courses in Brazil. **McGraw Hill** and **Dorling Kindersley** (*Hugo Portuguese in Three Months*) offer the best teach-yourself books. **Sonia Portuguese** (www.sonia-portuguese.com) is a useful online resource.

Money
Currency

→ *£1 = 3.41; €1 = 2.77; US$1 = R$2.12 (Dec 2012).*
The unit of currency is the **real**, R$ (plural **reais**). Any amount of foreign currency and 'a reasonable sum' in reais can be taken in, but sums over US$10,000 must be declared. Residents may only take out the equivalent of US$4000. Notes in circulation are: 100, 50, 10, 5 and 1 real; coins: 1 real, 50, 25, 10, 5 and 1 centavo. **Note** The exchange-rate fluctuates – check regularly.

Costs of travelling

Brazil is more expensive than other countries in South America. As a very rough guide, prices are about two-thirds those of Western Europe and a little cheaper than rural USA; though prices vary hugely according to the current exchange rate and strength of the real, whose value has soared since 2008 – with Goldman Sachs and Bloomberg considering the *real* to be the most over-valued major currency in the world in 2009-2010. It is expected to lose value; check on the latest before leaving on currency exchange sites such as www.x-rates.com.

Hostel beds are usually around US$15. Budget hotels with few frills have rooms for as little as US$30, and you should have no difficulty finding a double room costing US$45 wherever you are. Rooms are often pretty much the same price whether 1 or 2 people are staying. Eating is generally inexpensive, especially in *padarias* or *comida por kilo* (pay by weight) restaurants, which offer a wide range of food (salads, meat, pasta, vegetarian). Expect to pay around US$6 to eat your fill in a good-value restaurant. Although bus travel is cheap by US or European standards, because of the long distances, costs can soon mount up. Internal flights prices have come down dramatically in the last couple of years and some routes work out cheaper than taking a bus – especially if booking through the internet. Prices vary regionally. Ipanema is almost twice as expensive as rural Bahia. A can of beer in a supermarket in the south-east costs US$0.80, a litre of water US$0.60, a single metrô ticket in São Paulo US$1.60, a bus ticket between US$1 and US$1.50 (depending on the city) and a cinema ticket around US$3.60.

ATMs

ATMs, or cash machines, are common in Brazil. As well as being the most convenient way of withdrawing money, they frequently offer the best available rates of exchange. They are usually closed after 2130 in large cities. There are 2 international ATM acceptance systems, **Plus** and **Cirrus**. Many issuers of debit and credit cards are linked to one, or both (eg Visa is Plus, MasterCard is Cirrus). **Bradesco** and **HSBC** are the 2 main banks offering this service. **Red Banco 24**

Horas kiosks advertise that they take a long list of credit cards in their ATMs, including MasterCard and Amex, but international cards cannot always be used; the same is true of **Banco do Brasil**.

Advise your bank before leaving, as cards are usually stopped in Brazil without prior warning. Find out before you leave what international functionality your card has. Check if your bank or credit card company imposes handling charges. Internet banking is useful for monitoring your account or transferring funds. Do not rely on 1 card, in case of loss. If you do lose a card, immediately contact the 24-hr helpline of the issuer in your home country (keep this number in a safe place).

Exchange

Banks in major cities will change cash and traveller's cheques (TCs). If you keep the official exchange slips, you may convert back into foreign currency up to 50% of the amount you exchanged. The parallel market, found in travel agencies, exchange houses and among hotel staff, often offers marginally better rates than the banks but commissions can be very high. Many banks may only change US$300 minimum in cash, US$500 in TCs. Rates for TCs are usually far lower than for cash, they are harder to change and a very heavy commission may be charged. Dollars cash (take US$5 or US$10 bills) are not useful as alternative currency. Brazilians use *reais*.

Credit cards

Credit cards are widely used, although often they are not usable in the most unlikely of places, such as tour operators. **Diners Club**, **MasterCard**, **Visa** and **Amex** are useful. Cash advances on credit cards will only be paid in *reais* at the tourist rate, incurring at least a 1.5% commission. Banks in small, remote places may still refuse to give a cash advance: try asking for the *gerente* (manager).

Opening hours

Generally Mon-Fri 0900-1800; closed for lunch some time between 1130 and 1400. **Banks** Mon-Fri 1000-1600 or 1630; closed at weekends. **Government offices** Mon-Fri 1100-1800. **Shops** Also open on Sat until 1230 or 1300.

Safety

Although Brazil's big cities suffer high rates of violent crime, this is mostly confined to the favelas (slums) where poverty and drugs are the main cause. Visitors should not enter favelas except when accompanied by workers for NGOs, tour groups or other people who know the local residents well and are accepted by the community. Otherwise they may be targets of muggings by armed gangs who show short shrift to those who resist them. Mugging can take place anywhere. Travel light after dark with few valuables (avoid wearing jewellery and use a cheap, plastic, digital watch). Ask hotel staff where is and isn't safe; crime is patchy in Brazilian cities.

If the worst does happen and you are threatened, don't panic, and hand over your valuables. Do not resist, and report the crime to the local tourist police later. It is extremely rare for a tourist to be hurt during a robbery in Brazil. Being aware of the dangers, acting confidently and using your common sense will reduce many of the risks.

Photocopy your passport, air ticket and other documents, make a record of traveller's cheque and credit card numbers. Keep them separately from the originals and leave another set of records at home. Keep all documents secure; hide your main cash supply in different places or under your clothes. Extra pockets sewn inside shirts and trousers, money belts (best worn below the waist), neck or leg pouches and elasticated support bandages for keeping money above the elbow or below the knee have been repeatedly recommended.

All border areas should be regarded with some caution because of smuggling activities. Violence over land ownership in parts of the interior have resulted in a 'Wild West' atmosphere in some towns, which should therefore be passed through quickly. Red-light districts should also be given a wide berth as there are reports of drinks being drugged with a substance popularly known as 'good night Cinderella'. This leaves the victim easily amenable to having their possessions stolen, or worse.

Avoiding cons
Never trust anyone telling sob stories or offering 'safe rooms', and when looking for a hotel, always choose the room yourself. Be wary of 'plain-clothes policemen'; insist on seeing identification and on going to the police station by main roads. Do not hand over your identification (or money) until you are at the station. On no account take them directly back to your hotel. Be even more suspicious if they seek confirmation of their status from a passer-by.

Hotel security
Hotel safe deposits are generally, but not always, secure. If you cannot get a receipt for valuables in a hotel safe, you can seal the contents in a plastic bag and sign across the seal. Always keep an inventory of what you have deposited. If you don't trust the hotel, lock everything in your pack and secure it in your room when you go out. If you lose valuables, report to the police and note details of the report for insurance purposes. Be sure to be present whenever your credit card is used.

Police
There are several types of police: **Polícia Federal**, civilian dressed, who handle all federal law duties, including immigration.

A subdivision is the **Polícia Federal Rodoviária**, uniformed, who are the traffic police on federal highways. **Polícia Militar** are the uniformed, street police force, under the control of the state governor, handling all state laws. They are not the same as the Armed Forces' internal police. **Polícia Civil**, also state controlled, handle local laws and investigations. They are usually in civilian dress, unless in the traffic division. In cities, the **Prefeitura** controls the **Guarda Municipal**, who handle security. **Tourist police** operate in places with a strong tourist presence. In case of difficulty, visitors should seek out tourist police in the first instance.

Public transport
When you have all your luggage with you at a bus or railway station, be especially careful and carry any shoulder bags in front of you. To be extra safe, take a taxi between the airport/bus station/railway station and hotel, keep your bags with you and pay only when you and your luggage are outside; avoid night buses and arriving at your destination at night.

Sexual assault
If you are the victim of a sexual assault, you are advised firstly to contact a doctor (this can be your home doctor). You will need tests to determine whether you have contracted any STDs; you may also need advice on emergency contraception. You should contact your embassy, where consular staff will be very willing to help.

Women travellers
Most of these tips apply to any single traveller. When you set out, err on the side of caution until your instincts have adjusted to the customs of a new culture. Be prepared for the exceptional curiosity extended to visitors, especially women, and try not to overreact. If, as a single woman, you can befriend a local

woman, you will learn much more about the country you are visiting. There is a definite 'gringo trail' you can follow, which can be helpful when looking for safe accommodation, especially if arriving after dark (best avoided). Remember that for a single woman a taxi at night can be as dangerous as walking alone. It is easier for men to take the friendliness of locals at face value; women may be subject to unwanted attention. Do not disclose to strangers where you are staying. By wearing a wedding ring and saying that your 'husband' is close at hand, you may dissuade an aspiring suitor. If politeness fails, do not feel bad about showing offence and departing. A good rule is always to act with confidence, as though you know where you are going, even if you do not. Someone who looks lost is more likely to attract unwanted attention.

Tax

Airport departure tax The amount of tax depends on the class and size of the airport, but the cost is usually incorporated into the ticket.
VAT Rates vary from 7-25% at state and federal level; the average is 17-20%.

Telephone → *Country code: +55.*
Making a phone call in Brazil can be confusing. It is necessary to dial a 2-digit telephone company code prior to the area code for all calls. Phone numbers are now printed in this way: 0XX21 (0 for a national call, XX for the code of the phone company chosen (eg 31 for Telemar) followed by 21 for Rio de Janeiro, for example and the 8-digit number of the subscriber. The same is true for international calls where 00 is followed by the operator code and then the country code and number.

National calls
Cartões telefônicos (phone cards) are available from newsstands, post offices and chemists. Local calls from private phones are often free. *Cartões telefônicos internacionais* (international phone cards) are increasingly available in tourist areas and are often sold at hostels.

Mobile phones
Cellular phones are widespread and coverage excellent even in remote areas, but prices are extraordinarily high and users still pay to receive calls outside the metropolitan area where their phone is registered. SIM cards are hard to buy as users require a CPF (a Brazilian social security number) to buy one, but phones can be hired. When using a cellular telephone you do not drop the zero from the area code as you have to when dialling from a fixed line.

Time
Brazil has 4 time zones: Brazilian standard time is GMT-3; the Amazon time zone is GMT-4; the State of Acre is GMT-5; and the Fernando de Noronha archipelago is GMT-2. Clocks move forward 1 hr in summer for approximately 5 months. This does not apply to Acre.

Tipping
Tipping is not usual, but always appreciated. In restaurants, add 10% of the bill if no service charge is included; cloakroom attendants deserve a small tip; porters have fixed charges but often receive tips as well; unofficial car parkers on city streets should be tipped 2 reais.

Tourist information
The **Ministério do Turismo**, www.turismo. gov.br or www.braziltour.com, is in charge of tourism in Brazil and has information in many languages. **Embratur**, the Institute of Tourism, is in charge of promoting tourism abroad.
South American Explorers, www.sa explorers.org, is a non-profit educational

organization functioning primarily as an information network for South America.

National parks are run by the Brazilian institute of environmental protection, **Ibama**, www.ibama.gov.br. For information, contact **Linha Verde**, T0800-618080, linhaverde.sede@ibama.gov.br. National parks are open to visitors, usually with a permit from Ibama. See also the **Ministério do Meio Ambiente** website, www.mma.gov.br.

Visas and immigration

Visas are not required for stays of up to 90 days by tourists from Andorra, Argentina, Austria, Bahamas, Barbados, Belgium, Bolivia, Chile, Colombia, Costa Rica, Denmark, Ecuador, Finland, France, Germany, Greece, Iceland, Ireland, Italy, Liechtenstein, Luxembourg, Malaysia, Monaco, Morocco, Namibia, the Netherlands, Norway, Paraguay, Peru, Philippines, Portugal, San Marino, South Africa, Spain, Suriname, Sweden, Switzerland, Thailand, Trinidad and Tobago, United Kingdom, Uruguay, the Vatican and Venezuela. For them, only the following documents are required at the port of disembarkation: a passport valid for at least 6 months (or *cédula de identidad* for nationals of Argentina, Chile, Paraguay and Uruguay); and a return or onward ticket, or adequate proof that you can purchase your return fare, subject to no remuneration being received in Brazil and no legally binding or contractual documents being signed. Venezuelan passport holders can stay for 60 days on filling in a form at the border.

Citizens of the USA, Canada, Australia, New Zealand and other countries not mentioned above, and anyone wanting to stay longer than 180 days, *must* get a visa before arrival, which may, if you ask, be granted for multiple entry. US citizens must be fingerprinted on entry to Brazil. Visa fees vary from country to country, so apply to the Brazilian consulate in your home country. The consular fee in the USA is US$55. Students planning to study in Brazil or employees of foreign companies can apply for a 1- or 2-year visa. 2 copies of the application form, 2 photos, a letter from the sponsoring company or educational institution in Brazil, a police form showing no criminal convictions and a fee of around US$80 is required.

Extensions

Foreign tourists may stay a maximum of 180 days in any 1 year. 90-day renewals are easily obtainable, but only at least 15 days before the expiry of your 90-day permit, from the Polícia Federal. The procedure varies, but generally you have to: fill out 3 copies of the tax form at the Polícia Federal, take them to a branch of **Banco do Brasil,** pay US$15 and bring 2 copies back. You will then be given the extension form to fill in and be asked for your passport to stamp in the extension. According to regulations (which should be on display) you need to show a return ticket, cash, cheques or a credit card, a personal reference and proof of an address of a person living in the same city as the office (in practice you simply write this in the space on the form). Some offices will only give you an extension within 10 days of the expiry of your permit.

Some points of entry, such as the Colombian border, refuse entry for longer than 30 days, renewals are then for the same period, insist if you want 90 days. For longer stays you must leave the country and return (not the same day) to get a new 90-day permit. If your visa has expired, getting a new visa can be costly (US$35 for a consultation, US$30 for the visa itself) and may take anything up to 45 days, depending on where you apply. If you overstay your visa, or extension, you will be fined US$7 per day, with no upper limit. After paying the fine to Polícia Federal, you will be issued with an exit visa and must leave within 8 days.

Officially, if you leave Brazil within the 90-day permission to stay and then re-enter the country, you should only be allowed to stay until the 90-day permit expires. If, however, you are given another 90-day permit, this may lead to charges of overstaying if you apply for an extension.

Identification

You must always carry identification when in Brazil. Take a photocopy of the personal details in your passport, plus your Brazilian immigration stamp, and leave your passport in the hotel safe deposit. This photocopy, when authorized in a *cartório*, US$1, is a legitimate copy of your documents. Be prepared, however, to present the originals when travelling in sensitive border areas. Always keep an independent record of your passport details. Also register with your consulate to expedite document replacement if yours gets lost or stolen.

Warning Do not lose the entry/exit permit they give you when you enter Brazil. Leaving the country without it, you may have to pay up to US$100 per person. It is suggested that you photocopy this form and have it authenticated at a *cartório*, US$1, in case of loss or theft.

Weights and measures

Metric.

INDEX

CREDITS

Footprint credits
Editor: Felicity Laughton
Cover: Pepi Bluck
Colour section: Angus Dawson
Maps: Kevin Feeney

Publisher: Patrick Dawson
Advertising: Elizabeth Taylor

Photography credits
Front cover: Antonino Bartuccio/SIME/
4Corners Images
Back cover: fabio fersa/Shutterstock.com;
Eric Gevaert/Shutterstock.com; GARDEL
Bertrand/ hemis.fr
Inside front flap: Mark Schwettmann/
Shutterstock.com; Rafael Martin-Gaitero/
Shutterstock.com; Luiz Rocha/
Shutterstock.com; Carlos
Neto/Shutterstock.com
Colour pages: Alex Robinson p1, 2, 4, 8, 9, 13,
14, 15, 19, 21, 22, 25, 26, 27, 31, 32; AISPIX by
Image Source/Shutterstock p16; Alexandre
Fagundes de Fagundes/Dreamstime.com p3,
8, 10; Ammit Jack/Shutterstock p7; Antonio
de Azevedo Negrão/ Dreamstime.com p23;
Carlos Alberto Loff Fonseca/Dreamstime.com p3;
David Davis/Dreamstime.com p2; Dmitry V
Petrenko/Shutterstock p10; Eric Gevaert/
Shutterstock p20; Gary Yim/Shutterstock p27;
Giovanni de Caro/Dreamstime.com p23;
Aureli/ Dreamstime.com p23; LaurensT/
Shutterstock p9; Ldeavila/ Dreamstime.com
p15; Luis Carlos Torres/ Shutterstock p18; Luiz
Rocha/ Shutterstock p6, 9, 12; Mark Farrer/
Shutterstock p11; Marcus VDT/Shutterstock p7;
Mypix/ Dreamstime.com p2; ostill/ Shutterstock
p18, 24; Paulo Williams/ Shutterstock p20;
Pixattitude/ Dreamstime.com p11; Schmid
Christophe/Shutterstock p7; Spectral-design/
Dreamstime.com p16; Vinicius Tupinamba/
Dreamstime.com p22; Vtupinamba/
Dreamstime.com p17.

Printed in Spain by GraphyCems

Every effort has been made to ensure that
the facts in this guidebook are accurate.
However, travellers should still obtain
advice from consulates, airlines etc about
travel and visa requirements before travelling.
The authors and publishers cannot accept
responsibility for any loss, injury or
inconvenience however caused.

Publishing information
Footprint DREAM TRIP Brazil
1st edition
© Footprint Handbooks Ltd
February 2013

ISBN: 978 1 907263 668
CIP DATA: A catalogue record for this book
is available from the British Library

® Footprint Handbooks and the Footprint
mark are a registered trademark of Footprint
Handbooks Ltd

Published by Footprint
6 Riverside Court
Lower Bristol Road
Bath BA2 3DZ, UK
T +44 (0)1225 469141
F +44 (0)1225 469461
footprinttravelguides.com

Distributed in the USA by Globe Pequot Press,
Guilford, Connecticut